One of the weirdest heresies that has been generated in the last century pertains to the postulation of a hierarchical order within the members of the Trinity—as if there ever could exist a threat of discord or of misconduct that would require the exercise of authority within the oneness of the Godhead. This book not only exposes the agenda for the promotion of the subordinationist theory but also establishes its fallacy from both Scripture and from patristic history. By showing that subordinationism is a revival of a heresy that was systematically rejected by the non-Arian church, the author reinstates the classical orthodox doctrine of the Trinity in all of its scriptural majesty and grandeur.

— Gilbert Bilezikian, Wheaton College

Carefully gathering evidence from the Bible, the tradition (Athanasius, the Cappadocians, Augustine, Calvin, the Nicene, Constantinopolitan, and Athanasian creeds, and the Reformation confessions), and representative modern theologians such as Barth and Rahner, Kevin Giles aims to show that those contemporary evangelical theologians who argue for the subordination of women to men, based on a supposed eternal subordination of the Son to the Father in function and authority, have unwittingly embraced elements of ancient Arianism and have thus undermined the doctrine of the Trinity. Instead of allowing trinitarian doctrine to point us to God's eternal communion and freedom in order to direct us beyond the error of subordinating women to men, these contemporary evangelicals, Giles contends, actually end up redefining the trinitarian relations based on human experience and the ideology that derives from that experience. Giles skillfully places before us the stark choice which each generation of theologians must face: will we allow the Bible to speak its message about the Father, Son, and Holy Spirit to us, or will we use the Bible to advance our own agendas? There is no doubt that Kevin Giles has given us much that is worthwhile to think about in this important book, which certainly deserves to be widely read and carefully considered by all who are engaged in serious theology today.

—Paul D. Molnar, Professor of Systematic Theology,
St. John's University, Queens, New York

Other Books by Kevin Giles

JESUS
AND THE
FATHER

Modern Evangelicals
Reinvent the Doctrine of the Trinity

KEVIN GILES

ZONDERVAN.com/
AUTHORTRACKER
follow your favorite authors

We want to hear from you. Please send your comments about this book to us in care of zreview@zondervan.com. Thank you.

 ZONDERVAN®

Jesus and the Father
Copyright © 2006 by Kevin Giles

Requests for information should be addressed to:

Zondervan, *Grand Rapids, Michigan 49530*

Library of Congress Cataloging-in-Publication Data
Giles, Kevin.
    Jesus and the father : modern evangelicals reinvent the doctrine of the Trinity /
Kevin Giles — 1st ed.
      p. cm.
    Includes bibliographical references and index.
    ISBN-10: 0-310-26664-5
    ISBN-13: 978-0-310-26664-8
    1. Trinity — History of doctrines. 2. Evangelicalism. I. Title.
BT111.3.G45 2006
231'.044 — dc22
                                         2005034545
                                              CIP

Interior design by Nancy Wilson

Printed in the United States of America

---

06 07 08 09 10 11 12 13 • 18 17 16 15 14 13 12 11 10 9 8 7 6 5 4 3 2

CONTENTS

FOREWORD

Trinitarian life as portrayed in Scripture includes some patterns of subordination. In the economy of salvation, the Spirit, for example, sometimes appears to have little will of his own. He is comparatively unoriginal, an almost pure agent of the Father and the Son. Similarly, in John's gospel the Son and Father have one will, word, and work among us largely because the Son, by his own testimony, simply reproduces what comes to him from the Father: "Whatever I say is just what the Father has told me to say" (12:50); "the Son can do nothing by himself; he can do only what he sees his Father doing" (5:19). The Paraclete, in turn, just teaches the words of the Word (14:26; 16:14).

Most important is the sending pattern in the fourth gospel. The Father sends. The Son sends and is sent. The Spirit is simply sent. You never read that the Son or the Spirit send the Father on any missions.

What must we think of this? What does the subordination pattern tell us about the *eternal* life of God? Is God locked into the pattern we see in the drama of human redemption? Or is this pattern only a temporal measure?

The picture here is actually complicated. For one thing, we have to recognize that Jesus is the Son of God *incarnate*. Being incarnate involves certain humiliating limitations. Perhaps part of Jesus' subordination to his Father is owed to these limitations.

In fact, before his ascension Jesus seems subordinate to the Spirit as well—just the reverse of what we find in John's gospel. The Spirit conceives (Mt 1:18), compels (Mk 1:12), and inspires (Lk 10:21) Jesus. These facts deepen and complicate the portrait of the Holy Spirit, who, it appears, acts with the will and power of God.

Again, Paul sometimes uses language that suggests not that the center of the Holy Trinity is the Father, from whom the Son and Spirit are only radii. Not at all. Paul sometimes suggests that the divine life centers in the exalted Christ: "All things were created by him and for him ... in him all things hold together ... so that in everything he might have the supremacy" (Col 1:16–18). Even in John's gospel, the functional hierarchy is qualified by the fact that Father and Son *mutually* glorify each other (13:31–32).

Still further, in the lyric hymn of Philippians 2, Paul tells us of the preexistent Christ, "who, being in very nature God, did not consider equality with God something to be grasped, but made himself nothing, taking the very nature of a servant." For human beings jostling for position, volunteering and being sent are sometimes incompatible. The beauty of perfect trinitarian life is that they are the same, one will of God pulsing through triplicate personal life. Paul's servant Christ, who volunteers to make himself nothing, and John's Son of God, who is sent, are exactly the same person.

Bearing all these things in mind, and many others, Christians profess a holy mystery; namely, that "the Father is God, the Son is God, and the Holy Spirit is God; yet there are not three gods, but one God" (the Athanasian Creed). "One God" is the conclusion, but so is "the Holy Spirit is God." So is "the Son is God." Nothing we see in the Bible's story of salvation (including who sends whom on missions) detracts one iota from the dignity and gravity of the title "God" for the Son and Spirit as well as for the Father.

Of course, all this raises enormous and fascinating questions, on many of which Scripture is silent. That fact all by itself should make us hesitate to offer answers of our own. But the questions are still important. They remind us that the inner life of God is deep, and that there is much we do not understand about it—perhaps much we *couldn't* understand. And they keep us from using the doctrine of the Trinity as warrant for glib assumptions about fixed subordination arrangements among human beings—adult children being permanently subordinate to their aged parents, for instance, or slaves to masters, or women to men. None of these arrangements can be grounded inside a God in whom "nothing is before or after, nothing is greater or smaller" (the Athanasian Creed).

The equality of Father, Son, and Spirit is the first and great implication of the doctrine that each person is God. This implication anchors Kevin Giles's thinking about the Holy Trinity. While some recent evangelical writers have tried to establish women's subordination by seating it inside God, Giles rightly protests. (One wonders how a trinitarian Father-Son relationship is even relevant to a man-woman relationship.) Supported by the great ecumenical creeds, Giles joins centuries of Christians in preserving the doctrine of the coequality and coeternity of Father, Son, and Spirit within the mystery of the Holy Trinity, and in protecting the doctrine from hijackers with an agenda. In pursuit of this noble end, he has written a book of great power and beauty.

—Cornelius Plantinga Jr.
Calvin Theological Seminary

PREFACE

This book is not like any other book on the Trinity on the market today. It is not an academic outline on what the Bible teaches on the Trinity and how the doctrine of the Trinity has been developed across the centuries. It is rather a plea from the heart to my fellow evangelicals who in growing numbers in recent years have begun arguing for the eternal subordination in function and authority of the Son to the Father. I say to them, "Go back, you are going the wrong way." To set God the Son eternally under God the Father is to construe the Trinity as a hierarchy and thereby undermine the coequality of the differentiated divine persons, the core truth of the doctrine of the Trinity.

The counterparts to this book come from the fourth century, when men like Athanasius, the Cappadocian Fathers, Hilary of Poitiers, and Augustine poured out their soul in opposition to "the Arians,"[1] who eternally subordinated the Son to the Father in being, function, and authority. They concluded Arian teaching denied that Jesus was truly God and thus called into question the possibility of salvation in Jesus Christ. In about the year 360 when the Arians had gained the ascendancy, Jerome, the Latin translator of the original Hebrew and Greek Scriptures, exclaimed, "The whole world groaned in astonishment to find itself Arian."[2] Today the doctrine of the *eternal subordination of the Son* is in the ascendancy among evangelicals, and I for one groan in dismay. I groan in dismay because I am convinced that what is being taught by many of my fellow evangelicals on the Trinity is contrary to the most fundamental teaching of the New Testament and to what the best theologians of the past and present tell us is orthodoxy.

In my 2002 book, *The Trinity and Subordinationism: The Doctrine of God and the Contemporary Gender Debate*,[3] I sought to give a comprehensive rebuttal of the whole post-1970s' conservative evangelical case for the *permanent* subordination of women. One third of the book outlines how historic orthodoxy totally rejects the *eternal* subordination of the Son in role and authority to the Father, a doctrine developed

---

[1] This is a very broad category covering people and theological groupings with differing views on many things, united only by their common conviction that the Son is eternally subordinated to the Father in being, work/function, and authority. We will come back to this matter many times in what follows.

[2] Jerome, *Dialogue Against the Luciferians*, 19. Translation from W. H. C. Friend, *The Early Church* (Minneapolis: Fortress, 1965), 157.

[3] Kevin Giles, *The Trinity and Subordinationism: The Doctrine of God and the Contemporary Gender Debate* (Downers Grove, Ill.: InterVarsity, 2002).

late in the twentieth century to justify and explain the permanent subordination of women in role and authority to the men set over them in the church and in the home. Another third of my previous book critiques contemporary evangelical arguments for the permanent "role subordination" of women, showing them to be entirely novel and untenable. And the last third points out that Christians almost unanimously supported slavery until modern times. Indeed, nineteenth-century American Reformed evangelicals led the opposition to the emancipation of slaves, developing an impressive biblical case for slavery. For them the advice given in the Bible to slaves living in a culture that took slavery for granted was interpreted to speak of God's endorsement of slavery for all time. I thus asked, Are contemporary evangelicals making the same mistake when they oppose the emancipation of women by interpreting passages advising women how to behave in a patriarchal culture as God's ideal for all time, including our own egalitarian culture?

The evaluation of my book by some of the most significant evangelical theologians was very positive.[4] The response by those I sought to rebut was almost entirely negative and dismissive. Much to my surprise it was my work on the Trinity that upset my critics most of all.[5] Robert Doyle, head of the department of systematic theology at Moore College Sydney, thinks I have almost entirely misread the church fathers, Calvin, Barth, and Rahner on this doctrine. My work, he says is "tendentious, and consistently and grossly distorts the evidence from a long tradition of trinitarian reflection."[6] It is his belief that the Bible and the theologians just mentioned teach

---

[4] There is no need to go further than the comments by readers of my book on the back cover to substantiate my claim. However, see also the generally positive or very positive reviews: Duncan Reid, "*The Trinity and Subordinationism: The Doctrine of God and the Contemporary Gender Debate*," *The Australian Theological Book Review On Line*: www.atbr.openbook.com. au (August 2003); Max Davidson, "*The Trinity and Subordinationism: The Doctrine of God and the Contemporary Gender Debate* by Kevin N. Giles," *Evangelical Review of Theology* 28, no. 3 (2004): 287–88; V. Hiebert, "Kevin Giles. *The Trinity and Subordinationism: The Doctrine of God and the Contemporary Gender Debate*," *Didaskalia* (Fall 2004), 63–65; Stephen Dray, "*The Trinity and Subordinationism: The Doctrine of God and the Contemporary Gender Debate*," *Evangelical Quarterly* 77, no. 1 (2005): 94–95; Thomas R. Thompson, "The Trinity and Subordinationism," *Calvin Theological Journal* 40, no. 1 (2005): 134–37.

[5] In addition to the three very hostile responses I am about to discuss, here are other similar reviews: Peter R. Schemm, "Kevin Giles' *The Trinity and Subordinationism*," *Journal of Biblical Manhood and Womanhood* 7, no. 2 (2002): 67–78; Robert Letham, "Kevin Giles, *The Trinity and Subordinationism*," *Westminster Theological Journal* 65, no. 2 (2003): 383–87; Gerald Bray, "Review Article, *The Trinity and Subordinationism: The Doctrine of God and the Contemporary Gender Debate*," *The Churchman* 117, no. 3 (2003): 267–71; Mark Baddeley, "The Trinity and Subordinationism: A Response to Kevin Giles," *The Reformed Theological Review* 63, no. 1 (2004): 1–14.

[6] Robert Doyle, "Are We Heretics? A Review of *The Trinity and Subordinationism* by Kevin Giles," *The Briefing* 307 (April 2004): 11–19.

"the priority of the Father in intratrinitarian relations"[7] and the eternal subordination of the Son of God. He is convinced that I am dead wrong.

The American theologian Wayne Grudem, who has spent most of his working life arguing for the permanent subordination of women, is even more critical and condemnatory of my work on the Trinity. He says my understanding of the history of the development of this doctrine is "deeply flawed,"[8] I make "church tradition the supreme authority, an approach similar to Roman Catholicism,"[9] I reject the clear teaching of Scripture that eternally subordinates the Son to the Father,[10] and what I purport to be historic orthodoxy, "world renowned theologians and church historians" do not.[11]

Similarly, Bruce Ware argues that the "lethal failure" of my book is due to my "misreading" of the Bible and the tradition.[12] In reply he says, "The church fathers, both west and east" taught "the primacy of the Father in the immanent Trinity,"[13] and that the Son "stood in a subordinate position to the Father while sharing in the one divine essence."[14] My work, he believes, "signals a major departure from the evangelical, and certainly Reformational tradition."[15]

These comments, I must add, are mild and moderate in comparison to the many strongly worded emails I have had abusing me personally for dividing the evangelical community, for "ignoring" texts in the Bible that subordinate the Son to the Father, for "deliberately distorting" the historical evidence, and for seeking to overthrow the "orthodox doctrine" of the eternal subordination of the Son.

I have taken this onslaught in good heart even if it has been somewhat offensive. It inspired me to begin reading the Bible again and my historical sources, Athanasius, the Cappadocians, Augustine, Aquinas, and Calvin, to check on the veracity of what I had written. The work I had done for my first book gave me a solid base from which to go deeper and understand more adequately what the Bible was saying and how its teaching on the Trinity had been understood by the theologians I have just mentioned.

This book is the outcome of that work. It gives what I have learned from reading the Bible and my primary historical documents yet again. I have discovered much that adds to my earlier work, and with a deeper appreciation of my sources and the

---

[7] Ibid., 18.

[8] Wayne Grudem, *Evangelical Feminism and Biblical Truth* (Sisters, Ore.: Multnomah, 2004), 426.

[9] Ibid.

[10] Ibid., 426.

[11] Ibid., 427.

[12] Bruce Ware, "*The Trinity and Subordinationism: The Doctrine of God and the Contemporary Gender Debate* by Kevin Giles," *Religious Studies Review* 4, no. 29 (2003): 355.

[13] Ibid.

[14] Ibid.

[15] Ibid.

issues, I have been able to lay out my case much better. I am more convinced than ever that the *eternal* subordination of the Son is very dangerous teaching standing in direct opposition to how the best of theologians past and present and the creeds and Reformation confessions have understood what the Bible says on the Trinity. Most of the criticism made of my work on the Trinity has not been supported by any counter evidence at all, or if evidence has been given, it has lacked credibility. In what follows, these rebuttals will be considered. In reply to them I have quadrupled the factual evidence, outlining it, I hope, with greater clarity and force.

If my critics want to continue the debate, I ask them to interact at the same depth with Scripture and the writings of theologians of the caliber of Athanasius, the Cappadocian Fathers, Augustine, Calvin, Barth, Rahner, and Thomas Torrance. We cannot both be right. Either the Bible and the best of theologians across the centuries and the creeds and Reformation confessions exclude the idea that the Son of God is *eternally* subordinated to the Father, or they do not.

But Why All This Fuss about the Doctrine of the Trinity?

I suspect many Christians think that the doctrine of the Trinity is a very abstract and somewhat impractical doctrine of little importance. Nothing could be further from the truth. The doctrine of the Trinity, it cannot be denied, is a difficult doctrine to understand, but it is of huge importance and of great practical consequence. It is nothing less than the distinctive Christian doctrine of God. We Christians uniquely believe in one tripersonal God: Father, Son, and Spirit. It is this doctrine that explains how Jesus Christ and the Holy Spirit can be "coequal" God with the Father. Christ is God in revelation. Our saving knowledge of God is given solely through Jesus Christ. We worship Jesus Christ because we believe he is God. The Holy Spirit, we believe, likewise is God. When the Holy Spirit comes into our life as we become Christians, God comes into our life. If we think and believe anything less about Jesus Christ or the Spirit, we think less of God. If Jesus or the Spirit are in any way less than God, then we are mistaken in worshiping Jesus Christ as God in the power and presence of the Spirit of God.

To fail to correctly understand "our" distinctive and foundational doctrine of God can have catastrophic consequences. Almost, if not all, the so-called Christian sects either deny the doctrine of the Trinity or have a badly flawed understanding of it. The great Reformed theologian Herman Bavinck writes, "The confession of the Trinity throbs at the heart of the Christian religion: every error results from, or upon deeper reflection may be traced to, a wrong view of this doctrine."[16]

---

[16] Herman Bavinck, *The Doctrine of God*, trans. William Hendricksen (Grand Rapids, Mich.: Baker, 1977), 285.

What is more, how we formulate the doctrine of the Trinity has very practical outcomes. Because of its foundational nature, Christians like to appeal to the Trinity to justify other teaching or practice. Sadly, all too often concerns about other issues impact on how the doctrine of the Trinity is spelled out. Many examples could be given. A compelling example is basic to this book. One side argues that the Trinity should be understood as a hierarchy in which the Father rules over the Son and the Spirit, and on the basis of this belief the case is made that men should rule over women. The other side rejects this argument, claiming that historic orthodoxy has never accepted hierarchical ordering in the Trinity. The persons of the Trinity are to be understood as "coequal," each being alike "almighty" and "Lord," as the Athanasian Creed declares. This understanding of the Trinity, they insist, in no way justifies the permanent subordination of women, or unchangeable hierarchical social ordering in any context. As this particular debate impacts on a little more than half the human race, it would be hard to dispute that how we construe the doctrine of the Trinity is of huge practical consequences. The point seems beyond dispute. A right doctrine of the Trinity is needed for right belief and right behavior. No doctrine could be more important.

A Big God, Small Human Minds

The Athanasian Creed speaks of the triune God as "incomprehensible." By this it does not mean that nothing can be understood about God by human minds. The point is rather that no human mind can comprehend God—completely and exhaustively understand him. This is a basic insight that must never be forgotten. We will return to this matter many times in what follows. To say that the doctrine of the Trinity is divine "mystery" is to be understood in the same way. God is bigger, greater, and more profound than we can ever think or imagine, yet what is revealed can be trusted as true and sure knowledge of God. The Bible faithfully and accurately reveals God, but it reveals God in a way that our human minds can grasp. God is much greater than we can even imagine or human words can ever express. What we say about God is simply our best attempts as human beings to speak of the divine being on the basis of what he has revealed of himself.

In the process of revealing himself to human beings, God reveals in Jesus Christ and the subsequent giving of the Spirit that he is triune for all eternity. He is one and three, something that certainly extends the human mind beyond its limits. There is, however, no revealed *doctrine* of the Trinity. All attempts at formulating the doctrine of the Trinity are human attempts to explain how God can be one and three at the same time for all eternity. This does not mean that one attempt is as good as another. Far from it. After centuries of debate the church is basically agreed on what has to be clearly affirmed in any acceptable doctrine of the Trinity. This agreement is spelled out in the creeds and confessions. They endorse what has come to be recognized as central to what the Bible teaches on God as one and three, and they repudiate what has come to be seen as contrary to Scripture.

Thanks

This book was written over two years early in the morning, at night, and sometimes on days off while I have been the vicar (pastor) of St. Michael's, North Carlton, a vibrant growing "rebirthed" Anglican Church in inner Melbourne. It is a great privilege to lead this church and be part of the supportive Christian communal life it offers. I thank those who have prayed for me when they heard I was writing "another" book.

A big thanks also to my wife, Lynley, who also was part of this book and constantly supportive. I suspect that she was happy I was so busy, as her leadership of a large Christian ministry that prepares young couples for marriage and provides counseling and support for them afterwards involves her in long hours of work. As much as I love our four grown-up children, and the partners of the three that are married and the eight grandchildren, I do not think I can add them to those who have helped me get this book completed! I am, however, most appreciative of my youngest daughter Melissa's help with some of the computer glitches that arose from time to time while writing.

Because I was working alone and largely pioneering answers to the newly worded post-1970s' doctrine of the eternal subordination of the Son, I asked anyone I knew who seemed to be informed on the doctrine of the Trinity to comment on my work. Some said, "Yes, I will read what you have written," but most said no for one reason or another. I was particularly disappointed that my most strident critics, the members of Sydney Anglican Doctrine Commission, refused to read what I had written, although I offered to put the whole manuscript before them prior to sending it to the publisher.

Among those who read the manuscript in full I warmly thank Duncan Reid and John Capper, both careful scholars who are well versed in the doctrine of the Trinity. John went the extra mile, reading the whole manuscript the month before I sent it off, making innumerable constructive comments. Anne Hunt read my work at an early stage and told me to keep working! She was a constant source of encouragement and helped me understand a number of issues from her perspective as an informed Roman Catholic theologian. Among those who read one or more chapters I want to thank I. Howard Marshall and Gordon D. Fee, who read the chapter on the Bible; Paul Molnar and Gary Deddo, who read the chapters on Barth and on the immanent and economic Trinity; Peter Moore, who read the chapter on Barth;[17] and Neil Ormerod,

---

[17] His 2004 Australian College of Theology MTh thesis, *Karl Barth's Doctrine of Election in the Church Dogmatics Set in Its Theological and Historical Context*, is a good piece of work.

who read my work on Karl Rahner. Each one of these readers made helpful suggestions that I was pleased to take up.

It is, however, my critics whom I must thank the most. If they had not written so strongly against my earlier work, and in some cases entered into email correspondence with me, I would not have seen the key issues with half the clarity I now see them. I have in mind among others Andrew Moody, Matthew Paulson, Steven Boyer, Robert Forsyth, Mark Baddeley,[18] Peter Adam, Wayne Grudem, Robert Doyle, and the always polite and gracious Robert Letham.

Sadly, some of my critics have viewed me as a dangerous enemy to be opposed at all cost. Instead, I see myself as a friend saying to them, as fellow evangelicals, "Go back—you are going the wrong way."

Finally, as a postscript I would like to warmly thank the editorial and production team at Zondervan for their exemplary professionalism and courtesy. Katya Covrett, Brian Phipps, and Jack Kragt have corresponded with me regularly, and they have very positively contributed to the final outcome, but I know others have worked behind the scenes on my manuscript as well.

Kevin Giles
Melbourne, Australia

---

[18] Mark Baddeley asked to read my chapters on the economic–immanent Trinity debate and on Barth when I told him I was interacting with him in these pages. He only commented on my references to what he had published. He asked for a few corrections, which I gladly made.

CONTEMPORARY EVANGELICALS AND THE DOCTRINE OF THE TRINITY

In the past thirty years there has been an amazing resurgence of interest in the doctrine of the Trinity. Roman Catholics, mainline Protestants, and Eastern Orthodox theologians have published numerous studies and books on the Trinity, and they are continuing to appear. Evangelicals at first were not involved, but a change is under way, as this book and others written recently by evangelicals indicate.[1] After a long period of neglect, this doctrine is now on center stage as it should be, because it is nothing less than our distinctive Christian doctrine of God.

Most contemporary books on the Trinity have two foci. They look back to the historical sources to see how the doctrine was developed by the best of theologians across the centuries, and they look at the present to see how this fundamental doctrine can be best expressed building on all the work and thought that has gone before. Irenaeus, Tertullian, Athanasius, the Cappadocian Fathers, Augustine, Aquinas, and Calvin are the most commonly studied historical authorities. One of the most important developments in this doctrinal renaissance has been the recognition that there is much to learn from the early Greek-speaking theologians, particularly Athanasius

---

[1] For example, Millard Erickson, *God in Three Persons: A Contemporary Interpretation of the Trinity* (Grand Rapids, Mich.: Baker, 1995); Roger E. Olson and Christopher A. Hall, *The Trinity* (Grand Rapids, Mich.: Eerdmans, 2002); Stanley J. Grenz, *Rediscovering the Triune God: The Trinity in Contemporary Theology* (Minneapolis: Fortress, 2004); Brian Edgar, *The Message of the Trinity* (Leicester, England: Inter-Varsity, 2004); Robert Letham, *The Holy Trinity in Scripture, History, Theology, and Worship* (Phillipsburg, N.J.: P&R, 2004).

and the Cappadocian Fathers, who for centuries were somewhat forgotten by Roman Catholic and Protestant theologians. Right at the heart of their doctrine of the Trinity was the belief that God's triunity was to be understood communally. The three persons are the one God in the most intimate, self-giving fellowship. This development has led to a widespread move away from Tertullian, Augustine, and Aquinas's practice of speaking of God in unity as "one substance," an expression which sounds impersonal and abstract, even if this was not intended. In this prevailing "communal model" of the Trinity, the coequality of the divine three both in unity and in relation to one another as persons is very much to the fore.

Given this starting point for the doctrine of the Trinity, any suggestion that the divine three are ordered hierarchically, or divided in being, work, or authority, is unthinkable. Ted Peters in his 1993 book *God as Trinity: Relationality and Temporality in Divine Life*[2] describes contemporary thinking about the Christian God as "antisubordinationist trinitarianism." Similarly, the conservative evangelical Millard Erickson in his 1995 study, *God in Three Persons*, says that along with other contemporary theologians he believes in "the complete equality of the divine three."[3] David Cunningham in his 1998 book, *These Three Are One: The Practice of Trinitarian Theology*, is of much the same opinion. He speaks of "a radical, relational, co-equality" in modern trinitarian thinking.[4] In my opinion the finest study on the Trinity in the last ten years is that by Thomas F. Torrance, *The Christian Doctrine of God: One Being Three Persons*.[5] He too emphasizes the coequality of the differentiated divine persons. Building on the work of Athanasius and the Cappadocians, he makes the Trinity itself the *monarche* (sole source or origin) of the divine three and the Son the *monarche* of divine saving revelation. He is totally opposed to subordinationism in any form.

In the light of this contemporary stress on the coequality of the divine persons who are understood to be bound together in the most intimate bond of love and self-giving, it is of no surprise that some of the best contemporary expositions of the doctrine of the Trinity see the Trinity as a charter for human liberation and emancipation.[6] If no one divine person is before or after, greater or lesser because they are "coequal" (as the Athanasian creed says), this suggests, we are told, that all hierarchi-

---

[2] Ted Peters, *God as Trinity: Relationality and Temporality in Divine Life* (Louisville: Westminster, 1993).

[3] Erickson, *God in Three Persons*, 331.

[4] David Cunningham, *These Three Are One: The Practice of Trinitarian Theology* (Oxford: Blackwell, 1998), 113.

[5] Thomas F. Torrance, *The Christian Doctrine of God: One Being Three Persons.* (Edinburgh: T&T Clark, 1996).

[6] Leonardo Boff, *Trinity and Society* (New York: Orbis, 1988); Jürgen Moltmann, *The Trinity and the Kingdom* (New York: Harper and Row, 1981); Catherine LaCugna, *God for Us* (San Francisco: HarperSanFrancisco, 1991); Erickson, *God in Three Persons*.

cal ordering in this world is a human construct reflecting fallen existence, not God's ideal. God would like to see every human being valued in the same way. It is thus the Christian's duty to oppose human philosophies and structures that oppress people, limiting their full potential as human beings made in the image and likeness of God. Millard Erickson is one evangelical who is sympathetic to this agenda predicated on the belief that the persons of the Trinity relate as equals in self-giving love.[7]

Paradoxically, in this same thirty-year period many conservative evangelicals concerned to maintain the permanent subordination of women have been developing a doctrine of a hierarchically ordered Trinity in which the Father rules over the Son just like men are to rule over women in the church and the home. We are told that the Father is *eternally* "head over" the Son just as men are *permanently* "head over" women in the church and the home. On this model of the Trinity, the doctrine of the Trinity indicates that God has appointed some to rule and some to obey, and this is the ideal. It is not unfair to say that rather than being a charter for emancipation and human liberation, this doctrine of the Trinity suggests that social change and female liberation should be opposed.

The conservative evangelical theologians who think of the Trinity as hierarchically ordered with the Father commanding and the Son obeying insist that what they are teaching is what the Bible teaches and historic orthodoxy endorses. I am an evangelical, but I am convinced the opposite is the truth. The Bible and the interpretative tradition summed up in the creeds and Reformation confessions speak of a coequal Trinity where there is no hierarchical ordering.

When evangelical theologians are in dispute with one another about important doctrines such as baptism, eschatology, the church, the gifts of the Spirit, or women in leadership, resolution is seldom found. It is not found because there are no objective criteria to judge the competing interpretations of Scripture. There is no broad consensus among the great theologians of the past as to what the Scriptures are teaching on these doctrines and no defining comments in the creeds and confessions to which appeal can be made. It is very different with the doctrines of the Trinity and of Christ. How the Scriptures are to be interpreted on these two fundamental doctrines is discussed in great detail by the great theologians of the past such as Athanasius, the Cappadocian Fathers, Augustine, and Calvin, and their conclusions are now enshrined in the Nicene and Athanasian Creeds and in the Reformation confessions. Both evangelicals who endorse hierarchical ordering in the Trinity, and those who vehemently oppose hierarchical ordering, agree that this doctrinal tradition is the best guide we have for understanding what the Scriptures teach on the Trinity and the person of Christ. The dispute today among evangelicals is about what these authorities actually

---

[7] Erickson, *God in Three Persons*, 333.

say on these matters. The two sides both claim that the great theologians of the past and the creeds and confessions are on "their side." In this book we explore this dispute on the basis that we are agreed that we do have objective criteria in these authorities to judge who is reading Scripture aright.

The Post-1970s' Evangelical Doctrine of the Eternal Subordination of the Son

George Knight III in his highly influential book *New Testament Teaching on the Role Relationship of Men and Women*, published in 1977,[8] formulated an entirely new set of theological arguments in support of the permanent subordination of women. Men and women are created equal, yet women are differentiated from men by the fact that God has assigned to them a subordinate *role*. These differing *roles* given to men and women are based on the "order of creation," a hierarchical social order given by God before sin entered the world. For this reason male leadership and female subordination is the ideal. Thus the exhortations to women to be subordinate in the New Testament, unlike those to slaves, are transcultural and unchangeable. In developing his novel case, Knight also argued that this God-given *permanent* subordination of women in role and authority in the church and the home was supported and illustrated by the Trinity. For him the Son is *eternally* subordinated in role and authority to the Father, despite the fact that the Father and the Son are both fully divine. He thus speaks of a "chain of subordination"[9] and of an eternal subordination of the Son that has "certain ontological aspects."[10] This new teaching on the Trinity came to full fruition in 1994 with the publication of Wayne Grudem's *Systematic Theology: An Introduction to Biblical Doctrine*.[11] The impact of this book on evangelicals cannot be overestimated. Over 135,000 copies have been sold, and the abridged version, *Bible Doctrine*,[12] with exactly the same teaching on the Trinity and women, has sold over 35,000 copies. The former is now the most widely used systematic theology text in evangelical seminaries and Bible colleges in North America and most other English-speaking countries.

In this book Grudem has one chapter on the Trinity where he argues that the Father and the Son are both divine, yet the Son is eternally subordinated in role and authority to the Father. In another chapter on male and female relationships, he grounds women's permanent subordination on the eternal subordination of the Son.

---

[8] George Knight III, *New Testament Teaching on the Role Relationship of Men and Women* (Grand Rapids, Mich.: Baker, 1977).

[9] Ibid., 33.

[10] Ibid., 56.

[11] Wayne Grudem, *Systematic Theology: An Introduction to Biblical Doctrine* (Grand Rapids, Mich.: Zondervan, 1995).

[12] Wayne Grudem, *Bible Doctrine*, ed. J. Purswell (Grand Rapids, Mich.: Zondervan, 1999).

For Grudem the Son's *role subordination*, like that of women, is not a matter of who does certain things, as we might expect on seeing the word *role*, but rather the matter of who commands and who obeys. He writes, "The Father has the role of commanding, directing, and sending" and the Son has "the role of obeying, going as the Father sends, and revealing God to us."[13] These words disclose the key issue: the Son is set eternally under the *authority* of the Father. This understanding of the Trinity, he emphatically claims, is historic orthodoxy.[14]

The doctrine of the *eternal* subordination of the Son is also found paradoxically in the book *God Under Fire: Modern Theology Reinvents God*.[15] Here twelve leading conservative evangelical scholars argue that many modern-day theologians have replaced "the transcendent and relational God of historic Christianity"[16] with a God depicted according to their own thoughts on what God should be like. What they want to reaffirm is "catholic Christianity," "the tradition," or, "traditional theology,"[17] which reflects the plain teaching of Scripture. The chapter on the Trinity is written by Bruce Ware, the senior associate dean of the school of theology and professor of Christian theology at the Southern Baptist Theological Seminary in Kentucky. He claims that historic orthodoxy teaches that the Son of God is "equal in being, eternally subordinate in role." The Trinity is a "functional hierarchy." There is an "eternal relationship of authority and obedience grounded in the eternal immanent inner-Trinitarian relations of Father, Son, and Holy Spirit."[18] If God is rightly called "Father," then Ware holds the divine Father must be set over the divine Son, for human fathers always have authority over their sons.[19] It is contemporary theologians, he argues, who speak of a coequal Trinity who have broken with historic orthodoxy!

Wayne Grudem's *Systematic Theology* was the first systematic theology to enunciate the doctrine of the eternal subordination of the Son in function/role and authority.

---

[13] Grudem, *Systematic Theology*, 250.

[14] This teaching is most starkly expressed in Wayne Grudem's latest book, *Evangelical Feminism and Biblical Truth* (Sisters, Ore.: Multnomah, 2004), 405–43.

[15] Douglas S. Huffman and Eric L. Johnson, eds., *God Under Fire: Modern Theology Reinvents God* (Grand Rapids, Mich.: Zondervan, 2002).

[16] Ibid., 2. See the opening essay by Huffman and Johnson, "Should the God of Historic Christianity Be Replaced?" on pp. 1–42.

[17] Ibid., 29.

[18] Ibid., 270. See Bruce Ware's essay "How Shall We Think about the Trinity?" on pp. 253–77. At the proofreading stage of this book, Bruce A. Ware's study *Father, Son and Holy Spirit: Relations, Roles and Relevance* (Wheaton, Ill.: Crossway, 2006), appeared. At this point of time I could not include this book in the debate. What Professor Ware says in this work basically reflects his views as they are documented here and elsewhere in my book.

[19] Ibid., 270. He writes, "What *does* it mean that the Father is the eternal *Father* of the Son and the Son is the eternal *Son* of the Father? Is not the eternal and inner-Trinitarian Father-Son relationship indicative of some eternal relationship of authority *within* the Trinity itself?"

Now other major theological textbooks written by conservative evangelicals have appeared teaching much the same thing. The four-volume *Systematic Theology* by Norman Geisler,[20] another much published and well-known American evangelical theologian, is one example. In his chapter on the Trinity he says, "All the members of the Trinity are equal but they do not have the same roles ... some functions are subordinated to others." The Father's "function is superior."[21] The Son's "submission is eternal." He relates to the Father as a son, that is, subordinately. "This functional subordination in the Godhead is not just temporal and economical: it is essential and eternal."[22] I would say in reply that if the Son's subordination is "essential" and "eternal," then is it ontological? The Son's eternal subordination defines his person. It is what is "essential" to his being.

Another example of a weighty theological tome written by a conservative evangelical that endorses the doctrine of the eternal subordination of the Son is John Frame's book *The Doctrine of God: A Theology of Lordship*.[23] Most of what Professor Frame of Westminster Theological Seminary says on the Trinity is classic orthodoxy. He affirms unequivocally that the Father, Son, and Holy Spirit are divine, and he says he rejects "the ontological subordination of Arius."[24] However, in a separate section on "subordination," he argues for the Son's "eternal subordination of role."[25] He holds that this sub-ordering produces an "eternal hierarchy" within the Godhead.[26] The Son and the Spirit are "subordinate to the commands of the Father, because that kind of subordination is appropriate to the *eternal nature* of the persons, the personal properties that distinguish each one from the others."[27] These last words should be carefully noted. Professor Frame is not only arguing that the Son and the Spirit are eternally subordinated *in role or function and thus in authority*, but also that this subordination "constitutes part of the distinctiveness of each."[28] Their subordination defines

---

[20] Norman Geisler, *Systematic Theology*, Vol. 2 (Minneapolis: Bethany, 2003).

[21] Ibid., 290.

[22] Ibid., 291.

[23] John Frame, *The Doctrine of God: A Theology of Lordship* (Phillipsburg, N.J.: P&R, 2002). Most of what Frame says on the Trinity is completely orthodox and helpful. Many of his comments exclude the thought that the Son is eternally set under the Father's authority. I will appreciatively quote things he says a number of times in what follows. It is only in the four pages (719–22) in the subsection entitled "Subordination" that he goes off the track. His commitment to the permanent subordination of women leads him to argue for the eternal subordination of the Son to justify the former.

[24] Ibid., 720.

[25] Ibid., 719–22.

[26] Ibid., 721. Three times on this one page he speaks of the eternal Trinity as "hierarchy."

[27] Ibid., 723. To be quite fair it has to be acknowledged that John Frame has many comments alongside such quotes that are orthodox. This does not excuse what he says in error.

[28] Ibid.

"*the eternal nature of the persons.*" Is this not saying the divine persons are *ontologically* differentiated? That they are *not* one in being as the Nicene Creed affirms?

Grudem's *Systematic Theology* is noteworthy because it is the first major systematic theological textbook to spell out the doctrine of the eternal subordination of the Son in authority. Robert Letham's 2004 book, *The Holy Trinity in Scripture, History, Theology, and Worship*,[29] is likewise noteworthy. It is the first major study specifically on the Trinity to expound and commend this teaching, albeit in muted form. Like Professor Frame's book, most of what Letham says in his book is historic orthodoxy. His outline of biblical teaching on the Trinity and the historic development of the doctrine is by far the best written by any evangelical to this point. We agree on a great deal. I quote him with approval and appreciation on a number of points later in this book. Dr. Letham accepts that speaking of " 'the eternal subordination of the Son' is outside the boundaries of the tradition."[30] Instead he tells us he teaches "the submission of the Son eternally."[31] How this differs from "the eternal subordination of the Son" completely escapes me. Surely if the Son is and cannot be otherwise than the eternally submissive Son, he is the eternally subordinated Son. Letham's teaching on the doctrine of the eternal "submission" of the Son appears in just a few pages that stand in opposition to most of what he says prior to this point.[32] This section in his book parallels Professor Frame's short digression in his book from historic orthodoxy. The reason Letham takes up this matter, he tells us, is to counter "the feminist" agenda "to eliminate anything appearing to give credence to submission by the Son to the Father in the Trinity."[33] To deny that the Son is eternally submissive to the Father, as others and I do, he holds, leads to "a thoroughgoing homogenization of the [divine] persons in fully mutual relations."[34] This then becomes a way to underpin "ontologically" "complete reciprocity between male and female in human society."[35] I take it he believes the reverse is also true. An argument for the eternal "submissiveness" of the Son gives an "ontological" basis for men ruling over women. This is his agenda.

---

[29] Letham, *The Holy Trinity*. I have written a somewhat lengthy review of this book soon to be published in the *Evangelical Quarterly*. I suggested to the editor that he invite Dr. Letham to make a response for publication to be placed after my review, and Dr. Letham accepted this offer.

[30] Ibid., 490, cf. 399.

[31] Ibid., 398. It is true that theologians are not limited to using only words in the Bible, but I would ask, Is it legitimate to reject the defining biblical term *hypotasso* (Col 3:18, 1Co 15:28), which means "to stand under" or "to be subordinate," and replace it with another word that implies something different?

[32] Ibid., 392–404.

[33] Ibid., 392.

[34] Ibid.

[35] Ibid.

Dr. Letham is aware that he is treading on dangerous ground and so he "emphatically" asserts that he is not speaking "of 'command structures,' 'hierarchy,' and 'boss-servant relationships,' "[36] and he is definitely not suggesting that the Son is "inferior" to the Father.[37] Nevertheless, having said these things, he argues that "the Son submits in eternity to the Father," "being God he serves the Father,"[38] the obedience the Son renders to the Father is "unconditional obedience,"[39] and "his human obedience reflects his divine submission."[40] On this last matter he adds, "It is impossible to separate the human obedience of Christ from who he is."[41] I take it this means "his being." He is not just eternally submissive as the incarnate Christ, or functionally submissive, or temporally submissive. He *is* the eternally submissive Son who is set under the Father's authority. Letham quotes Barth in support for this teaching. It is true that Barth speaks of the eternal subordination and obedience of the Son, but always dialectically. The Son of God for Barth is eternally at one and the same time both the sovereign electing God and the elect man called to obedience, both Lord and servant.[42] He is never for Barth the subordinated Son *simpliciter*. This dialectical understanding of the Son of God, foundational to Barth's Christology, is missed by Letham. How what Letham teaches in these few pages significantly differs from what Grudem, Geisler, Frame, and other evangelicals are teaching also completely escapes me. What is first denied seems to me to be then unambiguously affirmed. The Son has to give "unconditional obedience to the Father"[43] just like women must give unconditional obedience to the men set over them. Women's subordination is grounded "ontologically" on a Trinity where the Father rules and the Son obeys.

In Australia this teaching on the eternal subordination of the Son in function and authority has almost overwhelmed evangelicals. The Sydney Anglican Diocese, one of the largest and most strongly Reformed-evangelical dioceses in the world, has officially adopted this position. In 1999 the synod of this diocese accepted the *Sydney Anglican Diocesan Doctrine Commission Report*, "The Doctrine of the Trinity and Its Bearing on the Relationship of Men and Women," which unambiguously endorsed the eternal subordination of the Son and hierarchical ordering in the immanent Trin-

---

[36] Ibid., 398.

[37] Ibid., 399.

[38] Ibid., 402.

[39] Ibid., 401.

[40] Ibid., 403.

[41] Ibid., 396.

[42] In chapter eight Barth's doctrine of the Trinity will be expounded in detail. In an earlier section of Letham's book (pp. 271–90), when the "feminist threat" is not in mind, Letham gives a first-rate exposition of Barth's doctrine of the Trinity. He praises Barth for emphasizing the equality of the divine persons and their differentiation.

[43] Ibid., 401.

ity with ontological overtones.[44] After first affirming the full divinity of Christ, this document says that eternal *role* subordination is "only true as far as it goes."[45] What has to be recognized is that "the obedience of the Son to the Father reflects *the essence of the eternal relationship* between them."[46] The Son's eternal subordination "arises from the *very nature of his being* as Son: he is incapable of doing other than the Father's will."[47] The idea that the Son's subordination seen in the incarnation is voluntary and temporal is "both inadequate and untrue."[48] The Son and the Spirit's subordination "belongs to the very persons in their *eternal nature*."[49] The Eastern tradition's emphasis of the "priority of the Father" is commended because it "ensures a hierarchical mode of conceiving God."[50] Most startling of all is the claim that the Athanasian Creed clearly witnesses to a belief in *"differences of being"*[51] between the divine persons, something most theologians have thought this creed explicitly excludes. Equally surprising is the assertion that the Arians only "overemphasised the subordinationist elements in the NT."[52]

In these quotations I highlight some of the most questionable assertions in this statement of faith. Alongside these stand other comments affirming the full divinity of the Son, divine unity, and acceptance of what the creeds teach. This document is undeniably self-contradictory. What explains this is that the report was drawn up to answer the claim that the orthodox doctrine of the Trinity called into question the permanent subordination of women. In reply the most learned and senior conservative evangelical theologians in the diocese of Sydney[53] compiled this statement of faith to give an authoritative ruling on what Sydney Anglicans should believe about the Trinity. In doing so they had one intent, namely to theologically ground the subordination of women by appeal to the doctrine of the Trinity. The tail wagged the dog. The primary doctrine of the Christian faith, the doctrine of God, was corrupted to

---

[44] *Sydney Anglican Diocesan Doctrine Commission Report*, "The Doctrine of the Trinity and Its Bearing on the Relationship of Men and Women," (1999), *Year Book of the Diocese of Sydney* (Sydney, NSW: Diocesan Registry, 2000), 538–50. I give this document in full in my book *The Trinity and Subordinationism* (Westmont, Ill.: InterVarsity, 2002), 122–37

[45] Ibid., par. 32.

[46] Ibid. Italics added.

[47] Ibid., par. 18. Italics added.

[48] Ibid., pars. 33 and 32.

[49] Ibid., par. 33. Italics added.

[50] Ibid., par. 23.

[51] Ibid., par. 25. Italics added.

[52] Ibid., par. 22.

[53] The key participants were Bishop Paul Barnett (chair), Archbishop Donald Robinson (retired), Archbishop Peter Jensen, Bishop Robert Forsyth, Dr. John Woodhouse (the principal of Moore College), Dr. Peter O'Brien (the head of New Testament, Moore College), Dr. Robert Doyle (the head of systematics, Moore College). Also on the committee were Michael Bowie and Stephen Williams (Sydney parish clergy), and Narelle Jarret (the principal of Mary Andrew's College).

serve a less than noble cause. When I pointed out in *The Trinity and Subordinationism* that many comments in this statement of belief directly contradicted clear biblical teaching and what the creeds affirm, I found myself under attack. The archbishop of Sydney, Peter Jensen, who had been on the doctrine commission, denounced my work as a "hostile reading" of the report, I had numerous accusatory emails, there were letters to church papers claiming that I was the heretic, and I was even threatened with legal action—on what basis I cannot imagine.

On reading this report the primate of the Australian Anglican Church, Peter Carnley, the archbishop of Perth, was shocked and dismayed. In his 2004 book *Reflections in Glass*,[54] he accused the Sydney evangelical theologians of falling into "the ancient heresy of Arianism,"[55] selectively quoting from the Bible, setting the will of the Son of God in opposition to that of the Father, and calling into question the Son's equal status with the Father.[56] After some exchanges with the primate, the archbishop of Sydney agreed to reconstitute the Sydney Doctrine Commission to evaluate what the report said. The newly formed commission met for about eighteen months, and when Peter Carnley retired as primate in the middle of 2005, it ceased meeting without any response being made public. All that Chairman John Woodhouse, the principal of Moore College, would tell me was that they had reached a common mind.

In seeking to clarify what the Sydney evangelical theologians believed, I had an ongoing correspondence by email with Bishop Robert Forsyth.[57] He was a leading member of the 1999 Sydney Anglican doctrine commission and was then a member of the reconstituted commission. I wanted to make sure that my outline of the Sydney position in this book was fair and accurate. He did not contest my summary of key problematic comments from this report as given above, although he thought the quotes were selective and needed to be read in the context of each paragraph. In my earlier book I published the whole report so this could be done,[58] and I encourage readers of this book to read the whole document. What he asked me to make emphatically clear is that none of the members of the 1999 commission "consciously intended" to embrace key elements of Arianism, or deny what the creeds teach, or directly contradict the basic theological principle enshrined in the Nicene and Athanasian creeds. In particular they did not "consciously" intend to deny that the

---

[54] Peter Carnley, *Reflections in Glass* (Sydney: HarperCollins, 2004), 232–43.

[55] Ibid., 234–35.

[56] Ibid., 241.

[57] At the end of our discussions I sent him this section on the Sydney position from the manuscript. He thanked me for making the additions or corrections he suggested and said, "You have been careful and represented what I believe we did say and still believe" (email dated April 4, 2005, on file).

[58] Giles, *The Trinity and Subordinationism*, 122–37.

three divine persons are "one in being" (*homoousios*) by speaking of "differences of being." When I asked would he now like to reword anything in the report, or admit that some comments were to say the very least unhelpful, he declined. He said that "properly understood" the report teaches what "we" believe.

Possibly the most significant contributor to the 1999 *Sydney Doctrine Report* was Dr. Robert Doyle, the head of systematic theology at Moore Theological College, Sydney. How he understands this synod-endorsed statement of faith is spelled out in detail in an article he wrote seeking to refute what I had said in *The Trinity and Subordinationism*.[59] He insists that historic orthodoxy teaches the Son's "eternal relational subordination,"[60] "the priority of the Father in intra-trinitarian relations,"[61] and that the subordination seen in the incarnation is to be read back into the eternal Trinity.[62] Like Professors Ware and Grudem, he makes frequent appeal to human relationships to explain divine relationships. He says the Father is a "real father" and the Son "is a real son. Neither names are metaphorical."[63] The title *father* indicates that the divine Father rules; he is the divine "monarch." The title *son* indicates that the divine Son "defines himself in subordination to that monarchy."[64] Any authority he has is delegated authority. The Trinity is to be understood as "a hierarchy of loving relations."[65] And, he says, he cannot see how terms "like 'essence,' 'being,' 'eternal nature'" can be avoided "in talking about who they are [the divine persons] in their differences."[66] Again we have divine differentiation ontologically grounded, this time with no balancing assertions. What is more, Doyle argues, Athanasius, Augustine, Calvin, Barth, and Rahner all teach the eternal subordination of the Son in authority. They give, he insists, no support to my argument that to eternally subordinate the Son of God in being, work, or authority is to break with historic orthodoxy.

Sydney Anglican evangelical theologians, however, are not the only ones who believe that the eternal functional subordination of the Son has ontological implications for the divine persons. We have just seen that the conservative Reformed theologian John Frame admits this, as do Norman Geisler and George Knight. The latter speaks unashamedly of the "ontological"[67] foundation for the eternal functional subordination of the Son in authority. Likewise John Dahms grounds the Son's

---

[59] Robert Doyle, "Are We Heretics? A Review of *The Trinity and Subordinationism* by Kevin Giles," *The Briefing* (April 2004): 11–19.

[60] Ibid., 17.

[61] Ibid., 18 and 13.

[62] Ibid., 15.

[63] Ibid., 14.

[64] Ibid., 13.

[65] Ibid., 17.

[66] Ibid.

[67] Knight, *New Testament Teaching*, 56.

eternal functional subordination on his ontological subordination in two articles in the prestigious *Journal of the Evangelical Theological Society*,[68] as does Robert Letham in an article in the *Westminster Theological Journal*,[69] although he now admits his wording was "unfortunate."[70] However, whether or not the expression "ontological subordination" or equivalents is used is a small point. It is my case that once the word *eternal* is added to the word *subordination*, you have ontological subordination. Letham concedes this point.[71] If the Son is *eternally* subordinated to the Father in function and authority, then this defines his person, as Doyle and the Sydney theologians so clearly see. Indeed, to intrinsically connect sonship and subordination, as virtually all these evangelicals do, has ontological implications. To argue that the Son—because he is a son and cannot be otherwise—must be subordinate says that the Son is a subordinated person, not just the Son who functions subordinately.

In England trinitarian subordinationism has had a lower profile among evangelicals because the leadership of the evangelical movement is given by well-informed biblical scholars, historians, and theologians who do not countenance the idea that the Son is eternally subordinated to the Father. Nevertheless this teaching is well known in English evangelical circles. It is given classic expression in Michael Harper's widely read book *Equal and Different: Male and Female in the Church and Family.*[72] It is his view that the Trinity is ordered hierarchically.[73] There is "a chain of command" among the divine persons.[74] "The Father has the leading role. He is the Head of the Trinity ... the Son submits to him."[75] And to underline the point he adds, "The Persons of

---

[68] John Dahms, "The Generation of the Son," *Journal of the Evangelical Theological Society* 32, no. 4 (1989): 493–501 and "The Subordination of the Son," *Journal of the Evangelical Theological Society* 37, no. 3 (1994): 351–64.

[69] Robert Letham, "The Man-Woman Debate: Theological Comment," *Westminster Theological Journal* 52 (1990): 65–78. He speaks of "the ontological relations of the persons of the Trinity" (68) and of the subordination of the Son "in the order of subsistence" (73).

[70] Letham, *The Holy Trinity*, 490, 493.

[71] Ibid., 399, 490.

[72] Michael Harper, *Equal and Different: Male and Female in the Church and Family* (London: Hodder and Stoughton, 1994). Harper is undeniably to be seen as an English conservative evangelical theologian despite the fact that he was a leader of the charismatic movement in the Anglican Church for many years and later joined the Orthodox Church when women were ordained. In this book he follows the post-1970s' novel view that men and women are equal yet have different permanent roles, meaning men are to lead, women obey, and he grounds this opinion on a permanently binding social order given in creation that applies only in the home and the church. He quotes with approval the work of Grudem and Piper.

[73] Ibid. Michael Harper uses the word *hierarchy* repeatedly, giving two extended discussions on this term on pp. 13–14 and 121–22. He says the word may be used of "a system with grades of status or authority ranking one above another in a series" (p. 14).

[74] Ibid., 121.

[75] Ibid., 156.

the Trinity are not an egalitarian relationship, for both the Son and the Spirit are in a relationship of submission to the Father."[76] He says the importance of this teaching cannot be "stressed too strongly" because it is only on this basis that the "headship" of human fathers can be upheld in today's world.[77]

Another example of this teaching from the English context is given by the Anglican evangelical theologian Tom Smail in his book *Like Father, Like Son*.[78] His thesis is that human relations should be modeled and prescribed by divine relations. He thus first warns of the danger of creating God in our own image: of depicting God in terms of fallen human realtionships.[79] Sadly he does just this himself. He begins by arguing that God has set men over women in creation; the man is the head of the woman.[80] Repeatedly he speaks of male "priority."[81] Men and women, he says, are equal in dignity and worth, but God has given "different roles" to each sex. Men as men are created to lead, women as women to obey. His doctrine of the Trinity exactly reflects this teaching. Historic orthodoxy, he claims, teaches "ontological equality and functional subordination" in the Trinity.[82] The divine persons are differentiated solely by their differing roles or functions.[83] The Father is distinguished as the Father by his "initiating sovereignty."[84] He is "the prototype of leadership."[85] The Son is distinguished as the Son by "his attentive obedience."[86] He gladly does as the Father commands. In divine relations and in the male-female relationship, there is, he says, "a hierarchy of headship."[87]

In other popular English publications the eternal subordination of the Son is also endorsed.[88] Most recently it was given expression in the conservative evangelical journal *The Churchman*, in an article by Peter Adam supporting the teaching of the Sydney Doctrine Commission.[89] In the Church of England this teaching on the

---

[76] Ibid., 161.

[77] Ibid., 2, 84, 155, 164–76.

[78] Thomas Smail, *Like Father, Like Son: The Trinity Imaged in Our Humanity* (Milton Keynes, Bucks.: Paternoster, 2005). See also Thomas Smail, *The Forgotten Father: Rediscovering the Heart of the Christian Gospel* (London: Hodder and Stoughton, 1980), 113–22.

[79] Ibid., 1–37.

[80] Ibid., 54.

[81] Ibid., 54, 247, 251, 258, 259, 260.

[82] Ibid., 76.

[83] Ibid.

[84] Ibid., 103

[85] Ibid., 161.

[86] Ibid., 104.

[87] Ibid., 260.

[88] See for example Werner Neuer, *Man and Woman in Christian Perspective*, trans. Gordon Wenham (London: Hodder and Stoughton, 1988), 111, 128; Bruce Ware, "Tampering with the Trinity," *Evangelicals Now* (April 2002).

[89] Peter Adam, "Honouring Jesus Christ," *The Churchman* 119, no. 1 (2005): 35–50.

eternal subordination of the Son has been taken up by "Reform," the vocal conservative faction among English evangelical Anglicans, who among other things are opposed to women in charge of parishes, and especially to women bishops.[90] The idea that the Son is eternally subordinated in function and authority is growing in influence in England as more and more evangelical theological colleges and Bible schools make Wayne Grudem's *Systematic Theology* a set text. This book, written and first published in the US, was published subsequently by Inter-Varsity Press in England.

Although all of these evangelical theologians say that they affirm unequivocally the divinity of Christ and the oneness in being of Father and Son in the immanent Trinity, and that they reject "Arianism" (a very imprecise term, as we will show), their position implies the eternal ontological subordination of the Son. If the Son's eternal functional subordination in authority defines his person, and the Father's eternal functional ruling role over the Son defines his person, then the Son *is* (not just functions as) the eternally subordinated Son of God and the Father *is* (not just functions as) the eternal monarch set over the Son. Most of those who take this position seem to recognize this, as we have just noted, despite their denials. But whether or not ontological language is used, one of the basic arguments of this book is that to speak of the *eternal subordination of the Son* in function and authority by necessity implies ontological subordinationism. The great theologians of the past and the creeds and confessions all recognize this and thus teach, as we will show, that the three divine persons are inseparable in operations or functions and indivisible in power and authority.

One of the more important things to note in this new doctrine of the Trinity is that it implies that the Father and the Son and by implication the Holy Spirit each have their own will. The Son has to submit his will to the Father's will, like a wife has to submit her will to that of her husband. If each divine person has his own will, the unity of the one Godhead is destroyed. For this reason orthodoxy with one voice insists that the three divine persons have one will and always work in perfect harmony and unison. By reformulating the doctrine of the Trinity by moving from the husband-wife relationship to the divine Father-Son relationship, the historic orthodox doctrine of the Trinity has been profoundly corrupted. As a result, not only is subordinationism embraced but so also tritheism.

---

[90] See for example the paper by Mike Ovey on the Reform Website, "Scripture and Authority" www.reform.org.uk/bb/defendingdesire.html. The Church of England Bishop Wallace Benn opposes the ordination of women by appealing to the Trinity, a position he outlines in an essay which is printed in Wayne Grudem, *Evangelical Feminism and Biblical Truth*, 541–43. In his review of my book *The Trinity and Subordinationism* in *The Churchman* 117, no. 3 (2003): 267–71, Gerald Bray agrees with my thesis that the Son is not to be thought of as eternally subordinate to the Father yet adds that he would endorse the eternal "submission" of the Son.

It is also to be noted that this novel doctrine of the Trinity openly and consistently endorses hierarchical ordering in the eternal or immanent Trinity.[91] The Father rules over the Son. The 1999 *Sydney Doctrine Report* commends the supposed Eastern tradition's emphasis of the "priority of the Father" that "ensures a hierarchical mode of conceiving God." In the conservative evangelical symposium *Recovering Biblical Manhood and Womanhood: A Response to Evangelical Feminism,*[92] hierarchical ordering in the male-female relationship and the divine Father-Son relationship is mentioned time and time again, and the two are related.[93] One contributor, Elisabeth Elliot, speaks of "a glorious hierarchical order of graduated splendour, beginning with the Trinity."[94] In 2004 Robert Doyle, a key contributor to the 1999 *Sydney Doctrine Report*, was still insisting on the "priority of the Father" and describing the Trinity as "a hierarchy of loving relations."[95] Similarly Professor John Frame speaks of an "eternal hierarchy of role within the Trinity,"[96] while J. Scott Horrell, professor of theology at Dallas Theological Seminary, speaks of "the hierarchy of the economic Godhead."[97] The English theologian Michael Harper makes hierarchical ordering in the immanent Trinity one of the most important and basic aspects of his doctrine of God.[98] Tom Smail is more circumspect, but he too speaks of a "hierarchy of headship" in divine and human relations.[99]

This evangelical preoccupation with fixed hierarchical ordering is somewhat paradoxical. It seems to reflect an attempt to reinstate a form of social ordering modern culture has largely repudiated. In contrast Athanasius, the Cappadocian Fathers, Augustine, Aquinas, and Calvin—who lived in thoroughly hierarchically structured social contexts—unambiguously and emphatically opposed hierarchical ordering in the Godhead, as we will show in due course. Aquinas quite explicitly says, "For among divine persons there is a kind of natural order but not hierarchic order."[100]

---

[91] Besides the other references given in this paragraph see James B. Hurley, *Man and Woman in Biblical Perspective* (Grand Rapids, Mich.: Zondervan, 1981), 167; Paul Barnett, *1 Corinthians* (Ross-shire, UK: Christian Focus, 2000), 200.

[92] John Piper and Wayne Grudem, eds., *Recovering Biblical Manhood and Womanhood: A Response to Evangelical Feminism* (Wheaton, Ill: Crossway, 1991).

[93] Ibid., 67, 83, 104, 130, 162, 163, 257, 282, 290, 293, 394, 412, 414, 415, 418, 462, 481, 492, 494, 500, 533, 534.

[94] Ibid., "The Essence of Feminity," 394.

[95] Doyle, "Are We Heretics?" 17.

[96] Frame, *The Doctrine of God*, 721.

[97] J. Scott Horrell, "Toward a Biblical Model of the Social Trinity: Avoiding Equivocation of Nature and Order," *Journal of the Evangelical Theological Society* 47, no. 3 (2004): 399–421.

[98] Harper, *Equal and Different*, 6, 14, 83, 153–63.

[99] Smail, *Like Father, Like Son*, 260.

[100] Thomas Aquinas, *Summa Theologiae*, trans. T. C. O'Brien (London: Blackfriars, 1975), 1.108.1 (p. 125).

These theologians were countercultural, because the Bible's clear teaching on the unity and equality of the divine persons forced them to break with their cultural and social norms when thinking about the triune God.

So pervasive and entrenched has the doctrine of the *eternal* subordination of the Son in function and authority become in conservative evangelical circles that it is hard to find evangelical theologians who openly oppose this teaching, recognizing its heretical nature. It is now widely thought that this is "what the Bible teaches" and what historic orthodoxy affirms. Those who argue otherwise are accused of "tampering" with the orthodox doctrine of the Trinity and introducing a novel doctrine of the Trinity![101] Besides an excellent article by Professor Gilbert Bilezikian,[102] I know of no other specific protest to this teaching by evangelicals.[103]

How Could Evangelicals Get Their Doctrine of the Trinity So Wrong?

The central thesis of this book is that the contemporary evangelical case for the eternal subordination of the Son is a clear breach with historic orthodoxy. It is impossible, I will argue in what follows, to reconcile what is being taught with what Athanasius, the Cappadocian Fathers, Augustine, Calvin, the Nicene and Athanasian creeds, and the Reformation confessions teach on the Trinity. For Western Christians the Athanasian Creed has been understood for fifteen centuries to sum up the orthodox or catholic doctrine of the Trinity. This creed directly excludes what too many conservative evangelicals believe about the Trinity. It declares that the three divine persons are "coequal," "none is before or after another, none greater or less than another," all three are "almighty" and "Lord." If this is the case, then the question arises: How is it that so many evangelicals believe what is patently counter to the Christian faith as it has been defined in the past?

Three things have led to this disastrous outcome. First of all, this new and dangerous doctrine of the Trinity has gained wide support among evangelicals because they have not recognized that this teaching is an old heresy in a new form. This has been possible because evangelicals have tended to be weak on historical theology in general and on the historical development of the doctrine of the Trinity in particular. On this last matter evangelicals have not been alone in their ignorance, even if it has

---

[101]Ware, "Tampering with the Trinity," and Grudem, *Evangelical Feminism*, 416.

[102]Gilbert Bilezikian, "Hermeneutical Bungee-Jumping: Subordination in the Godhead," *Journal of the Evangelical Theological Society* 40, no. 1 (1997): 57–68. Reprinted in *Community 101* (Grand Rapids, Mich.: Zondervan, 1997), 187–202.

[103]It is to be noted, however, that the respected conservative evangelical theologian Millard Erickson is totally opposed to the eternal subordination of the Son and to hierarchical ordering in the Trinity (*God in Three Persons*). He simply does not engage with the "woman question." Similarly Grenz, *Rediscovering the Triune God*, opposes subordinationism but does not engage directly with his fellow evangelicals who are subordinationists.

been more pervasive than in Catholic and mainline Protestant circles. Until the resurgence of interest in the doctrine of the Trinity initiated by Karl Barth, it is often said the doctrine of the Trinity was in "exile." It was a doctrine wandering in the wilderness that few were interested in. Second, this new doctrine has gained support among evangelicals because in many nineteenth- and twentieth-century evangelical theological texts comments can be found that endorse subordinationism, or can be read to do so. Evangelicals have thus assumed that the eternal subordination of the Son is sound evangelical theology. Third and most important, the doctrine of the eternal subordination of the Son in function and authority was developed by respected evangelical theologians whom other evangelicals assumed had it right. I now spell out in more detail these three contributing factors that have led to the widespread acceptance of this new and dangerous doctrine of the Trinity among evangelicals.

The Trinity in Exile

From the time of Thomas Aquinas in the twelfth century for Roman Catholics and from the time of John Calvin in the sixteenth century for Protestants, very little if any fresh thought was given to the doctrine of the Trinity.[104] In theological texts it became common for the doctrine of the one God and his attributes to be formally discussed at great length before an outline of the doctrine of the Trinity was given, almost as an addendum.[105] Not surprisingly in this bleak time for the doctrine of the Trinity, informed discussions on the historically developed doctrine of the Trinity were rare, and trinitarian heresies flourished. Some theologians embraced unitarianism, some modalism, and some subordinationism. Most were simply confused, being ignorant of the content of historical orthodoxy. The nineteenth and early twenty-first centuries are usually singled out as the bleakest period for the doctrine of the Trinity. Evangelicals, possibly more than any other section of the church, reflected this confusion about and neglect of the historic doctrine of the Trinity that characterized this period.

For most of the nineteenth and twentieth centuries evangelicals showed little interest in the doctrine of the Trinity. When I studied systematic theology at

---

[104]Claude Welch, *The Trinity in Contemporary Theology* (London: SCM, 1953), 3–34, and William C. Placher, *The Domestication of Transcendence* (Louisville: Westminster, 1996), 164–78. Richard H. Muller, *The Triunity of God*, vol. 4, *Post-Reformation Reformed Dogmatics* (Grand Rapids, Mich.: Baker, 2003), however, argues that the post-Reformation Reformed scholastics did make an important contribution. Despite his scholarship I was not convinced. From his own work I note that the post-Reformation scholastics consistently argued for the primacy of the Father (200, 254, 265, 269) and developed the idea that the Son was subordinated in order (84, 324) and subordinated in divine operations (84, 255, 263, 269).

[105]On Roman Catholics see Karl Rahner, *The Trinity* (London: Burns and Oates, 1970), 10–20, and on Catholics and Protestants Placher, *Domestication*, 75–79.

seminary in the mid-sixties, the Trinity was only one of many doctrines introduced, and if I remember it was covered in two lectures. It was not recognized that this is the primary doctrine of the Christian faith, our doctrine of God. The evangelicals I have spoken to about this in England and North America tell me this was their experience as well. In the famous twelve-volume work *The Fundamentals*, produced between 1910 and 1915, which purported to be an exposition of "the central doctrines" of Christianity, the Trinity is not even discussed. In 1982 Carl Henry, whom some call "the father of modern conservative evangelicalism," says that evangelicals have not yet "contributed significant literature to the current revival of trinitarian interest."[106] Robert Letham in his 2004 book *The Holy Trinity*, in an attempt to put right this problem, says, "Sadly from the time of Calvin, little of significance has been contributed to the development of Trinitarian doctrine by conservative Reformed theologians.... This lacuna on the part of conservative Christianity is little short of tragic."[107]

However, it is not just that evangelicals have shown little interest in the historically developed doctrine of the Trinity; they have all too often also got it wrong. Subordinationism in one form or another has all too often been endorsed by evangelical theologians, or ambiguously dealt with. This is still the case today.

Contemporary evangelicals who teach the eternal subordination of the Son in function and authority can thus find quotes from evangelical worthies from the past that seem to support what they are teaching today. So the compilers of the 1999 *Sydney Doctrine Report* assert that "the Calvinists (Edwards, Berkhof, Hodge, Dabney, Packer, and Knox)"[108] and T. C. Hammond[109] all embrace "a certain subordination as to the manner of subsistence" of the Son and the Spirit. In his 1995 *Systematic Theology*, Wayne Grudem says C. Hodge and A. H. Strong teach what he teaches, the eternal functional subordination of the Son apart from his ontological subordination.[110] In his 2004 book *Evangelical Feminism*, he adds to these names Benjamin B. Warfield, Philip Schaff, and Geoffrey Bromiley.[111]

In response to this list of evangelical worthies who supposedly support the eternal subordination of the Son in function and authority, three things need to be said. First, some of the people listed do not embrace subordinationism in any form. They in fact oppose this idea. Calvin and Warfield definitely fit this category. I suspect so too does

---

[106]Carl Henry, *God, Revelation and Authority: God Who Speaks and Shows*, vol. 5 (Waco, Tex: Word, 1982), 212.

[107]Letham, *The Holy Trinity*, ix–x.

[108]*Sydney Doctrine Report*, par. 26.

[109]Ibid., par. 15.

[110]Grudem, *Systematic Theology*, 252.

[111]Grudem, *Evangelical Feminism*, 422.

Jonathan Edwards.[112] Second, in regard to nineteenth- and twentieth-century evangelical theologians, I think the above list is too short. The idea that somehow the Son of God is subordinated in the eternal or immanent Trinity is endemic in evangelical writings past and present. In the past this occurred because most theologians seem to have been largely ignorant of what the great theologians such as Athanasius, the Cappadocians, Augustine, and Calvin actually taught on the Trinity. In the present it is driven by the concern to find a theological basis for the permanent subordination of women. Third, before accepting uncritically that all the people listed are *consistent* subordinationists, or in particular that they *endorse the eternal subordination in function and authority* of the Son apart from ontological subordination, the writings of these theologians should be carefully studied. Where they are consistent subordinationists they invariably teach a subordination in being *and* function, and where they are not they are simply confused or ambiguous in wording, often giving contradictory statements in near proximity. None of those quoted speak of *the eternal role or functional subordination of the Son apart from subordination in being.* This is an idea Wayne Grudem invented.

Charles Hodge, the nineteenth-century staunchly conservative Presbyterian theologian who was for fifty years professor of systematic theology at Princeton Seminary,[113] was definitely a subordinationist. For him three "essential facts" sum up the

---

[112]On his views see Richard M. Weber, "The Trinitarian Theology of Jonathan Edwards: An Investigation of Charges Against Its Orthodoxy," *Journal of the Evangelical Theological Society* 44, no. 2 (2001): 297–318. See also Amy Plantinga Pauw, *The Supreme Harmony of All: The Trinitarian Theology of Jonathan Edwards* (Grand Rapids, Mich.: Eerdmans, 2002).

[113]Princeton Seminary was the most influential theological training institute in the United States in the nineteenth century. From its inception in 1812 the main theological text studied was Francis Turretin, *The Institutes of Elenctic Theology*, ed. J. T. Dennison, trans. G. M. Giger, vol. 1 (Phillipsburg, N.J.: P&R, 2002). Turretin, a learned scholastic Reformed theologian, was a successor to Calvin in Geneva. This work was widely used in Europe as well. Turretin's exposition of the doctrine of God is as far away from Calvin's as you could imagine. After nearly a hundred pages on the one true God that examines almost every philosophical issue and logical distinction imaginable, Turretin comes to the doctrine of the Trinity. At first I suspected him of modalism because he argues "the persons differ from the [one divine] essence not 'really' or 'essentially' but 'modally'" (278). However, on turning the page, I then suspected him of subordinationism. He writes, "With respect to (that) order a certain pre-eminence is attributed by theologians to the Father, not indeed as to essence and deity (because the persons being consubstantial the highest equality exists among them), but as to mode (both in subsisting and in working): because both as to order and as to origin, he precedes the Son and the Holy Spirit" (280).

This language is certainly confusing and seemingly contrary to the Nicene and Athanasian Creeds, but what is most surprising is that most of the discussion is divorced from virtually any reference to Scripture, or to how Scripture has been understood by the trinitarian theological luminaries such as Athanasius, the Cappadocians, Augustine, and Calvin. For a more positive estimation of Turretin's work on the Trinity see Muller, *The Triunity of God*, 109, 174–76, 193–94.

doctrine of the Trinity: "unity of essence, distinction of persons, and subordination."[114] He mostly speaks the language of the trinitarian orthodoxy, but repeatedly (thirteen times) he insists on "the principle of subordination of the Son to the Father, and the Spirit to the Father and the Son"[115]—hierarchical ordering in the Trinity. This subordination, he says, is in "the mode of subsistence and operation of the persons."[116]

Subordination in "modes of operation" indicates that the Son does as the Father directs and the Spirit does as the Father and the Son direct. In their functions or work, the Son and the Spirit are set under the Father. The Father is first, the Son is second, and the Spirit is third in authority.[117] The concept of subordination in "subsistence" is a little more complex. Hodge's definition of the Trinity as "one divine being [who] subsists in three persons, Father, Son and Holy Spirit" helps explain things.[118] "To subsist" means "to exist in or as." For Hodge there is one divine substance who "subsists" in, or as, the Father, Son, and Holy Spirit. In the technical terminology of trinitarian discourse, one may speak of either three divine "persons," or "hypostases," or "subsistences." Hodge is thus claiming that in his eternal personal existence as the Son, the second person of the Trinity is subordinated to the person of the Father, and in his personal existence as the Holy Spirit, the third person of the Trinity is subordinated to the first and second persons in the immanent or eternal Trinity. The Father is first not only in his operations or works (functional superiority) but also first in his "subsistence"—personal existence as the Father (ontological superiority)—and the Son second, and the Spirit third. He thus speaks of the Son as "inferior in rank."[119] Hodge is depicting the eternal Trinity as an ontological and operational hierarchy. Paul Jewett says that Hodge's doctrine of the Trinity is "remarkable in its confusion."[120] In ordering the divine three hierarchically, Hodge unashamedly reflected his own social presuppositions more than those of the Bible or historic orthodoxy. Hodge believed that God had instituted a hierarchically ordered society where whites ruled over blacks and men over women. He was the most important evangelical voice for the biblical case for slavery.[121]

---

[114] Charles Hodge, *Systematic Theology*, vol. 1 (Edinburgh: T&T Clark, 1960), 467.

[115] Ibid., 460. See also 445, 461, 462, 464, 465, 467, 468, 474.

[116] Ibid., 445, 461. Muller, *The Triunity of God*, 184, explains how the Reformed scholastics came to speak of "the modes" of subsistence and operations, rather than just subsistence and operations.

[117] Ibid., 445. See Benjamin Warfield, *Biblical Foundations* (Grand Rapids, Mich.: Eerdmans, 1958), 110–11, for a clear and concise explanation of what is meant by "operational subordination," something he utterly rejects.

[118] Ibid., 444, 445, 454.

[119] Ibid., 469.

[120] Paul Jewett, *God, Creation and Revelation* (Grand Rapids, Mich.: Eerdmans, 1991), 317.

[121] For more on this see my book *The Trinity and Subordinationism*, 74, 215–23.

Hodge is correctly quoted as supporting subordinationism but not as supporting the contemporary evangelical teaching on the eternal *role* subordination of the *Son apart from his subordination in being*. Hodge speaks of the eternal subordination of the Son in his "mode of subsistence *and* operations," in his person as the Son and in what he does as the Son. He teaches an eternal subordination in being *and* function. He thinks these two things are the two sides of one coin. Because the Son is eternally subordinated in subsistence, he is eternally subordinated in operations or functions. Grudem may claim Hodge endorses his position, but the truth is Hodge gives no support whatsoever to the idea that you can have eternal role or operational subordination apart from ontological subordination. He is of the opposite opinion. The eternal ontological subordination of the Son implies his eternal operational subordination and vice versa.

Among those quoted as supporting the eternal subordination of the Son, the most significant name next to Hodge is Louis Berkhof, possibly the most influential conservative Reformed theologian of the twentieth century in the English-speaking world. In his extended discussion on the Trinity in his *Systematic Theology* he closely follows Herman Bavinck's *Gereformeerde Dogmatiek,* volume 2.[122] Bavinck was totally opposed to all expressions of subordinationism. As a general rule so too is Berkhof. Thus he commends both Augustine for "entirely eliminating" subordinationism[123] and Barth, who "does not allow for any subordination."[124] He says his own opinion is that there can be "no subordination as to essential being of the one person in the Godhead to another, and therefore no difference in dignity,"[125] and "there are never works of one person exclusively, but always works of the divine being as a whole."[126] Nevertheless, he makes a couple of passing comments that can be read to suggest subordinationism. First he speaks of a "subordination in respect to order and relationship,"[127] and a little later he says that the generation of the Son and the procession of the Spirit "imply a certain subordination as to the manner of personal subsistence, but no subordination as far as the possession of the divine essence is concerned."[128] These words could be taken to refer to hierarchical ordering in the eternal or immanent Trinity or simply to a subordination in the economy of salvation and sanctification—the historical work of the Son and the Spirit in the world. If the former is the case, then in these

---

[122]This book was first published in Dutch in 1897. In 1957 it was translated by William Hendricksen as *The Doctrine of God* (Grand Rapids, Mich.: Baker). All references to this work are to the English translation.
[123]Louis Berkhof, *Systematic Theology* (London: Banner of Truth, 1958), 83.
[124]Ibid., 84.
[125]Ibid., 88.
[126]Ibid., 89.
[127]Ibid., 88.
[128]Ibid., 89.

comments we see a reflection of Hodge's influence. As a young man Berkhof studied at Princeton for two years. I personally think the latter is the case. But whatever we decide on this, one thing is clear. Berkhof gives no support whatsoever to the idea that the Son of God is eternally subordinated in function but not in being. The whole idea is completely foreign to him, and we should not read it into what he says.

T. C. Hammond (1877–1961), the Irish-trained evangelical theologian, who in 1935 became the principal of Moore Theological College, Sydney, is equally ambiguous on this matter. He is frequently quoted in the Australian context as endorsing the eternal subordination of the Son before the "women question" arose. His little introduction to Christian doctrine, *In Understanding Be Men*, first published in 1936,[129] was republished many times and was used in innumerable theological colleges, seminaries, and Bible colleges around the world. In his brief synopsis of the doctrine of the Trinity, Hammond gives an excellent summary of orthodoxy in which he emphasizes the full divinity of the three persons, rejects any "opposition between the persons," and speaks of the persons of the Trinity as "coequal."[130] To conclude his brief discussion on the doctrine of the Trinity, he gives a three-point summary. The doctrine of the Trinity demands belief in "the unity of the Godhead," "the full deity of the Son," and "the subordination of the Son and the Spirit to the Father."[131] This last comment comes as quite a surprise. It does not reflect anything he has said previously. It seems unlikely that he is speaking of a subordination in the eternal or immanent Trinity because he rejects ontological subordinationism, and nowhere does he mention functional or role subordination. It could be he is only speaking of a temporal subordination in operations in the work of the Son and the Spirit for our salvation and sanctification. What he believed is unclear, but it cannot be denied that this comment is ambiguous. Again he offers not one scintilla of support for eternal role subordination apart from ontological subordination.

The quoting of comments by respected evangelical theologians of the past that supposedly endorse the contemporary evangelical doctrine of the eternal subordination of the Son have naturally impacted on current evangelical thinking. It has encouraged evangelicals to believe that the eternal subordination of the Son in function and authority is sound evangelical theology. The truth is that no one before 1970 had ever spoken of *eternal* role subordination, and orthodoxy has never endorsed the eternal subordination of the Son of God in work, operations, functions, or authority that can somehow be accepted without compromising ontological equality. Professors George Knight and Wayne Grudem invented this idea. Historic orthodoxy has

---

[129]T. C. Hammond, *In Understanding Be Men* (London: IVF, 1936). Printed and revised numerous times. My copy used at Moore College, Sydney, in the 1960s is dated 1961.
[130]Ibid., 53–57.
[131]Ibid., 57.

always insisted that if the Son is *eternally* subordinated in his works/operations/functions or authority then he must be ontologically subordinated and vice versa. His work or functions speak of who he is — his being. Hodge was correct in seeing this connection.

I say again, it is because evangelicals have not been strong on historical theology in general and on the historical development of the orthodox doctrine of the Trinity in particular that this new form of an old heresy has flourished. Without the wisdom that history gives, many contemporary evangelicals have embraced subordinationism thinking it is evangelical orthodoxy.

Evangelicals Who Did Not Get Lost in the Exile

Grudem quotes B. B. Warfield as one of those who supports the eternal subordination of the Son in function apart from ontological subordination, but nothing could be further from the truth. Warfield directly opposes this understanding of the Trinity. He is one of the very few theologians of the late nineteenth and early twentieth centuries who had a firm grasp of the historical development of the doctrine of the Trinity, and thus he stands as a bright light in a dark period for evangelical thinking on the Trinity. His detailed study of Calvin's doctrine of the Trinity is an exceptional piece of work.[132] He tells us he writes on the Trinity to "reassert the principle of equalization."[133] He is totally opposed to the idea that the Son of God is eternally subordinate to the Father in "subsistence and operations," but he never openly speaks against Hodge or his ideas. For him the Son's subordination in "the redemptive process" is completed on the cross.[134] It is not to be read back into the eternal "modes of subsistence" — the eternal being of the Son in the immanent Trinity. To do this, he says, would "impair the [Son's] complete identity with the Father in being and the *complete equality with the Father in power.*"[135] In speaking of the Son's subordination in the "redemptive process" and in calling this a "functional subordination," possibly for the first time, he reflects the terminology and thought world of his own context, but in the last case not without possible confusion. There is no problem in saying that Christ is "functionally" subordinated to the Father in his temporal work of redemption as the second Adam. A problem only arises if it is claimed that he is eternally functionally subordinated. He is subordinated on earth and in heaven.

Another clear and unambiguous account of trinitarian orthodoxy, given by an evangelical before the contemporary renaissance of interest in this doctrine, is given

---

[132]B. B. Warfield, "Calvin's Doctrine of the Trinity," in B. B. Warfield, *Calvin and Augustine* (Philadelphia: Presbyterian and Reformed, 1956), 189–284.

[133]B. B. Warfield, "Biblical Doctrine," 116.

[134]Ibid., 110.

[135]Ibid., 112. Italics added.

by the Dutch Reformed theologian Herman Bavinck (1854–1921) in his *Dogmatics*, translated into English in abbreviated form as *The Doctrine of God*.[136] In this work Bavinck not only gives an excellent outline of the historic development of the orthodox doctrine of the Trinity but also forcefully argues against the acceptance of any form of modalism or subordinationism.[137] For him Arianism is only one form or expression of the heresy called "subordinationism."[138] He says that in Augustine "all subordinationism is banished."[139]

Cornelius Van Til, longtime professor of apologetics at Westminster Seminary, Philadelphia, also wrote in opposition to the eternal subordination of the Son in being or function well before the question of women's emancipation had come onto center stage for many conservative evangelicals. Paradoxically, some of the most significant present-day American advocates of the permanent subordination of women and the eternal subordination of the Son trained at Westminster Seminary (e.g., George Knight, Wayne Grudem, John Frame, and Robert Letham). Professor Van Til does not allow that divine equality and divine differences can be set in opposition, as if one had to be chosen over the other. For him the Trinity resolves the age-old debate over the one and the many. In the Trinity the one and the three are both ultimate.[140] In reply to those who read back into the eternal Trinity the subordination seen in the incarnation, he says, "All heresies with respect to the Trinity may be reduced to one great heresy of mixing the eternal with the temporal."[141] And in answer to those who quote the Bible to prove that the Son of God is eternally subordinated to the Father, he says, "A consistent biblical doctrine of the Trinity would imply the complete rejection of all subordinationism."[142]

None of the general introductions to the doctrine of the Trinity written by conservative evangelicals in the "post-exilic period" for this doctrine, it is pleasing to note, give any encouragement to the idea that God the Son is eternally subordinated to God the Father. The books by Christopher Kaiser,[143] Charles Sherlock,[144] Gerald Bray,[145]

---

[136]Herman Bavinck, *The Doctrine of God*, trans. William Hendricksen (Grand Rapids, Mich.: Baker, 1979).

[137]See ibid., 280, 281, 283, 288, 313–14.

[138]Ibid., 288–89.

[139]Ibid., 283.

[140]Cornelius Van Til, *The Defense of the Faith* (Philadelphia: Presbyterian and Reformed, 1955), 25–28.

[141]Cornelius Van Til, *An Introduction to Systematic Theology* (Phillipsburg, N.J.: Presbyterian and Reformed, 1971), 220.

[142]Cornelius Van Til, *A Christian Theory of Knowledge* (Philadelphia: Presbyterian and Reformed, 1969), 104.

[143]Christopher Kaiser, *The Doctrine of God* (London: Marshall Morgan and Scott, 1982).

[144]Charles Sherlock, *God on the Inside* (Canberra, Aust.: Acorn, 1991).

[145]Gerald Bray, *The Doctrine of God* (London: Inter-Varsity, 1993).

Roger Olson and Christopher Hall,[146] Stanley Grenz,[147] and Millard Erickson[148] all consider subordinationism to be a dangerous error. With one voice they argue that the Bible and creedal orthodoxy speak of a "coequal" Trinity where no one person is eternally set under another. Many other respected contemporary evangelical theologians, in briefer discussions on the Trinity, also insist on the full equality of the three persons, rejecting all forms of subordinationism.[149] What none of these books do, except for the one by Erickson and then very briefly, is address directly the contemporary evangelical doctrine of the eternal role or functional subordination of the Son. These authors simply speak in opposition to subordinationism, which they think is an old heresy, no longer a pressing threat to the modern church. No warning is given to the fact that to eternally subordinate the Son in his work, functions, or roles implies by necessity ontological subordinationism.

Why the Doctrine of the Eternal Subordination of the Son Has Flourished

When the question of the status and ministry of women suddenly erupted in the late 1960s and early 1970s, conservative evangelicals were ill-prepared to deal with the theological and hermeneutical issues this raised. At first it seemed that to accept the emancipation of women would involve rejecting what the Bible taught, something no evangelical could do. It was some decades before the majority of evangelicals concluded that the *interpretation* of biblical teaching on women that they had inherited was not what the Bible actually said. At first the best response to the emancipation of women for evangelicals seemed to be the pioneering reformulation of the old position by George Knight III that I have already outlined. He linked women's permanent subordination in role with the eternal role subordination of the Son. Following Knight's book, evangelicals committed to the permanent subordination of women made much of this supposed parallel between the Son's *eternal* subordination and women's *permanent* subordination. This connection with the Trinity seemed to give the knockout blow to those evangelicals who were arguing that women should be seen as partners in marriage and be free to use God-given gifts of leadership in the church.

It is this "great cause," the permanent subordination of women, that generated this new doctrine of the Trinity. For some evangelicals "the woman question" is the

---

[146]Roger Olson and Christopher Hall, *The Trinity* (Grand Rapids, Mich.: Eerdmans, 2002).

[147]Stanley Grenz, *Rediscovering the Triune God: The Trinity in Contemporary Theology* (Minneapolis: Augsburg Fortress, 2004). Also see his *Women in the Church: A Biblical Theology of Women in Ministry* (Downers Grove, Ill.: InterVarsity, 1995), 114, 151–56.

[148]Erickson, *God in Three Persons.*

[149]So Donald Bloesch, *God the Almighty* (Downers Grove, Ill.: InterVarsity, 1995), 199–204; Paul K. Jewett, *God, Creation and Revelation* (Grand Rapids, Mich.: Eerdmans, 1991), 75–78, 83, 86–89, 146–52, 322–25; Bilezikian, *Community 101,* 187–202.

apocalyptic battle of our age. They are convinced that the Bible gives "headship" ("leadership" in plain speak) to men, and if this principle were abandoned because of cultural change, the authority of the Bible would be overthrown and the door would be opened to homosexual marriages, homosexual clergy, and other disastrous social changes. The redefined and reworded doctrine of the eternal subordination of the Son in role and authority has thus become for some evangelicals the bastion that holds back the attacking and mistaken egalitarians. Virtually every evangelical theologian who has written in support of the eternal subordination of the Son in function and authority is committed to the permanent subordination of women in the church and the home. Because the subordination of women and the subordination of the Son are inextricably united in the minds of those with whom I am debating, getting them to consider honestly and openly what they are saying on the Trinity is almost impossible. Too much for them is at stake. Some of them have said to me quite openly, "We will never give way on the Trinity, because this would be the first step in giving way on our case for the subordination of women." Professor Wayne Grudem is firmly of this opinion. He says "the most decisive factor" in the case for the permanent subordination of women is "a proper understanding of the doctrine of the Trinity," by which he means understanding the Trinity as hierarchically ordered so that the Son is bound to obey the Father.[150] Nothing is more important "in the whole universe," he says, than maintaining "the equality of being together with authority and submission to authority" in the relationship between the Father and the Son in the immanent Trinity.[151]

In this book I do not want to discuss this primary issue, the permanent subordination of women, but why it is so important to my debating opponents must be understood. For them two fundamental issues are at stake: one is openly admitted; the other never mentioned and usually denied. The first is biblical authority. Their case in essence is this: the authority of the Bible is the most important doctrine, the Bible teaches the permanent subordination of women—this is not an interpretation but what the Bible says—therefore to allow that women may share in decision making in the home and in leadership in the church is a rejection of biblical authority. To reject women's permanent subordination is thus seen as an attack on what is foundational to their faith, namely the authority of the Bible. In reply, evangelical egalitarians such as myself say, we are not questioning biblical authority, just your *interpretation* of Scripture that we think is wrong.[152] My debating opponents cannot accept this

---

[150]Grudem, *Evangelical Feminism*, 411 and n. 12.

[151]Ibid., 429.

[152]See my book *The Trinity and Subordinationism*, 141–269, and on other evangelical egalitarians the recent scholarly evangelical symposium Ronald W. W Pierce, Rebecca Merrill Groothuis, Gordon D. Fee, eds., *Discovering Biblical Equality: Complementarity without Hierarchy* (Downers Grove, Ill.: InterVarsity, 2004).

distinction. What they teach, they insist, is not an interpretation; it is what the Bible says. They have failed to see that every attempt to give meaning to the words on the pages of our Bibles is an interpretative exercise. There are only good, bad, and indifferent interpretations.

The second fundamental issue, the one never mentioned, is male hegemony. To concede that women should be given equality of consideration and their leadership accepted would invalidate the claim that men should have the final say in the home and leadership in the church. This part of the agenda is extremely emotive and complex because it merges biblical teaching with the male psychological will to power and the desire to control. With this powerful double agenda lying behind any discussion of the male-female relationship and the divine Father-Son relationship, communication is almost impossible. To question either male "headship" or the Father's "headship"—in plain speak the leadership of men and the Father—only evokes strong passions and hostility. I have thus set myself an almost impossible task. I am writing to ask my fellow evangelicals with whom I am debating to put their concerns about women to one side to examine and assess what they are teaching about the Trinity. The doctrine of the Trinity is the primary doctrine of the Christian faith. It is our doctrine of God. We can get this right only if other agendas are left to one side.

It took me some time to realize that almost all the ingredients in the contemporary case for the eternal subordination of the Son are entirely novel. Those who were making this case had developed ideas and terms not found in the tradition, or if the terms are found in the tradition, they have given them new content. These novel ideas and terms came directly from the post-1970s' case for the permanent subordination of women. Instead of saying women are "inferior" to men, as Christians had said for centuries, conservative evangelicals intent on maintaining the subordination of women began saying that women are "equal" with men; they simply have "different roles." The role that defines a man as a man is "headship"; the role that defines a woman as a woman is obedience. Women are not subordinated in person or being, only subordinated in "role" or "function." "Role differentiation," meaning in reality the leadership of men and the subservience of women, is what differentiates the sexes. If this role differentiation in authority is not maintained, then sexual differentiation itself is blurred or obliterated. We are thus told frequently that the relationship between men and women is "hierarchically ordered" and "asymmetrical."

Building on this new case for the subordination of women, with its carefully crafted temninology, the doctrine of the Trinity was reformulated and reworded. The three divine persons are "equals," we were told, yet they are eternally role differentiated. The Father commands, the Son obeys. It is this difference in role and function (in plain speech, difference in authority) that primarily distinguishes the divine persons. If this specific difference is not maintained, modalism follows. Finally, it is claimed, like the man-woman relationship, the Father-Son-Spirit relations are ordered hierachically and are asymmetrical.

The Tail Wagging the Dog

Once it is seen that a doctrine of the Trinity has been construed to prove a prior belief or commitment, our "heresy antenna" should come into play. It could be that the Christian doctrine of God has been subverted. Miroslav Volf, in his important book *After Our Likeness: The Church as the Image of the Trinity*,[153] argues that all too often appeals to the Trinity to prove another doctrine or to support a social agenda are based on prior beliefs that have determined how the Trinity is understood. It is his case that such theologizing is always circular in nature. First the Trinity is defined in a way that will support what is already believed, and then an appeal to this doctrine of the Trinity is made to support what is already believed. It is a central tenet of the case put in this book that far too many contemporary evangelicals have done just this. They have let their passion to maintain the permanent subordination of women dictate how they understand the doctrine of the Trinity. Beginning with what they think is the most important theological issue of the day, the permanent subordination of women, they have reformulated the doctrine of the Trinity to prove what they already believe. In doing this they have depicted divine relations in terms of human relations, and this is idolatry.

In contemporary theological texts on the Trinity we hear of "Rahner's rule,"[154] "Pannenberg's principle,"[155] and "LaCugna's corollary."[156] I would like to add another slogan called, "Giles's ground rule," or "Giles's guideline." It is this: "Whenever the Trinity is construed to support a prior belief, then the orthodox doctrine of the Trinity is invariably corrupted and distorted."

Terminological Confusion

Professor R. P. C. Hanson says, "The search for the Christian doctrine of God in the fourth century was in fact complicated and exasperated by semantic confusion so that people holding different views were using the same words as those who opposed them, but, unawares giving them different meanings from those applied to them by their opponents."[157]

---

[153]Miroslav Volf, *After Our Likeness: The Church as the Image of the Trinity* (Grand Rapids, Mich.: Eerdmans, 1998).

[154]This is given and explained in chapter 7 to follow.

[155]On this see Grenz, *Rediscovering the Triune God*, 96–97.

[156]On this see Peters, *God as Trinity*, 124.

[157]R. P. C. Hanson, *The Search for the Christian Doctrine of God: The Arian Controversy 318–381* (Edinburgh: T&T Clark, 1988), 181. J. N. D. Kelly, *Early Christian Doctrines* (London: Adam and Charles Black, 5th rev. ed., 1977), 253, says much the same thing. "Every alert reader

The problem was this: the pro-Nicene theologians used the key terms with one meaning and the Arians used the same terms with another meaning. It is the same today. One group of evangelical theologians uses the key terms in the tradition as they have always been understood from the time of the Council of Constantinople in 381, while other evangelical theologians use terms not in the tradition, or if they are, in novel ways, not in accord with any dictionary definition. This terminological confusion is one of many close parallels between what took place in the fourth century and what has taken place among evangelicals in the last few years.

Late in the fourth century the Cappadocian Fathers sorted out much of the terminological confusion in the debate of their age and in doing so paved the way for the consensus reached at the Council of Constantinople in 381. If any resolution of the contemporary evangelical debate on the Trinity is to be found, it must also involve coming to an agreement on the use and meaning of the key terms. If the same words are used by each side yet each understands them differently, the painful rending apart of the evangelical fraternity over the doctrine of the Trinity will never be overcome. Words can have a range of meanings, but the meanings of words cannot be dictated arbitrarily. When there is a dispute over the meaning of a word, our arbitrator is the dictionary. I thus ask my debating opponents to do two things. First, to give the key terms the meanings found in our dictionaries and confirmed by everyday speech. And second, to make clear what they mean by the words they use. If a word has more than one meaning, then state openly the meaning intended. What is needed as much as anything in this dispute among evangelicals is greater terminological clarity and precision, and this will be achieved only if we each know what the other is saying and meaning to say when certain words are used. The key terms in the contemporary debate given differing meanings by each side include the following.

Role

In everyday speech the word *role* refers to actions people perform, for example in the home who cooks, cuts the lawn, goes to work, and so forth.[158] One's role does not define one's person. Roles can change. In evangelical literature supporting the permanent subordination of women in the home and the church, the word *role* (and its synonym *function*) has another meaning. It is a gender-and-person-defining category. A woman's role, which is nothing other than her subordination in authority

---

must have noticed, and been astonished by, the extent to which theological division at the time [the fourth century] was created and kept alive by the use of different and mutually confusing terminology."

[158]For a fuller treatment of the way certain key terms are used in contemporary evangelical literature advocating the permanent subordination of women see my book *The Trinity and Subordinationism*, 179–93.

to men, defines who she is. She *is* the subordinated sex. Her role or function defines her *being*: it can never change. A man's role is to lead. It is this "role" that defines him as a man. When this special and novel meaning of the words *role* and *function* are applied to the Son of God, we have major problems. If the divine Son is *eternally* subordinated in role or function, he is a subordinated divine person. His subordination as it is eternal defines his person. In other words, he is subordinated in *being*. Simply to protest loudly that this is not the case does not overcome the logical force of this observation. In historic orthodoxy the things the Father, Son, and Spirit do are usually called their "work," "acts," or "operations." In early twentieth-century America, the word *function* appears as another term, and for the first time in the late 1970s the word *role* is used—and then only in evangelical literature.[159] In orthodoxy these differing works, acts, operations, functions, or roles do not imply eternal subordination in being or authority of any of the persons, or any separation or division. Every work by one divine person is also a work of the other two, even if particular works are the works primarily of one person, and each makes a distinctive contribution. The three divine persons are always understood to work in unison and in perfect harmony. They have one will and they indwell or interpenetrate one another. This is called "the doctrine of inseparable operations." Inseparable operations does not mean identical operations.

I would plead that this insupportable use of the word *role* be repudiated. In the dictionary and sociological usage the word *role* is not a person-defining term. What is more, to define male and female identity in terms of differing roles is contrary to biblical revelation. In the Bible men and women are defined by their God-given sexual identity as man or woman, not by what they do or by the authority they exercise or do not exercise (Ge 1:27). To differentiate the Father and the Son on the basis of differing roles, as we will see, is contrary to historic orthodoxy. In orthodoxy the divine three are always understood to operate or function inseperably and have indivisible authority. I have asked my debating opponents for nearly thirty years to desist from using the word *role* because their usage obfuscates rather than clarifies what is being said by them, and it is without biblical or theological warrant, but to no avail. This term and its special meaning is basic to their whole case.

Difference

Another key term in evangelical literature advocating the subordination of women and the Son of God is *different/difference*. In everyday speech these cognate words mean "other than" or "not the same." In the writings of my debating opponents they imply

---

[159]Frame, *The Doctrine of God*, 719, is simply mistaken when he says that theologians have "debated for many centuries ... eternal subordination in role."

or mean "subordinated." If anyone denies women are permanently subordinated, or the Son is eternally subordinated, they are accused of denying differentiation itself. In the historic trinitarian tradition, differentiating the divine persons is an issue of fundamental importance. To exclude modalism, the *eternal* differences between the Father, Son, and Spirit are stressed. There is one God who is eternally three "persons." Divine unity/equality and divine threeness/difference are both made absolutes. As we will see, historic orthodoxy has sought ways to underline divine differentiation without allowing any subordination or hierarchical ordering in the Trinity, or any separating or dividing of the divine "persons." In stark contrast to the tradition, contemporary evangelicals have reconceptualized the doctrine of the Trinity, seeing it as a hierarchy in authority, and they want us to believe that the word *difference* implies "subordination." To be differentiated is to be subordinated. Thus when egalitarians deny that the Son is eternally subordinated to the Father, they are accused of denying divine differentiation itself: of being "modalists." No matter how strongly I or others stress eternal divine differentiation, once eternal subordination is questioned, my debating opponents are sure differentiation itself is being questioned. This novel and unsupportable use of the word *difference* cannot be endorsed. In everyday speech the word *difference* does not mean subordination, and in the historic trinitarian tradition the unequivocal affirmation of difference does not imply in any way subordination of any of the divine persons in the eternal Trinity.

With this special meaning of the word *difference* in mind, those with whom I am debating have made the slogan "equal and different" a positive-sounding brief summary of their position. The English theologian Michael Harper in fact calls his book arguing for the permanent subordination of women and the eternal subordination of the Son *Equal and Different*.[160] This is all very confusing, because all orthodox theologians believe that the divine persons are "equal and different." In this debate the truth is that absolutely no one is denying divine differentiation. The divide at this point is over the meaning of the word *different*. For my debating opponents, "equal and different" means that the three divine persons are equal in divinity but differentiated, because the Son and the Spirit are subordinated to the Father in function and authority, and for some, being as well. In contrast, in historic orthodoxy the words "equal and different" mean that the divine three are equal in being, function, and authority but are not to be identified. The Father is eternally the Father, the Son eternally the Son, and the Spirit eternally the Spirit. They are differentiated as persons. What has to be acknowledged is that it is not the matter of sexual and divine differentiation that divides evangelicals today. To suggest this is disingenuous. What divides evangelicals

---

[160]Harper, *Equal and Different*.

today is whether women are permanently subordinated to men and whether the Son of God is eternally subordinated in function and authority to the Father.

Inferior

In everyday speech the words *inferior* and *subordinate* mean much the same thing. In almost every dictionary we are told a subordinate is an inferior and an inferior is a subordinate. In contrast, in contemporary evangelical literature we are frequently told that the word *subordination* does not mean "inferior." Those with whom I am debating repeatedly say we reject that women are inferior to men, or the divine Son is inferior to the Father, which would be Arianism. It is true that someone holding an inferior or subordinate position is not necessarily in their person (ontologically) inferior. They may well be in the subordinate or inferior position because they lack the gifts, training, or experience needed for the superior position. They would only be personally inferior if they could never hold the superior position whatever their gifts, training, or experience might be. Thus the private in the army, while inferior in role, is not in his person an inferior because he can become an officer, and the officer who is superior in role is not in his person superior to the private, because he can be demoted. But in the case of women and the divine Son in evangelical theological texts supporting the permanent subordination of women and the eternal subordination of the Son, the subordinate status is irrevocable and intrinsic: it can never change. It defines the person. If women are *permanently* subordinated to men and the Son is *eternally* subordinated to the Father, they are in some way less than the one who is always over them. To emphatically deny that teaching the *eternal* subordination of the Son in function and authority and in some cases being as well does not indicate the Son is "inferior" to the Father is an assertion without substance. The Son is either superior to the Father (and both sides reject this suggestion), or equal with the Father (as I would argue), or inferior to the Father. There are no other options. If the Son is eternally set under the Father in function and authority, he is less in some way than the Father. In plain English, he is inferior to the Father. In this usage the words *subordinate* and *inferior* are synonyms.

Order

When the English word *order* and the Greek word it translates, *taxis*, are used to speak of the relationship between one or more things or people, it is not self-explanatory.[161] To give content to this word, how the persons or things are related has to be made clear. The word *order* used relationally always implies the question, what order? Is it hierarchical, vertical, circular, horizontal, sequential, chronological, or

---

[161]See the very good analytical discussion of the concept of order by P. G. Kuntz, "Order," *New Catholic Encyclopaedia* 10 (Washington, D.C.: Catholic University of America, 1967), 721–23.

simply according to a given plan or pattern? In this last sense it is a synonym for the word *dispose*, meaning to arrange in a proper, given, or prescribed way. It is taken as axiomatic that the relations between the divine three persons are ordered because nothing in God is random or arbitrary. No one denies order in God. The division is over the question of how the divine three are ordered. According to the conservative Reformed theologian Robert Letham, the great divide in the fourth century was between the Arians, who thought the divine three were ordered hierarchically, and the pro-Nicene theologians, who emphatically denied hierarchical ordering. He writes, "The Orthodox and the Arians used the word *taxis* [order] in different ways. The Arians used it to support their heretical idea that the Son was of lesser rank or status than the Father. The pro-Nicenes used the word in the sense of fitting and suitable disposition, not hierarchy."[162]

The divide is exactly the same today. Evangelicals committed to the permanent subordination of women and the eternal subordination of the Son almost invariably take the word *order* to mean "hierarchy" or "sub-ordering," Letham being the notable exception. Thus when they say God has "ordered" the man-woman and the Father-Son relationship, they mean "hierarchically ordered," or "sub-ordered." Robert Doyle makes the point explicitly. He says, "Order does mean hierarchy."[163] The word *hierarchy* indicates differing rank, graded importance, superiors and inferiors, above and below.

When orthodox theologians affirm divine order they are never endorsing hierarchical order in the Godhead. For them hierarchical ordering in the Trinity in being, work or function, or authority is an Arian error. Robert W. Jenson says the great achievement of the Cappadocian Fathers was to conceptualize the order of the three divine *hypostases* (persons) not hierarchically, as Origen had done, but horizontally.[164] There are a number of ways orthodoxy affirms divine order.[165] First it is recognized that the Bible reveals God in a sequential order. The Father is revealed first, then the Son, and last the Holy Spirit as a distinct divine person.[166] This economic or revelational order is the basis of the structure of the Apostles' and Nicene Creeds. In this order the

---

[162]Letham, *The Holy Trinity*, 400. See similar comments by him on pp. 383, 480, 482, 491.

[163]Robert Doyle, "God in Feminist Critique," *Reformed Theological Journal* 52, no. 1 (1993): 21.

[164]Robert W. Jenson, *The Triune Identity: God According to the Gospel* (Philadelphia: Fortress, 1982), 106.

[165]I found the best discussions on divine order in Thomas Marsh, *The Triune God: A Biblical, Historical and Theological Study* (Dublin: St. Columba, 1994), 170; William J. Hill, *The Three-Personed God* (Washington, D. C.: Catholic University, 1982), 278–82; and Torrance, *The Christian Doctrine of God*, 175–76, 179–80. However, none are comprehensive treatments of this matter.

[166]The Spirit of God is frequently mentioned in the Old Testament, but it is only in the New that he is revealed as the third person of the Trinity, as in some way differentiated from God the Father and God the Son.

Father is introduced first as the creator, the Son is mentioned next primarily in relation to his work of revelation and redemption, and last the Spirit is said to be given to all believers after Christ's ascension. Second, since the time of Athanasius, orthodox theologians building on clear biblical teaching have spoken of an operational order among the divine persons. "Each act of God," says Basil, is "initiated by the Father, effected by the Son, and perfected by the Spirit."[167] The divine three work inseparably but not identically. Third, and closely connected with the last point, the church fathers speak of the God-human, human-God relationship as ordered. God's relation with us proceeds from the Father through the Son in the Spirit. Our relation with God is in the Spirit through the Son to the Father. Fourth, orthodoxy speaks of an order in how the divine three are related by differing origination. The Father is spoken of as "unbegotten," the Son as "begotten," and the Spirit as "proceeding." These terms are all metaphors that defy precise definition.[168] Nevertheless, all orthodox theologians agree that the word *begotten* does not mean created, or created in time. The words *begotten* and *proceeding* speak of eternal generation, and thus differing relations of origin.[169]

What all these ways of speaking of divine order in the Trinity seek to underline is that while divine unity must never be compromised, the divine persons must never be identified. They are equal in being, work, and authority, yet eternally differentiated as Father, Son, and Spirit. Thomas Torrance says, "Inner trinitarian order is not to be understood in an ontologically differentiated way, for it does not apply to the Being or the Deity [and I would add "authority"—and I am sure Torrance would agree as the last of the alternatives below indicate] of the divine Persons which each individually and all together have absolutely in common, but only to the mysterious 'disposition or economy' which they have among themselves within the unity of the Godhead, distinguished by position and not status, by form and not being, by sequence and not power, for they are fully and perfectly equal."[170]

Asymmetrical

The word *asymmetrical* is occasionally found in modern orthodox texts on the Trinity to describe the Father-Son relationship, but it is not a common technical term in the

---

[167]Basil, *The Holy Spirit*, 16.38. I give the translation I found in Gerald O'Collins, *The Tripersonal God: Understanding and Interpreting the Trinity* (Mahwah, N.J.: Paulist, 1999), 134. For the same idea expressed in archaic wording see *The Nicene and Post Nicene Fathers of the Christian Church* (henceforth *NPNF*), ed. Philip Schaff and Henry Wace (Grand Rapids, Mich.: Eerdmans, 1971), 8:16 (p. 23).

[168]We will come back to this matter and these terms many times in what follows. At this point I do not substantiate what is asserted.

[169]These words may well mean very little to some readers at this point. In discussing later how the divine persons are differentiated they will be fully explained.

[170]Torrance, *The Christian Doctrine of God*, 176.

tradition like the word *order*.[171] In speaking of sub-ordering and divine differentiation in the Trinity, conservative evangelicals committed to the subordination of the Son frequently describe the Father-Son relationship as "asymmetrical." Like the word *order*, this term says very little until we are told what is in mind. The antonyms *symmetrical* and *asymmetrical*, like the word *order*, speak of the relationship between one or more persons or things. For my evangelical debating opponents the word *asymmetrical* is intended to indicate that the Father and Son (and men and women) have differing authority. In this usage the word is a synonym for hierarchically ordered, or differentiated in authority. It is, in other words, an obfuscating way of speaking of the eternal subordination in authority of the Son to the Father (or of the permanent subordination in authority of women in the home and the church). In contrast, when rightly used in orthodoxy, the word *asymmetrical* speaks of the distinguishing and irreversible relations of the divine persons. The Father is the Father of the Son, and the Son is the Son of the Father, and the Spirit proceeds from the Father, or the Father and the Son. The Father begets and sends the Son, and the Son is begotten and sent. In orthodoxy, as I have already pointed out, divine differentiation never implies the subordination of one or more persons in the Trinity.

Again using the one term to indicate two different things is problematic, to say the least. I give an example. In a public forum on the Trinity in my home city of Melbourne in July 2004,[172] Dr. Peter Adam made the claim that what distinguished his position from mine was that whereas we both affirmed divine equality, he also affirmed "asymmetry." No matter how much I protested that I too endorsed asymmetry in the sense that divine relations differentiated the persons and could not be eradicated or glossed over, he would not budge. I was in error. Later he published his lecture in the English conservative evangelical journal *The Churchman*, without clarifying what he meant by using the word *asymmetrical*.[173]

It is my view that the term *asymmetrical* should not be used in trinitarian discourse unless it is used specifically to speak of the irreversibility of divine relations. A symmetrical relationship implies harmony, correspondence, equivalence, and complementarity in the relationship between two people or things that cannot be identified. I suspect this describes exactly how we should think the differentiated persons in the Trinity interact with one another, and how the best of marriages work. When the

---

[171] Most expositions of the doctrine of the Trinity do not use this term as far as I can see. In their glossary of the more important terms used in trinitarian discourse, O'Collins, *The Tripersonal God*, 204–7, and Letham, *The Holy Trinity*, 497–503, do not list this word.

[172] Called and chaired by the primate of the Australian Anglican Church, Archbishop Peter Carnley. The papers in revised form from this conference were published in the Australian journal, *St Marks Review* 198 (July 2005).

[173] Peter Adam, "Honouring Jesus Christ," *The Churchman* 119, no. 1 (2005): 35–50.

letter *a* is added to this word, it means these things are lacking, or they are negated. To suggest that the best of marriages and the divine persons are asymmetrical relationships seems to me to be very problematic. This implies the persons involved are not equals, they lack symmetry in their relationship, they are set over against one another in an uneasy tension, and there is a real lack of correspondence and harmony. I prefer the terms *reciprocal, complementary, differentiated, ordered*, and *irreversible* to describe the perfect and unchanging relationship between the Father, Son, and Spirit.

Egalitarian

Egalitarian is another word that means something for one side in this debate and another thing for those on the opposite side. For most contemporary Western Christians the words *equal* and *egalitarian* are entirely positive words. We value democracy predicated on the principle of the equal value and dignity of every person, and most Christians think the Bible demands that we consider everyone of equal worth and dignity and grant them equality of opportunity. In contrast, those who speak of the permanent subordination of women and the eternal subordination of the Son invariably give this word a negative connotation. An egalitarian is someone to be condemned for denying the differences between the sexes and the differences between the divine persons. How affirming the equality of the divine persons suggests the denial of divine differentiation—that one is a "modalist"—escapes me. Does not the New Testament twice speak of the Father and the Son as "equal" (Jn 5:18; Php 2:6)? And does not the Athanasian Creed commend just this idea when it speaks of a "coequal" Trinity where none is before or after another, where none is greater or less than another?

My Special Use of Words

Because those with whom I am debating have moved the goalposts by introducing terms not found in the tradition, or by giving new meanings to key terms found in the tradition, I have needed to equate two or to be exact three words basic to their case with technical words in the tradition so that we do not pass like two ships in the dark. The first of these are the synonyms *role* and *function*. In everyday usage these two words refer to what people do: the things they specifically undertake. I thus equate them with the terms, operations, acts, and works which are the words used in the interpretative tradition of what the persons of the Trinity do: the works they specifically undertake.

The second term is *authority*. In the tradition we find theologians consistently speaking of God as all-powerful and of the divine three having the one power. All orthodox theological textbooks are in agreement that the Father, Son, and Spirit are equally omnipotent—alike all powerful. One of the most important things that defines the triune God for the Christian is his omnipotence. Not to be omnipotent would mean not to be God. Thus in orthodoxy the divine three are thought of as indivisible in power because they are indivisibly God. In the post-1970s' evangelical theology that speaks of the eternal subordination of the Son, the term *authority* rather than *power* is used. Men have "authority" over the women set under them, and the divine Father has "authority" over the Son. *Authority* carefully defined implies that someone has the right to exercise leadership, whereas the word *power* implies the ability to assert leadership or achieve an end. However, the words may be used synonymously and often are in everyday speech. For this reason, I have taken the liberty to equate the terms *power* and *authority* in what follows. I assume that when those with whom I am debating speak of the differing authority of the Father and the Son they mean much the same as if they had spoken of the differing power of the Father and the Son. This equating of these two words should not be disputed, because if each divine person is all powerful without distinction, then each must have all authority without distinction.

Terms for What Is One and Three in God

Before concluding this discussion on technical terms used in discourse on the Trinity, a comment on the words used to speak of divine unity and divine differentiation is needed. The terms referring to what is one in God and what is three in God are both diverse and numerous. In each case the precise technical meaning of these terms evolved, as did agreement on their synonyms.[174] These two sets of terms should not be confused, as they invariably are in evangelical literature.[175] I set them out in a chart (see table on the following page).[176]

What the inclusion of the Greek term *homoousios* (one in being/substance, or consubstantial) into the Nicene Creed did was to link inextricably what God is in his oneness with what God is in his threeness. If God is a monad (ultimately unitary), he must be one in being, work, and authority. It is because Christians believe that God is both one and three (a triunity) that the question is asked, Are the divine three one in being, work, and authority? To confess that the Father, Son, and Spirit are *homoousios* gives the answer unambiguously. The divine persons cannot be differentiated by who they are—their being—and if they are one in being, they must be one

---

[174] The best discussion on terminology I found was by Gerald E. Bray, *Christian Theological Language* (Oxford: Latimer House Studies, 1989). Bray's schema is more complex than mine. He points out that one Greek or Latin term was often made the equivalent of more than one term in the other language.

[175] So Van Til speaks of God as "one person" (*An Introduction to Systematic Theology*, 220, 229); Frame speaks of subordination "in the eternal nature of the persons" (*The Doctrine of God*, 721); and the Sydney theologians speak of a subordination of the person of the Son in "the very nature of his being" (*Sydney Doctrine Report*, par. 18), or of "differences in being" in the one God (ibid., par. 25).

[176] I got the idea of this chart from Frame, *The Doctrine of God*, but have modified it by adding terms.

Terminology for the Divine Unity and Divine Differentiation

	Greek	Latin	English
One	*ousia*	*substantia*	being/substance
		essentia	essence
	physis	*natura*	nature
Three	*prosopa*	*personae*	persons
	hypostases	*subsistentiae*	subsistences, modes of subsistence
	tropos hyparxeos		modes or ways of being/existing

in work/function and authority. What the one God is as being-in-unity, the divine persons are as being-in-relation.

To sum up this section I say again, no progress can be made in this painful debate among evangelicals until there is agreement on the meaning and force of the technical terms being used. To use terms incorrectly, or to give them meanings not found in any dictionary, or to obfuscate what is really being said, does not further the cause of truth or meaningful communication.

One Thing Is Needed before Progressing Further

If the reader cannot separate the question of what is the orthodox doctrine of the Trinity from their belief that women are permanently subordinated to men in the home and the church, they should not bother to read on. This last matter will be mentioned from time to time in passing in subsequent chapters, but the focus will be entirely on what the Bible teaches and what the interpretive tradition says on the Trinity. In other words, from this point on the woman question needs to be bracketed off if we are going to hear what the Bible and the historical tradition says on the Trinity. I say this because my basic thesis is that the novel contemporary evangelical doctrine of the eternal subordination of the Son in function and authority reflects more of a concern to keep women subordinated than a concern to be faithful to the orthodox doctrine of the Trinity. To get our theology right we have to reverse this order. We have to make the doctrine of the Trinity our primary concern. This is the most important Christian doctrine: our doctrine of God.

Before we turn to the Bible and the interpretative tradition to see if what I have just set out is what should be believed by those who want to call themselves "catholic" or "orthodox" Christians, there are some issues still needing to be spelled out or clarified. We deal with these in the next chapter.

CHAPTER

GETTING THINGS STRAIGHT:
THE ISSUES IN CONTENTION

Before we turn to the Bible and to the historical sources to see what they say about the Trinity, a number of preliminary issues have to be sorted out. What is the essence of the error called "subordinationism"? Does human fatherhood help explain divine fatherhood? What is the connection between biblical exegesis and evangelical systematic theology, often called Christian doctrine? How should the doctrine of the Trinity be construed, depicted, or modeled? What preeminence does the Father have? And finally, who are the people who formulated the historic doctrine of the Trinity, and what did they write on this matter?

What Is Subordinationism?

In the contemporary evangelical literature advocating the eternal subordination of the Son, we are told that there is a fully orthodox subordinationism and a heretical subordinationism, called Arianism. This is asserted time and time again. Grudem spells out the point. "The heresy of subordinationism, which holds that the Son is inferior in being to the Father, should be distinguished from the orthodox doctrine that the Son is eternally subordinate to the Father in role or function."[1] Similarly, the authors of the 1999 *Sydney Anglican Diocesan Doctrine Commission Report* claim that there is an

---

[1] Wayne Grudem, *Systematic Theology: An Introduction to Biblical Doctrine* (Grand Rapids, Mich.: Zondervan, 1995), 245n. 27.

orthodox subordinationism that affirms both the equality of the divine persons and the subordination "in the very nature" of the Son and the Spirit,[2] which we are told is supported by "Calvin, and the Calvinists (Edwards, Berkhof, Hodge, Dabney, Packer, Knox),"[3] and the Nicene and Athanasian Creeds.[4] This is to be distinguished from unorthodox Subordinationism (to be spelled with a capital "S") represented by the Arians, "who overemphasised the subordinationist elements of the NT."[5]

Despite differences in detail between evangelicals arguing for the eternal subordination of the Son in function and authority, they are agreed on one thing. So long as you say you endorse the creeds, affirm the deity of Christ, speak of the Son as having the same essence or being as the Father in the eternal or immanent Trinity, and state that you reject "Arianism" or the extremes of "Arianism," you are orthodox. If only it were so simple.

In reply we need to ask, Is what the creeds say really being affirmed without equivocation, and what are the implications of teaching the eternal subordination of the Son in function and authority? The supposed endorsement of the creeds illustrates the first point. I am of course aware that the Eastern Orthodox Churches do not endorse the Athanasian Creed, but for 1500 years it has been the standard for Trinitarian and Christological orthodoxy for Western Christians. Those who I am opposing tell me they accept this creed, but when I press them on specific wording, they become evasive. Yes, they say, the Father and the Son are "coequal," but the Father still rules over the Son! Yes, Father, Son, and Spirit are "Lord" and "almighty," but they quickly add, not in the same way.[6] If I press on, the next response is to start questioning the authority of this creed. What has to be especially noted is that affirming the deity of Christ does not avoid the error of subordinationism. All the so-called fourth-century "Arians" could agree that Jesus is God. What they could not confess was that Jesus was "true God,"[7] one in being, work,

---

[2] Sydney Anglican Diocesan Doctrine Commission Report, "The Doctrine of the Trinity and Its Bearing on the Relationship of Men and Women," (1999), par. 18. M. E. Bauman, "Milton, Subordinationism, and the Two-Stage Logos," Westminster Theological Journal 48 (1986): 177–82, also distinguishes between heretical and orthodox forms of subordinationism.

[3] Ibid., par. 26. See also pars. 14 and 15.

[4] Ibid., par. 25. This assertion is not endorsed. Calvin was certainly not a subordinationist in any sense, and the Nicene and Athanasian creeds I believe exclude what is being claimed.

[5] Ibid., par. 22. See also par. 8.

[6] I am not speaking hypothetically. When I asked a Sydney evangelical theologian and bishop on the Sydney doctrine commission whether he accepted that all three divine persons were equally "lord" and "almighty" as the Athanasian Creed said, he replied, "Yes, the three divine persons are almighty, but the Father is more almighty than the Son." Apparently the word almighty is not a superlative!

[7] Lewis Ayres, Nicaea and Its Legacy: An Approach to Fourth-Century Trinitarian Theology (New York: Oxford, 2005), 14.

and authority with the Father.[8] To say Jesus Christ is not "inferior" to the Father, simply *eternally subordinated*, does not help in any way. If the Son of God is eternally subordinated to the Father, he is the Father's "inferior" in some way. Even to say, "I reject Arianism" says very little. The best of contemporary studies on the trinitarian debates of the fourth century are agreed that *Arianism* is a very imprecise term. There was not one theological position reflecting the teaching of Arius that was opposed by Athanasius, the Cappadocians, and others, but a theological trajectory with many variations that with one voice emphasized the differences between the Father and the Son, always placing the Son under the Father in being, work, and authority, both in the incarnation and in eternity. All the so-called Arians of the fourth century were subordinationists in that they eternally subordinated the Son, but in detail they differed, as do contemporary evangelical subordinationists. What then is the substance or essence of the theological error called "subordinationism"?

Everyone without exception can agree that at a minimum the error of subordinationism involves denying that the Father, Son, and Holy Spirit are one in being/essence/nature/substance in the eternal or immanent Trinity and thus are not "coequal" God. It is my argument that you can give lip service to belief in the oneness of being of the three persons and the coequality of the three divine persons, yet deny this by other things that are said. In other words, you can be a subordinationist and be ignorant of this fact. Four key elements in the contemporary evangelical understanding of the Trinity that I am opposing imply that the three divine persons are not one in being and thus coequal God.

1. The use of the word eternal

First of all I argue that *eternal* functional or role subordination involves by necessity ontological subordinationism. Once the word *eternal* is used, it indicates that the subordination ascribed defines the person. If the Son of God is *eternally* subordinated in function, and cannot be otherwise, then in his *being/essence/nature/substance* he is in some way less than the Father. He is not fully "coequal" as the Athanasian Creed affirms. Here it should be noted that the Bible, all the church fathers, and virtually all mainline contemporary theologians insist that the being *and* the works (functions) of Father, Son, and Spirit are one. "Inseparable operations" is one of the fundamental elements of the Nicene faith.[9] Orthodoxy affirms that each divine person has works that are distinctly his own. Their works are not identical, yet they work inseparably. No one divine person does anything apart from the other two, and the divine three have

---

[8] Throughout this book I argue and demonstrate that subordination in being, function, and authority always went together in fourth-century Arianism.

[9] Ayres, *Nicaea*, 236.

one will, always working as one.[10] To reply that most definitions of subordinationism do not mention "eternal functional or role subordination" is not altogether true or relevant. The fact that the words *function* or *role* are not mentioned in most historic texts defining subordinationism or orthodoxy is of no significance. The term *function* did not come to be used in trinitarian discourse until the late nineteenth century and the word *role* until the late twentieth century. Before this time theologians spoke of the operations, acts, or works of the divine persons. As far as I can see, the conservative Reformed scholar, Benjamin B. Warfield, who wrote at the turn of the twentieth century, was the first to equate the terms *operations* and *functions* when speaking of what God does.[11] After this time we do find definitions of subordinationism that mention eternal subordination in function as an error. In the article on the heresy of "subordinationism" in the *Dictionary of Religion and Ethics* published in 1921, we are told this error involves subordinating the Son or the Spirit "in function or essence."[12] Similarly, putting the case for orthodoxy, the conservative evangelical Wayne House writing in 1992 says "orthodox Trintarianism" unhesitatingly affirms "Father, Son and Holy Spirit as co-equal and co-eternal with regard to divine essence and function."[13] The expression the eternal "*role* subordination" of the Son did not appear until the 1970s, being used first of all by George Knight III.[14] We would therefore not expect any historic texts to endorse or oppose this idea specifically. However, in the *Evangelical Dictionary of Theology*, first published in 1984, eternal role subordination is discussed as one form of the heresy of subordinationism.[15] The specific words used are, however, not an important issue. It is of no significance whether or not we speak of the *eternal* subordination of the Son in his works, acts, operations, functions, or role because whatever words are used to permanently set the Son under the Father in work divides who God is (his being) from what God does (his works). This division breaches divine unity, equality, and "simplicity."[16] It suggests that in the immanent Trinity the divine

---

[10] I make no attempt at this stage to validate this claim or most others in this section. The evidence is given in the substance of the book.

[11] Benjamin B. Warfield, "The Biblical Doctrine of the Trinity," in *Biblical Foundations* (London: Tyndale, 1958), 79–116. See especially p. 110.

[12] S. Matthews and G. M. Smith, eds., *Dictionary of Religion and Ethics* (New York: Macmillan, 1921), 429.

[13] Wayne House, *Charts of Christian Theology and Doctrine* (Grand Rapids, Mich.: Zondervan, 1992), 47.

[14] George Knight III, *New Testament Teaching on the Role Relationship of Men and Women* (Grand Rapids, Mich.: Baker, 1977).

[15] R. C. Kroeger and C. C. Kroeger, "Subordinationism," in *Evangelical Dictionary of Theology*, ed. Walter A. Elwell (Grand Rapids, Mich.: Baker, 1984), 1058.

[16] A comment on the word *simplicity* is needed. "Simplicity" is the first divine attribute discussed by Aquinas in the *Summa Theologiae*. For him it indicated that there was no composition in the one substance or nature of God—no physical elements, no parts or division, no

three do not work as one. To speak of the *voluntary* and *temporal* "functional or role subordination" of the Son in the work of salvation is acceptable, but the minute the word *eternal* is introduced, a profound theological error is embraced. The word *eternal* indicates that the Son does not merely function subordinately in the incarnation; he *is* eternally subordinated to the Father. His subordination defines his person. As the Son he is subordinated to the Father—subordinated in his person or *being*. Millard Erickson agrees. He says, "A temporal, functional subordination without inferiority of essence seems possible, but not an eternal subordination."[17]

2. The teaching that the Son must obey the Father

Second, I argue that to teach that the Son must always obey the Father, that he is eternally subordinated in authority to the Father, also implies his ontological subordination. If the Son must always obey the Father, he is not the Father's equal in power. What makes God God is his omnipotence—his absolute power. If Jesus is not omnipotent in exactly the same way as the Father because he is eternally set under the Father's authority, then he is not fully God. All my debating opponents with one voice hold that the Son must obey the Father. There is a hierarchy of authority in the immanent Trinity. For them the Son's subordination in authority prescribes who he is—his *being*. This is what differentiates him from the Father. He *is* the eternally subordinated Son and cannot be otherwise. If this is not ontological subordination-ism I don't know what is. Here it must be pointed out that arguing that the Son of God is eternally subordinated in authority to the Father is a denial of the primary Christian confession, "Jesus is Lord." The New Testament teaches that after his resurrection the Son of God reigns as equal God, not subordinated God. It is also a denial of the Athanasian Creed's affirmation that Father, Son, and Spirit are alike "Lord" and "almighty." All the various fourth-century "Arians" argued that the Son was

---

distinction between form or matter, no substance and accidents—and in particular, God and his attributes are one and the same. On this see John Frame, *The Doctrine of God: A Theology of Lordship* (Phillipsburg, N.J.: P&R, 2002), 225–30. Frame is rightly critical of much of what Aquinas says on this matter, but he argues divine simplicity is a biblical idea. The Bible makes it clear that God has no physical parts, and he and his attributes are one and the same. Divine simplicity makes the point that although God is triune, he is a unity, and this must never be denied. Ayres, *Nicaea*, 142, 280–81, approaches this matter differently. He points out that divine simplicity was a basic category for all the pro-Nicene theologians who emphasized this in refuting the Arians who divided the one Godhead. For them, he argues, divine simplicity was not a carefully defined concept. Negatively, it excluded the idea that there "were degrees of divine existence," and positively, it affirmed that the divine persons were one in being, work/function, and authority.

[17] Millard Erickson, *God in Three Persons: A Contemporary Interpretation of the Trinity* (Grand Rapids, Mich.: Baker, 1995), 309. He adds that arguing for eternal subordination and denying this implies inferiority are "contradictory" assertions.

subordinated in authority, and apparently some of the sixteenth-century subordinationists with whom the Reformers battled taught this. So the Second Helvetic Confession condemns the "blasphemy" of those who teach that the Son is "subordinated"
(i.e. less in being), or "subservient" (less in authority) to the Father.[18]

3. Differentiating the divine persons by nature, being, essence, or substance

Third, I argue that to teach that the divine persons are *eternally* differentiated on the basis
of differing "nature,"[19] "being,"[20] essence,[21] or "subsistence,"[22] ontologically divides the
one Godhead, opening the door to subordinationism; while to argue that the Son must
be subordinate and obedient because he is a son leads immediately to subordinationism.[23] Differing the divine persons by nature, being, essence, or subsistence denies the
homoousian principle enshrined in the Nicene Creed. What the inclusion of the Greek
term *homoousios* (one in being/substance, or consubstantial) into the Creed did was to
link inextricably what God is in his oneness with what God is in his threeness. If God is a
monad he must be one in being, work, and authority. It is because Christians believe that
God is both one and three that there have always been those who have asked whether
or not the three are one in being, work, and authority. To confess that the Father, Son,
and Spirit are *homoousios* gives the answer unambiguously. The divine persons cannot be
differentiated by who they are—their being—and if they are one in being they cannot
be divided in work/function or authority. What God is as being-in-unity he is as being-

---

[18] See the English translation given by A. C. Cochrane, *Reformed Confessions of the Sixteenth Century* (London: SCM, 1960), 220.
[19] Robert Doyle explicitly says that the divine three are differentiated in "essence," "being," and their "eternal nature" ("Are We Heretics? A Review of *The Trinity and Subordinationism* by Kevin Giles," *The Briefing* [April 2004]: 17). Frame, *The Doctrine of God*, 723, differenti-ates the Father and the Son on their differing "nature."
[20] Doyle, ibid. See also the *Sydney Doctrine Report*, pars. 18, 24, 25.
[21] I do not use quotation marks here because Norman Geisler's own word in his *Systematic Theology*, vol. 2 (Minneapolis: Bethany, 2003), 291, is "essential." The Son of God, he argues, is not just only eternally functionally subordinated: "it is essential."
[22] This is the word popularized by Charles Hodge, *Systematic Theology*, vol. 1 (Edinburgh: T&T Clark, 1960), 455–74. Grudem consistently says he is arguing only for the eternal functional subordination of the Son, but he frequently quotes Hodge in support, as do many other evangelicals who follow Grudem. Does this mean they too accept the eternal subordination of the Son in his personal existence as the Son?
[23] Most of those I am debating with argue that because Jesus is a true son, not just functions as a son, he is by nature subordinated to the Father. His sonship defines his being. I will discuss and document this argument next in what follows. I of course agree that to be the Son is not to be the Father and vice versa. Their indelible identities as Father and Son eternally distinguish them. What I am arguing is that it is dangerous to distinguish the Father primarily on the basis that because he is a father, he rules over the Son, and the Son on the basis that because he is a son, he is subordinated to the Father and is bound to obey.

in-relation—as the divine "persons." Yes, the divine three are eternally and indelibly differentiated as Father, Son, and Spirit, but in orthodoxy differentiation never implies subordination, or differences in being/nature/essence/substance.

4. Reading the incarnation back into the eternal Trinity.

Fourth, I argue that to claim that the subordination seen in the incarnation (the economy of salvation) should be read back into the eternal or immanent Trinity is also an expression of the error of subordinationism. This reasoning denies what Paul so clearly teaches in Php 2:4–11, namely that the Son is equal God before the incarnation; in the incarnation he humbled himself, taking the form of a servant, and then after his ascension he was exalted to reign as Lord. Both sides in this debate agree that in the incarnation the Son was subordinated to the Father. The difference on this matter is that one side thinks the subordination seen in Jesus' earthly ministry reflects what is eternally true: the Son is forever set under the Father; he is subordinated in the immanent Trinity. In contrast, the other side that I represent holds that the subordination seen in Jesus' earthly ministry is temporal, limited to the time of his incarnate ministry when he was in "the form of a servant." Cornelius Van Til, the learned and influential onetime professor at Westminster Theological Seminary, argues that reading back what was seen in the incarnation into the eternal or immanent Trinity is the root of all trinitarian heresies. He says, "All heresies with respect to the Trinity can be reduced to one great heresy of mixing the eternal and the temporal."[24]

If I wanted to write a concise statement that excluded any suggestion that the Son is *eternally* subordinated to the Father in any way whatsoever I do not think I could do better than what is said in the Athanasian Creed. All three divine persons are "almighty" and "Lord" (no subordination in authority); "none is before or after another" (no hierarchical ordering); "none is greater or lesser than another" (no preeminence for any one person); all are "coequal." "Such as the Father is, such is the Son, such is the Spirit." In all of these affirmations the Athanasian Creed seeks to exclude the subordination of the Son or the Spirit in the eternal or immanent Trinity in any way whatsoever. An adequate definition of the heresy of subordinationism must describe it as the rejection explicitly or implicitly of what this creed affirms on the coequality of the divine persons.

To sum up, my own brief definition of the theological heresy called subordinationism is this: to explicitly or implicitly teach that the Son and/or the Spirit are *eternally* subordinate to the Father in being, function, or authority.

---

[24] Cornelius Van Til, *An Introduction to Systematic Theology: Class Syllabus Notes* (1955), 234, and *The Defense of the Faith* (Philadelphia: Presbyterian and Reformed, 1955), 25.

Before leaving the matter of definition, one final observation needs to be made: all expressions of subordinationism imply tritheism. Athanasius was first to recognize this when among other things he accused the early Arians of being "polytheists."[25] Not all tritheists are subordinationists, but all subordinationists are tritheists. The essence of tritheism is the dividing and separating of the one Godhead. All subordinationists stress the differences between the divine three and thus divide and separate the "persons." This is very much the case in the contemporary evangelical form of this error. Both the idea that the Son functions differently and separately from the Father and that the Father commands and the Son obeys breach divine unity and imply tritheism. This is most clearly evident in the latter issue. If in the immanent Trinity the Son must always obey the Father, then the Father and the Son, and by implication the Spirit, each have their own will. The existence of three wills in the Trinity is the logic of the "chain of command" model of the Trinity. Absolutely basic to the conservative evangelical case for the eternal subordination of the Son in function and authority is a paralleling of the Father-Son relationship with the husband-wife relationship. In the hierarchical model of marriage, when there is a clash of wills the wife should always submit to her husband. Proof that this is how Christian marriages should operate is given by appeal to the doctrine of the Trinity. The Son, it is argued, always obeys the Father. If the Son of God gladly submits to the Father's will in obedience, so too should wives. To reply that this teaching does not suggest that the Father and the Son have separate wills because the Son can only do as his Father wills, does not help. If this is the case, his actions are not free obedience; he acts under necessity and compulsion. It is also to be noted that this argument undermines the Father-Son, husband-wife parallel basic to their case. Wives are obviously free to disobey. To avoid both subordinationism and tritheism, orthodoxy stresses divine unity, insisting that the divine three have one will; they work as one and have the same authority. Calvin excludes all forms of subordinationism and tritheism when he says he will allow only a "distinction, not a division" between the divine three.[26] Barth in his extended repudiation of "every form of subordinationism" says the essence of subordinationism consists of two things: the dividing of "the one single and equal God," and depicting "the one who reveals himself [as] the kind of subject we ourselves are."[27]

---

[25] Philip Schaff and Henry Wace, eds., *The Nicene and Post-Nicene Fathers of the Christian Church*, vol. 4, *St. Athanasius: Selected Works and Letters* (Grand Rapids, Mich.: Eerdmans, 1971), 3.15 (p. 412).

[26] John Calvin, *Institutes of the Christian Religion*, ed. John T. McNeill, trans. Ford Lewis Battles (London: SCM, 1960), 1.13.17 (p. 142).

[27] Karl Barth, *Church Dogmatics* (Edinburgh: T&T Clark, 1975), 1.1 (pp. 381–82).

Does Human Fatherhood Explain Divine Fatherhood? The Problem of Analogical Correlation

One of the most common arguments found in the evangelical literature in support of the eternal subordination of the Son is that the divine Father-Son relationship is to be understood in terms of the human father-son relationship. So Professor Wayne Grudem in his *Systematic Theology* says, "The Father and the Son relate to one another as a father and a son relate to one another in a human family: the Father directs and has authority over the Son and the Son obeys."[28] Later he makes exactly the same point and adds, "The Father has greater authority. He has a leadership role among all the members of the Trinity."[29] Similarly, Professor Peter Schemm defines the divine Father-Son relationship in terms of the relationship between a human father and a junior son. He asks, "What exactly does the name 'Father' signify in the Godhead if not relational priority and relational authority?"[30] Professor Bruce Ware also wants us to believe that the human father-son relationship explains the divine relationship. He argues the terms *father* and *son* when used of the first two persons of the Trinity should be taken literally. His case is as follows. In using masculine language for God, the Bible prescribes male leadership—it presupposes males are always to lead. The Bible uses the titles *father* and *son*, he reasons, because it wants human beings to infer that the divine Father and Son relate to each other like human fathers and sons. The divine Father like a human father has authority over his Son. He asks, "What does it mean that the Father is the eternal Father of the Son, and the Son is the eternal Son of the Father? Is not the Father-Son relationship within the immanent Trinity indicative of some eternal relationship of authority within the Trinity itself?"[31]

Robert Doyle, the senior systematic theologian at Moore College Sydney, also argues that the father-son language used of God should be taken literally. He says, "The Father is a real father and the triune Son is a real son. Neither names are metaphorical."[32] He then explains what he means. Just like an earthly (patriarchal) father, the divine Father is the ruler. He has ultimate authority. "The Son defines

---

[28] Grudem, *Systematic Theology*, 249.

[29] Ibid., 459.

[30] Peter Schemm, "Kevin Giles: *The Trinity and Subordinationism*: A Review Article," *Journal of Biblical Manhood and Womanhood* 7, no. 2 (2002): 76.

[31] Bruce Ware, "Tampering with the Trinity: Does the Son Submit to the Father?" in *Biblical Foundations for Manhood and Womanhood*, ed. Wayne Grudem (Wheaton, Ill.: Crossway, 2002), 242. This quote seems mixed up to me. "The immanent Trinity" is "the Trinity itself." I wonder if Ware meant to say the "economic Trinity" and wrote the "immanent Trinity" by mistake?

[32] Doyle, "Are We Heretics?" 14.

himself in subordination" to the Father's authority and rule.[33] For Doyle, what must be stressed above all else is "the priority of the Father in intra-trinitarian relations."[34] Human fathers have priority on earth, and the divine Father has priority in heaven. The English theologian Michael Harper argues in exactly the same way. He repeatedly parallels the authority of the human father over his wife and children and the divine Father's authority over the Son.[35]

How human beings may speak about God has been a contentious issue since the time of Arius. If there is a God, we would imagine that human language could be used to speak of him, although not necessarily adequately or perfectly. Thomas Aquinas put his able mind to work on this problem.[36] He argued that human speech used of God could be one of three things: (1) It could be *univocal*. To say God loves me means the same as to say my dad or wife loves me. If our language of God is univocal, it would mean that God is just like a human person. (2) It could be *equivocal*. To say God loves me means something altogether different from saying my dad or wife love me. If our language used of God is equivocal, we could not say anything factual about God. (3) It could be *analogical*. To say God loves me tells me something true about God, but it captures only part of the reality. If our language used of God is analogical, as Aquinas argued, it means we can speak of and understand God in the categories of human thought but never fully comprehend him. In his discussion of human language used of God, Aquinas said, "It seems that no word can be used literally of God. For as we have already said that every word used of God is taken from our speech about creatures, as already noted, but such words are used metaphorically of God."[37] In this quote he makes the term *metaphorical* an equivalent of the term *analogical*. In modern discussions of religious language it is acknowledged that the meaning of the two words overlap, but it is generally held that the word *metaphorical* has a wider range of meanings and uses than the more technical and precise term *analogical*.[38]

Recently this issue of the nature of human language and thought about God has become a critical issue among evangelicals because some evangelicals have been

---

[33] Ibid., 13.

[34] Ibid., 18.

[35] Michael Harper, *Equal and Different: Male and Female in Church and Family* (London: Hodder and Stoughton, 1994), 2, 59–62, 84, 153–62, 164–76.

[36] Thomas Aquinas, *Summa Theologiae* 3, trans. H. McCabe (London: Blackfriars, 1964), 47–93. I give the traditional summary of what Aquinas is thought to be saying. In more detail and with an alternative reading of Aquinas on this matter see Alan J. Torrance, *Persons in Communion: Trinitarian Description and Human Participation* (Edinburgh: T&T Clark, 1996), 120–212.

[37] Ibid., 57. For a similar point see also 67, 69.

[38] For a good summary of this discussion see J. W. Cooper, *Our Father in Heaven* (Grand Rapids, Mich.: Baker, 1998), 167–80.

depicting God in very human terms, advocating what is called "Open Theism."[39] In contrast to historic orthodoxy, which thinks of God as sovereign, working all things according to his own will, the open theists think of God as contingent, responding to human wills and changing his mind. As proof of their doctrine of God, they appeal to passages in the Bible where God is said to repent or change his mind. In reply, other evangelical theologians argue that what we have in open theism is an attempt to define God in human categories, and in support the Bible is read *univocally*. This is rejected. They say (I believe rightly) that when the Bible speaks of God changing his mind, this turn of phrase must not be understood literally in human terms. It is *analogical* language. God is like human beings in some ways but profoundly different in other ways. Only biblical revelation can help us see what are the similarities and what are the differences. Moving from human experience to the divine only leads to error. God is then understood in human terms. So the conservative evangelical A. B. Caneday insists that "all of God's self-revelation is analogical and anthropomorphic." "The Bible is God's speech to humans in human language."[40] If God were to speak in divine language, human beings would not be able to understand what he was saying. For us to understand God in revelation he must speak to us in human language and categories. In saying this, the point is being made that what is said in Scripture about God must *not* be understood *univocally*, or in colloquial terms "literally."

One of the theologians who has written against "Open Theism" is Bruce Ware, an evangelical committed to the permanent subordination of women and the eternal subordination of the Son.[41] When he explains the force of the divine Father–Son language in the Bible, he argues it should be taken literally. The divine Father like all fathers rules over his Son. However, when he explains what the Bible means by speaking of God changing his mind and "repenting," he argues the language is metaphorical and anthropomorphic. It is not "literal." It is hard not to see special pleading at work here.

Whenever God is defined from below by analogy, God is invariably brought down to a human level. The correct way to go is from God to humankind. Our

---

[39] For example, see Clark H. Pinnock, ed., *The Openness of God: A Biblical Challenge to the Traditional Understanding of God* (Downers Grove, Ill.: InterVarsity, 1994). In reply see *God's Lesser Glory: The Diminished God of Open Theism* (Wheaton, Ill.: Crossway, 2000); John Piper, Justin Taylor, Paul K. Helseth, eds., *Beyond the Bounds: Open Theism and the Undermining of Biblical Christianity* (Wheaton, Ill.: Crossway, 2003).

[40] A. B. Caneday, "Veiled Glory: God's Self-Revelation in Human-Likeness — A Biblical Theology of God's Anthropomorphic Self-Disclosure," in *Beyond the Bounds*, 160.

[41] Bruce Ware, "An Evangelical Reformulation of the Doctrine of the Immutability of God," *Journal of the Evangelical Theological Society* 29, no. 4 (1986): 431–46, quote p. 441. In the 2003 evangelical symposium against "open theism," *Beyond the Bounds*, he has another article in opposition to this teaching, "The Gospel of Christ," 309–36.

relationships should be Godlike. In contemporary evangelical literature advocating the permanent subordination of women and the eternal subordination of the Son, it is invariably claimed that this order is being followed. God's headship over the Son is the model for the husband's headship of his wife and men's in the church, but in reality the argument flows the other way—from the human to the divine. As I have explained earlier, first of all the historic doctrine of the Trinity was redefined and restated in the very terms invented in the post-1970s' case for the permanent subordination of women. Then this novel doctrine of the Trinity was used to justify and explain the permanent subordination of women. Women are subordinated to men just like the Son is to the Father. The circular nature of this reasoning and the fact that it starts with the human relationship is to be recognized.

There is yet another problem for conservative evangelicals who seek to define the husband–wife relationship in terms of the divine Father–Son relationship or vice versa: the analogy is not a good fit. The husband–wife relationship is twofold; trinitarian relations are threefold. The husband–wife relationship is a male–female relationship; the divine Father–Son relationship is depicted analogically as a male–male relationship. The husband–wife relationship anticipates offspring; the divine Father–Son relationship does not. Why the Father–Son relationship should inform the human husband–wife relationship or vice versa is thus not logically clear. There seems to be a slip in the argument somewhere. If anything you would think the divine Father–Son relationship would inform, at least in the first instance, the human father–son or father–child relationship.

What we learn from all this is that the evangelical theologians' normative concern to avoid human experience as a basis for theological formulations is based on good grounds. In this case, when this rule is breached, profound error follows. I therefore ask my debating opponents to begin their thinking about the Trinity not with the husband–wife relationship but with what is expressly taught in Scripture. There is some correlation between human life and divine life. If there were not, our talk about God would be meaningless, but only revelation can give this content. Barth argues that presupposing an analogy of being between humans and God is the primary error of Roman Catholic theology.[42] What is so surprising is that the conservative evangelicals who claim that they have the highest view of the Bible are those most prone to this error. They are so certain that Scripture must teach what they have concluded from human experience that they cannot hear what Scripture is in fact saying.

Paradoxically this way of doing theology is exactly that of Arius. He defined the divine Father–Son relationship in human terms. In speaking of the Son as "begotten,"

---

[42] On this see my book *The Trinity and Subordinationism* (Downers Grove, Ill.: InterVarsity, 2002), 90–91, 109–10.

he wanted the church to accept that the Son of God was a creature brought forth in time like any human son. Thus the Son was less in dignity and authority than his Father. Athanasius, the Cappadocian Fathers, Augustine, and Karl Barth in modern times all oppose such reasoning. In speaking of Arius, Alasdair Heron says, "By a curious irony, on which Athanasius was not slow to remark, Arius seemed to possess a good deal of privileged information. But where had he got it from? Athanasius was in no doubt about the source: the Arians had fabricated the divine being out of their own minds, thus making their own intellects the measure of ultimate reality and assigning to Christ, the Word made flesh, the place their minds could make for him."[43]

Robert Gregg and Dennis Groh make a similar point. They say, "The Arian understanding of the terms 'Son' and 'Father' derive from the empirical ... the example of human relationship and experience."[44] On this basis the Father was thought of as "prior, superior and dominant" in relation to the Son, who is marked by "dependence rather than co-equality."[45]

How Does the Bible Inform and Contribute to Systematic Theology or Doctrine?[46]

For all evangelicals the Bible is the supreme authoritative guide as to what we should believe and do as Christians. In more conservative evangelical circles it is often suggested that what we believe, our doctrine, springs immediately from Scripture. We are told, "Everything I believe is based entirely on the Bible." This is not true. All the important doctrines of the Christian faith are in fact the product of centuries of reflection on Scripture, heated debate, and creative conceptual thinking. They are grounded in Scripture, but they are always more than just an ordered compilation of texts drawn from Scripture. Nowhere is this truer than with the doctrine of the Trinity. The great Reformed theologian Abraham Kuyper called claims to the effect that one's theology is based entirely on the inductive study of Scripture

---

[43] Alasdair Heron, "*Homoousios* with the Father," in *The Incarnation*, ed. T. F. Torrance (Edinburgh: Hansel, 1981), 70.

[44] Robert C. Gregg and Dennis E. Groh, *Early Arianism: A View of Salvation* (Philadelphia: Fortress, 1981), 84.

[45] Ibid., 91.

[46] On this section see in more detail my "Evangelical Systematic Theology: Definition, Problems, Sources," in *The Fullness of Time: Biblical Studies in Honour of Archbishop Donald Robinson*, eds. David Peterson and John Pryor (Homebush, Aust.: Lancer, 1992), 255–76. See also Stanley J. Grenz, *Revisioning Evangelical Theology: A Fresh Agenda for the 21ˢᵗ Century* (Downers Grove, Ill.: InterVarsity, 1993); Stanley J. Grenz and John R. Franke, *Beyond Foundationalism: Shaping Theology in a Postmodern Context* (Louisville: Westminster, 2001); and I. Howard Marshall, *Beyond the Bible: Moving from Scripture to Theology* (Grand Rapids, Mich.: Baker, 2004).

"unscientific," "grotesque," and "utterly objectionable."[47] He goes on to say, "There is, to be sure, a theological illusion abroad ... which conveys the impression that, with the Holy Scriptures in hand one can independently construct his [sic] theology ... [T]his illusion is a denial of the historic and organic character of theology, and for this reason is inwardly untrue. No theologian following the direction of his own compass would ever have found by himself what he now confesses and defends on the ground of Holy Scripture. By far the largest part of his results is adopted by him from theological tradition, and even the proofs he cites from Scripture, at least as a rule, have not been discovered by himself, but have been suggested to him by his predecessors."[48]

How then is evangelical theology "done"? To answer this question three disciplines must be distinguished and defined.

1. *Exegesis.* Exegesis seeks to discover how the original hearers would have understood a text or passage in Scripture. It seeks to give the *historic meaning* of what is written down. Knowledge of the various contexts that gave rise to these words and the meaning of the language used are key tools in this endeavor. Exegesis is basically analytical in nature and inductive in methodology.

2. *Biblical theology.* Biblical theology is also concerned primarily with historical meaning, but it is a synthetic activity.[49] The biblical theologian seeks to understand the overall thought of particular biblical writers and possibly how what he says relates to what other biblical writers say. A study of the "light" motif in John's gospel, or of ideas of creation in the Old and New Testaments, would be two examples of biblical theology. Because biblical theology, defined in this manner, is concerned exclusively with the thought of the biblical writers, it does not aim to directly address the present. There is a dialectical relationship between exegesis and biblical theology. Exegesis informs biblical theology, and biblical theology informs exegesis.

3. *Systematic theology.* Systematic theology—sometimes called dogmatics or doctrine—in contrast to the two disciplines just mentioned aims to speak to the present. Its primary goal is to answer the question, What should Christians do or believe in the historical context in which they find themselves? In seeking to answer this question, the conclusions of exegesis and biblical theology are

---

[47] Abraham Kuyper, *Principles of Sacred Theology* (Grand Rapids, Mich.: Baker, 1980), 564–65, 574.

[48] Ibid., 574–75.

[49] Like everything in biblical studies there is a debate about what exactly is biblical theology. My definition closely follows that given by George Eldon Ladd, *A New Testament Theology* (Grand Rapids, Mich.: Eerdmans, revised edition 1993), 20–28. In more detail and with more nuances see I. Howard Marshall, *Beyond the Bible.*

a starting point and of primary importance for the evangelical theologian, but they are not the sole source of guidance. Most evangelical theologians hold that what the best of theologians from the past and the creeds and confessions teach should also be taken into consideration and followed (this is called "tradition"), unless Scripture dictates otherwise, and that human wisdom (reason) can also contribute to systematic theology.

"Doing" systematic theology has to be more than just collecting or systematizing what is in Scripture for a number of reasons. First, because using a concordance does not produce theology. The various comments in Scripture on virtually any issue do not say exactly the same thing. One of the primary tasks of the theologian is to find some coherence in the varied and sometimes seemingly contradictory teaching in Scripture on the matter under discussion. Then second, because Scripture often does not directly answer a question asked in later generations, theologians have to extrapolate from what it does say. For example, when the question arose in the fourth century, Was God the Son really one in divinity with God the Father?, the theologians at the Council of Nicea in 325 decided in favor. To make clear that what they believed was implied in Scripture they decided to include in the creed of Nicea the Greek word *homoousios*, meaning one in being, to define the Father-Son relationship. In doing this they went beyond what was explicitly stated in Scripture. They made an objective advance in theological definition. Third, systematic theology must be more than simply quoting Scripture, because often questions asked in later times are not answered by anything specifically in Scripture. For example, the Bible says nothing directly on abortion, euthanasia, or gambling, yet the Christian theologian has to direct Christian thinking on such matters. In doing so deductions have to be made from texts that are thought to give the guidance needed.

There is, however, a fourth and important way in which systematic theology is more than just what the Bible says. Systematic theologians are constantly seeking to make sense of what is given in Scripture. They are engaged in a creative and generative work. Their constructs are insightful ways of seeing the parts as a whole, and in doing so creating something hitherto not recognized. For this reason theological formulations are often called "models" or "paradigms." Nowhere is this creative contribution of redeemed human reason seen more clearly than in theological work on the Trinity. All attempts at formulating the doctrine of the Trinity are mind-expanding "models" of how God is one and three at the same time. B. B. Warfield clearly recognized the creative contribution of redeemed reason. In speaking of the "science" of systematic theology he wrote, "The mind brings to every science something which, though included in the facts, is not derived from the facts considered in themselves alone, as isolated data."[50]

Just as exegesis and biblical theology are dialectically related, so too are systematic theology, biblical theology, and exegesis. Evangelical systematic theology begins with the Bible, but how the Bible is read is governed to a large degree by one's sometimes implicit systematic theology. This means that the theology we bring to Scripture tends to determine what we take from Scripture. For this reason it is of utmost importance that theologians come to the Bible with good theology, and with the Trinity and Christology there is no better place to begin than with the teaching of the creeds and confessions (authoritative tradition).

The Bible and Tradition

As horrified as Grudem might be that I said in *The Trinity and Subordinationism* that on the Trinity and other doctrinal issues the Bible can be read in more than one way, I stand by what I said. I think my assertion is irrefutable.[51] He and I do not agree on how the Bible should be read on the Trinity. He holds that all comments that speak of the subordination of the Son in the incarnation should be read back into the immanent Trinity, and I take the opposite opinion. Athanasius and those he designated "Arians" also disagreed on exactly the same issue. Much of Athanasius' "Discourses Against the Arians" are taken up with his interpretation of passages the Arians interpreted to support the eternal subordination of the Son in being, function, and authority. One of the painful things evangelicals must honestly face is that a high view of biblical authority does not necessarily lead to unanimity in doctrine. No one should be more convinced of this than Dr. Grudem. Despite his valiant efforts over a working lifetime, he has not been able to convince the majority of evangelicals that the Bible teaches the permanent subordination of women. Most think his interpretations of the key texts that he appeals to for support are forced and mistaken.[52]

I do not hold—as I said explicitly in my earlier book and as Grudem notes—that the Bible can mean anything. I believe very firmly that one reading of Scripture on any issue is correct and one is not. This is where tradition is so important. Over the centuries a way of reading the Bible on key matters has emerged, and in the case of

---

[50] B. B. Warfield, "The Idea of Systematic Theology," in *The Necessity of Systematic Theology*, ed. John J. Davis (Grand Rapids, Mich.: Baker, 1978), 131.

[51] Wayne Grudem, *Evangelical Feminism and Biblical Truth* (Sisters, Ore.: Multnomah, 2004), 426. He thinks by suggesting this I "effectively silence" God's Word.

[52] See in particular the scholarly conservative evangelical reply to what Grudem teaches, Ronald W. Pierce and Rebecca Groothuis, eds., *Discovering Biblical Equality: Complementarity without Hierarchy* (Downers Grove, Ill.: InterVarsity, 2004).

the Trinity and Christology this way has been codified in the creeds. This agreed interpretation of Scripture, which is called "the tradition," is not of equal authority with Scripture. It is a secondary authority not to be ignored, particularly so when codified in creeds and confessions, yet always subject to the correction of Scripture. Grudem is simply not being fair when he says I make "the tradition of the church the supreme authority, an approach similar to Roman Catholicism but contrary to the Reformation *sola scriptura* ("Scripture alone"), and contrary to beliefs of evangelical Protestants."[53] I give no authority to "church tradition"—feast days, saints, vestments, and so on. When I use the word *tradition* I am always speaking of the historic interpretative tradition, that is, what the best of theologians in the past and the creeds have concluded is the plain meaning of the Bible.

The Reformers held to exactly the same high view of the interpretative tradition and the same low regard for "church tradition" as I do. The expression *Sola Scriptura* did not mean for them either that the Bible alone gave the answer to every question asked, or that it was self-interpreting so that how others had interpreted it was of no interest or help.[54] This slogan spoke rather of the *supremacy of Scripture* over church traditions. For the Reformers the best guide to rightly interpreting Scripture was the work of those who had carefully studied and debated its meaning before them. In attacking me for my appeal to the interpretative tradition, Grudem is being disingenuous. The truth of the matter is that he and I consider tradition, as I have carefully defined it, in exactly the same way. If he did not greatly value tradition, why does he claim time and time again that his view of the Trinity is what the great theologians of the past and the creeds teach,[55] and that his view of women is "traditional"? Because he cannot convince evangelicals of contrary opinion to him on both matters simply by appeal to the Bible alone, he claims the tradition is on his side: he is reading the Bible as the great theologians of the past have done. On the Trinity, we will show in what follows that what he teaches is directly in opposition to what the best of theologians of the past and the creeds teach. In regard to the subordination of women, the situation is not the same. Both he and I have in fact broken with the "weak tradition" that spoke uniformly for eighteen centuries of the "inferiority" of women and the "superiority" of men, and of women being more prone to sin and error.[56]

---

[53] Wayne Grudem, *Evangelical Feminism and Biblical Truth* (Sisters, Ore.: Multnomah, 2004), 426.

[54] See further on this my "Evangelical Systematic Theology," 268. On the meaning and force of the expression "*Sola Scriptura*" see in more detail G. C. Berkouwer, *Holy Scripture* (Grand Rapids, Mich.: Eerdmans, 1975), 299–326; and Craig D. Allert, "What Are We Trying to Conserve? Evangelicals and *Sola Scriptura*," *Evangelical Quarterly* 76, no. 4 (2004): 327–48.

[55] In Wayne Grudem's latest book, *Evangelical Feminism and Biblical Truth*, 415–22, he gives eight pages to attempting to prove the tradition is on his side.

[56] On all this see my book *The Trinity and Subordinationism*, 156–93.

I call the interpretative tradition that has the Bible teaching that women are inferior to men and more prone to sin a "weak" tradition because across the centuries until very recently there never has been any profound theological reflection on the status and ministry of women. Theologians simply reflected the same values and ideas that everyone held in a patriarchal culture where women were not educated and were not in control of their own fertility. It was only in the post-1970s' period that Christian theologians began to work on this issue in depth. This led all involved to reject the central tenets of the inadequately thought out tradition. Even those who wanted to keep women subordinated insisted that they were not teaching that women are inferior or more prone to sin, even if what they said seemed to imply just this. With the doctrine of the Trinity, in contrast, "the tradition" is very strong. No doctrine has been so widely discussed by the best of theologians across the centuries, and no doctrine has been more fully and explicitly defined. It is my case that we cannot ignore what the best of theologians in the past and the creeds and confessions say on the Trinity. How they have concluded that Scripture should be read and understood weighs heavily on us. Only with overwhelming scriptural evidence and the consensus of other informed orthodox Christian brothers and sisters should we consider opposing or correcting in part or in whole the received tradition on the Trinity.

In stark contrast to Grudem, who represents the most socially and theologically conservative wing of evangelicalism, often called "fundamentalism," Robert Letham, a conservative Reformed theologian, stresses the importance of the tradition in seeking to understand and enunciate the doctrine of the Trinity. He writes, "While our supreme authority is Holy Scripture, we should also listen seriously and attentively to the Fathers as did Calvin, the Reformers, and John Owen. In a culture where rugged individualism flourishes, we need to be " 'submitting to one another out of reverence for Christ' (Eph 5:21) recognizing that we are all liable to error."[57]

Professor Lewis Ayres in his very important book *Nicaea and Its Legacy: An Approach to Fourth-Century Trinitarian Theology* puts the case for the careful study of the tradition even more strongly. He says the stormy theological controversies of the fourth century "produced some of the basic principles of classical Trintarianism and Christological doctrine, the most important creed in the history of Christianity, and theological texts that have remained points of departure for Christian theology in every subsequent generation."[58] To ignore or reject this rich tradition, he holds, is

---

[57] Robert Letham, *The Holy Trinity in Scripture, History, Theology, and Worship* (Phillipsburg, N.J.: P&R, 2004), ix. Richard H. Muller, *The Triunity of God*, vol. 4, *Post-Reformation Reformed Dogmatics* (Grand Rapids, Mich.: Baker, 2003), 17–19, 21–3, 61, similarly argues that this high regard for the interpretative tradition is characteristic of Calvin and the post-Reformation Reformed theologians.

[58] Ayres, *Nicaea*, 1.

one of the most foolish and unhelpful things any modern theologian can do. I completely agree.

Last, I quote Professor Craig Allert, speaking on the Reformers' attitude to the interpretative tradition. He says, "Luther and the other magisterial reformers . . . were working to conserve the traditional doctrines of the church like the Holy Trinity. They believed that the traditional understandings of the ecumenical Councils of Nicea (325) and Constantinople (381) were correct interpretations of Scripture."[59]

Reading and Interpreting Scripture

The thesis that evangelical systematic theology or Christian doctrine is always more than simply accumulating biblical texts is fundamental to the argument of this book. What Scripture teaches is absolutely basic to all evangelicals, but because how the Scriptures should be read and interpreted is what divides the two sides in this debate about the Trinity, and because it is obvious that developed doctrine of the Trinity says more than what the Scriptures explicitly say, a way of going beyond disputing the meaning of specific texts must be found. My protagonists show the way forward. They repeatedly and consistently claim that what they teach on the eternal subordination of the Son is what the great theologians of the past and the creeds teach. It is their case that if these secondary authorities endorse how they are reading Scripture they must be right. People like me they say are the innovators. I am more than pleased to respond on this basis. I agree that how the Bible has been understood on the Trinity by the best of theologians in the past and codified in creeds and confessions gives the best guidance possible for reading Scripture aright today.

In the next chapter I study in detail what the Scriptures say about the divine Father, Son, and Spirit and their relationships with one another, but I admit from the outset that I am reading the Bible in the light of what I understand to be historic trinitarian orthodoxy—the tradition. If an entirely opposing understanding of the Trinity were presupposed and the Bible read with these "spectacles" on, other answers would be found. This cannot be denied, because this is exactly the position at the moment. One group of evangelicals is saying on their reading of the Bible the Son is *not* eternally subordinated to the Father in being, function, or authority; and the other side is saying on their reading of the Bible the Son *is* eternally subordinated in function, authority, and—possibly for some—in being as well.

All this indicates that reading and interpreting Scripture is more complex than some evangelicals want to admit. It suggests that although we may have an objective text, and a common high view of the Bible, there is a degree of subjectivity in interpretation. In the many books on hermeneutics written by evangelicals in the

---

[59] Allert, "What Are We Trying to Conserve?": 342.

past twenty years, it has come to be recognized that what we bring to Scripture, our presuppositions of various kinds, tends to determine what we take from Scripture.[60] In the debate in which we are involved I believe the alternatives are crystal clear. We can either come to Scripture seeking to find evidence for a doctrine of the Trinity that supports the permanent subordination of women, or we can come informed by the teaching of the creeds and confessions expecting that Scripture will basically confirm the teaching on the Trinity given in these documents. When this latter course is taken, what we discover about the Trinity may or may not support our view of women or anything else, but it will not simply mirror our own contemporary presuppositions, beliefs, and concerns. Because I am convinced that the tradition, as I have carefully defined this term, offers the key to the right reading of Scripture, especially on the doctrines of the Trinity and Christology, most of this book is concerned with the tradition. This should not lead anyone to conclude that I think tradition is more important than Scripture. Rather, it should be seen as indicating that I believe that the best guide available for a right reading of Scripture, especially in regard to the Trinity and Christology, is the tradition. This tells us how the best of theologians in the past have concluded the Scriptures should be read and understood.

Within the Bounds of Orthodoxy: Differing Models of the Trinity

After centuries of debating and thinking about the Trinity, some matters are settled and others are not. The diagram following helpfully begins our discussion of what may be considered orthodoxy.

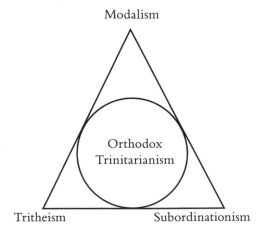

This diagram allows that within the bounds of orthodoxy some "models" or explanations of the doctrine of the Trinity move more towards tritheism. They

---

[60] I particularly commend Kevin J. Vanhoozer, *Is There Meaning in This Text?* (Grand Rapids, Mich.: Zondervan, 1998).

emphasize the individual persons and are called "social models" of the Trinity. Other models move more towards modalism, the idea that there is only one undifferentiated God. Augustine, Barth, and Rahner all move towards this corner of the triangle, yet stay within the circle of orthodoxy. And finally, some models of the Trinity move towards the subordinationism corner. Invariably they do this by emphasizing the priority and preeminence of the Father and consequently the differences between the divine persons. Many suggest that the Cappadocians, Basil in particular, and most Eastern Orthodox theologians could be placed near this corner. Judging when a formulation of the doctrine of the Trinity has moved outside the bounds of orthodoxy is not easy, because invariably lip service is given to other corners of the triangle not central to the model advocated. What has to be asked in each case is, Has this model, despite the words used, undermined divine unity/equality, or differentiation/three-ness, and thus moved outside the bounds of orthodoxy?

In this one-dimensional triangle modalism, tritheism, and subordinationism are given as three opposing corners. However, tritheism and subordinationism could be listed together at one end of a line or continuum with modalism at the other end. Modalism conceives of God as an absolute unity; both tritheism and subordinationism conceive of God like three separate persons. Classic tritheism thinks of God as three divided yet equal divine persons. Classic subordinationism thinks of God as three divided and unequal divine persons. Or to put it another way, tritheism has the divine three "standing apart" although equal in being, work, and authority; subordinationism has the divine three "standing apart" with one above another. In the first case they are ordered horizontally; the second hierarchically. Because subordinationism and tritheism both breach divine unity, historic orthodoxy has emphasized divine unity to exclude both errors and then sought ways to preserve divine differentiation that do not breach divine unity. When divine unity is stressed, both tritheism and subordinationism are of little danger. It is an emphasis on differentiation that opens the door to these two errors that are "half-brothers." The so-called "social model" of the Trinity—which has had a lot of support in recent years—veers towards tritheism, having to work hard to show how the divine three are still one. The conservative evangelical model of the Trinity in which the Father is eternally set over the Son in authority, I argue, actually moves outside the circle of orthodoxy, embracing both the errors of subordinationism and tritheism. The Father is the God who rules; the Son is the God who does what the Father commands.

Other Options: Eastern and Western Models of the Trinity

Another way that many discussions on the Trinity distinguish theologies of the Trinity within the bounds of orthodoxy is to contrast Eastern and Western models. The argument is that the traditional Eastern Orthodox model of the Trinity begins with the three persons and then seeks to explain how the divine three are one.[61] In contrast, the traditional Western model begins with the one divine substance before speaking of the persons. There is really very little to commend in this popular simplification if the primary evidence for it is to be drawn from the third, fourth, and early fifth centuries.[62] In the early church, the great theologians of the western and eastern sides of the Roman Empire seem to have felt free to draw on one another's writings. In seeking to expound the doctrine of the Trinity, each says some things that are quite distinctive, and each builds on the work of those before them wherever they are located. Thus Tertullian was a Western theologian, but George Prestige notes his dependence on Eastern theology.[63] It is the same with Irenaeus. His thinking is enriched both by theologians in the eastern and western ends of the empire. Athanasius is from the East but is exiled to Rome more than once. He distinctively argues that God is not a monad but a triad from all eternity, yet he stresses divine unity. Hilary of Poitiers was from the West and was exiled to the East and knew at least the writings of Basil. The Cappadocians follow Athanasius in some matters and in others take their own path. Augustine does not read Greek with ease but knows the work of the Eastern theologians and Hilary. He does not think of himself as moving in a new direction. Even his reflections on the soul as an image of the triune God in his *De Trinitate* only develops what Gregory of Nyssa had first suggested.[64] Lewis Ayres cogently argues that Augustine stands squarely in the pro-Nicene tradition exemplified by Athanasius and the Cappadocians.[65] Calvin is not conscious of any contrast between Eastern and Western doctrines of the Trinity but notices differences between various theologians and draws from whoever he finds most helpful on any issue.

In the contemporary theological texts in English and European languages, a sharp East-West divide on the doctrine of the Trinity is also hard to find. The general trend in discussions on the Trinity over the last thirty years has been to draw from the best of theological work from Eastern and Western theologians. Modern works on the Trinity are characteristically eclectic.

In dissenting from the thesis that there is a clear and sharp separation between Western and Eastern models of the Trinity in either the early church or today, I am not denying that from the time of Augustine, and to some extent due to him, theo-

---

[61] Letham, *The Holy Trinity*, 2–5, 250–51, endorses this approach, making much of the East-West divide in the early church and today.

[62] On all this see especially Michel Rene Barnes, "De Regnon Reconsidered," *Augustinian Studies* 26 (1995): 55–71. On the early church see Ayres, *Nicaea*, 1, 2, 302–4, 365–83. Barnes points out that in fact De Regnon's contrasts were between the "patristic" and "scholastic" models of the Trinity, the latter beginning with Augustine.

[63] George Leonard Prestige, *God in Patristic Thought* (London: SPCK, 1959), xxv.

[64] Ayres, *Nicaea*, 291.

[65] Ibid., 364–83.

logians in the East and the West did draw apart. Nor am I denying that there remain deep divisions between most Western theologians and most Eastern theologians over important issues,[66] particularly the *filoque* clause, but even on this matter there is movement today.[67]

Options within the Bounds of Orthodoxy on Who or What Is First?

Notwithstanding what has just been said on the growing consensus in contemporary theological work on the Trinity, there is a significant difference on where thinking about the Trinity should begin, and this matter bears profoundly on the present debate among evangelicals. Do we begin with the Father, or the divine three, or the one divine substance, or the divine three in communion? Contemporary theologians differ on their answer to this question.

One approach is to begin with the Father. This was the starting point of the Apologists, Tertullian, Irenaeus, Arius, and the Cappadocians, each in their own way. We will explain the ideas of these people later. For the moment I very briefly give the Cappadocians' position. They argued that the Father is to be understood as the source (*arche*) or cause (*aitia*) of the being of the Son and the Spirit. For them this did not imply hierarchical ordering or the subordination of the Son and the Spirit in any way. All three divine persons share in the one being, they interpenetrate one another, they work as one, and they have the same power and authority. In this model of the Trinity, the Son and the Spirit proceed from the Father alone. For most Eastern Orthodox theologians, the idea that the Father is the *monarche* (sole source) of divinity is a dogmatic axiom and not debatable. In recent years making the *monarche* of the Father the starting point for thinking about the Trinity has been given fresh support by the Greek Orthodox theologian and bishop John Zizioulas in his important book *Being As Communion*.[68] Western theologians are generally critical of this approach because they think by giving a certain pre-eminence to the Father it conceptually implies subordinationism. They also note that in the Bible the Spirit is sent by the Son, even if what he gives has been received from the Father (Jn 16:7; Lk 24:49; Ro 8:9–11).

Nevertheless, some Western theologians do begin with the Father. The Roman Catholic theologians Karl Rahner[69] and Walter Kasper[70] are examples. This is perfectly acceptable, because in revelational order the Father is first, as both the Apostles'

---

[66] See further on this Duncan Reid, *Energies of the Spirit* (Atlanta: Scholars, 1997).

[67] The problem of the *filioque* clause will be discussed later in the book.

[68] John Zizioulas, *Being As Communion* (Crestwood, N.Y.: St. Vladimir's, 1993).

[69] Karl Rahner, *The Trinity* (London: Burns and Oates, 1970). And for a discussion of this see N. Omerod, "Wrestling with Rahner on the Trinity," *Irish Theological Quarterly* 66, no. 3 (2003): 213–27.

[70] Walter Kasper, *The God of Jesus Christ* (London: SCM, 1983).

and Nicene Creeds allow, and because orthodoxy speaks of the Father as "unbegotten", and the Son as "begotten," terminology that suggests a distinctive creative
initiative of the Father, albeit without temporal priority. Western theologians who
begin with the Father, however, generally do not endorse the *monarche* of the Father.
Following the Nicene and Athanasian creeds, they confess that the Father *and* the Son
are the *source* (*arche*) of the Spirit. In Roman Catholic dogma, the Father is understood
to be the first principle or *principium* of the Godhead, but this is not exactly the same
as speaking of the Father as the *monarche*. At the Council of Florence (1438–45) it was
agreed that "all that the Father is, and all that he has, he does not derive from another,
but from himself, he is the principle that has no principle."[71]

This model of the Trinity is not explicitly taught by the Nicene Creed as formulated in 381, yet this creed can be appealed to for support. The Father is named first
and the Son is said to be "eternally begotten of the Father, God from God, Light from
Light, true God from true God," although this wording was originally included not
to teach derivation but to explain and support the primary point that the Father and
the Son are "one in being." The Son is "true God." In the later Western version of
the Nicene Creed where it is said the Spirit proceeds from the Father and the Son,
the doctrine that the Father alone is the source of the being of the Son and the Spirit
is excluded. The idea that the Father is the *monarche* of the Son and the Spirit, or
that the Father holds some preeminence in the Trinity, finds no support at all in the
Athanasian Creed. It declares that, "Such as the Father is, such is the Son, and such
is the Holy Spirit."

Conservative evangelicals who speak of the eternal subordination of the Son
always want to begin with the Father. They are often ignorant of the finer points
of historically developed trinitarian theology, but their great cause to uphold the
authoritative headship of males leads them to this conclusion. They want to give
whatever precedence and priority to the Father that is possible so that by analogy this
can be transferred to men. In every conversation and debate I have had with evangelicals with whom I disagree on the doctrine of the Trinity, I find always that the
priority and preeminence of the Father is to the fore. They want him to stand apart
and be "first" in the Trinity. Doyle says the *monarchy* of the Father must be upheld at
all cost.[72] What these evangelicals need to heed is the warning of the learned Roman

---

[71] Yves Congar, *I Believe in the Holy Spirit: The River of Life Flows in the East and the West*, vol. 3
   (London: G. Chapman, 1983), 133–40, has a very informative chapter on "The Father, the
   Absolute Source of Divinity." In his attempt to find bridges between East and West, Congar
   favors making the Father the source of divinity because he is to be understood as pure love.

[72] Doyle, "Are We Heretics?" 12–18. Similarly, J. Scott Horrell, "Toward a Biblical Model of
   the Social Trinity: Avoiding the Equivocation of Nature and Order," *Journal of the Evangelical
   Theological Society* 47, no. 3 (2004): 399–421.

Catholic theologian Edmund Fortman. Speaking of theologies of the Trinity that start with the Father, seeing him as the cause of the other two divine persons, he says, "This approach is entirely orthodox and has many advantages, but if ineptly handled it can easily involve subordinationism."[73]

A second possible approach would be to begin with the divine three. Many think this is the primary distinguishing characteristic of the so-called Eastern doctrine of the Trinity.[74] So Robert Letham says, "The East consistently starts with the three divine persons."[75] It is immediately apparent that this assertion stands in stark tension to the claim that Eastern theologians begin with the *monarche* of the Father. Both cannot be right. When we turn to the Cappadocians, what we find in fact is that they begin with the *monarche* of the Father and stress divine unity. What is distinctive about their doctrine of the Trinity is not that they start with the three divine persons but rather that they start their thinking about the Trinity by conceptualizing the one being of God relationally and communally.[76] The one God for them is the three persons bound together in mutual self-giving love, perichoretically[77] interpenetrating one another. In the contemporary scene, possibly Jürgen Moltmann comes closest to making the divine three the starting point for all thinking about the Trinity.[78] As a consequence he is often accused of bordering on tritheism or of falling into this error.[79]

In support of the idea that all thinking about the Christian God should begin with the divine three, the New Testament and the Nicene Creed could be quoted. Both clearly put the divine "persons" to the fore, but in both the primary belief is that God is one. Monotheism is the premise. What they are seeking to explain is how the Father, Son, and Spirit can be that one God yet distinct "persons." As far as the

---

[73] Edmund Fortman, *The Triune God* (Grand Rapids, Mich.: Baker, 1972), 282. Letham, *The Holy Trinity*, 3, 377, 500, says much the same thing.

[74] This contrast goes back to the late nineteenth-century French theologian Theodore De Regnon. For a critique of his work see Michel Rene Barnes, "De Regnon Reconsidered," *Augustinian Studies* 26 (1995): 55–71 and Ayres, *Nicaea*, 1, 2, 302–4, 365–83.

[75] Letham, *The Holy Trinity*, 251.

[76] At this point I do not document the evidence for these comments. Later in the book we will carefully explore what in fact the Cappadocians say on these and other matters.

[77] *Perichoresis* is the technical term to speak of the mutual interpenetration, or coinherence, of the three divine persons suggested by Jn 10:30, 38; 14:11; 17:21. It implies a perfect communion in being and work in divine triune existence.

[78] Jürgen Moltmann has written widely on the Trinity. Possibly *The Trinity and the Kingdom* (New York: Harper and Row, 1981) is his most comprehensive work on this doctrine. Ted Peters, *God as Trinity: Relationality and Temporality in Divine Life* (Louisville: Westminster, 1993), 103, says that in Moltmann's writings "divine threeness is given priority."

[79] So Letham, *The Holy Trinity*, 307–9; Paul Molnar, *Divine Freedom and the Doctrine of the Immanent Trinity* (Edinburgh: T&T Clark, 2003), 201–2.

historical tradition goes, none of the major contributors to the doctrine of the Trinity begin with the divine three. They all begin with divine unity.[80]

A third possible way to begin thinking about the Trinity is to begin with a "one substance." From the time of Tertullian, Western theologians have commonly defined the Trinity as "one substance and three persons" (*una substantia tres personae*). Augustine was an heir to this definition, and a common interpretation of Augustine is that he makes the one divine substance the foundation and commencement point for thinking about the Trinity. So Thomas Marsh says that Augustine "leaves the reader in no doubt what his starting point is.... the unity of the one divine substance."[81] My reading of Augustine leads me to think that he thought of the one substance as triune.[82] It cannot, however, be contested that following his time, culminating in Aquinas, that the one divine substance was thought of as the starting point for all thinking about the Trinity. An excellent contemporary example of a theology of the Trinity commencing with the one divine substance is seen in Edmund Hill's *The Mystery of the Trinity*.[83] One major problem with this approach is that the English word *substance* sounds very abstract and impersonal. In answer it may be said that the Latin word it translates, *substantia*, has a more dynamic element, and that in the East the term *ousia* ("being") was accepted as its synonym, but this does not completely negate the objection to using this term to speak of God in unity.

The Athanasian Creed is often said to support the idea that the commencement point for all thinking about the Trinity is God as one substance, but I am not convinced. In the fourth sentence of this creed it is true that we are called to confess "the Trinity in unity, neither confounding the persons, nor dividing the substance," but this is the only time the word *substance* is used. From this point on in the Creed God is always confessed as the three divine persons in unity, distinguished only by their given identities and differing origins.

A fourth approach is to begin with the Trinity itself. The Christian God is triune from all eternity. This insight was first articulated by Athanasius. In contemporary thinking about the Trinity, this conceptual foundation and starting point is endorsed by Thomas F. Torrance, *The Christian Doctrine of God*;[84] Leonardo Boff,

---

[80] In a later chapter on divine differentiation this assertion will be substantiated.

[81] Thomas Marsh, *The Triune God: A Biblical, Historical, and Theological Study* (Dublin: Columba, 1994), 132.

[82] In fact Augustine says just this. See "Letter 120," in *Saint Augustine's Letters*, vol. 2 (83–130), trans. Sister Wilfred Parsons (Washington, D.C.: Catholic University Press, 1953), 306, 310, 313, 314. After reaching this conclusion by reading Augustine, I was pleasantly surprised to find it ably argued and confirmed by Ayres, *Nicaea*, 364–72.

[83] Edmund Hill, *The Mystery of the Trinity* (London: Chapman, 1985).

[84] Thomas F. Torrance, *The Christian Doctrine of God: One Being Three Persons* (Edinburgh: T&T Clark, 1996).

Trinity and Society;[85] Catherine LaCugna, *God for Us*;[86] and Alan J. Torrance, *Persons in Communion*,[87] among others. For each of these theologians, divine being is relational and communal, and the Trinity itself is the *monarche* of the three persons. They argue that thinking about the Christian God should not begin with the Father, or the three divine persons, or the one divine substance, but with the eternally triune communal God.[88] To conceptualize the Trinity in this way does not diminish the divine Father in any way, or minimize the differences between the divine persons. The Father remains the begetter of the Son, whom he sends to reveal and save, and whom he raises after the crucifixion, exalting him to reign as Lord. The Son remains he who willingly took human flesh to become the Savior of all who call on his name. It is he who reveals the Father, and it is he who now rules as Lord. And the Holy Spirit remains the Spirit who empowers and transforms those whom Christ is saving to the glory of God the Father. On this view the Father is the *monarche* of the person of the Son (he is the Father *of* the Son), the Son is the *monarche* of saving revelation, and triune being-in-communion is the *monarche* of being-in-relation, the divine persons.

The Nicene Creed does not presuppose this model, but no words exclude it. The three divine persons are given equal status and dignity, and nothing is said explicitly of the *monarche* of the Father. In the 381 text of the Nicene Creed it is true that the Spirit is said to "proceed" from the Father, but from the Council of Toledo in 589, Western versions of this creed have the Spirit proceeding from the Father and the Son. The Athanasian Creed could also be quoted in support of this model even more sympathetically than the one-substance model.

Within this fully communal and relational understanding of divine being, which makes the Trinity itself the *monarche*, two schools of thought can be seen. In what I call for want of a better term the "weak" model, or perhaps better "the communal model," divine unity is given equal weight with divine threeness. The divine three have one center of consciousness and one will. Thomas F. Torrance is the classic representative of this position. This is the model I would endorse. I set this apart from the "strong" version, which is represented by those theologians who are said to embrace a "social model" of the Trinity. In this approach threeness is very much to the fore. Each divine person is thought of as a center of consciousness. Here the danger is tritheism. Among mainline Protestant theologians Jürgen Moltmann possibly gives

---

[85] Leonardo Boff, *Trinity and Society* (New York: Orbis, 1988).

[86] Catherine LaCugna, *God for Us* (San Francisco: HarperSanFrancisco, 1991), 288–305.

[87] Alan J. Torrance, *Persons in Communion: An Essay on Trinitarian Description and Human Participation* (Edinburgh: T&T Clark, 1996).

[88] See the excellent discussion on all this in Stanley J. Grenz, *Rediscovering the Triune God* (Minneapolis: Fortress, 2004), 120–47.

the clearest example of the strong version of social trinitarianism.[89] Among evangelical scholars the "social" model of the Trinity is advocated and defended by Cornelius Plantinga Jr.,[90] Millard Erickson,[91] and J. Scott Horrell,[92] each of whom wants to exclude any suggestion of tritheism.

Most evangelicals at this point would hope that by appeal to the Bible one of these four starting points, each with variant expressions, could be shown to be "biblical" and the others not so. If only it were so easy! The one-substance model can probably be excluded, but the others are neither equivocally supported nor rejected by Scripture. What this means is that the theologian has to decide which of the options that are within the bounds of Scripture and the tradition is the most conceptually powerful in putting together what is clearly revealed in Scripture about the one-in-three God we Christians worship. I personally have concluded that starting our thinking about the Trinity with a belief that God is triune from all eternity yet profoundly one is the best approach, albeit without forgetting that in economic (revelational) order the Father is to be thought of as first. He is thus named first in the Apostles' and Nicene Creeds and is said to beget the Son and send the Son and the Spirit. Orthodoxy, as we will show, does not understand economic order to imply either hierarchical order or subordination in the eternal or immanent Trinity. In the work of revelation Christ is "first," and in the work of empowerment for ministry and sanctification the Spirit is "first."

Introducing the Cast of Players

In what follows we will meet a number of theologians time and time again. It thus seems appropriate to introduce the more important ones at this point so that we know who they are and something of what they taught. My primary authorities for the tradition are Athanasius, the Cappadocian Fathers, Augustine, and Calvin; and my primary exponents of the historic subordinationist position are the Arians. I also discuss the contribution of Karl Barth and Karl Rahner, often thought to be the two most influential trinitarian theologians of the twentieth century, and for this reason alone they cannot be ignored.

The Theologians Prior to the Council of Nicea in 325

Before the advent of Arius many of the key issues needing to be resolved in formulating a theologically adequate doctrine of the Trinity were not recognized, or if they

---

[89] Jürgen Moltmann, *The Trinity and the Kingdom of God* (Minneapolis: Augsburg, 1993). This is only one of several books he has written on the Trinity. See further on this Peters, *God as Trinity*, 103–10.

[90] Ronald J. Feenstra and Cornelius Plantinga Jr, eds., "Social Trinity and Tritheism" in *Trinity, Incarnation and Atonement* (Notre Dame, Ind.: Notre Dame Press, 1989), 21–47.

[91] Erickson, *God in Three Persons*.

[92] Horrell, "Toward a Biblical Model."

were, not dealt with satisfactorily. In outlining this early period I mention first the *Apologists*, a group of second-century Christian writers who attempted to give a reasoned defense of the Christian faith to unbelievers. They include Aristides, Tatian, Athenagoras, Theophilus, and most importantly Justin Martyr (c. 100–165). Tertullian (160–225) is numbered among them, but he is a bridge figure going beyond the other Apologists in his theological writings. These men were all ardent monotheists who thought of God the Father as a monad who became three for the purpose of creation and redemption.

Indebted to the Apologists but again going beyond them was Irenaeus (c. 130–200), the Bishop of Lyons. He writes mainly against the Gnostics, yet in passing comments he says some very important things about the Trinity. All these writers naively subordinate the Son to the Father thinking this safeguarded the *monarchy* (the sole rule) of the Father, whom they considered to be God in the ultimate sense of this term.

In the light of subsequent developments in the doctrine of the Trinity, we may judge the attempts by second-century theologians in construing this doctrine as inadequate, but what has to be acknowledged is that they laid the groundwork on which others built. Their best insights were adopted by later Catholic theologians, and once their mistakes were seen, the path could be taken that led to better answers.

Athanasius (296–373)

Athanasius was not the most likeable of people, or the most gracious Christian, but he was certainly a great theologian. While still in his early twenties he wrote *The Incarnation*, a profound study of how God became man in Jesus of Nazareth. In 325 he attended the Council of Nicea as the secretary to Alexander, the bishop of Alexandria, succeeding him as bishop in 328. Five times his theological and political opponents saw him exiled from Alexandria. He was the most important, most consistent, and possibly the most able opponent of "Arianism."[93] Between 339 and 359 he wrote a series of works defending the faith of Nicea and opposing Arianism in any form, the most significant being his "Discourses Against the Arians," traditionally given as four in number, but critical scholars today think he wrote only the first three himself. What characterizes his writings is a constant appeal to Scripture and a complete rejection of any suggestion whatsoever that the Son is eternally subordinated to the Father in being, work, or authority. Athanasius stands out head and shoulders over most other theologians because of his numerous innovative and breathtaking theological insights.

The vast majority of my quotes from Athanasius are taken from *The Nicene and Post-Nicene Fathers of the Christian Church*, vol. 4, *St. Athanasius: Selected Works and*

---

[93] We will explain the force of this collective term a little later.

Letters, eds. Philip Schaff and Henry Wace (Grand Rapids, Mich.: Eerdmans, 1971). I do, however, sometimes quote from C. R. B. Shapland's translation of *The Letters of Saint Athanasius Concerning the Holy Spirit* (London: Epworth, 1951). In quoting from the translations of Athanasius' writings edited by Schaff and Wace, I have at times taken the liberty of conservatively modernizing the English (e.g., "worketh" to "works," the divine "Him" to "him," and so on). The Greek text of Athanasius' writings is found in J. Migne, ed., *Collected Works, Athanasius* (1857), vols. 25G, 26G, 27G, 28G.

Because referencing quotations from the *Nicene and Post-Nicene Fathers of the Christian Church* is not without its problems, I have given all references twice, once with volume number (always succeeded by a colon), then "the book," and lastly, if given, the section numbers and once with page numbers. References are hard to find in these volumes because often a section goes for more than one page and there are no verse numbers, and because in a few instances in the Cappadocian Fathers the title given at the top of the page differs from the section title. I followed this practice with Augustine and Calvin to remain consistent and because sections in their works also often go for more than one page.

The Cappadocian Fathers

This title is usually restricted to Basil (330–97), his brother Gregory of Nyssa (d. 394), and their friend Gregory of Nazianzus (329–90), three important anti-Arian philosophical theologians who all lived in Cappadocia, Asia Minor. They differ from one another on some matters about the Trinity, but they have so much in common that they are invariably grouped together. They were responsible for bringing about an understanding of the Trinity that the bishops assembled in Constantinople in 381 could endorse and see codified in what is known today as the Nicene Creed. They were not wedded to one formula, or to a group of words to define orthodoxy, yet it was they who established the definition of the Trinity as "one being and three hypostases." In my reading of books about the development of the doctrine of the Trinity, I often found references to the Cappadocians' *hierarchical* understanding of the Trinity. To my surprise I did not find one passage in their writings that suggested this and dozens that explicitly excluded this idea. The Cappadocians are not easy to read. Their writings are voluminous, they are long-winded and often repetitive, and abstract philosophical discussions can go on for pages.

In working on the Cappadocians I had open before me *The Nicene and Post-Nicene Fathers of the Christian Church*, vol. 5, *Gregory of Nyssa*; vol. 7, *Gregory of Nazianzen*; and vol. 8, *Basil*, eds. Philip Schaff and Henry Wace (Grand Rapids, Mich.: Eerdmans, 1971). The Greek text is given in J. Migne, *Collected Works* (1857), vols. 29G, 30G, 31G, 32G, 35G, 36G, 37G, 38G.

Augustine (354–430)

Augustine, who became bishop of Hippo in North Africa in 396, was a man of deep spirituality, massive intellect, and great theological ability. No one has influenced the course of theology among Catholics and Protestants more than he has. He wrote widely on the Trinity, but his most important work is *De Trinitate* (*The Trinity*), a volume divided into fifteen "books," or chapters, as we would call them today. He tells us he began this work as a young man and completed it twenty years later as an old man. *De Trinitate* is in two parts, books 1 to 7 and 8 to 15. The first part can also be divided between the first four "books," which are basically an attempt to read the Bible theologically in relation to the Trinity, and the next three "books" that raise and discuss philosophical and linguistic issues. Augustine recognized that the central issue in appealing to the Bible to build a doctrine of the Trinity was that there appeared to be a contradiction between statements that spoke of the equality of the Father, Son, and Spirit, and those that suggested the Son was subordinated to the Father. His answer was that the Scriptures had to be read holistically and theologically (*canonically* was his word). Augustine's primary canonical rule was that all texts that spoke of the Son's divine status and equality with the Father spoke of him "in the form of God," his eternal status, and all texts that spoke of his subordination spoke of him "in the form of a servant," his temporary status during the incarnation.

In the chapters that follow I only occasionally refer to "books" 8 to 15 of *De Trinitate*, where Augustine looks for analogies of the Trinity within human personality, or in the "soul," as many say. The function of these "books" is not to prove by reason that God is triune, since for Augustine Scripture is the authority for this belief. It is rather to facilitate understanding at a deeper level of the absolute unity and equality of the divine three who are somehow also distinct persons. These chapters are difficult and often dismissed by evangelicals as speculative reason, but they disclose the greatness of Augustine's mind, possibly more than anything else he wrote. Ayres argues that in this section of *De Trinitate* Augustine develops ideas found in the Cappadocian Fathers, especially in Gregory of Nyssa's reflections on the soul as the image of God.[94]

Most of my references to Augustine are drawn from Edmund Hill's excellent translation of *De Trinitate*, *The Trinity* (Brooklyn: New City Press, 1991). My Latin text to check word usage was R. Hurter, *De Trinitate* (London: David Nutt, 1881).

Pro-Nicene

A term is needed to designate all those from the fourth and early fifth century who opposed Arianism. It is not altogether fair or helpful simply to call them the

---

[94] Ayres, *Nicaea*, 291.

representatives of orthodoxy, because the whole controversy was about what is orthodoxy. It is in hindsight that we see them as the champions of what eventually was
defined as orthodoxy, or the catholic faith. I have thus chosen a more neutral term,
"the pro-Nicene theologians." I am aware that in the prolonged debate there was
development in theological thought on the issues in contention and there were significant differences between those opposed to "Arianism," but I think "pro-Nicene"
is the best option available.[95] Professor Ayres says, "Fundamental to all pro-Nicene
theologies" was the belief that "God is one power, glory, majesty and rule."[96]

"The Arians"

Until recently those that Athanasius, the Cappadocians, and Augustine opposed
because they eternally subordinated the Son to the Father were called by theologians
and historians "Arians." Indeed, often the term "Arianism" was used pejoratively to
refer to any perceived deviation from trinitarian orthodoxy across the centuries, even
of those straying towards or into modalism. Careful critical study of the fourth-century
debates over the Trinity in the past thirty years has demanded a more nuanced use of
this term.[97] It is now recognized that so-called fourth-century Arianism was a diverse
and complex phenomenon. All the different groupings lumped together and once
called "Arians" were all subordinationists, but they did not have one body of agreed
beliefs, and most did not see themselves as disciples of Arius. I offer a simplified outline
of the picture that may help clarify things a little.

Arius (c. 256–336) was a presbyter in the city of Alexandria who fell out with
his bishop, Alexander, over his teaching on the Son. We have no more than three letters, a few fragments, and possibly a quotation from his *Thalia* from his own hand.[98]
Most of our information on what he taught comes from the writings of his opponents,
especially from the pen of Athanasius, his bitterest foe. In his "Discourses Against
the Arians," Athanasius depicts him as the leader of a heretical grouping which he
calls "the Arians" or the "Ariomaniacs."[99] Robert Gregg and Dennis Groh call these
people "the early Arians," arguing that they held in common certain key beliefs,

---

[95] Ayres, *Nicaea*, 6, uses the term "pro-Nicene" primarily to refer to "theologies appearing
from the 360s to the 380s" that formed the basis of the creed agreed to at the council of
Constantinople in 381. However, on p. 167 he says he also uses the term "to refer to the
precursors of that theology." To be exact it would be best to speak of early pro-Nicene
theology, say up to 360, and later more developed pro-Nicene theology from 360 onwards.
Ayres categorically argues that Augustine stands clearly in the pro-Nicene tradition.

[96] Ibid., 279.

[97] See R. P. C. Hanson, *The Search for the Christian Doctrine of God: The Arian Controversy,
318–381* (Grand Rapids, Mich.: Baker, 2005) *passim*, and Ayres, *Nicaea, passim*.

[98] See in more detail Hanson, *The Search*, 5–6.

[99] See in more detail Ayres, *Nicaea*, 105–16.

and besides Arius lists Asterius the Sophist (d. c. 341) and Eusebius of Nicomedia (d. c. 342) as comprising this grouping.[100] In what follows in this book we call these people "Arians," following Athanasius, or "early Arians" when there is a need to be specific.

The Cappadocians also wrote against those they called "Arians," but contemporary scholars hold that it is more accurate to speak of the Cappadocians' theological opponents as "Neo-Arians." The leading Neo-Arians were Aetius (d. c. 370) and his more prolific disciple Eunomius (c. 330–94). Hanson speaks of them as "the radical left wing of Arianism."[101] Ayres calls them "the most subordinationist wing" of the so-called Arians.[102] Like the early Arians, they insisted that the Father alone is true God and that the Son is eternally subordinated in being, work, and authority. Their teaching on these matters was characterized by a very literal interpretation of key biblical terms, by a confidence that God's being or essence can be perfectly comprehended by humans, and by rational philosophical argumentation.[103]

The third main grouping of the so-called Arians are today usually referred to as the "*Homoians*." They argued that the Son was "like" the Father in being or essence (*homoios*, "like"). Hanson says the "main pillar" of their position was the "incomparability of God the Father."[104] He alone is true God, perfectly good, all-powerful, and immortal. Their goal was to find a middle way between those who said the Father and the Son were *homoousios* (one in being) and those who absolutely rejected this confession. They failed in this because in denying that the Father and the Son were one in being and power, they divided the one Godhead, making the Son a God less in being and authority.[105] For this reason the old designation of them as "semi-Arians" is inaccurate and unhelpful.

Although the early Arians, the Neo-Arians, and the *Homoians* differ on significant details, and the *Homoians* and the Neo-Arians do not think of themselves as followers of Arius, they are alike subordinationists. They cannot concede that "the God" (the Creator, the Father) and the Son of God share the same being; or that the Father and the Son work/function as one, or that the Father and the Son are equal in power and authority. For all three groupings the human father-son relationship defines the divine Father-Son relationship, and the subordination seen in the incarnate Christ is to be read back into the eternal or immanent Trinity.[106]

---

[100]Gregg, *Early Arianism*, ix.

[101]Ibid., 598.

[102]Ayres, *Nicaea*, 432.

[103]For more detail see Hanson, *The Search*, 598–636.

[104]Ibid., 563.

[105]For more detail see ibid., 557–97.

[106]All of this will be demonstrated in detail in subsequent chapters.

To sum up then, Arianism was in the fourth century a collective term used by Athanasius, the Cappadocians, and others allied with them to designate the teaching of various theologians who held to a common belief in the eternal subordination of the Son in being, work, and authority, yet differed on other secondary matters.

John Calvin (1509–64)

It is generally agreed that Calvin was the greatest theologian among the sixteenth-century Reformers, and one of his major areas of interest was the doctrine of the Trinity. Time and time again throughout his ministry he found himself in debate on this doctrine, and invariably the issue in question was whether or not the Son was eternally subordinated to the Father. What he opposed was the idea that the Son *derived his divinity* from the Father and thus was subordinated to, or less than, or inferior, to the Father in being and authority. He wrote more in opposition to this idea in his chapter on the Trinity in the *Institutes* than on any other aspect of this doctrine. In expounding his understanding of the Trinity, Calvin's aim was, as with all other doctrines, to formulate his position on the basis of Scripture as it had been understood by the best of theologians from the past, unless the Bible itself dictated otherwise. In his hermeneutical methodology he is neither a naive biblicist who thinks that doctrines can be formulated apart from tradition like the radical anti-Nicenes of his day, nor a committed traditionalist who appeals to the Scriptures simply to substantiate church teachings like the Catholics of his day. What is of particular interest to note is that in his appeal to the church fathers Calvin draws on both theologians from the east and west of the Roman Empire. His reading and comprehension of their writings is impressive. This is illustrated when Calvin casually mentions that Hilary of Poitiers speaks of three "substances" in God "more than a hundred times."[107] My English text for Calvin was *Institutes of the Christian Religion*, ed. John T. McNeill, trans. Ford L. Battles, 2 vols. (London: SCM, 1960). I also quote from his commentaries from time to time.

Karl Barth (1886–1968)

When I started writing this book I had no intention of interacting in any detail with modern discussions of the Trinity. I wanted to put the case for historic orthodoxy. However, I have had to abandon that plan. The strident Australian evangelical critics of my first book on the Trinity unexpectedly made Barth the test case. They argued that Barth eternally subordinates the Son in authority in a similar way to them. If the greatest theologian of the twentieth century embraced the eternal obedience of the Son, they asked, how could they be wrong? If they are not in error then I must be the one in error.

---

[107]John Calvin, *Institutes of the Christian Religion*, ed. John T. Neill, trans. Ford Lewis Battles (London: SCM, 1960), 1.13.5 (p. 126).

Moreover, they said, I had deliberately and "completely misread" Barth to further my own case.[108] In the face of such an attack in "positional" publications that allowed me no reply, I decided that I would need to give a chapter to Barth in this book. Seeking to master Barth's thinking is something no one can confidently claim to have done, and I am no exception. In attempting to make a reply to my critics I read carefully and noted several volumes of Barth's *Church Dogmatics* and parts of other volumes. This involved me in a lot of extra work, but I am very glad that I was forced to do this. Barth is unquestionably the most important theologian of the twentieth century. If he does in fact teach the eternal subordination of the Son in authority in a way similar to contemporary evangelicals, my case is less than convincing. I argue in agreement with most Barth scholars that he does not.

Karl Rahner (1904–84)

My critics also claim that Karl Rahner, whom I quoted in my earlier book mainly in reference to his so-called rule, "*The 'economic' Trinity is the 'immanent' Trinity and the 'immanent' Trinity is the 'economic' Trinity*,"[109] is on their side, not mine. They argue this rule implies the eternal subordination of the Son.[110] If Christ truly reveals God and he is subordinated in the incarnation (the economy of salvation), then he must be subordinated in eternity (the immanent Trinity). I give less space to Rahner than to Barth in answering my critics. I discuss him in a chapter that considers the whole matter of the relationships between the economic Trinity (what is revealed of God in history) and the immanent Trinity (God as he is apart from history). As Rahner is thought to be one of if not the most important Roman Catholic theologian of the twentieth century, I was pleased to interact with him as well.

Omissions

In preparing to write this book I read and noted Hilary of Poitier's book on *The Trinity* (*De Trinitate*). However, I decided not to make Hilary a major debating partner because, first it would have made each chapter too long, and second because he is seldom discussed in the popular historical introductions to the doctrine of the Trinity. Hilary (c. 315–67) is of particular interest because he was the most respected and learned Latin theologian of his day, yet it seems he spoke Greek and from his time in exile in the East knew the writings of Athanasius and at least those of Basil among the Cappadocians. He is a consistent and unrelenting opponent of Arianism, yet on key issues he frequently develops his own arguments. I also read Thomas Aquinas's

---

[108]I document what my critics have said in chapter 8.

[109]Karl Rahner, *The Trinity*, trans. J. Donceel (London: Burns and Oates, 1970), 22, 34.

[110]I document what my critics said on Rahner in chapter 7.

Summa Theologiae on the Trinity in preparation, but again I decided not to make this great theologian (c. 1225–74) a debating partner. He is implacably opposed to subordinationism in any form, and to hierarchical ordering in the eternal Trinity, but evangelicals generally do not count him as an authoritative voice from the past. What he says on the Trinity is predominately analytical and philosophical, and the issue of how biblical teaching forms and is informed by the doctrine of the Trinity is not a major concern in his work.

One thing that fascinated me in reading these theologians was that all of them found communicating with subordinationists almost impossible. I have discovered exactly the same thing today. It seems that once someone has become convinced that the Son is somehow less than the Father no argument can sway the mind, and no creed or confession can be read to oppose what is already believed. Athanasius and the Cappadocians seem to have had little success in convincing their opponents. They were more successful in winning over the confused and confirming and informing the faith of those who wanted to adhere to the Nicene faith. Augustine begins *The Trinity* by discussing this problem. He argues that those who cannot accept the teaching on the Trinity given in the catholic faith are "misguided by their love of reason," or have tried to "transfer what they have observed about bodily things to incorporeal and spiritual things." By these means "they block their own road to genuine understanding by asserting too categorically their own presumptuous opinions, and then rather than change their own misconceived opinion they have defended, they prefer to leave it uncorrected."[111] Calvin also speaks of his inability to convince the subordinationists he battled with. He blames Satan for stirring up "great battles" "during nearly all ages" over the Trinity. Because Calvin found his opponents would not listen, he says he addresses only the "teachable."[112]

A Note on the Reading of These Sources

In the somewhat bitter debate I have had with fellow evangelicals after the publication of my book *The Trinity and Subordinationism*, one thing has become clear. There are two ways of reading the Bible and of reading the thousand and thousands of pages written on the Trinity by theologians past and present. One is to read what has been written with the sole goal of seeking to understand what the author says; the other is to read solely to find comments that would support what is already believed. No fallen human being in debate can completely avoid the second approach, but to read with this aim alone in mind does not promote the cause of truth. I must admit that more

---

[111] Edmund Hill, *The Mystery of the Trinity* (London: Chapman, 1985), 1.1 (p. 65).
[112] Calvin, *Institutes*, 1.13.21 (p. 145).

and more I have become convinced that those who speak of the eternal subordination of the Son deliberately follow the second path. They turn to the Bible, the historical sources, and the writings of modern theologians simply to find comments that would support what they already believe or to refute their critics.

The quotes from the great theologians of the past that have been brought to my attention supposedly supporting the eternal subordination of the Son have not convinced me. Invariably the words cited are simply affirmations of divine differentiation or order. Orthodoxy never allows that divine differentiation and divine order imply subordination. The church fathers are agreed that the Father is not the Son, and the Son is not the Father, and the Spirit is not the Father or the Son, and that some things said of the Father or the Son or the Spirit cannot be said of any other divine person. Thus the Father sends the Son and not vice versa, the Son reveals the Father and not vice versa, and the Spirit directs attention to the Son and not vice versa. The persons are eternally differentiated and relate in a fixed and ordered manner. Divine differentiation and order do not involve the sub-ordering of the Son and the Spirit. It is admitted, nevertheless, that in the vast body of historical material, occasional comments are found that may imply or allow the eternal subordination of the Son. I think I have had every one of them pointed out to me by one critic of my position or another. In reply I simply say that a passing comment, possibly poorly worded, or even added by a scribe, should not be taken to express the dominant view of the author. A holistic reading of any ancient or modern text is demanded. I am sure there will be many a slip in wording here and there in this book.

It will now be obvious that what follows is not an entirely neutral reading of the Bible and the tradition. This is of no surprise because no such thing is possible. Every reader comes to a text with preconceptions, and every Christian theologian has theological convictions that in part determine what is seen in the text. I confess my commitments openly. I am setting out to read the Bible and the tradition in the light of the Nicene and Athanasian Creeds and the Reformation confessions, which I believe give the best guide to how the varied comments in this body of writings should be interpreted and understood. About a hundred years ago the great Reformed scholar B. B. Warfield wrote on the Trinity "vigorously to reassert the principle of equalization," because his fellow evangelicals were all too commonly embracing subordinationism.[113] I write with the same agenda in a similar context. This commitment does not mean I am slavishly bound to what these creeds and confessions say, but it does mean that I think they are basically correct in what they affirm, and if on some detail I dare to differ from them, I will do so only tentatively, suggesting that the truth enunciated might have been expressed better in some other way.

---

[113] Warfield, "The Biblical Doctrine of the Trinity," 116.

Those whose views I am opposing of course also read the Bible with their commitments. It is my argument that their primary commitment is to the permanent subordination of women. They want to justify and explain this social ordering by arguing that the Son is eternally subordinated to the Father in function and authority. The way they have changed traditional language used of the Trinity to parallel the language they have created to make their post-1970s' case for the permanent subordination of women indicates this.

CHAPTER

WHAT THE BIBLE SAYS ABOUT THE TRINITY AND WHAT IT DOES NOT SAY

In the fourth century one of the most bitter and painful theological disputes the church has known took place. It was basically about how Jesus Christ the Son of God should be understood in relation to God the Father. Were these two divine "persons" to be considered equally God or not? Right at the heart of this controversy stood the problem of biblical interpretation—hermeneutics, as we would call it today.[1] The contending parties held the same high view of the Scriptures;[2] both read the Scriptures in much the same way, and both found passages that seemed to support their position, especially in John's gospel.[3] Exactly the same situation exists today in the early twenty-first century among evangelicals. One side argues that the Bible clearly teaches that the Son of God is eternally set under the Father in function and authority, and they have their list of texts in support. In opposition stand others who argue that the Bible does not eternally set the Son under the Father; they are two different yet "coequal" divine persons.

In both the 1999 *Sydney Anglican Diocesan Doctrine Commission Report*, drawn up by evangelical biblical and systematic theologians, and in the writings of Professor

---

[1] Further on this see R. P. C. Hanson, *The Search for the Christian Doctrine of God: The Arian Controversy, 318–381* (Grand Rapids, Mich.: Baker, 2005), especially 824–48; and Lewis Ayres, *Nicaea and Its Legacy: An Approach to Fourth-Century Trinitarian Theology* (New York: Oxford, 2005), 31–40, 335–41.

[2] Hanson, *The Search*, 825, says both thought of the Bible as "inerrant."

[3] See especially T. E. Pollard, *Johannine Christology in the Early Church* (Cambridge: Cambridge University Press, 1970).

Wayne Grudem, the most significant evangelical advocate in America of the eternal subordination of the Son in function and authority, we have the constantly reiterated claim that all that they are teaching on the eternal subordination of the Son exactly captures the plain teaching of Scripture. The Sydney theologians say, "*The Scriptures themselves* bear witness to a subordination which belongs to the eternal relationship between the persons of the Trinity, and not only to the humanity of Jesus in the incarnation, or even in the broader work of redemption. This applies to the Spirit as well ... unity, equality and subordination characterise the life of the Trinity."[4]

Similarly, Wayne Grudem constantly claims that all that he teaches on the eternal subordination of the Son in function and authority, and on the "differing roles" of the Father and the Son, perfectly reflects the teaching of Holy Scripture.[5] For every point he makes he quotes biblical texts that supposedly endorse exactly what he is saying. In reply to those like me who argue that he is reading into the Scripture his own views and directly contradicting how the best of theologians in the past have interpreted these texts, he says it is "we"[6] who have not proven our case by appeal to Scripture. This is not a very convincing argument for rejecting what Professor Gilbert Bilezikian and I have written previously, because we wrote mainly to refute his *historical* claim that orthodox theologians from the council of Nicea onwards have taught the eternal subordination in role and authority of the Son.[7] In this chapter for the first time I will carefully examine what the Scriptures themselves say.

As we come to consider first of all what the Scriptures themselves actually teach on the Father-Son relationship in the eternal Trinity, we cannot ignore history. How the best of theologians in the fourth century resolved the very same "battle of the texts" may well offer the way forward today. Athanasius, the Cappadocians, and

---

[4] Par. 17. The whole document is reprinted in my book *The Trinity and Subordinationism* (Downers Grove, Ill.: InterVarsity, 2002), 22–137. Italics added.

[5] These assertions are constant in all Wayne Grudem's writings, but I think they come out most strongly in his *Evangelical Feminism and Biblical Truth* (Sisters, Ore.: Multnomah, 2004), 405–43.

[6] Ibid., 425–29. He is referring to my book *The Trinity and Subordinationism*, and Gilbert Bilezikian, "Hermeneutical Bungee-Jumping: Subordination in the Godhead," *Journal of the Evangelical Theological Society* 40, no. 1 (1997): 57–68. He also criticizes Millard Erickson, *God in Three Persons: A Contemporary Interpretation of the Trinity* (Grand Rapids, Mich.: Baker, 1995), for not depending primarily on Scripture, but again this argument is hardly to be taken seriously. The doctrine of the Trinity does not spring immediately from the pages of Scripture. It is an historically developed doctrine. And Erickson has far more solid biblical exegesis—three full chapters—than we find in any of Grudem's writings on the Trinity. Grudem mainly gives lists of texts that supposedly endorse his views, or quotes texts that when examined say nothing about *the eternal role subordination of the Son*—a concept not mentioned anywhere in the Bible.

[7] Wayne Grudem, *Systematic Theology: An Introduction to Biblical Doctrine* (Grand Rapids, Mich.: Zondervan, 1995), 251. See for a parallel claim his *Evangelical Feminism*, 415.

Augustine employed three strategies in reply to their "Arian" opponents who adamantly believed the Bible was on their side, quoting it profusely.

First of all they appealed to "the tradition of the Fathers."[8] Initially for Athanasius this tradition was the teaching on the Trinity by the great theologians who had preceded him. Later for him, the Cappadocians, and Augustine it was the creed of Nicea. Their argument was that the way the "Arians" were interpreting the Bible contradicted how the tradition indicated that the Scriptures should be read. Second, they sought to give a better exegesis of the texts in contention than their adversaries. Much of Athanasius' famous "Discourses Against the Arians" is taken up with the exposition of Scripture. He seeks to give alternative interpretations to the texts Arius and those he called "Arians" interpreted in ways to support their ideas. And third, Athanasius and Augustine argued that a correct hermeneutic had to be found in Scripture itself to make sense of the diverse and sometimes seemingly contradictory comments within Scripture. If this was not done, they could see no resolution would ever be found in the battle of the texts. Each side would simply go on quoting isolated texts giving their own interpretation of them. In what follows in subsequent chapters we will explore what in fact is "the tradition"—the way the best of theologians from the past and the creeds and confessions have thought the Scriptures should be understood. In this chapter the second and third matters will be explored. What hermeneutical principles should be followed as we struggle with the diverse comments in Scripture on the Father-Son relationship, and what is the best and most plausible interpretation of the key texts in contention?

The Debate Today

In the present-day debate among evangelicals, there are a number of matters on which there is full and complete agreement. Both sides believe the Trinity is foreshadowed in the Old Testament and that God is one and yet three "persons," Father, Son, and Spirit. Both sides also profess the divinity of Christ and the Holy Spirit. On these matters where we agree we may assume scriptural support. The main points of disagreement today, as in the fourth century, are how the Father Son relationship is to be understood and how the divine persons may be eternally differentiated without falling into the errors of tritheism, subordinationism, or modalism. It is on these questions we concentrate. The Spirit is not forgotten, but he does not get the attention he deserves. Again as in the early fourth century, the Father-Son relationship and how the Father and the Son are to be differentiated are the primary issues.

As we turn to the pages of the New Testament, the following key questions are to be kept in mind. These are the ones that sharply divide evangelicals today.

---

[8] Hanson, *The Search*, 778, 827–28, 847–49; Ayres, *Nicaea*, 218–20, 420–23, 425–29.

1. How should the Bible be read as a whole, because some texts seem to indicate that God the Son is subordinated to God the Father, and other texts seem to indicate that God the Son is one and equal with God the Father?

2. Is there anything in the Bible that suggests that the Son of God is eternally subordinated in function and/or authority under the Father?

3. Does the Bible suggest that the Father, the Son, and the Spirit are eternally ordered hierachically in being, function, or authority?

4. What are we to understand by the human terms *father* and *son* when used of the first two persons of the Trinity? Do these titles imply that the divine Father always has authority over the Son, or are they chosen to convey something other than this?

5. How are the Father, Son, and Spirit differentiated in the Bible? (We agree they are eternally differentiated; we disagree on *how* they are eternally differentiated.)

The Big Picture

In contemporary biblical studies, the narrative nature of so much of the Bible is recognized and stressed. Whatever else the Bible might be, it is a narrative or story of God's dealings with humankind. The big story is made up of lots of individual stories and teaching. No one passage is properly understood unless it is set in the light of the whole divine drama that unfolds from Genesis to Revelation, and yet each story is what generates the big picture. In other words, the micro informs the macro and vice versa. This principle is also true for the didactic parts of Scripture such as we have in the New Testament epistles. The overall teaching of any author is always the best guide to understanding specific passages in his writings. This hermeneutic counts against taking verses in isolation to prove anything. The big picture is always what is most important.

In saying this we are embracing the fact that there is a rich diversity in the Scriptures. This diversity is of the very nature of Scripture, because each author has particular and distinctive things to say and is addressing specific problems. Even within the writings of one author, we often find comments not easily reconciled with other comments. Nowhere is this truer than in reference to what the Bible says about the divine Father, Son, and Spirit and their relationship with one another. Limiting ourselves just to the Gospels at this point, we see on the one hand Jesus lying in a cradle, growing as a man, learning, subject to hunger, tiredness, sorrow, ignorance, and finally death (Lk 2:7; 2:40; Mk 2:15; 13:32; 14:33; 15:34; Jn 11:35). He is said to be "sent" by the Father, and shown as dependent on the Father and praying to the Father. On the other hand, the Gospel writers also speak of him doing the things only God can do (forgiving sins, offering salvation, giving life, creating, raising the dead, and so on), and John the evangelist declares him to be God (Jn 1:1; 20:28). How, we must ask, can these two contrasting pictures of Christ be reconciled? This is not a new question. It was clearly seen and addressed in the patristic age by Athanasius and Augustine, and we begin with their solution.

Athanasius and Augustine on the Diversity in Biblical Teaching on the Trinity[9]

The Arians amassed a great list of texts that could be read to teach the Son's subordination in being, work/function, and authority.[10] In reply to their selective proof-text approach, Athanasius countered with a holistic hermeneutic that began with the big picture and read the problematic texts in this light. His understanding of the content of this big picture, what he calls "the scope of Scripture," came from two sources: what he had received from those before him, "the traditions of the fathers,"[11] and what he himself perceived to be primary and central in Scripture. Most of his "Discourses Against the Arians"[12] are taken up with the exposition of the many passages the Arians quoted in support of their case.[13] He judges their hermeneutic to be selective, "devious," "irreligious,"[14] and not "from our fathers."[15] To grasp the true meaning of Scripture, he argues, the whole "scope" (*skopos*) of the Bible has to be embraced. In regard to the Son of God he says, "The scope and character of Holy Scripture ... is this: it contains a double account of the Savior; that he was ever God and is the Son, being the Father's *Logos* and Radiance and Wisdom; and that afterwards for us he took the flesh of a virgin ... This scope is to be found throughout inspired Scripture."[16]

This "double account" of the Savior, he argues, is most clearly enunciated in Jn 1:1, 14 and Php 2:5–11. First, the apostle John makes this plain when in the opening

---

[9] In the next chapter and subsequent chapters, the writings of Athanasius and Augustine will be carefully studied. They are introduced here because of their contribution to biblical hermeneutics.

[10] For the early Arians and the Neo-Arians—as we will demonstrate in due course—subordination in being, work/function, and authority went hand in hand.

[11] Athanasius, "On the Councils," in *The Nicene and Post Nicene Fathers of the Christian Church* (henceforth *NPNF*), ed. Philip Schaff and Henry Wace (Grand Rapids, Mich.: Eerdmans, 1971), 4:1.54 (p. 479). Also "Discourses against the Arians," in *NPNF* 4:1.3 (p. 307), 1.4 (p. 308), 3.29 (p. 409).

[12] Prevailing scholarly opinion is that the fourth discourse was not written by Athanasius, despite the fact it is consistently anti-Arian and Athanasian in outlook.

[13] On the Arian use of the Bible and the orthodox reply see Hanson, *The Search*, 824–49. In relation to the key texts from John's gospel see particularly Pollard, *Johannine Christology*.

[14] Athanasius, "Discourses," in *NPNF* 4:1.1–5 (pp. 306–8).

[15] Ibid., 1.8 (p. 310), "On the Councils," in *NPNF* 4:2.14 (p. 457).

[16] Athanasius, "Discourses," in *NPNF* 4:3.29 (p. 409).

chapter of his Gospel he juxtaposes the statements "the Word was God" (Jn 1:1) and "the Word became flesh" (Jn 1:14), and second, when Paul says Christ "was equal with God but emptied himself, taking the form of a servant, being found in the human likeness."[17] These texts, Athanasius maintains, give the interpretative key to the reading of the whole of Scripture. They indicate that texts found anywhere in the Bible speaking of the subordination of the Son refer to him as the incarnate Son. They allude to his freely chosen servant ministry in the flesh. Texts that speak of him as divine and all-powerful speak of him as God for all eternity. For Athanasius, the Son is God *eternally* one in being with the Father, and in his incarnate ministry *temporally* subordinate to the Father by reason of him taking human flesh. Athanasius had no problems with the many texts that spoke of the Son's frailty, prayer life, obedience, or death on the cross. For him these texts affirmed unambiguously that the Son assumed human flesh and the limitations this involved for us and our salvation. Such human traits, he argued, are not to be ascribed to Jesus as the divine Son for all eternity.

Similarly, Augustine's aim in writing *The Trinity* was to confirm on the basis of Scripture the catholic faith as it had been delivered to him.[18] In setting out on this task he is acutely aware of the seeming "contradictions"[19] and "multifarious diversity"[20] in the Bible on the issues he is addressing. To establish the catholic faith on the basis of biblical teaching, he recognizes, like Athanasius, that he must articulate a way of reading Scripture that makes sense of the whole. He thus formulates a number of "canonical rules" for correct interpretation, the most important of these being that all texts speaking of Christ as equal in divinity, majesty, and authority with the Father refer to the Son "in the form of God," and all texts speaking of Christ's human limitations, subordination, and obedience refer to him in "the form of a servant," as the incarnate Son.[21] This hermeneutical rule he found spelled out in Php 2:5–11. However, Augustine recognized that this one rule was not adequate in itself. A comprehensive "trinitarian hermeneutic" was needed.[22] He thus identified and distinguished three kinds of trinitarian comment on the relationship between the Father and the Son in the New Testament.

1. "Many" texts that speak of "the unity and equality" of the Father and the Son in "substance" and "work."[23]

---

[17] Ibid. He returns to these passages time and time again. In his exposition of key texts, he begins with Php 2:9–10. See ibid., 1.37–45 (pp. 327–33).

[18] Augustine sets out his goals in writing in *The Trinity*, trans. Edmund Hill (Brooklyn: New City Press, 1991), 1.2.7 (p. 69).

[19] Ibid., 1.4.22 (p. 82).

[20] Ibid., 2, prologue, 1 (p. 97).

[21] Ibid., 1.3.14–21 (74–81).

[22] Further on this see J. Pelikan, "The Trinitarian Hermeneutics of Augustine," in *Collecta Augustiniana*, eds. J. C. Schnaubelt and F. Van Fleteren (New York: Peter Lang, 1990), 327–43.

[23] Augustine, *Trinity*, 2.1.3 (pp. 99–100).

2. A few texts that speak of "the Son as the lesser because of the form of a servant," that is, while he was incarnate.[24]

3. "Lastly,... others which mark him neither as less nor equal, but only intimate
   that he is *from* (Latin *de*) the Father."[25] Later in discussing what it means when
   Scripture speaks of the Son as "begotten" and "sent," he argues these comments fall within this third category.[26]

Athanasius and Augustine show the right approach in seeking answers from
the Scriptures on any doctrinal issue, especially one hotly debated. It is first of all
to ask, What is the "tradition"—how has the Bible been understood by the best
of theologians of the past on this topic? And then second, How can the primary
theological answer to the question in contention be discerned in the various and
sometimes seemingly contradictory comments in Scripture? Both Athanasius and
Augustine had no doubts as to what was the catholic faith or tradition in regards to
the Trinity. The Father, Son, and Spirit were equally God, one in being, work, and
authority, and yet in taking human flesh the Son had willingly subordinated himself
to the Father for our salvation. They held that the Scriptures were to be read on
the basis of this given theology. They were to be interpreted not only to confirm
what was believed but also to inform what was already believed. In this reading
added evidence might be found for what was already believed, new insights might
be gained, and aspects of the tradition might be corrected. In what immediately
follows I embrace their methodological presuppositions. I too will read the Bible in
the light of the received tradition as codified in the creeds and confessions, assuming this to be the best guide to how the Scriptures as a whole should be understood.
Nevertheless, I remain open to the possibility of learning something new about the
Trinity from the Bible and of the Bible calling into question aspects of the Trinity
tradition.

Resolving Diversity in Biblical Teaching on the Trinity Today

For an evangelical biblical scholar today, the best solution to the seemingly contradictory portrayal of Christ in the New Testament is to explain it in terms of the very
structure of the New Testament story which envisages three stages or epochs in the
ministry of the Son of God:[27] (1) his preexistent glory, (2) his humiliation for a short

---

[24] Ibid. (p. 99).

[25] Ibid.

[26] Ibid., 4.5.27 (p. 173), 4.5.29 (p. 174), cf. 2.2.9 (p. 1030).

[27] I. H. Marshall, "Incarnational Christology in the New Testament" in *Christ the Lord: Studies
in Christology Presented to Donald Guthrie*, ed. H. H. Rowdon (Leicester, UK; Inter-Varsity,
1982), 1–16 and on Paul, Ben Witherington III, *Paul's Narrative Thought World* (Louisville:
Westminster, 1994), 11–119.

period in the incarnation, and (3) his exaltation to reign as Lord. This three-fold schema is nowhere more clearly spelled out than in Php 2:5–11, a passage commonly taken to be a pre-Pauline "hymn." There has been much debate on the background to this hymn, its overall interpretation, and the meaning of several key terms used in it. Peter O'Brien in his commentary on Philippians does a brilliant job sorting through these questions and explaining the text.[28] In my brief discussion of this key christological passage I follow him closely, not only because of the strengths of his exegesis, but also to exclude the charge that I have interpreted this passage to serve my own ends. Dr. O'Brien was a member of the 1999 Sydney Doctrine Commission that ruled that the Son of God was compulsorily and eternally set under the Father in function and authority.[29]

Transition

Verse 5. This verse is transitional. It concludes the moving appeal of vv. 1–4 and introduces the "hymn" that speaks of Christ's preexistent glory, humiliation, and exaltation beginning at v. 6. The apostle asks his readers to have the same mind as "was in Christ Jesus." In their behavior as Christians he wants them to make Jesus their exemplar.

The First Stage: Christ as Preexistent God (Verse 6)

Verse 6. "This magnificent passage begins by asserting that Christ Jesus, who existed in the form (*morphe*) of God and shared his glory, did not regard his equality with God as something to be used for his own advantage."[30] The Greek term *morphe*, translated as "form," refers to that "which truly and fully expresses the being which underlies it."[31] In saying that Jesus had "the form of God," Paul is asserting that the preexistent Christ was God and shared God's glory, majesty, and authority. The sentence begins with a participial phrase, "who, being in the form of God." Paul uses a participle rather than an infinite verb because he wants to make it clear that Christ is forever God. The equality Jesus has with the Father before he became man is qualified by a sentence using the rare and disputed Greek word *harpagmos*. The word can mean grasping after something not one's own, or not holding onto something one already

---

28 Peter O'Brien, *The Epistle to the Philippians* (Grand Rapids, Mich.: Eerdmans, 1991). I also had open before me as I worked through the text, Gordon Fee, *Paul's Letter to the Philippians* (Grand Rapids, Mich.: Eerdmans, 1995), another excellent commentary.

29 It seems to me it is impossible to reconcile what Dr. O'Brien endorses in this document as a theologian concerned to uphold the permanent subordination of women and what he says as an exegete when his only concern is to expound the text of Scripture.

30 O'Brien, *Philippians*, 206.

31 Ibid., 210.

possesses. The context demands the latter. Paul has just said Christ "was in the form of God." Now he says that Christ did not regard his divine status and authority as something to be held onto and used "for his own advantage."[32] To be God did not mean clutching onto what he had but giving it up. In this hymn's opening verse we are told of Christ's status prior to his stepping down from heaven. Before becoming incarnate he was God in all glory, majesty, and authority.

The Second Stage: Christ Empties Himself and Becomes Man (Verses 7–8)

Verse 7. Instead of holding onto what he had, O'Brien says, "Christ *voluntarily* chose the path of obedient humiliation that led to his incarnation and death." The emphatic "himself" (*heauton*) and the use of the aorist active Greek verb *ekenosen*, translated as "emptied," he says, indicates this self-humbling was freely chosen.[33] What the pre-existent Christ emptied himself of is not stated. Paul does not suggest at any time he gave up his divinity. We simply are told what this self-emptying involved. It involved "taking the form (*morphe*) of a slave, being born in human likeness."

In using the word *morphe* a second time to speak of Jesus' humiliated status, Paul is saying Christ really became a slave. He did not function as a slave or take the role of a slave; he became a slave. He did this "voluntarily,"[34] O'Brien says, and thereby showed clearly "what it meant to be God."[35] The second phrase, "being born in human likeness," spells out more precisely what his voluntary self-emptying involved. He truly became man, but he did not cease to be God.[36] He was the same as we are in his humanity, but he was different from us in that he never ceased to be "equal with God."

The NRSV translation of the following phrase, "and being found in human form," is not ideal. The word translated this time as "form" is *schema*, not *morphe*. This Greek word speaks of what makes something or some person recognizable. Having stated that Christ became man, Paul now says Jesus was clearly identifiable as a man.

Verse 8. At this point Paul explains what this self-emptying of the Son of God involved. It involved taking the path of obedience even to death on a cross. According to O'Brien, the reflexive pronoun (he humbled *himself*) is used once again to underline that "the action was free and voluntary."[37] He then quotes with warm approval Barth's citing of Kierkegaard's words, "Christ humbled himself—not he was humbled." O'Brien notes that to whom or to what Christ is obedient is not mentioned.

---

[32] Ibid., 215.
[33] Ibid., 217.
[34] Ibid., 218.
[35] Ibid., 224.
[36] Ibid., 226.
[37] Ibid., 228.

He is not convinced it is to the Father. I suspect he does not want to concede this seemingly natural conclusion because he opposes the idea made by some scholars that the hymn as a whole depicts Christ as the second Adam. We may agree with him on this yet concede that at this point in the "hymn" Christ is thought of as the second Adam who is completely obedient to the will of the Father. He is the perfect human being fully pleasing to God. If this is the case, then we have here a parallel with Ro 5:19.[38] Ralph Martin, who adopts this position, says, "His [Christ's] obedience is a sure token of his deity and authority for, as Lohmeyer says in a brilliant insight, only a divine being can accept death as *obedience*; for ordinary men it is a necessity."[39] O'Brien quotes the German theologians J. Schneider and E. Kasemann, who make a similar point. They "argue that a differentiation between Jesus and all other human beings is made in the hymn in that the incarnate Christ accomplished what no other person could do, that is, render complete obedience."[40]

The Third Stage: Christ Exalted to Reign as Lord (Verses 9–11)

Verse 9. This verse clearly marks the third transition point in the unfolding narrative about Christ. In response to the Son's voluntary obedience and self-humbling, God the Father "therefore" (*dio*) exalted him.[41] O'Brien says the inclusion of the second Greek conjunction *kai* and the position of the emphatic *him* (*auton*) indicates reciprocity. "He humbled himself, and God exalted him."[42] O'Brien continues, "Jesus' self-humbling reached the absolute depths in his most shameful death on a cross. But now by way of vindication and approval of Jesus' total self-humbling, the Father has magnificently exalted his Son to the highest station and graciously bestowed on him the name above all other names, that is, his own name, LORD (=Yahweh).... In his exalted state Jesus now exercises universal lordship."[43]

Twice on this one page O'Brien speaks of God the Father's action in exalting Christ as indicating "reciprocity" and once as a "reciprocal response."[44] These cognate words introduce the ideas of mutuality, correspondence, giving and receiving, and of one action having its counterpart in another. The Son voluntarily humbled himself, and in response the Father exalted him. O'Brien says that in exalting the Son the

---

[38] Fee, *Philippians*, 216.

[39] Ralph Martin, *The Epistle of Paul to the Philippians* (London: Tyndale, 1964), 102.

[40] O'Brien, *Philippians*, 225.

[41] Neil Richardson, *Paul's Language about God* (Sheffield: Academic, 1994), 244, notes that Paul most commonly speaks of God the Father raising Christ. Before too much is made of the passive verbs, it should be noted what the Father does is a response to what the Son has done willingly. We have here reciprocal actions.

[42] O'Brien, *Philippians*, 333.

[43] Ibid., 233.

[44] Ibid.

Father gave him nothing that he did not already have. "All authority in heaven and on earth were his by nature as well as by gift (Mt 28:18; cf. Eph 1:20–21)."[45]

Verses 10–11. The final two verses speak of a universal homage that will be given on the last day to Jesus the Lord. The believers in Philippi already acknowledge the lordship of Christ, even as believers do today, but universal recognition of Jesus as Lord must await the final consummation. The hymn begins by speaking of Christ as equal with God (the Father) and concludes by saying that his exaltation leads "to the glory of God the Father." What Paul seems to be saying is that in exalting the Son to reign as Lord over the universe and in making him the focal point of homage the Father himself is glorified. We now see why O'Brien twice says, "The hymn reveals not only what Jesus is truly like, but also what it means to be God."[46] The passage focuses on Jesus, his glory and self-humbling, but ultimately it reveals a new understanding of God. The God revealed in Jesus Christ is both Lord and servant. He is the all-powerful God who gladly humbles himself for the salvation of men and women. There is no hint here of a Son eternally subordinated to the Father in being, function, or authority. Instead, there is a bold revelation of the Father and the Son reciprocally related in giving and receiving, ruling and serving.

Conclusion

This three-stage Christology so clearly spelled out in Php 2:5–11 may be presupposed throughout the New Testament.[47] Jesus is the incarnation of the preexistent Son of God, who voluntarily stepped down from heaven, assuming the subordination this demanded, so as to win our salvation, and then was raised to rule as Lord over all creation. Before and after the incarnation, he is God in all glory, majesty, and authority; during the incarnation, he is God subordinated by the flesh he chose to assume. Thus a contemporary critical biblical theology comes to much the same conclusions as those reached by Athanasius more than sixteen hundred years ago. There is "a double account" of the Savior in Scripture. He is depicted both as God in the flesh, God in *kenotic* (self-emptied form), subordinated God; and as God in all his glory, majesty, and authority, the Lord of all. It is a serious mistake to think that what the biblical writers say of the Son of God incarnate, in kenotic form, says all that needs to be said of him.

The Apostle Paul on the Trinity

With the big picture established, we can now turn to Paul's specific comments about the Father, Son, and Spirit, concentrating on his teaching addressing the questions

---

[45] Ibid., 238.

[46] Ibid., 216, 224, and, similarly, 252.

[47] It is acknowledged that some would dispute this, arguing that Mark and Luke for example do not speak of the preexistence of Christ.

outlined at the beginning of this chapter and the passages most quoted today to suggest that the Son is eternally subordinated in function and authority to the Father.[48]

Whatever Paul may say about Christ, the Son of God, and the Holy Spirit, he remains a monotheist. He speaks only four times of the "one God" (Ro 3:30; 1Co 8:4–6; Eph 4:6; 1Ti 2:5), but the idea seems close at hand in many other passages (e.g., 1Th 1:9–10; 1Co 1:9). About forty times he speaks of God as Father, seventeen times of God the Son, and sixteen times of God the Spirit. Every one of his epistles begins with a greeting or opening blessing in which God is designated as "our Father" or "the Father" or "the Father of our Lord Jesus Christ." The last of these, "the Father of our Lord Jesus Christ," is particularly common (Ro 1:7; 1Co 1:3; 2Co 1:2; Gal 1:3; etc.). It is a phrase that identifies both parties and relates them intimately together. I. Howard Marshal says, "naming Jesus alongside God as the source of spiritual blessings" in these epistolary greetings "assigns to him the same role as that of God" [the Father].[49] One of the interesting facets of Paul's use of "Father" language is that he almost never allows the term to stand alone. When Paul refers to "our Father," it is always coupled with the word God—either "God our Father" or "our God and Father." What this coupling suggests is that the term Father is for him not simply an equivalent for the term God (theos), but the identification of one divine person.[50]

When Paul refers to God's Son he uses the definite article. Christ is "the Son (of God)." His relationship with the Father is unique. A survey of Paul's usage of this title shows how it functions for him. In several instances the title Son indicates his royal status and work. Thus in Ro 1:3–4 the Son is identified as "the seed of David according to the flesh" (KJV) who has now been appointed as Son of God in power

---

[48] Most books on the Trinity say something about biblical teaching on this topic, usually in brief summary. The most detailed study is Arthur Wainwright, The Trinity in the New Testament (London: SPCK, 1962). This is an excellent source, and while he finds subordination in a few texts as he interprets them, it is to be noted that he does not support subordinationism. See also Ben Witherington III and Laura Ice, The Shadow of the Almighty: Father, Son and Spirit in Biblical Perspective (Grand Rapids, Mich.: Eerdmans, 2002); Brian Edgar, The Message of the Trinity: Life in God (Downers Grove, Ill.: InterVarsity, 2005); and C. F. D. Moule, "The New Testament and the Doctrine of the Trinity," Evangelical Theology 88 (1976): 16–20. Good summaries of biblical teaching on the Trinity are also found in Erickson, God in Three Persons, 46–72 and Robert Letham, The Holy Trinity in Scripture, History, Theology, and Worship (Phillipsburg, N.J.: P&R, 2004), 17–85. On Paul's doctrine of the Trinity see Gordon Fee, God's Empowering Presence: The Holy Spirit in the Letters of Paul (Peabody, Mass.: Hendrickson, 1994), 827–45, and Gordon Fee, "Paul and the Trinity: The Experience of Christ and the Spirit for Paul's Understanding of God," in The Trinity: An Interdisciplinary Symposium on theTrinity, eds. S. Davis, D. Kendall, G. O'Collins (Oxford: Oxford University, 1999), 46–72. See also Richardson, Paul's Language about God.

[49] I. Howard Marshal, New Testament Theology (Downers Grove, Ill.: InterVarsity, 2004), 427.

[50] Witherington and Ice, The Shadow, 33.

by the resurrection (cf. 2Sa 7:12–16). Hurtado also finds this motif in 1Th 1:9–10 and 1Co 15:24–28.[51] In at least three other passages Paul speaks of the Son's redemptive death. In Gal 2:20 he speaks of "the Son of God, who loved me and gave himself for me," in Ro 5:10 of being reconciled to God "through the death of his Son," and in Ro 8:32 of God (the Father) "who did not withhold his own Son, but gave him up for all of us." Cullmann sees here a parallel with Jesus' own understanding of his Sonship, "the Son of God carries out the divine plan of salvation in his life, but above all in his death.... To be God's Son means to suffer and to die."[52]

Paul's designation of the resurrected Jesus as "Lord" is very significant.[53] He calls Jesus "the Lord" about 180 times. It seems he took over this title from the earliest Jewish Christians who in Aramaic prayed, *Maranatha*, "Our Lord, come!" (1Co 16:22). The title *lord* (*kurios*) in everyday usage in the first century designated someone in authority. A lord is characteristically set over servants or slaves. In the Greek translation of the Old Testament (the Septuagint or LXX), it is used to translate the Hebrew name for God, *Yahweh*, and Paul continues this usage (2Co 6:16, 18; Ro 14:11; etc). What is surprising is that Paul and other New Testament writers freely give this title to Jesus as well. Nowhere is this seen more clearly than when Old Testament texts that spoke of Yahweh as the Lord are used in reference to the resurrected Jesus (Ro 10:13; 1Co 1:31; 10:26; 2Co 10:17; etc. cf. Ac 2:21). This transference of the name of God to Jesus comes to the fore in eschatological texts. In the Old Testament the end of this world as it is known entails the final visitation of *Yahweh* in judgment. In the New Testament Paul speaks of the visitation in judgment of "our Lord Jesus Christ" (1Th 5:23; 4:15–17; 1Co 1:7–8; 4:1–5; etc.). What this indicates is that although Paul continued to affirm monotheism, he no longer thought of God as a solitary unitary being. His understanding of monotheism included the Father, Son, and Spirit. Nowhere is this expanded monotheism more clearly seen than in 1Co 8:5–6, where Paul confesses both "one God, the Father" and "one Lord, Jesus Christ." In this bold association of the Father and Christ, Paul adapts the wording of the foundational Jewish confession, the *Shema*, from Dt 6:4, "Hear, O Israel, the LORD our God is one LORD" (KJV). He keeps the "one" intact as a monotheist but confesses that he believes the Father and the Son are this one God. At this point the Spirit is not mentioned.

At the very least the title *lord* indicates that after the resurrection Jesus was seen to "function" as God. If this is the case, then Paul knew nothing of a functionally subordinated Christ after Easter. Christ is no longer the obedient servant set under

---

[51] Larry Hurtado, "Son of God," in *Dictionary of Paul and His Letters*, eds. Gerald Hawthorne, Ralph Martin, and Daniel Reid (Downers Grove, Ill.: InterVarsity, 1993), 904.

[52] Oscar Cullmann, *The Christology of the New Testament* (London: SCM, 1963), 292–93.

[53] Hurtado, "Lord," in *Dictionary of Paul*, 560–69.

the Father. The resurrected and ascended Christ reigns as God. Christ functions as Yahweh whose name he bears in all majesty, glory, and authority. Why is this? It must be that he functions as God because he *is* God.

The most elevated teaching on Christ in the Pauline corpus is found in Col 1:15–20, and its echo in Col 2:9–10. Here Christ is said to be "the image (*eikon*) of the invisible God" (1:15). This means "he replicates God."[54] O'Brien says Paul depicts Christ as one with God the Father ontologically and functionally.[55] Schreiner says the passage "emphasises the supremacy of Christ over all."[56] After describing Christ as the image of God, Paul then adds that he is "the first born of all creation." Arius took these words to mean that Jesus was one of God's creatures, a subordinate God.[57] This interpretation is impossible. The word *firstborn* (*prototokos*) carries the meaning of "temporal priority and sovereignty of rank."[58] It speaks of a father's honoring of his eldest son. The allusion is to Ps 89:27, where God says of the messianic king, "I will make him the firstborn, the highest of the kings of the earth." Furthermore, Paul then goes on to say that "in him [Christ] all things in heaven and on earth were created" (v. 16). The preposition *in* indicates that Christ is the agent of creation. God the Father creates, just as he elects (Eph 1:4), "in Christ," not apart from him.[59] Far from being a creation, the resurrected Christ is over all creation. He has "first place in everything" (v. 18). This is so because "in him all the fullness of God was pleased to dwell" (v. 19). In him the completeness of deity was present. Paul makes it clear that at this point he is thinking of Christ in his incarnate existence, because immediately he goes on to speak of the reconciliation achieved through Christ's death on the cross (v. 20).

In Col 2:9–10 Paul reiterates his lofty view of Christ. He says, "In him the whole fullness of deity dwells bodily," and he "is the head of every ruler and authority." While in Jewish apocalyptic thought the overthrow of all evil forces was expected to take place on the last day, here Paul thinks of Christ ruling over the material and spiritual world at this present time. He now reigns as "the head of every ruler and authority."

Exaltation and Enthronement

In the next chapter of Colossians Paul takes up one of his most important christological motifs. He speaks of the Christ being exalted in the resurrection to rule

---

[54] I. Howard Marshall, *New Testament Theology: Many Witnesses, One Gospel* (Downers Grove, Ill.: InterVarsity, 2004), 368. Similarly Fowl, "Image of God," in *Dictionary of Paul*, 427.

[55] Peter O'Brien, *Colossians and Philemon* (Waco, Tex.: Word, 1982), 44.

[56] Thomas R. Schreiner, *Paul, Apostle of God's Glory in Christ* (Downers Grove, Ill.: InterVarsity, 2001), 167.

[57] So Athanasius, "Discourses," 2.21.63 (p. 382).

[58] O'Brien, *Colossians*, 44.

[59] Ibid., 45.

"seated at the right hand of God" (3:1). These words reflect Ps 110:1, the most often quoted Old Testament text in the New Testament. Grudem in an extended discussion covering four pages interprets the phrase "sitting at the right hand" to indicate that Jesus is second to God the Father in authority.[60] He concludes, "Supreme authority always belongs to the Father. The egalitarian claim that Jesus was subject to the Father only during his lifetime is simply wrong."[61] In direct contradiction to what Grudem asserts, the conservative Reformed theologian Louis Berkhof says that the imagery of Christ sitting at the right hand of God speaks of Christ in his office as King, of his "participation in government," and of his direct exercise of divine authority.[62] In surveying the scholarly literature on the writings of Paul, I found no one that gave the interpretation that Grudem gives of the phrase "sitting at the right hand of God." Virtually all spoke of these words as "figurative language" or as a metaphor, indicating that after his resurrection Christ reigns with supreme authority. I quote O'Brien again, who is certainly not biased to my point of view but is an excellent exegete. He says we are not to take these words "literally" but "figuratively," understanding that they "point to the centrality and supremacy of Christ in the heavenly realm." As the exalted Christ "he is in a position of supreme authority."[63] John Maile interprets this expression in virtually identical words but helpfully goes on to say that the imagery indicates that the resurrected Jesus as Lord "now shares with the Father dominion over all creation."[64]

In contrast to Grudem, who thinks that there is no significant change in Christ's status after the resurrection, the New Testament makes this event epoch changing. The lowly, subordinated, suffering Christ is exalted to reign forever as the Lord. In his exaltation he leaves behind all the limitations that his taking flesh involved. Rather than his continuing existence as God and man making him a little less than equal God, his glorified state makes his humanity God-like. Thomas Torrance speaks of the resurrection as solving the "bewildering enigma of Jesus." It "discloses and gives access" to the true identity of the historical Jesus. He is coequal God, the Lord, who is to be worshipped.[65]

---

[60] Grudem, *Evangelical Feminism*, 410–14.

[61] Ibid., 412.

[62] L. Berkhof, *Systematic Theology* (London: Banner of Truth, 1958), 351–53, 406–11.

[63] O'Brien, *Colossians and Philemon*, 163.

[64] John Maile, "Exaltation and Enthronement," in *Dictionary of Paul and His Letters*, 275–78, quote 277. See also K. N. Giles, "Ascension," *Dictionary of Jesus and the Gospels*, eds. J. B. Green and I. H. Marshall (Downers Grove, Ill.: InterVarsity, 1992), 46–50.

[65] Thomas Torrance, *The Christian Doctrine of God: One Being Three Persons* (Edinburgh: T&T Clark, 1996), 46–47.

Paul the Trinitarian Theologian

At least thirty times Paul associates the Father, the Son, and the Holy Spirit together within a few lines in his epistles, suggesting that he thought of them as equal in divine dignity and authority and working together in perfect harmony.[66]

Possibly the most important text is 2Co 13:13. This remarkable early benediction takes us right into the heart of Paul's *theo-logy* proper (i.e., his understanding of God). In concluding what we know today as his second letter to the Corinthians, he speaks almost in passing of the work of the Son, the Father, and the Spirit in that order. Marshall says in these words Paul indicates their "closeness to one another and their *joint function* as the source of blessing for believers."[67] In this prayer the apostle places the three divine persons on an equal footing, yet making it clear that "the grace of our Lord Jesus" is what has brought salvation to them, revealed the love of God, and united them in the fellowship of the Holy Spirit.

Brian Edgar writes, "Each of the three phrases in Paul's trinitarian benediction connects an attribute of God with one member of the Trinity. They are then put in order which reflects the experience of the believer: that is, it is through encounter with the *grace of Christ* that we come to know God's *love*, and thus participate in divine life and *fellowship through the Spirit*. Of course grace is not exclusive to Christ but also comes from the Father, and love is not restricted to the Father as it is also an attribute of Christ, and fellowship is not only found in the Spirit but also in Christ. Yet the distinctions are made very appropriately as they describe the distinctive and primary work of each member of the Trinity."[68]

The second highly significant trinitarian text is 1Co 12:4−6. In this passage Paul urges the Corinthians to broaden their perspective by recognizing the rich diversity of the Spirit's manifestations in their midst (over against their apparently singular interest in *glossolalia*). The Spirit, the Lord, and the Father are the givers of the "gifts," "ministries," and "activities" that can be seen when they assemble. The implication is that the diversity of ministry reflects the diversity in God. The passage underlines the common work of the three divine persons. They act or function as one in equipping the church for ministry.

---

[66] Jane Schaberg, *The Father, the Son, and the Holy Spirit: The Triadic Phrase in Matthew 28:19b* (Chico, Calif.: Scholars, 1982), 6, says that triadic New Testament texts can be classified as (1) triadic formulas; (2) triadic thought patterns; (3) triadic schema or ground plans that may be seen in a given passage; and (4) narratives that mention all three persons, for example Jesus' baptism. I do not make any attempt to categorize the passages I give from Paul. Letham, *The Holy Trinity*, 61−85, has a good discussion on these triadic texts in Paul, especially as they are found in Ephesians.

[67] Marshall, *New Testament Theology*, 430. Italics added.

[68] Edgar, *The Message of the Trinity*, 36.

The third of the more important Pauline trinitarian texts to be highlighted is Eph 4:1–6. In an almost creedal formulation Paul speaks seven times of what is "one" for Christians. Among these are "one Spirit," "one Lord," and "one God and Father of all, who is above all and through all and in all." This threefold pattern is also to be seen in many other places in the Pauline epistles.[69]

Divine Order

In these many Pauline triadic comments no one order among the persons can be detected, and this randomness in how the persons are listed is common to the New Testament as a whole.

Every sequential order possible is found several times.[70] For example, sixteen Pauline passages put Jesus/Christ/Son/Lord first, nine put the Spirit first, and six put God/Father first (see table).[71] If the order in the eternal Godhead were Father, Son, and Spirit, we would expect it to be reflected in Scripture. Warfield concludes that this variation in order indicates that the Father-Son-Spirit order does not embody "the very essence of the doctrine of the Trinity."[72]

Order of Persons in Paul

Person Listed First	Passages
Jesus/Christ/Son/Lord (16 passages)	Ro 8:1–3; 15:16, 18–19, 30 1Co 2:2–4; 6:11, 17–20 2Co 1:19–22; 3:3, 16–18; 13:13 Gal 3:1–5 Eph 2:17–18, 20–22 Php 3:1–5 Col 3:16 (cf. 1Pe 4:14)

---

[69] Ro 5:1–4; 8:1–3, 9–11, 16–17; 14:17–18; 15:16, 18–19, 30; 1Co 1:4–7; 2:2–4; 6:11, 17–20; 2Co 1:19–22; 3:3, 16–18; Gal 3:1–5; Eph 1:14–17; 2:17–18, 20–22; 3:6–19; 4:4–6; 5:18–19; Php 3:1–5; Col 1:3–8; 3:16; Col 1:6–8; 1Th 1:4–6; 2Th 2:13; 2Ti 1:7–8; Tit 3:4–6.

[70] Gerald Bray, *The Doctrine of God* (London: Inter-Varsity, 1993), 146, sets the alternatives out in columns, but does not give the references. Wainwright, *The Trinity in the New Testament*, 238–46, gives a list of triadic texts. Gordon Fee adds others from Paul. This list is my own.

[71] The exact number of passages in each category can be disputed. In several cases members of the Godhead are mentioned more than once in the one context, and so where one begins and ends, the selected passage determines the answer.

[72] Benjamin B. Warfield, "The Biblical Doctrine of the Trinity," in *Biblical Foundations* (London: Tyndale, 1958), 108.

Person Listed First	Passages
Spirit (9 passages)	Ro 8:9–11, 16–17; 14:17–18 1Co 12:4–6 Eph 2:18–20; 3:16; 4:4–6; 5:18–20 Php 3:3 (cf. Jude 19–21)
God/Father (6 passages)	Eph 3:14–17 Col 1:6–8 1Th 1:4–6 2Th 2:13 2Ti 1:7–8 Tit 3:4–6 (cf. Mt 28:19; 1Pe 1:2)

This evidence suggests that Paul did not believe the three divine "persons" are ordered hierarchically. The Father is always "first" and the Son "second" in precedence and power. Indeed it seems he would agree with the words of the Athanasian Creed, "in this Trinity none is before or after, none is greater or less than another." This is not to suggest, however, that Paul denied divine order as such. For Paul there is nothing arbitrary or random in how God the Father and God the Son work or function. He indicates that he believed they always work cooperatively in an orderly manner. There is a given divine disposition. God the Father creates through God the Son (Col 1:16); judges through the Son (Ro 2:16); justifies sinners through the Son (Ro 5:1, 21; cf. 1Th 5:9); elects to salvation through the Son (Eph 1:5); reconciles through the Son (2Co 5:18; Col 1:20); and pours out the Spirit through the Son (Tit 3:6). In reverse order Christians come to God the Father through God the Son. They thank God the Father through God the Son (Ro 1:8; 7:25; Col 3:17), glorify God the Father through God the Son (Ro 16:27), and have access to God the Father through God the Son (Eph 2:18). Such order does not imply the subordination of any party. Rather, it envisages harmonious and agreed ways of cooperatively and reciprocally working together. God the Father does nothing apart from God the Son and vice versa. They are distinct "persons," yet they work as one in an ordered, in the sense of orderly, manner.

Differentiation of the Divine Persons

It would be hard to dispute that Paul spoke of the Father, the Son, and the Spirit in fully personal terms and in some sense thought of them as "persons." As "persons" they continue in time with each other. God the Father is eternally the Father of our

Lord Jesus Christ; God the Son who becomes incarnate is the eternal Son of the Father (Php 2:6; Gal 4:4; Col 1:15) and now rules over all; God the Spirit is the Spirit that was active in Old Testament times and then was poured out on all believers after Easter. Each has distinctive work, although Paul would have them always working together inseparably and cooperatively. It is the Son who voluntarily and freely humbles himself to become man and die on the cross for our salvation, not the Father or the Spirit. It is the Father who raises the Son to reign as Lord. It is through faith in Christ our Savior that we are justified. It is the Spirit who apportions the *charisma* given by the Father (1Co 12:28) and the Son (Eph 4:8), and produces "the fruits" such as love, joy, and peace (Gal 5:22). There is little if anything in Paul that would encourage modalism.

Headship in 1 Corinthians 11:3

In Col 2:10 Paul says that Christ is now "the head (*kephale*) of every ruler and authority" (cf. Eph 1:22). Christ rules over all. The Father is not mentioned at this point. In 1Co 11:3 this same word *kephale* appears, but this time we are told that "God is the head of Christ." It is true that we have in 1 Corinthians and Colossians two very different writings from different periods, but how might these two passages be reconciled?

In the patristic debates about the Trinity and in Calvin, 1Co 11:3 gains little attention. In the contemporary evangelical case for the eternal "headship" of the Father over the Son, in contrast, 1Co 11:3 is highlighted and much discussed. Grudem tells us this verse is "decisive" for his understanding of the Trinity and women.[73] He says that Paul here refers to a "relationship of authority between God the Father and God the Son, and he is making a parallel between that relationship in the Trinity and that between a husband and wife in marriage."[74] Basic to Grudem's case is his thesis that the Greek word *kephale* when used metaphorically (usually translated into English as "head") always means a "person in authority over." Grudem's premise seems to be that words have one fixed meaning and that the context in which they are found does not matter. Virtually all linguists are of another opinion. Any given word has a range of meanings, and the context is the most important indicator of that meaning. Thiselton holds that Paul is playing on the "multiple meanings" of *kephale* in 1Co 11:3ff.[75] No one meaning for the word can be dictated, but whatever it means in v. 3, he says,

---

[73] Wayne Grudem, *Biblical Foundations for Manhood and Womanhood* (Wheaton, Ill.: Crossway, 2002), 47. The importance of this verse for this case is seen in that there are eleven references to 1Co 11:3 in the "Scripture References" at the back of the book, most of them discussing this verse for over a page.

[74] Ibid., 49.

[75] A. C. Thiselton, *The First Epistle to the Corinthians* (Grand Rapids, Mich.: Eerdmans, 2000), 812–23, quote p. 820.

"it does not seem to denote a relation of 'subordination' or 'authority over.' "[76] If Paul was arguing that women, not simply wives as Grudem holds,[77] were set under men in authority, it is unlikely he would then say in v. 4 that women can lead in prayer and prophesy in church, the two most important ministries, so long as they cover their "heads." On a theological level, it is also worth noting that whatever it means for man to be the "head" of woman, it cannot be exactly the same for the God-Son pairing, or the Christ-man pairing. The human example cannot be used to univocally define the divine relationship. The Father and the Son do not relate to one another in exactly the same way as a man and a woman might do, and to suggest so is bad theology.

In 1Co 11:3 Paul does not allude to a fourfold hierarchy, God-Christ-man-woman, but to three paired relationships in which in each case one party is the *kephale* of the other. They are not ordered hierarchically. Paul speaks first of Christ and man, then man and woman, and last of God and Christ. Rather than subordinating the persons in a descending "chain of command,"[78] or "hierarchy of headship"[79] Paul is differentiating the persons paired to introduce the main point he wants to make in the whole passage, namely that men and women are differentiated by God. This sexual differentiation is to be demonstrated by what they have or do not have on their head when leading in public worship. First Corinthians 11:3 is a difficult text to understand, but to interpret it to mean that the Father eternally has authority over the Son is unconvincing. Such an idea is nowhere else suggested by Paul and would contradict his teaching that Christ now reigns as Lord, the head of every ruler and authority.

1 Corinthians 15:24–28

Another text much quoted by contemporary evangelical subordinationists is 1Co 15:24–28. Bernard de Margerie in his substantial study *The Christian Trinity in His-*

---

[76] Ibid., 816.

[77] Throughout this passage Paul has, at least in the first instance, men and women in mind, not husbands and wives. The evidence is as follows: (1) he is here ruling on how men and women as such should dress when leading in church; marriage never comes into view; (2) he speaks of "every man" and "every woman" in vv. 3, 4, 5; (3) in vv. 11–12 men as such are born of women, not husbands of wives; (4) there were unmarried women in the church at Corinth (cf. 1Co 7:8, 25), and we know from Acts that some women prophets were unmarried (Ac 21:9). George Knight III, *New Testament Teaching on the Role Relationship of Men and Women* (Grand Rapids, Mich.: Baker, 1977), 35n. 13, gives seven reasons why the Greek nouns *andros* and *gune* that can mean either man and woman or wife and husband must mean in this passage man and woman in general.

[78] Michael Harper, *Equal and Different: Male and Female in the Church and Family* (London: Hodder and Stoughton, 1994), 121.

[79] Thomas Smail, *Like Father, Like Son* (Milton Keyes, Bucks.: 2005), 260. Paul Barnett, *1 Corinthians* (Ross-shire, UK: Christian Focus, 2000), 200.

tory writes this is "the favorite text" for "subordinationists of all times."[80] This is not an easy text for anyone concerned with what the New Testament teaches as a whole. Taken in isolation it can be read to indicate that Paul is teaching that Christ's reign is limited to the period between his resurrection and his return at the end of history, and/or that the Trinity one day will cease to exist. On the last day the triune God will become one in the person of the Father. Both ideas are impossible to sustain because of what is said elsewhere in Scripture.

In the fourth century, Marcellus, Bishop of Ancyra (d. 374), caused a theological storm when he argued that in this passage Paul was teaching that at the end of all things the Son of God would be absorbed back into God, who would once again become a monad. On that day, the Son's rule of the universe would cease. To counter Marcellus's teaching, the Council of Constantinople in 381 added to what we call today the Nicene Creed the words "and his [the Son's] kingdom will have no end." The bishops at Constantinople did so with good biblical warrant.

Any suggestion that the rule of the Son one day comes to an end directly contradicts many texts that speak of the Son's reign as "forever" (2Sa 7:12–16; Isa 9:7; Lk 1:33; 2Pe 1:11; Rev 7:10–12; 11:15; cf. Eph 1:20). Kreitzer finds the nearest parallel in wording to 1Co 15:28 in Eph 1:10. In the Ephesian passage it is Christ who at the end "gathers up all things" into himself, "things in heaven and things on earth."[81] This text is eschatologically christocentric, not theocentric. Elsewhere in his writings Paul speaks of Christ *extending his rule* at the consummation, not of it ending. When Jesus comes he will sit in judgment (2Co 5:10). Then believers will be "glorified with him" (Ro 8:17), be "with [him] forever" (1Th 4:17), and reign with him (Ro 5:17).[82]

The best exegetical treatment of this passage I found was by Joseph Plevnik. He argues that in verses 24 to 27 Paul first of all has an entirely Christocentric focus.[83] It is Christ who delivers the kingdom to God the Father, it is Christ who destroys every rule, and it is Christ who reigns over all except the Father. Between his resurrection and the end, Christ progressively triumphs over all persons and powers opposed to his rule; the last enemy to be conquered by him is death. A transition to a theocentric focus takes place in the second half of v. 27 when Paul makes it plain that it is God

---

[80]Bernard de Margerie, *The Christian Trinity in History* (Petersham, Mass.: St. Bedes, 1982), 75.

[81]T. J. Kreitzer, *Jesus and God in Paul's Eschatology* (Sheffield, UK: Academic, 1987), 159.

[82]J. D. G. Dunn, *The Theology of Paul the Apostle* (Grand Rapids, Mich.: Eerdmans, 1998), 255, speaks of "the christologizing of traditional theistic eschatology." H. Ridderbos, *Paul: An Outline of His Theology* (Grand Rapids, Mich.: Eerdmans, 1975), 560, argues that Paul's eschatology, at least in its terminology, does not form a closed system. "He gives expression to the same matter in various ways, even though this sometimes involves the appearance of mutual contradiction."

[83]Joseph Plevnik, *Paul and the Parousia: An Exegetical and Theological Investigation* (Peabody, Mass.: Hendrickson, 1997), 125–34.

the Father who is subjecting everything to Christ. The conclusion to his exposition is worth quoting.

> Thus, although it is true that Christ must put all things under his own feet, it is also true that it is God who puts all things under Christ's feet. In v. 28 Paul again affirms that God is the one who is subjecting everything to Christ and that ultimately the Son himself will submit to God "so that God may be all in all." The ultimate completion is God himself. God's reign is meant to bring about the kingdom of God and the sovereignty of God. The passage thus first focuses on the activity of Christ, before the end, then on God's activity through Christ, and then on the kingdom of God as the ultimate goal.... Hence, the Father's and the Son's actions are not separated. The Son does not act independently of the Father but rather in the power the Father gave him. As God is subjecting all things to Christ, Christ is destroying all powers that are hostile to God, thus establishing the dominion of God.[84]

Another approach in dealing with this difficult text is to let wider theological commitments determine the meaning of this one problematic text. Later we will give classic examples of this approach from the pens of Augustine and Calvin. Calvin's suggestion that the text is speaking not of the end of Christ's rule as the second person of the Trinity but of the end of his rule as the God-man Mediator has been followed by many Reformed theologians. It is adopted by F. W. Grosheide in his commentary on 1 Corinthians.[85] He argues that in specifically designating the Savior as "the Son" in v. 28, in contrast to his consistent use of the title *Christ* up to this point, Paul alerts his readers to a change in focus. He is now speaking of the Son as the Mediator of salvation and suggesting that at the end his work is complete and thus "he lays down his office at the feet of the Father."[86] Paul, he insists, is not teaching that the Son as the Son "will be subjected to the Father."[87] The American conservative theologian Robert Reymond also adopts this characteristically Reformed interpretation in slightly different wording.[88] After the resurrection, he argues, what is new is that Christ reigns as Lord as "the divine-human Messiah."[89] At the end he yields "up to the Father not his Sonship but his delegated authority as the Messiah and his special mediatorial dominion." Then "the universal and eternal dominion of the triune God" will be reestablished.[90]

---

[84] Ibid., 133–34.

[85] F. W. Grosheide, *Commentary on the First Epistle to the Corinthians* (London: Marshall, Morgan and Scott, 1953), 369–70.

[86] Ibid., 369.

[87] Ibid.

[88] Robert Reymond, *A New Systematic Theology of the Christian Faith* (Nashville: Thomas Nelson, 1998), 280–81.

[89] Ibid., 280.

[90] Ibid., 281.

Another theological interpretation of this difficult passage is given by Wolfhart Pannenberg. I find this far more convincing than the one just enunciated. Whereas most orthodox theologians are somewhat embarrassed by 1Co 15:28, Pannenberg gives pride of place to this text in his daring reinterpretation of the doctrine of the Trinity. This text, he maintains, demonstrates that the Father and the Son are distinguished by their mutual dependence. At the resurrection the Father gives all rule to the Son, and at the end the Son hands back rule to the Father. He writes, "In the handing over of lordship from the Father to the Son, and in its handing back by the Son to the Father, we see mutuality in their relationship."[91] Pannenberg gives no exegetical basis for this claim. Support for this reading of 1Co 15:24–28 may, however, be found in the text. The Greek verb translated "subjected" in v. 28 can be read in the middle voice, "Christ subjects himself," or in the passive voice, "Christ is subjected by God the Father." Richards argues the former is to be preferred because this means what happens at the end parallels what took place in the incarnation when the Son voluntarily subordinated himself for our salvation.[92] If this is the case, then what Paul is teaching is that at the resurrection God the Father freely makes God the Son ruler over all, and at the end, God the Son freely gives back this rule to God the Father.[93] Rather than speaking of fixed roles, or of an eschatological subordination of the Son, or of the demise of the Trinity, this text indicates a changing of roles in different epochs by two omnipotent divine persons.

No one can deny that 1Co 15:24–28 is a difficult text to interpret. In these words Paul takes us into the presence of God on the last day, stretching our human minds beyond their limit. Here I think—more than anywhere else in Paul's writings—our attempts to understand the apostle are penultimate and inadequate.

The Obedience of Christ in Paul and Hebrews

In Arian teaching the Son of God was not only less than the Father in being; he was also less than the Father in authority.[94] He is the eternally obedient Son. In the present debate among evangelicals over the Trinity, the eternal subordination in authority of the Son to the Father is the central issue.

Paul certainly speaks of the obedience of Christ. In Php 2:8 we have already noted he says the incarnate Christ was "obedient to the point of death—even death on a cross." In Ro 5:12ff. he develops this idea, making it plain that he thinks of

---

[91] Wolfhart Pannenberg, *Systematic Theology*, vol. 1 (Grand Rapids, Mich.: Eerdmans, 1991), 313.

[92] W. L. Richards, *"Hupotagesetai* in 1 Cor 15:28b," *Andrew University Seminary Studies* 38, no. 2 (2000): 203–6.

[93] Pannenberg, *Systematic Theology*, vol. 1, 308–15.

[94] For more on this, see the next chapter.

Christ as the second Adam,[95] representative humanity (or man), who does not fail like the first Adam. He is obedient even to the point of death. "The first Adam" through his act of disobedience brought condemnation; Christ, the second Adam, through his perfect obedience brought justification. He writes, "For just as by the one man's disobedience the many were made sinners, so by the one man's obedience the many will be made righteous" (Ro 5:19; cf. 1Co 15:22). In speaking of Christ as the second Adam, Paul underlines his true humanity that made it possible for him to die on the cross.[96] In his death his work as the second Adam was fulfilled. In these theologically pregnant texts Christ is depicted as representative humanity (or man), the counterpart of Adam. He is obedient whereas Adam was disobedient. In his death on the cross Christ's obedience is completed.

In Heb 5:7–9 Christ's obedience is also mentioned. "In the days of his flesh, Jesus offered up prayers and supplications, with loud cries and tears, to the one who was able to save him from death, and he was heard because of his reverent submission. Although he was a Son, he learned obedience through what he suffered; and having been made perfect, he became the source of eternal salvation for all who obey him."

"In the days of his flesh" indicates the time of the incarnation, when "the Word became flesh and dwelt among us" (Jn 1:14; cf. Heb 5:7; 1Pe 4:1). Throughout this time, the incarnate Son demonstrated his dependence on and communion with his Father in heaven by prayer and supplication (cf. Mk 1:35; 6:46; Lk 5:16; etc.). Most commentators think his "loud cries and tears" allude to the story of Jesus at prayer in the Garden of Gethsemane just before his arrest. In this last trial yet again he was obedient. The reference to his "learning obedience" does not imply that at one point he was not, or not fully, obedient to his Father. Rather it suggests that with each victory over temptation he was strengthened for the next testing. John Murray says the wording points to the true humanity of the Son. "The moment we think of human nature we must posit growth, development and progression."[97] This growing obedience, the author of Hebrews adds, took place "though he was a Son." He sees it as paradoxical that the eternal Son of God had to learn obedience through suffering.

---

[95] Paul once calls Jesus "the last Adam" (1Co 15:45), but he never actually calls him "the second Adam," although the idea is close at hand. In using this expression I follow common practice.

[96] John Murray, "The Obedience of Christ," in *Collected Writings of John Murray*, vol. 2 (London: Banner of Truth, 1977), argues that the obedience of Christ fulfills the servant prophecies of Isaiah. This "office" as the servant, he says, "implies commission by the Father, subjection to, and fulfillment of, the Father's will. All of this involves obedience" (p. 151). However, he adds, "It was in human nature that Christ rendered the obedience required by his commission and office" (p. 152). It was as a man he obediently fulfilled the law's demands and won our salvation.

[97] Ibid., 153.

This was what the incarnation involved. His suffering was not limited to the cross. Nevertheless it was on the cross that he was "made perfect [and] became the source of eternal salvation to all who obey him" (cf. Heb 2:10). Philip Hughes says, "This perfection was progressively achieved as he moved toward the cross which marked *the consummation of his suffering and obedience*."[98]

Later in Hebrews the author makes plain that the incarnate Son's will was always to do the Father's will. "Consequently, when Christ came into the world, he said, 'Sacrifices and offerings you have not desired, but a body you have prepared for me; in burnt offerings and sin offerings you have taken no pleasure.' Then I said, 'See, God, I have come to do your will'" (Heb 10:5–7).

Here the Son's obedience is related solely to the incarnation. It took place "when Christ came into the world" and while he was in "a body." It was completed when he died on the cross.

In the epistles of Paul and the epistle to the Hebrews, Jesus' obedience is exclusively related to his incarnate life culminating in his death on the cross. Leon Morris says, wherever and whenever Jesus' death comes into view in the New Testament, Jesus as man is the focus.[99] If this is so, then the comments in these epistles about the obedience of Christ say nothing at all about an obedience that is *eternal*. Rather they speak of the incarnate Christ as the obedient second Adam and the perfect priest who wins our salvation by the sacrifice of himself for our sins and then is raised to rule as Lord.

Paul certainly embraced a fully trinitarian understanding of God, but what he says does not resolve many questions about divine triune identity that others after him would ask. These would occupy the minds of countless theologians across the centuries. Nevertheless, says Richardson, "There is no great gulf between the theology of Paul and the later theology of the creeds and councils of the patristic period."[100]

John's Gospel and the Synoptics

In the Arian debates the gospel of John provided the chief arsenal for both sides.[101] This is not at all surprising, for in John's gospel we have the boldest affirmations that the Son is less than and subject to the Father and the boldest affirmations that the Father and the Son are one in divinity, function, and authority. So on the one hand in John's gospel Jesus starkly says, "The Father is greater than I" (14:28), and that the Son is sent by the Father (3:17, 28, 34, etc.) and does the Father's will (4:34; 5:30; etc.). On the other hand

---

[98] Philip Hughes, *A Commentary on the Epistle to the Hebrews* (Grand Rapids, Mich.: Eerdmans, 1977), 187. Italics added.

[99] Leon Morris, *The Cross in the New Testament* (Exeter, UK: Paternoster, 1967), 373.

[100] Richardson, *Paul's Language*, 314.

[101] On this see Pollard, *Johannine Christology*, and Hanson, *The Search*, 824–29.

it is said that Jesus is God (1:1; 20:28), that he does only what God can do—namely save, judge, raise the dead, etc.—and that he is one with the Father (10:30; 17:11, 21). Exegesis resolves some of the apparent tension between these comments, but ultimately the tension has to be resolved hermeneutically and theologically.

In the gospels it may be argued that the title "Son of God" is the most important.[102] According to the Synoptic Gospels, Jesus understood himself to be the Son of God in a unique sense, although he was reluctant to publicly claim the title. In contrast, in John's gospel Jesus openly and frequently speaks of himself as the Son of God. How this title is to be understood is critical. What is given in the Gospels must answer this question, not our human experience of sonship. The first indication of how Mark understands this title is found in the words from heaven at Jesus' baptism, "You are my Son, the Beloved; with you I am well pleased" (Mk 1:11; which combines words from Ps 2:7 and Isa 42:1).[103] "You are my Son" gives Jesus the highest status imaginable. He is designated the royal Son who is destined to rule as king. "The beloved" speaks of the unique and intimate relationship shared between *the* Son and *the* Father. "With you I am well pleased" indicates that despite his lofty status, he will fulfill the ministry of the suffering servant. In this one declaration given in all the Synoptic Gospels, right at the commencement of their narratives of the life and ministry of Jesus, the evangelists set Jesus apart from all who have gone before and above all angelic intermediaries. Robert Guelich sees in these words from heaven "a juxtaposition of role and relationship."[104] Jesus in terms of his role is the anointed King called to serve, and in terms of relationship, he is the Father's only beloved Son. There is no indication whatsoever in this fundamental definition of divine Sonship that this status implies eternal subordination in function and authority. The words of Scripture in fact suggest just the opposite. Jesus is the royal King with divine authority. The triadic nature of the baptismal story should not be missed. The Father addresses the incarnate Son to whom the Spirit is given. From this time on it is evident that Jesus sees himself as the Son of God in a unique sense. So he speaks of "my Father" (Mt 7:21; 10:32), addressing him in the intimate form, *Abba* (Mk 14:36; cf. Ro 8:15; Gal 4:6), and he speaks to the disciples of "your Father" (Mt 5:45; 6:6), but never of "our Father" collectively.

In John's gospel the titles *Father* and *Son* come onto center stage. The title *Father* appears 120 times, and when the Father is mentioned, the Son is usually mentioned in

---

[102]See D. R. Bauer, "Son of God," in *Dictionary of Jesus and the Gospels*, 769–75. See also Cullmann, *Christology*, 276.

[103]I assert this predominant opinion, but I am aware of the debate over whether or not these are the Old Testament texts that are reflected. On this see Robert Guelich, *Mark 1–8:26* (Dallas: Word, 1989), 33–34.

[104]Ibid., 34.

close proximity.[105] So Professor Marianne Thompson asks the question, is it possible to think of John talking "about God as Father apart from talking about Jesus as the Son?" She replies in the negative, arguing that for John "it is only in relation to the Son that God is 'Father.'"[106] Again it is of fundamental importance that we seek to understand this relationship in terms of how John understands it and not in terms of our human experience of human father-son relationships. John emphasizes the unity and inseparability of the Father and Son. They are both called God (1:1; 20:28). They are said to be one (10:30; 17:11, 21), to indwell one another (14:10–11; 17:21), and to work as one (5:19b). The Father is said to love the Son (3:35; 5:20; 10:17; 17:23) and the Son to love the Father (14:31). Jesus is the unique and beloved Son (*monogenes*) (1:14; 3:35), who is "close to the Father's heart" (1:18). It thus seems that in the Gospels, and in John in particular, the divine titles *Father* and *Son* speak of mutuality, love, and intimacy, not of the rule of the Father over the Son.

In John's gospel Jesus says the Father is the one who sent him (8:42; 17:3, 23), and he refers to himself as the one who has been sent by the Father (3:17; 5:30; 7:29; etc.). From our cultural perspective this could be read to suggest that Jesus is subordinated in authority to the Father. He has to do as the Father commands. Some contemporary evangelicals interpret this language exactly in this manner. This is not a new opinion. The Arians drew the same conclusion from human experience as well. Augustine's reply was to argue that the language of sending is simply human language that differentiates the divine persons: it does not subordinate the one sent to the sender.[107] It is always tempting to interpret the Scriptures on the basis of human experience, but good exegesis should begin by seeking to discover what the biblical author himself had in mind when he wrote. A more plausible interpretation of this sending language is that it reflects the Jewish *Shaliach* concept.[108] In Judaism the one sent (the *Shaliach*) has the same authority as the one who sends him: he is as the sender himself. In the Rabbis the principle is stated many times: "The one who is sent is like the one who sent him."[109] In this case the one sent is none other than the Father's only Son. Thus

---

[105]Marianne Thompson, *The Promise of the Father: Jesus and God in the New Testament* (Louisville: Westminster, 2000), 56, and with more nuance, Marianne Thompson, *The God of the Gospel of John* (Grand Rapids, Mich.: Eerdmans, 2001), 57. Witherington and Ice, *The Shadow*, 51, suggest the principle that "the higher the Christological reflection, the more likely the proliferation of Father language for God … the more one says about the Son, the more one needs to explain about the Father, lest one think the Father has been eclipsed or supplanted or has faded from the scene."

[106]Thompson, *The God*, 71.

[107]*The Trinity*, 4.5.27 (pp. 172–73). We will return to Augustine's treatment of these sending comments several times in discussing his teaching on the Trinity in subsequent chapters.

[108]See C. G. Kruse, "Apostle," in *Dictionary of Jesus and the Gospels*, 30.

[109]m. Ber. 5:5; b. B. Mesʿia 96a; b. Hag. 10b; b. Menah. 93b; b. Naz. 12b, etc.

Jesus says, "Anyone who does not honor the Son does not honor the Father *who sent him*" (5:23, italics added). This means that the sending terminology in John is best understood as underscoring the unity between the Father and the Son in their work (5:17–18; 10:29–30), and as explaining how the words of the Son are the words of the Father (3:34; 12:50; 14:10–11). The human language of sending distinguishes the persons—the Father is the one who sends, the Son the one who is sent—but the emphasis falls on the authority of the Son as expressing the authority of the Father.

Another interpretation of the sending texts is suggested by Larry Hurtado, who writes to explain how as strict monotheists the early Jewish Christians could so readily come to worship Jesus as God.[110] He argues that they were able to worship Jesus as God because the Jews believed that God could have an agent (Wisdom, Logos, Angel, etc.) who represented him. On this basis Jesus is identified as *the one sent* by God—God's own agent or representative. It was then a small step to think that Jesus is God's equal. In John's Gospel, Hurtado believes, we see this development well established. Here we find a "commitment to the uniqueness of the biblical God, together with an unprecedented treatment of Jesus in terms otherwise reserved for God."[111] It is against this backdrop of thought, he argues, that the tension in John's gospel between passages that speak of the Son as one with God the Father and those that seem to suggest he is subordinate in some way to the Father can be made to "fit together." John holds that the Son is to be honored and worshiped in the same way as the Father precisely because he perfectly represents the Father, yet he is not the Father.[112] If Hurtado is right, then the sending language in John's gospel does not suggest that the Son is the eternally obedient servant of God the Father, but rather that the Son perfectly represents God the Father, sharing his divinity and authority.

What those who make much of the scriptural comments on the Father sending the Son fail to mention is that there are also numerous comments on the lips of Jesus where he speaks of his own decision to come. For example, he says, "Let us go on to the neighboring towns, so that I may proclaim the message there also; for this is what I came out to do" (Mk 1:38); "I have come to call not the righteous but sinners" (Mk 2:17); "For the Son of man came not to be served but to serve, and to give his life a ransom for many" (Mk 10:45); and "I came to bring fire to the earth" (Lk 12:49; cf. 12:51, par. in Mt 10:34–35). In the prologue of John's gospel where most of the important themes in the fourth gospel are introduced, John says, "He [Jesus/the

---

[110]Larry Hurtado, *Lord Jesus Christ: Devotion to Jesus in Earliest Christianity* (Grand Rapids, Mich.: Eerdmans, 2003), 392–96. Thompson, *The God*, 140, comes close to what Hurtado argues. She argues that John sees Jesus as "the mediator of God's life and, hence also of God's sovereign authority in this world."

[111]Hurtado, *Lord Jesus Christ*, 379.

[112]Ibid., 393.

Word] came to what was his own, and his own people did not accept him" (Jn 1:11). Later in John's gospel this very human language of sending and coming is associated together when Jesus declares, "I have come down from heaven, not to do my own will, but the will of him who sent me" (Jn 6:38).

Doing the Father's Will

Arius seems to have been the first to use the story of Jesus' struggle in prayer in the Garden of Gethsemane as proof that the Son always has to submit to his Father's will (Mk 14:32–42; pars. Mt 26:36–46; Lk 22:40–46; cf. Jn 12:27; Heb 5:7–8).[113] In the garden Jesus prays, "Abba, Father, for you all things are possible; remove this cup from me; yet not what I want, but what you want" (Mk 14:36). Certainly the text indicates a real struggle for Jesus. The thought of going to the cross filled him with dread. It is also clear at this point in time Jesus faced a conflict between what he willed and what he knew the Father willed. As a full human being he feared the suffering that lay ahead and he wished to avoid it. In this scene it is the incarnate Son in the form of a servant who prays to his Father in heaven for strength and courage to fulfill the mission he has freely undertaken for the salvation of men and women. Possibly no other story in the New Testament so profoundly presents what it meant for him who was equal with God to become man. To suggest that from this earthly story set unambiguously in the time of the Son's humiliation we learn something of the eternal heavenly relationship of the Father and the Son is a mistake. In any case, this story does not depict a battle of wills where the Father prevails over the Son. It depicts rather the incarnate Son praying for strength to do the Father's will despite his fear of the suffering this would entail.[114]

In John's gospel Jesus prays a rather different prayer just before his arrest. Clearly echoing the Garden of Gethsemane prayer of the Synoptics, Jesus prays, "Now my soul is troubled. And what should I say—'Father, save me from this hour'? No, it is for this reason that I have come to this hour" (Jn 12:27). In John's gospel, Jesus' prayer is entirely a declaration of his intent to do his Father's will. We see no struggle in this text between the Son's will and that of his Father. The Son's will is solely to do the Father's will. This interpretation of Jesus' prayer perfectly matches the way John the evangelist thinks of the Father-Son relationship.

In John, the Son does the Father's will (4:34; 5:30; 6:38–39; etc.), but the evangelist never suggests that Jesus is under compulsion to do as the Father commands. Rather, says Thompson, John thinks of Jesus as the "instrument or expression of the

---

[113]See Athanasius, "Discourses," 3.26.26 (p. 408).

[114]See John Frame, *The Doctrine of God: A Theology of Lordship* (Phillipsburg, N.J.: P&R, 2002), 695n. 14.

Father's will."[115] The word *obedience* is never actually used in connection with the Father-Son relationship in John. Furthermore, John allows that the Son has authority in his own right. Jesus says, "For this reason the Father loves me, because *I* lay down *my* life in order to take it up again. No one takes it from *me*, but *I* lay it down of *my* own accord. *I* have power to lay it down, and *I* have power to take it up again. *I* have received this command from my Father" (10:17–18, italics added). The last words of this quote, "I have received this command from my Father," seem at first thought to almost contradict what is said immediately before. This is not the case, says Thompson. In John's gospel "the Father not only gives the Son his life, but grants it to him to dispose of as he wills."[116] John never envisages a disjunction in will or work between the Father and the Son. He consistently teaches that the Son does the works of the Father (5:17, 19; 10:32, 37; 14:10–11). What Jesus does the Father does and vice versa. They work as one. C. K. Barrett speaks of "the complete continuity between the work of the Father and the work of the Son."[117] *Rather than suggesting the functional subordination of the Son, John implies the functional equality of the Father and the Son.*

This is not of course to imply that John does not clearly distinguish the two divine "persons." The Son comes from the Father (3:31; 6:33–42) and returns to the Father (13:1–3; 14:28; 16:28). The Father is the one who sends, and the Son is he who is sent by the Father. The Son does the Father's will not vice versa. However, as we have just seen, none of this language subordinates the Son to the Father. It differentiates them, certainly, and allows for no confusing of the persons, but it does not negate their profound unity and equality. Indeed it suggests that the Father and the Son always work harmoniously and reciprocally together in an orderly manner. Augustine holds that such comments indicate neither that the Son is "less nor equal, but only intimate that he is from the Father."[118]

"The Father Is Greater Than I"

What Jesus had in mind when he said "the Father is greater than I" (Jn 14:28) has stretched the minds of theologians across the centuries. These words are not easy to reconcile with what Jesus says earlier in this same chapter of John's gospel, "Whoever has seen me has seen the Father" (14:9). The same tension appears in chapter 10 where we read something very similar. First Jesus says, "The Father ... is greater than all" (10:29 KJV), and then immediately after, "The Father and I are one" (10:30; cf. 17:11, 22). In what way the Father is greater than the Son is not defined. In the early church

---

[115]Thompson, *The Promise*, 150.
[116]Thompson, *The God*, 95, offers a helpful explanation in John's thought.
[117]C. K. Barrett, *The Gospel According to St. John*, 2d ed. (Philadelphia: Westminster, 1978), 260.
[118]Augustine, *The Trinity*, 2.1.3 (p. 98).

one group of church fathers (Tertullian, Hilary, Gregory of Nazianzus, etc.) argued this "greatness" referred solely to the differentiation of the persons in relation to origination. The Son is "begotten" whereas the Father is "unbegotten." Another group (Cyril of Alexandria, Ambrose, Augustine, etc.), argued that the Father is "greater" than the Son only while he is incarnate. In the form of man the Son is less than the Father. In both cases the Arian debate determined how this passage was explained, yet both interpretations have supporters today, albeit with a stronger contextual and exegetical basis.

Marianne Thompson gives a modified version of the origination interpretation. She argues that these words are best understood against the backdrop of John's theme that the Father gives life to the Son (5:26). The disciples should rejoice that Jesus is "going" to the Father, since he came from the Father. In the sense that the Father gave to the Son his incarnate life he is greater than the Son.[119] Don Carson in contrast restates the incarnational interpretation. He says the text should not be read to place Jesus on a lower rung in a hierarchical order because John "places Jesus on a level with God (1:1, 18; 5:16–18; 10:30; 20:28)."[120] The preceding comments about Jesus departing to be with the Father and that the disciples should be joyful about this, he sees as the clue to a right understanding of this difficult text. Jesus is telling the disciples that "if they truly loved him, they would be glad that he is returning to the Father, for he is returning to the sphere where he belongs, to the glory he had with the Father before the world began (17:5), to the place where the Father is undiminished in glory, unquestionably greater than the Son in his incarnate state."[121] I would add one further exegetical insight. Part of the answer to this tension in John's thought between Jesus as God in all his glory, majesty, and authority and Jesus as the obedient incarnate Son lies in what John Frame calls "a major theme in the Gospel of John," "mutual deference."[122] The Son always defers to the Father and the Father always defers to the Son. So Frame notes in John a "mutual glorification" motif, what he describes as "an intra-trinitarian deference" of each divine person to the other.[123] The Son glorifies the Father (7:18; 14:13; 17:1, 4; 21:19), and the Father glorifies the Son (1:4; 8:50, 54; 12:23; 16:14; 17:1, 22, 24).

Coequality of the Divine Persons

This discussion of the texts that have been read to subordinate the Son in John's gospel should not obscure for a moment the fact that the predominant emphasis is on the

---

[119]Thompson, *The God*, 94.

[120]D. A. Carson, *The Gospel According to John* (Leicester, UK: Inter-Varsity, 1981), 507.

[121]Ibid., 508.

[122]Frame, *The Doctrine*, 695.

[123]Ibid., 695, 696. On the motif of mutual glorification in John see also Hurtado, *Lord Jesus Christ*, 374–81.

oneness in person and work (function) of the Son and the Father. John begins (1:1, 3) by declaring that "in the beginning was the Word, and the Word was with God [pre-existence], and the Word was God [true God, one in being].... All things came into being through him [he is the agent of creation, he functions as one with the Father]." And the Gospel comes to a conclusion with Thomas confessing Jesus as "My Lord and my God" (20:28). Everything in John's gospel is framed by these two declarations that Jesus *is* God. However, the oneness of the Father and the Son in deity is also affirmed in the body of the gospel. Repeatedly Jesus speaks of himself as "I am" (8:24, 28; 13:19; 6:35; etc.)—the self-designation of Yahweh in the Old Testament (Ex 3:14). John also says that Jesus shares God's glory[124] and bears his name, comments which indicate the Son is thought to be truly God.[125] However, it is not only that Jesus is depicted as God in John's gospel; he is also depicted functioning as God, as we have already seen. He does what only God can do. He creates (Jn 1:3, 10), raises the dead (5:21; 6:40; 11:1–44), bestows eternal life (5:24–27; 10:28–29), saves (3:16; 4:42; 5:24), judges (5:22, 27–29; 8:16; 9:39), and heals (4:46–54; 5:1–9; 9:1–12). So his opponents perceptively accuse him of "making himself equal to God" (5:18).[126] The conclusion the reader is supposed to draw is that since Jesus functions as God, he *is* God in all his majesty, glory, and power. We may agree with Barrett that John "more than any other New Testament writer lays the foundation for a doctrine of a co-equal Trinity."[127]

The Holy Spirit in John

For John, the Holy Spirit is God at work in the world. He calls him in Greek the *paraclete* (14:16, 26; 15:26; 16:7), etymologically suggesting that he is "the one called alongside," variously translated as the counselor, the advocate, or the comforter. In John the Spirit is always spoken of in personal terms. He first of all comes on Jesus to "reveal" him as the one who will baptize with the Holy Spirit (1:33–34). Jesus himself says the Holy Spirit will only be given to his disciples after he has been glorified (16:7). John's first comment about the work of the Spirit is that the Spirit gives life (3:3, 5–6; cf. Eze 36:23–28). This is what the Father and the Son likewise do (Jn 5:25–26). In John, Jesus speaks of the Spirit as "another" (*allos*—of the same kind) *paraclete* (14:16), who will come when he departs "to be with you forever." However, John does not suggest that the Spirit replaces Jesus after his resurrection, but rather that he reminds the disciples of Jesus' teaching (14:26), testifies to Jesus (15:26–27), and discloses Jesus (16:14). It would seem that John thinks of the Spirit as mediating Jesus' and the Father's presence to the disciples after Easter (14:23). So Jesus says that

---

[124]On the profound significance of this detail see Hurtado, *Lord Jesus Christ*, 374–81.
[125]Again on this see ibid., 381–92.
[126]See further Thompson, *The God*.
[127]Barrett, *The Gospel*, 92.

after his departure the Spirit "will glorify me, because he will take what is mine and declare it to you" (16:14). Just as the Father-Son relationship is ordered harmoniously and reciprocally, so too is the Son-Spirit relationship.

When Jesus ascends into heaven, the Spirit continues the work of the Son. He functions in much the same way as the Son: Jesus teaches, and so does the Spirit (14:26); Jesus gives testimony (5:31–32; 7:7; 8:13–14), and so does the Spirit (15:26); Jesus speaks of what he has heard (7:17; 8:26; 14:10), and so does the Spirit (14:26; 16:13–14); Jesus discloses and reveals (1:18; 4:25), and so does the Spirit (16:13). However John also holds that some functions ascribed to the Father are also functions of the Spirit. The Father testifies to Jesus (5:37; 8:18), so does the Spirit (15:26–27); the Father glorifies Jesus (5:44; 8:54; 12:23), so does the Spirit (16:14); the Father will be with the disciples (14:23; 15:26; 17:11), and so will the Spirit (14:17). This over-lapping in function is also evidenced in how John speaks of the Son and the Spirit coming to be with the believer after Easter. Sometimes Jesus says he will come to be with his disciples (14:3, 18, 20, 28), and sometimes he says the Spirit will come to be with them (14:16; 15:26; 16:7). We are thus not at all surprised to note that often John speaks of the Father, Son, and Spirit in the closest association, in what might be called triadic comments (1:33–34; 14:16, 26; 16:15; 20:21–22; cf. 1Jn 4:2, 13–14).

The Son Reveals the Father

Before leaving John's gospel one final theological point must be made. In John the Son reveals the Father. There is no saving knowledge of God apart from the Son (1:18; 8:19; 12:44–45; 14:7, 9; 16:3; 17:3; etc.). This means that the Father is revealed in the Son's words, works, and in his humble service and self-giving (cf. 13:1–20). The Father is not other than what is seen in the Son. The Father is the Father and not the Son, and the Son is the Son and not the Father, yet they are not divided: they are one (Jn 10:30; 17:11, 22). "Whoever has seen me has seen the Father" (Jn 14:9), says Jesus in John's Gospel. The God John wants his readers to know and believe in is a majestic God who stoops to save. He is both high and humble, Lord and servant. No cost is too great for him to make for the salvation of men and women. The revelation in the Son tells us this.

The Great Commission

Before leaving the Gospels, a brief comment on Mt 28:19 is needed. In what is commonly called the Great Commission, Matthew has Jesus send out his followers to make disciples, baptizing them "in the name [singular] of the Father and of the Son and of the Holy Spirit." The expression "in the name" means something like "in reference to." The singular "name" indicates that the divine three are somehow one, and the definite article before each person suggests distinctive and differentiated identities. Many think these words reflect the most developed understanding of the

Trinity in the New Testament. The wording implies there is one God who is three "persons," and the three persons stand on an equal footing. In this one text the three great trinitarian heresies are implicitly excluded—modalism, tritheism, and subordinationism.

The Book of Revelation

In the book of Revelation the Son reigns on the one throne with the Father "forever and ever" (7:10–12; 11:15; cf. 1:6, 18). This is affirmed in doxologies in which Jesus the triumphant Lamb is worshiped conjointly with God the Father. In 3:21, 22:1, and 22:3 Jesus is also said to share God's throne. The pairing of God and Christ is reflected in other ways too. Jesus and God the Father are both to be worshiped (5:8–14; 7:10). The eschatological kingdom belongs jointly to "our Lord [or God] and his Messiah" (11:15; 12:10). God the Father designates himself as "the Alpha and Omega" (1:8), as does Jesus (22:12–13). Christians hold to both the Word of God and the "testimony of Jesus" (1:2, 9; cf. 12:17).[128] It is also to be noted that in the book of Revelation the Son has a certain priority in the divine plan of redemption and judgment. The final act cannot proceed until the Lamb has conquered, and then it is he alone who is able to open the scroll with its seven seals (5:1–5).

John the Seer clearly believed that Jesus is to be worshiped with the Father, but he cannot allow any suggestion that there are two Gods. He remains a monotheist. Where he mentions God the Father and Christ together he uses in the Greek a singular verb (11:15) or singular pronouns (22:3–4). And he does not suggest modalism. God the Father and God the Son are clearly differentiated, although they are never set in opposition or divided. It is, however, to be noted that in a few instances there are comments that could be read to stand in tension with John the Seer's primary emphasis on the Father and the Son as equal God. John begins by saying that the revelation for the church is given to Jesus by the Father (1:1), and the risen Jesus himself says he has received his authority from his Father (2:28), although in 12:10 a loud voice from heaven ascribes authority to the Son in his own right. It is also to be noted that twice Jesus speaks of the Father as "my God" (3:12, 21). Exegesis cannot harmonize these texts-in-tension. If there were not this diversity within Scripture, the debate about the doctrine of the Trinity would not have challenged the minds of the best theologians for centuries.

Back to the Beginning

At the commencement of this chapter the five most important questions to be put to the New Testament in relation to whether or not the Son is eternally subordinated

---

[128]Larry Hurtado, "Christology," in *Dictionary of Later New Testament Writings*, eds. Ralf P. Martin and Peter H. Davids (Downers Grove, Ill.: InterVarsity, 1997), 177.

to the Father in being, function, or authority were listed. We are now in a position to answer them.

1. Yes, the Bible is to be read holistically and theologically in working out any doctrinal or ethical question, because diversity is of the very nature of Scripture. Proof-texting proves nothing. This was true in the fourth century and it is true today. Read from the vantage point given by Php 2:5–11, the Son's subordination is restricted to his voluntary taking of human flesh (the incarnation).

2. Rather than suggesting that the Son is functionally subordinated to the Father, the New Testament depicts Christ as functioning as God—because he is God. In his ministry on earth he does the works that only God can do. After his resurrection he functions as Lord, the supreme ruler, because he is *the* Lord. From cover to cover the Bible speaks of God revealing himself by what he does. Thus his being and actions cannot be divided. To eternally subordinate the Son (or the Spirit) on the basis of what he does, his functions, makes him less than the Father. It is a denial that he is equal and fully God.

3. Nothing in Scripture indicates that the Father-Son-Spirit are eternally hierarchically ordered in being, work/function, or authority. Rather, the Bible indicates that Father, Son, and Spirit are one in divinity, work/function, and authority. Their relationship is ordered but not sub-ordered.

4. The titles *Father* and *Son* are not used in the New Testament to suggest that the divine Father always has authority over the Son. They speak rather of an eternal correlated relationship marked by intimacy, unity, equality, and identical authority. In his detailed study on the force of the title *Son* in the Bible, John Frame concludes that that title *Son* when used of Jesus speaks of his authority and lordship and of his unique relationship with his Father. He says, "There is considerable overlap between the concepts Lord and Son.... But each encompasses the emphasis of the other. Lordship presupposes sonship, and sonship implies lordship."[129]

5. The Father, Son, and Spirit are primarily differentiated in the Bible by their individual identities. The Father is the Father and not the Son or the Spirit, Jesus is the Son and not the Father or the Spirit, and the Spirit is the Spirit and not the Father or the Son. The logic of this is that they have differing relations. The Father is the Father *of* the Son, the Son is the Son *of* the Father, and the Spirit is *from* the Father and the Son. Differentiating the divine three on the basis of differing origination seems to be more a post New Testament theological construct than something clearly taught in Scripture. In

---

[129]Frame, *The Doctrine*, 661.

the New Testament the divine three are also clearly distinguished by their specific work. For example, the Father sends the Son, the Son becomes man and dies on the cross, and the Spirit is poured out on all believers after Christ is resurrected. We found no evidence that they were separated or divided by function or differentiated by asymmetrical power and authority. Rather, they are depicted as working complementarily in perfect harmony and unity, exhibiting the same power and authority.

With this study completed on what the Bible says on the key issues that divide evangelicals in reference to the doctrine of the Trinity, we now turn to consider how the most important theologians in the centuries after the New Testament was completed developed what we now call "the orthodox doctrine of the Trinity."

CHAPTER

THE ETERNAL
SUBORDINATION
OF THE SON OF GOD

For a large number of contemporary conservative evangelicals, the eternal subordination of God the Son to God the Father in function and authority is a doctrine of great importance, not to be questioned but rather passionately defended. It is what "Bible believing" Christians who want to remain faithful to historic orthodoxy should believe. The support cited for this belief is twofold. First, it is said this is what the Scriptures clearly teach; and second, it is claimed this is what orthodox theologians "throughout history" have taught and the creeds endorse.[1] In reply I argued in my book *The Trinity and Subordinationism*[2] that the "tradition" (what orthodox theologians throughout history have concluded the Scriptures teach) in fact indicates just the opposite. The best of theologians across the centuries and the creeds and Reformation confessions all oppose the idea that the Bible teaches the eternal subordination of the Son. Without engaging with the historical evidence in any detailed way that I cite in my previous book, Grudem dismisses me perfunctorily. He says, "Unfortunately Giles' understanding of the historic view of the church [on the Trinity] is deeply flawed."[3] Similarly, Robert Doyle, my principal debating opponent in

---

[1] I have substantiated this claim quoting in detail from those who speak of the eternal subordination of the Son in the introductory chapter. On the historical claim made by all evangelical subordinationists see in most detail Wayne Grudem, *Evangelical Feminism and Biblical Truth* (Sisters, Ore.: Multnomah, 2004), 415–22.

[2] Kevin Giles, *The Trinity and Subordinationism* (Westmont, Ill.: InterVarsity, 2002).

[3] Grudem, *Evangelical Feminism*, 426.

Australia, thinks my reading of the tradition is mistaken, a distortion of the truth, and dismisses it categorically.[4]

In the previous chapter what the Scriptures say on the relationship between the Father and the Son was outlined. What we found among other things was that the New Testament testifies to the full divinity of Christ, his subordination in the incarnation, his present Lordship, and an intimate relationship between the divine Father, Son, and Spirit so profound that the divine three can be associated together on an equal footing. The early Christians were agreed that there is one God who is eternally three divine "persons." We also discovered that there are occasional comments in the New Testament that seem at first discordant, and that the New Testament does not answer directly every question about the Trinity that would be asked in later times. We now begin to explore how the best of theologians subsequent to the completion of the New Testament resolved these tensions within Scripture and how they attempt to answer questions raised by people about the Trinity on which the Scriptures are silent. In other words, we are studying the historical development of the doctrine of the Trinity which in its final form says more than what is explicitly said in Scripture. This historically developed doctrine of the Trinity emerged in the heat of controversy. It was in response to explanations of how the divine three were related that seemed to deny important teaching in Scripture that better answers emerged.

In this chapter I concentrate specifically on what the interpretative tradition says on *the eternal subordination of the Son*. As we listen to what Athanasius, the Cappadocians, Augustine, and Calvin teach, and what the creeds and Reformation confessions prescribe, the following questions should be kept in mind.

1. Is it permissible to think of the Son as in any way whatsoever as less than the Father, or *eternally* subordinated to the Father in being, work, or authority?
2. Are the Father, Son, and Spirit ordered hierarchically?
3. Can a division be made between the one being/essence/nature/substance of the divine three and what they do—their works/operations/functions/roles?
4. Can any division or separation be made between what the Father does and what the Son does? In other words, are they differentiated on the basis of differing functions/roles and authority?
5. Does the confession that Jesus is "begotten of the Father," or that the Father may be called the *monarche* (sole source) of the person of the Son (and the Spirit), or that the Son can be said to be "God from God, Light from Light, true God from true God" (the Nicene Creed) suggest that the Son is dependent on the Father for his divinity, being, or authority?

---

[4] Robert Doyle, "Are We Heretics? A Review of *The Trinity and Subordinationism* by Kevin Giles," *The Briefing* (April 2004): 11–19.

In the next chapter we will consider in detail whether or not tradition allows or indicates that the Son is eternally subordinated *in authority* to the Father. In this chapter we only touch on this question. In chapter 6 we deal with how the tradition *differentiates* the divine persons.

The First Inadequate Explanation: There Is Really Only One God

One of the earliest solutions to the *trilemma* of how the divine three are related was called *Monarchianism* in the West of the Roman Empire and *Sabellianism* in the East.[5] Concerned with safeguarding the unity of God at all cost, some argued that the Father, the Son, and the Holy Spirit were merely successive *modes of revelation* of the one God, a monad. So in later times this error was called *modalism*. This answer upheld the biblical truth that God is one, but it undermined the eternal personal distinctions of Father, Son, and Spirit which the Bible also emphasizes. This solution was rejected by the church fathers and by subsequent orthodox theologians down to our day. It is believed that to be loyal to biblical revelation, the doctrine of the Trinity must affirm without equivocation the unity of God *and* the eternal, personal coexistence of Father, Son, and Holy Spirit as eternally differentiated divine "persons."

A Second Inadequate Explanation: One God and Two Lesser Gods

Another early suggestion made by second- and early third-century theologians was that God the Creator and Father, a monad, is God in the fullest sense.[6] The Son is the *Logos* or Word of God always in the Father who was brought forth for creation and redemption along with the Holy Spirit. This *Logos* "model" of the Trinity safeguarded the unity of God, and affirmed the personal distinctions of Father, Son, and Spirit, but it implied that the Son and the Spirit were secondary and tertiary subordinates. The theologians who depicted the Trinity in this way began with the premise that God the Father was God in the primary sense of this word and then sought to show how the Son or Logos and the Spirit who come on the scene at creation might also be thought of as God. On this basis they read the Bible. The problem was that this "model" of the Trinity inevitably implied a subordinate status of the Son and the Spirit.

These two early attempts at formulating a conceptual doctrine of the Trinity cannot be endorsed, yet those who proposed them helped later theologians

---

[5]For more detail see J. N. D. Kelly, *Early Christian Doctrines*, 5th ed. (London: Adam and Charles Black, 1977), 119–23.

[6]I speak of the Apologists, Irenaeus, Tertullian, and Novatian. See further my book *The Trinity*, 60–62. In a later chapter when discussing the differences between the divine persons I spell out these matters in more detail. I think George Leonard Prestige, *God in Patristic Thought* (London: SPCK, 1959), 112–55, gives one of the best and most helpful discussions of these writers. See also Edmund Hill, *The Mystery of the Trinity* (London: Chapman, 1985), 47–54, who is also helpful.

Where they were seen to have grasped rightly what the Bible was saying, those who followed after built on their insights. Where what was proposed was seen to be problematic or dangerous, it was rejected. This is how conceptual thinking usually develops. Early attempts to explain complex phenomena prepare the way for better explanations.

A Big Step Forward: God Is Eternally Triune

A better way to read the Bible was needed, one that captured the trinitarian presuppositions of the New Testament itself. This was provided by Origen of Alexandria (185–254).[7] He argued that God for all eternity is triune, and if the primary name for God is Father, then a Son is always implied. Father and Son are eternal correlatives. In his *First Principles*, he says, "No one can be a father without having a son."[8] On this basis he speaks of the eternal generation or begetting of the Son, whom he identifies as the Logos or Wisdom. Can anyone, he asks, "suppose or believe that God the Father ever existed, even for a moment of time, without having generated his Wisdom?"[9] And noting that the New Testament consistently speaks of the Father, Son, and Spirit together, he concludes that the Spirit likewise is eternal.[10] Thus for him the Trinity is three eternally existing "persons" or *hypostases*. Modalism is absolutely excluded. For the first time the conception of the Christian God as eternally three "persons" emerges. However, Origen eternally subordinates the Son and the Spirit in being and work. He is led to do this on the basis of his middle Platonic philosophy, which determines his theology as much as the Bible does. In middle Platonism, a cause is always superior to what is caused, because what is caused does not participate fully in the being of the ultimate cause. Once he decided that God the Father was to be understood as "the fountainhead of deity" (*pege tes Theotetos*)[11] and as the origin or source (*arche*) of the Son and the Spirit, the ultimate cause of everything, the ontological subordination of the Son and the Spirit necessarily followed. Ontological subordinationism naturally led to functional subordinationism. The Son and the Spirit obediently do the work of their superior, the Father. So Professor Ayres says

---

[7] Because of contradictory comments in Origen's works and the uncertainty on what he actually wrote, there is much debate about his theology. On this see Kelly, *Early Christian Doctrines*, 128–32; Peter Widdicombe, *The Fatherhood of God from Origen to Athanasius* (Oxford: Clarendon, 1994), 7–92; R. P. C. Hanson, *The Search for the Christian Doctrine of God: The Arian Controversy, 318–381* (Grand Rapids, Mich.: Baker, 2005), 60–70.

[8] Origen, *De Principiis*, 1.2.10, in *The Writings of Origen*, vol. 10, *The Ante Nicene Library*, eds. A. Roberts and J. Donaldson (Edinburgh: T&T Clark, 1895), 28. See also Widdicombe, *The Fatherhood of God*, 10–92.

[9] Origen, ibid., 1.2.2 (p. 19).

[10] Ibid., 1.3.4 (p. 37).

[11] Ibid., 2.3 (p. 20).

that Origen thinks of the three hypostases having "specific roles or activities in the world" in hierarchical order.[12]

A Big Step Backwards: Arius (c. 250–336)

Early in the fourth century Arius, a presbyter in Alexandria, popularized the subordinationist strand that we have just noted in Origen's teaching,[13] denying that the Son is eternally one in being, work, and authority with the Father. Arius had his own distinctive ideas, as did the various later groupings of theologians lumped together and loosely called "fourth-century Arianism," yet says Hanson in his definitive study of this phenomenon, there were "certain characteristic ideas"[14] held in common by all who were called "Arians."

1. The first and most important of these was ontological subordinationism. The Son (and the Spirit) is subordinate to the Father in his being/nature/essence. This observation comes as no surprise, for most know that ontological subordinationism was the primary characteristic of what is commonly known as "Arianism." On this basis, all the so-called Arians emphasized the differences between the divine three, especially between the Father and the Son.[15]

2. What is of surprise to many is that for all the so-called "Arians," this ontological subordinationism *always* had as its corollary the eternal functional subordination of the Son. Hanson says the Arians consistently taught that the Son "does the Father's will and exhibits obedience and subordination to the Father, and adores and praises the Father, not only in his earthly *ministry but also in Heaven.*"[16] The last words are highlighted because they pinpoint a key issue. The Arians assumed that the subordination of the Son evident in the incarnation was to be read back into the eternal Trinity. Earthly subordination implied heavenly subordination in being, work/function, and authority, they argued.

3. Hierarchical ordering. From the first two basic characteristics of Arianism follows a third. The Father, Son, and Spirit are understood to coexist in

---

[12] Lewis Ayres, *Nicaea and Its Legacy: An Approach to Fourth-Century Trinitarian Theology* (New York: Oxford, 2005), 28.

[13] The relationship between Origen's teaching and that of Arius is complex and disputed. On some things they agree and on others they disagree. What has to be recognized is that Origen influenced all fourth-century theologians in one way or another. See Rowan Williams, *Arius: Heresy and Tradition* (London: Darton, Longman and Todd, 1997), 131–48 and Ayres, *Nicaea*, 15–30.

[14] Hanson, *The Search*, 99. The list given is my own compilation.

[15] On the emphasis on "difference" see particularly Ayres, *Nicaea*, 42, 56, 80. Divine differentiation is discussed in chapter 6 following.

[16] Hanson, *The Search*, 99.

a descending order of being and authority. They are sub-ordered. Robert Letham says that one of the key issues that divided the pro-Nicene and Arian theologians was how they understood divine order. For the Arians, divine order was a hierarchical order. For the pro-Nicene theologians, order among the divine three spoke of "a fitting and suitable disposition"[17] that existed between them.

4. Jesus is divine. Arius and all who were called Arians in the fourth century could confess that Jesus is "God." What they could not confess was he is "true God," one in being with the Father. For them God the Father alone was "true God." He alone is *autotheos*—God of himself.

5. The human father-son relationship explains and defines the divine Father-Son relationship. God is to be understood in terms of human family relationships.

6. The Bible taught what they believed. Arius in particular, and all the "Arians" of the fourth century in general, appealed to the Bible in support of their beliefs. They pointed to the texts that either seemed to subordinate the Son, or actually did subordinate him in the incarnation, arguing that this subordination was to be read back into the immanent Trinity. It was eternal.

Athanasius' Reply to the Early Arians

Athanasius was one of the greatest theologians of all times.[18] His theological acumen is breathtaking.[19] In opposition to Arius and the "early Arians"[20] he pioneered a way of understanding the Trinity that modern-day scholars now recognize for its brilliance. He was the first to give the "model" of an eternal "coequal" Trinity where the three divine persons are differentiated yet profoundly one, and the Son and the Spirit

---

[17] Robert Letham, *The Holy Trinity in Scripture, History, Theology, and Worship* (Phillipsburg, N.J.: P&R, 2004), 400.

[18] T. F. Torrance is definitely of this opinion. See his books *The Trinitarian Faith: The Evangelical Theology of the Ancient Catholic Church* (Edinburgh: T&T Clark, 1993) and *The Christian Doctrine of God: One Being Three Persons* (Edinburgh: T&T Clark, 1996) and the chapters "The Doctrine of the Holy Trinity According to Athanasius" in *Trinitarian Perspectives: Toward Doctrinal Agreement* (Edinburgh: T&T Clark, 1999), 7–21, and "Athanasius: A Study in the Foundations of Classical Theology," in *Theology in Reconciliation* (Grand Rapids, Mich.: Eerdmans, 1975), 215–66. See also John Behr, *The Nicene Faith: Part One, True God of True God* (Crestwood, N.Y.: St. Vladmirs, 2004), 163–68.

[19] Helpful introductions to Athanasius' theology include Hanson, *The Search*, 421–58; Widdicombe, *The Fatherhood of God*, 145–71; Ayres, *Nicaea*, 41–126; Behr, *The Nicene Faith*, 164–255; and Alwyn Petterson, *Athanasius* (London: Chapman, 1995).

[20] As I pointed out in chapter 2, Athanasius wrote in opposition to those he calls "the Arians," and he equates their ideas with those of Arius himself. Whether or not he creates this entity is a moot point. On this see Ayres, *Nicaea*, 105–10. I call this entity "the early Arians" when I want to differentiate Athanasius' opponents from those of the Cappadocians, but usually I simply call them "Arians."

are not subordinated to the Father in being, function, or authority.[21] He was able to do this because of his profound grasp of Scripture and his revolutionary insight that to interpret the Bible rightly, it must be read holistically with what is theologically central and basic determining the meaning of isolated seemingly discordant texts.[22] Much of his "Discourses Against the Arians" are taken up with the exposition of the many biblical passages the Arians quoted in support of their case.[23] He judges their hermeneutic to be selective, "devious," and "irreligious."[24] Two passages he came to see offered the key to grasping what he called the "scope" of Scripture—the overall story line, we might say—were the prologue to John's gospel, especially verses 1 and 14, and Php 2:5–11. The first passage teaches that "the Word was with God" and "the Word became flesh," and the second that the Son "was equal with God but emptied himself." These two texts give what he calls "a double account of the Savior"—one temporal and one eternal.[25] He gladly accepts that there are many passages in Scripture that speak of the Son's subordination and obedience to the Father. These, he holds, emphasize the reality of the incarnation. They highlight the Son's voluntary and temporary subordination for our salvation. In his eternal being, however, there could be no subordination at all.

Athanasius attributes the human frailties seen in the incarnate Son solely to his taking of human flesh. He writes, "When he is said to hunger, and to thirst, and to toil, and not to know, and to sleep, and to weep, and to ask, and to flee and to be born, and to deprecate the cup, and in a word to undergo all that belongs to the flesh ... these affections may be acknowledged as not proper to the very Word by nature, but proper by nature to the very flesh.... The Word himself is impassible, and yet because of that flesh, which he put on these things are ascribed to him."[26]

This explanation of the incarnation enabled Athanasius to reject the Arian argument that the limitations and weaknesses of the incarnate Son were proof of his eternal subordination to the Father and to avoid the idea that God himself could suffer. Later orthodox theologians would follow his lead by insisting that the human characteristics of the incarnate Son should not be read back into the eternal Trinity,

---

[21] It is true that he owed much to his mentor and predecessor as Bishop of Alexandra, Alexander (d. 328). On Alexander's theology see Widdicombe, *The Fatherhood of God*, 123–44.

[22] My primary source is *The Nicene and Post Nicene Fathers of the Christian Church* (henceforth *NPNF*), eds. Philip Schaff and Henry Wace (Grand Rapids, Mich.: Eerdmans, 1971).

[23] On the Arian use of the Bible and the orthodox reply, see Hanson, *The Search*, 824–49 and Ayres, *Nicaea*, 1–3, 31–42. In relation to the key texts from John's gospel see particularly, T. E. Pollard, *Johannine Christology in the Early Church* (Cambridge: Cambridge University Press, 1970).

[24] Athanasius, "Discourses," in *NPNF* 4:1.1–5 (pp. 306–8).

[25] Ibid., 4:3.26.29 (p. 409).

[26] Ibid., 4:3.26.34 (p. 412).

but they would embrace more strongly than Athanasius did the full hypostatic union between the human and the divine in the one Christ.[27]

In direct opposition to the Arians, Athanasius spoke of the Christian God as triune from all eternity, following Origen and his mentor Bishop Alexander (d. 328). He says God is "not a Monad first who afterwards becomes a Triad,"[28] and we "Christians acknowledge the blessed Triad as unalterable and perfect and ever what it was."[29] However, it was the Father-Son relationship that Athanasius concentrated on, because this stood at the heart of his dispute with Arius and the early Arians. First of all, Athanasius insisted on calling the first person of the Trinity "Father." He particularly disliked the Arian designation of God as "the Unoriginate" (*agenetos*), a title they equated with "the Unbegotten" (*agennetos*). Athanasius could accept that from his "works" (i.e., creation) God may be called "the Unoriginate," but not in relation to the Son. He says this designation of God is "unscriptural." It is more "pious" to use the language of the Bible and speak of "Father," because this word envisages a Son.[30] If God is Father from all eternity, and he is, then it follows that the Son is also eternal. The Father cannot be the Father without the Son, and the Son cannot be the Son without the Father. On this basis he thinks it is absurd to argue that "once the Son was not," as his opponents did. If there was a time when the Son was not, there must have been a time when the Father was not, and this is impossible. To put it succinctly, for Athanasius the Father and the Son are eternally correlated. The Father never stands alone or works alone. Pannenberg states that "Athanasius' *most important argument* [was] that the Father would not be the Father without the Son (*Contra Arian* 1.29)."[31]

The words *begotten* and *offspring* are for Athanasius helpful terms to use of the Father-Son relationship because they "signify a Son ... And beholding the Son we see the Father."[32] He rejects that these human words when applied to the Son suggest he is created by or is subordinated to the Father. This does not convince the Arians. They want to understand the titles *Father* and *Son* in the way these words are understood when used of human fathers and sons. For them the title *Son* indicated that Jesus must be less than the Father, because all human sons are less than their fathers. Athanasius summarily dismisses this argument by pointing out that human sons are in fact *one in being* with their father.[33] Athanasius will not allow that it is possible to

---

[27] For a strong defense of Athanasius' Christology see Behr, *The Nicene Faith*, 169–207, 215–31.

[28] Athanasius, "Discourses," in *NPNF* 4:1.6.17 (p. 316).

[29] Ibid., 4:1.6.18 (p. 317).

[30] Ibid., 4:1.34–35 (p. 326).

[31] Wolfhart Pannenberg, *Systematic Theology*, vol. 1 (Grand Rapids, Mich.: Eerdmans, 1991), 273. Italics added.

[32] Athanasius, "Discourses," in *NPNF* 4:1.5.16 (p. 316).

[33] Ibid., 4:1.8.27–28 (p. 323).

define divine relations in terms of human relations. Although he does not use the words *analogical* or *metaphorical*, he argues that human language used of God should not be taken literally, although it conveys truth.[34] More than once in answer to the Arians' literal or "univocal" understanding of the terms *father* and *son* he says, "God is not man."[35] Contemporary evangelicals follow the Arian logic when they argue that because human fathers have authority over their sons, so the divine Father has authority over his Son.[36]

How Athanasius relates to the much-debated idea that the Father is the *monarche* of the Son (and the Spirit) is important. The first part of this word *mon* (a contracted form of the Greek word *monos*) means "only," "sole," or even "isolated by itself." The Greek word *arche* means "source," "origin," or "authority." I find no examples of the combined word *monarche* in Athanasius' writings, but he does frequently use *arche* in relation to the Father and the Son, always it seems with the meaning "source" or "origin." However, he does occasionally use, possibly following Tertullian, the cognate combined word *monarchia*, which can mean, literally understood, "sole rule." In this chapter we explore what Athanasius said on God as the *arche* and in the next what he says on God as the *monarchia*, or sole ruler.

Peter Widdicombe[37] asserts that Athanasius thought of the Father as the *monarche*, "sole source" or "sole beginning," of the Son and the Spirit, but he does not expand on this matter. It is true that Athanasius repeatedly speaks of the Father as "unbegotten" and the Son as "begotten," saying explicitly that "the Father is the Origin of the Son and begat him,"[38] but it is too much to claim as Widdicombe does that Athanasius thinks of the Father as "the font of divinity."[39] It seems rather that Athanasius does not have a developed and consistent understanding of the Father as the *arche* (source, or beginning) of the Son and the Spirit. He frequently uses the word *arche* in reference to the Father and the Son, but in every case the debate he is engaged in, or the point he wants to make, determines how he uses the word.

When he is opposing the Arian argument that if the Father and the Son are both eternal they must be brothers, as if they were "generated from some pre-existing

---

[34] Ibid., 4:2.18.34–35 (pp. 366–67). Athanasius, "On the Councils," in *NPNF* 4:42 (p. 472).

[35] Ibid., 4:2.28–33 (p. 367).

[36] Robert Doyle, "Are We Heretics?" 14, asks, "If the Father is not the final locus of authority, how indeed can he really be a 'father.'" Then he says, the "Father is a real father and the triune Son a real son. Neither names are metaphorical."

[37] Widdicombe, *The Fatherhood of God*, 175, 255.

[38] Athanasius, "Discourses," in *NPNF* 4:1.14 (p. 314).

[39] Widdicombe, *The Fatherhood of God*, 175. On p. 255 he speaks of the Father as the "fount of the Godhead."

origin or source (*arche*)," he replies in the words just quoted, "The Father is the origin (*arche*) of the Son who begat him."[40] Later opposing much the same idea, he says, "The Father's essence (*ousia*) is the origin (*arche*) and root and fountain of the Son."[41] In this exchange he speaks of the *eternal* Father as the origin of the *eternal* Son to avoid allowing that there is anything prior to God, but to make one of two eternal divine persons the source of the other is very difficult, if not logically impossible.[42]

In the context of his wider debate with the Arians, Athanasius seeks to exclude absolutely Origen's middle Platonist premise that a cause is always superior to what is caused. On this premise the Son does not fully *participate* in the divinity of the Father. Athanasius totally opposes this idea. Time and time again he insists that the Son fully *participates* (the Greek words are *methexis*, *metousia*, *metoche*) in the divine life.[43] The Father and the Son are one in being (*homoousios*). Meijering says, "Athanasius is completely opposed to any hierarchy in God,"[44] which he regards as "idolatry."[45]

It is thus of no surprise to find that at times Athanasius denies that the Son has an *arche*. After agreeing that all creatures have a beginning in time, he says the Son has no such beginning. He writes,

> The Word has his beginning (*arche*) in no other beginning (*arche*) than the Father whom they allow to have no beginning (*anarche*), so he too exists without beginning (*anarche*).[46]

And then to complicate things even more, Athanasius introduces the revolutionary and visionary idea that the whole Godhead is in fact the *arche* of the three persons. He says,

> We know of but one origin (*arche*); and the all-framing Word we profess to have no other manner of Godhead, than that of the only God, because he is born from him.... For there is but one form of Godhead, which is also in the Word. For thus we confess God to be one through the Triad.[47]

---

[40] Athanasius, "Discourses," in *NPNF* 4:1.14 (p. 314).

[41] Athanasius, "On the Councils," in *NPNF* 4:45 (p. 474), cf. 4:51 (p. 477).

[42] Hanson, *The Search*, 435n. 65, says, "It is doubtful whether the word 'cause' can have any meaning when applied to two eternally existing divine persons."

[43] On this concept see Williams, *Arius*, 215−29 and Widdicombe, *The Fatherhood of God*, 189−92. For Athanasius' views see especially his "On the Councils," in *NPNF* 4:51−52 (pp. 476−78).

[44] E. P. Meijering, *Orthodoxy and Platonism in Athanasius: Synthesis or Antithesis* (Leiden, Neth.: Brill, 1974), 129.

[45] Ibid., 131.

[46] Athanasius, "Discourses," in *NPNF* 4:2.57 (p. 379).

[47] Ibid., 4:3.15 (p. 402), cf. 4:3.1 (p. 394), "Synodal Letter," in *NPNF* 4:11 (p. 494), "On Luke 10:22," in *NPNF* 4:6 (p. 90), "Statement of Faith," in *NPNF* 4:1−4 (pp. 84−85).

Later in his "Synodal Letter to the People of Antioch" he reiterates this point. He says there is

... a Holy Trinity but one Godhead, and one beginning (*arche*), and that the Son is co-essential with the Father ... while the Holy Spirit [is] proper to and inseparable from the essence of the Father and the Son.[48]

Then in the disputed fourth "Discourse Against the Arians," we read,

For the Word, being Son of the One God is referred to him of whom also he is; so that the Father and the Son are two, yet the Monad of the Godhead is indivisible and inseparable. And thus too we preserve one beginning (*arche*) of the Godhead and not two beginnings (*archai*), whence there is strictly a monarchy (*monarchia*). And of this very beginning (*arche*) the Word is by nature Son, not as if another beginning (*arche*), subsisting by himself.[49]

In these passages Athanasius speaks of the Godhead as the *arche*, rather than the Father alone as the *arche*.[50] Torrance says that for Athanasius the *monarche* "is identical with the Trinity."[51] In trying to get our minds around all this, Athanasius' most fundamental insight offers the key. For him the Father is never alone. The Father cannot exist without the Son, or the Son without the Father. Father and Son are correlatives. He says, "When we call God Father at once with the Father we signify the Son's existence."[52] Hanson says, "In the Father we have the Son: this is a summary of Athanasius' theology."[53] Frequently Athanasius draws on biblical images to illustrate this unbreachable correlation between the Father and the Son. The Son "is the Father's image and Word eternal, never having not been, but being ever, as the eternal Radiance of a light which is eternal."[54] To the Arians who say, "there was a once when he was not," Athanasius replies, they rob the Father "of his Word like plunderers," suggesting that "he was once without Radiance, and the Fountain was once barren and dry."[55] The imagery of God as a fountain is common in Athanasius. It is his argument that if the fountain is destitute of Life and Wisdom (identified as the Son), "it is not a fountain."[56]

---

[48] Athanasius, "Synodal Letter," in *NPNF* 4:5 (p. 484).

[49] Athanasius, "Discourses," in *NPNF* 4:4.1 (p. 433).

[50] See further on all this Meijering, *Orthodoxy and Platonism in Athanasius*, 8; and in more detail Torrance, *The Christian Doctrine of God*, 183; and *The Trinitarian Faith*, 78–79, 241–42. Hanson, *The Search*, 434–35, comes to the same conclusion.

[51] Torrance, *The Christian Doctrine of God*, 183.

[52] Athanasius, "Discourses," in *NPNF* 4:3.6 (p. 397).

[53] Hanson, *The Search*, 426.

[54] Athanasius, "Discourses," in *NPNF* 4:1.13 (p. 314).

[55] Ibid., 1.14 (p. 315). See also most of 1.20 (p. 318).

[56] Ibid., 1.19 (p. 317).

The description of the Son as the Father's "Radiance" and as "Light from Light"[57] are significant. These metaphors both distinguish the Father and the Son and affirm their indivisible unity. "For what the light enlightens, that the radiance irradiates; and what the radiance irradiates, from the light is its enlightenment. So when the Son is beheld so is the Father for he is the Father's radiance; and thus the Father and Son are one."[58]

Contemporary evangelicals often suggest that the "from" in "light *from* light" implies the Son's derivation from the Father. He is thus dependent on the Father for his existence. This is not the intent of Athanasius or the compilers of the creed of Nicea or the Nicene Creed. It is what Michel Barnes calls "the X from X" argument.[59] "The Son is God from God, Light from Light, true God from true God."[60] The Father and the Son are to be distinguished, but one is as truly God in every way as the other.

In his earlier writings Athanasius uses a number of terms[61] to denote the ontological unity of the Father and the Son, the least common of which is *homoousios* (one being or substance) that was so important at the Council of Nicea (325). In his "Discourses Against the Arians," written probably between 339 and 345, he uses the word only once. It was only when this word was repudiated in the 350s by Athanasius' opponents that he came to see it must be defended at all cost to guarantee the apostolic faith. In reply to those who objected to the term, *homoousios*, seeing in it the danger of modalism which collapses the distinctions within the Godhead, Athanasius argued that the term spoke both of the unity of being of the one God who is eternally a Triad, and of the eternal distinctions of the three persons — only differing things or persons can be said to be *homoousios*. His insistence on this term to sum up the "scope" of Scripture discloses not only his theological concerns, but also his epistemological concerns. This word emphatically signifies that in and through the Son (and in the Spirit) God communicates himself. *How* we know and *what* we know of God the Father is through the Son. In Athanasius "the whole Godhead" is complete in the Son as much as it is in the Father. God is God the Son as much as he is God the Father. From this follows what we might call "Athanasius' rule," an idea he repeats many times with some variation in wording, "the same things are said of the Son which are said of the Father except for calling him Father."[62]

---

[57] Ibid., 1.9 (p. 311), "On the Opinion of Dionysius," in *NPNF* 4:15 (p. 182).

[58] Athanasius, "Discourses," in *NPNF* 4:3.13 (p. 401).

[59] Michel Barnes, *The Power of God: Dunamis in Gregory of Nyssa's Trinitarian Theology* (Washington, D.C.: Catholic University of America, 2001), 119.

[60] The Nicene Creed.

[61] For a list of these expressions see Hanson, *The Search*, 437.

[62] Athanasius, "Discourses," in *NPNF* 4:3.4 (p. 395), 3.5 (p. 395); see also 3.6 (p. 396) and "The Councils," in *NPNF* 4:3.49 (twice, p. 476).

Athanasius opposed Arianism principally because it presupposed *a difference in being and authority* between the Father and the Son. Right at the heart of Arius' theology was ontological subordinationism that presupposed functional subordination. For Arius and his followers, the Son could only be called God in a secondary sense. He was subordinated God who owed his existence to the Father, he was dependent on the Father, and his works were not the same as the Father's. In reply Athanasius argued that to deny that the Father and the Son are eternally one in being *and* work is to deny what is essential to Christian faith and salvation. "For must not he be perfect who is equal to God? And must not he be unalterable who is one with the Father, and his Son proper to his essence?... For this is why he who has seen the Son has seen the Father, and why the knowledge of the Son is knowledge of the Father."[63]

Athanasius will not allow any disjunction between the Father and the Son. The two affirmations of Jesus he quotes the most are "I and the Father are one" (Jn 10:30) and "He who has seen me has seen the Father" (Jn 14:9). For him the unity of the three divine persons was so profound that it implied their coinherence, or mutual indwelling.[64] Building on the words of Jn 14:11, "I am in the Father and the Father is in me," he reasoned that at all times there is a complete mutual indwelling in which each divine person—while each remains what he is by himself as Father, Son, or Holy Spirit—is wholly in the others as the others are wholly in him. He did not use the word *perichoresis*. It had not yet been coined, but it was he who developed the concept of the mutual coinherence of the persons of the Trinity. This insight was later recognized to be yet another of his many important pioneering contributions to trinitarian theology. Once this complete coinherence of the persons of the Trinity is recognized, it follows that the works of the divine three cannot be divided. Because the Father is always in the Son and the Son is always in the Father, they must work as one.

Professor Lewis Ayres says that Athanasius was the first to recognize that the unity in being of the Father and the Son implied a unity of will and work. He thus can be seen as the originator of one of the most basic Pro-Nicene theological principles, namely that the Father and the Son work inseparably.[65] On this principle Professor Richard Hanson says that for Athanasius, "As the Son acts so the Father acts inseparably."[66] Time and time again the Alexandrian bishop insists that what the Father does the Son does and vice versa. He writes:

Wherefore through him [the Son] does the Father create and in him reveal himself to whom he will, and illuminate them.... For where the Father is, there

---

[63] Athanasius, "Discourses," in *NPNF* 4:1.35 (p. 327).
[64] This is a much-repeated motif; see especially ibid., 3.2–6 (pp. 394–97).
[65] Ayres, *Nicaea*, 113–15.
[66] Hanson, *The Search*, 427. So also Widdicombe, *The Fatherhood of God*, 205; and Ayres, *Nicaea*, 113.

is the Son and where the light, there is the radiance, and what the Father works, he works through the Son, and the Lord himself says, "What I see the Father do, that I do also"; so also when baptism is given, whom the Father baptizes, him the Son baptizes.[67]

When the Son works, the Father is the worker, and the Son coming to the saints, the Father is he who comes in the Son.... Therefore also ... when the Father gives grace and peace, the Son also gives it.[68]

What God speaks, it is very plain. He speaks through the Word and not through another, and the Word is not separate from the Father, nor unlike and foreign to the Father's essence, what he works, those are the Father's works.[69]

In his letters to Bishop Serapion, Athanasius speaks for the first time of the inseparable operations of all three divine persons, a doctrine that would become one of the basic planks of the pro-Nicene theology. First Athanasius speaks of the "works" of the Father, Son, and Spirit, and then he says, "But if there is such co-ordination and unity within the holy Triad, who can separate either the Son from the Father, or the Spirit from the Son or from the Father himself?"[70]

In recognizing that in being and work the Father and the Son are one, Athanasius yet again demonstrates his profound grasp of biblical thought. He clearly saw that in the Bible what God does reveals who God is, and in particular that the works of the Son are the works of the Father and vice versa (Jn 5:36; 9:3−4; 10:25; 10:37; 14:10). In enunciating this principle Athanasius captures biblical thinking. This unity of being and action between the Father, Son, and Spirit, first spelled out by Athanasius, is a constant theme from this point on in the orthodox doctrine of the Trinity. On this basis it is held that to *eternally* subordinate the Son or the Spirit in work/opera-tion/function by necessity implies their ontological subordination. If the Son (and the Spirit) on the basis of his personal identity alone must *always* take the subordinate role and always be obedient to the Father, then he must be a subordinated person, less than his superior in some way. Athanasius' denial of the eternal functional subordination of the Son does not entail a denial of or confusing of the eternal distinctions between the Father and the Son (or the Holy Spirit). For him, "They are two, because the Father is Father and is not also Son, and the Son is Son and not also Father."[71]

---

[67] Athanasius, "Discourses," in *NPNF* 4:2.41 (p. 370).

[68] Ibid., 3.11 (p. 400).

[69] Ibid., 3.14 (p. 402).

[70] *Letters of Saint Athansius Concerning the Holy Spirit*, trans. C. R. B. Shapland (London: Epworth, 1951), 1.20 (p. 113). This comment needs to be read in context to get its full force. On this matter see Ayres, *Nicaea*, 212−14.

[71] Athanasius, "Discourses," in *NPNF* 3:3.4 (p. 395).

It naturally follows for Athanasius that if the Father and the Son are inseparably one in being and function, then they must be inseparably one in authority, but this is a matter we will take up in the next chapter.

For Athanasius and the Nicene theologians, the doctrine of "inseparable operations" does not imply *identification* in operations or functions. Each divine person has their distinct contribution to make to every common work that they do. In other words, Athanasius follows the New Testament by endorsing divine operational order, or disposition. So he says, "Through the Son does the Father create"; "he works through the Son," and he "speaks through the Son." In his letters to Bishop Serapion, this motif is given full trinitarian expression. He says, "The Father does all things *through* the Word *in* the Holy Spirit. Thus the unity of the Holy Triad is preserved."[72] In these words Athanasius is not speaking of sub-ordering, or of hierarchical ordering in the Trinity. He never hierarchically orders the Trinity in any way. The Son is "first" just as much as the Father is "first."[73] Rather he is speaking of the distinct contribution of each divine person in every common work in an ordered pattern.[74] Athanasius affirms distinctions within the one God, but he will not allow any division or separating of the divine persons.

Nowhere is Athanasius' rejection of hierarchical ordering in the Trinity more eloquently expressed than in the following quotation. The allusion is to the cherubim and seraphim, who stand nearer to God than any other praising him continually in the words, "Holy, holy, holy," yet no one has ever suggested that in

> The first utterance of the word, Holy, the voice is raised aloud, while in the second it is lower, but in the third, quite low,—and that consequently the first utterance denotes lordship, the second subordination, and the third marks a yet lower degree. But away with the folly of these haters of God and senseless men. For the Triad, praised, reverenced, and adored, is one and indivisible and without degrees (*aschematistos*). It is united without confusion, just as the Monad also is distinguished without separation. For the fact of those venerable living creatures (Isa. vi; Rev. iv. 8) offering their praise three times, saying "Holy, Holy, Holy," proves that the three Subsistences are perfect, just as in saying "Lord," they declare the One Essence. They then that depreciate the Only-Begotten Son of God, blaspheme God, defaming his perfection and accusing him of imperfection, and render themselves liable to the severest chastisement. For he who blasphemes any one of the Subsistences shall have no remission.[75]

---

[72] Athanasius, *Letters*, 1.28 (p. 135).

[73] Athanasius, "Discourses," in *NPNF* 4:3.9 (pp. 398–99). He says, "For as the Father is first, so also is he [the Son] as the image of the first."

[74] Behr, *The Nicene Faith*, 235, says, "For Athanasius, as the works done by the Son in the Spirit demonstrate their own identity of essence with the Father, their mediating activity effects the immediate presence of the Father."

[75] Athanasius, "On Luke 10:22," in *NPNF* 4:6 (p. 90).

There is no uncertainty or ambiguity. In Athanasius we find the most thorough repudiation of the idea that the Son is in any way eternally subordinated to the Father. For him, without any caveats, the Father and the Son and the Holy Spirit are one in being, work/function, and authority. In answer to the Arians Athanasius completely rejects the idea that the Trinity is to be understood as a hierarchy in any form. He could not allow any diminution in the Son's divinity, majesty, or authority, neither in who he is or in what he does. Many times he repeats his "rule," "The same things are said of the Son that are said of the Father, except for calling him Father."[76] As far as Athanasius was concerned, the Arians did not merely "overemphasise the subordinationist elements in the NT," as the 1999 *Sydney Anglican Diocesan Doctrine Commission Report* states;[77] they undermined the very foundations of Christianity. By arguing that the Son is *different in being, works, and authority* from the Father, they impugned the full divinity of Christ, the veracity of the revelation of God in Christ, and the possibility of salvation through Christ.[78]

In Pannenberg's estimation, "Athanasius vanquished subordinationism, insisting that we cannot think of the Father as Father without the Son and the Spirit. He left no place for causally related graduations in the fullness of the divine being."[79]

The Cappadocian Fathers

The Cappadocian Fathers developed their trinitarian theology largely independently of Athanasius, although they knew his work and utilized some of his insights. Like Athanasius they were totally opposed to any suggestion that the Son is eternally subordinated to the Father in being, work/function, or authority.[80] Most of their writings seek to counter the teaching of two radical subordinationists, Aetius (d. c. 370), and his more prolific disciple Eunomius (c. 330–94), who are best-designated "Neo-Arians."

The Cappadocians like Athanasius conceive of God not as a Monad who becomes a Triad but as one Godhead who is eternally triune. In the secondary literature, it is often said they begin with the divine three and then attempt to show how they are one.[81] On reading their works I was surprised to find that in fact they consistently

---

[76] Athanasius, "Discourses," in *NPNF* 4:3.4 (p. 395), 3.1 (p. 395), 3.6 (p. 396), 4.3 (p. 434), "Councils of Ariminum," in *NPNF* 4:49 (p. 476 twice), "On Luke 10:22," in *NPNF* 4:3 and 4 (pp. 88–89).

[77] *Sydney Doctrine Report*, par. 22.

[78] So Athanasius argues. See "Discourses," in *NPNF* 4:1–10 (pp. 306–12).

[79] Pannenberg, *Systematic Theology*, vol. 1, 275. So also Meijering, "Athanasius," 11.

[80] This is not to suggest that they were not also opposed to Sabellianism (modalism). This error is never ignored, but it is not given the same emphasis as the error of subordinationism.

[81] And so it is argued they have a "social" doctrine of the Trinity. In reply see S. Coakley, " 'Persons' in the Social Doctrine of the Trinity: A Critique of Current Analytic Discussion"

begin with the one Godhead (*Theotes*), who is for them eternally triune. What is distinctive is their recognition that the one God is the divine three persons in communion. Gregory of Nazianzus writes,

> To us there is one God, for the Godhead is one ... though we believe in three persons.[82]

> Let us adore the one Godhead in the three.[83]

> One Godhead and power, found in the three in unity.[84]

Similarly Gregory of Nyssa says,

> Since we cannot find any diversity in their nature, we not unreasonably define the Holy Trinity to be one Godhead.[85]

> We say that the Godhead of the Father and of the Son and of the Holy Spirit is one, and we forbid men to say, "there are three Gods."[86]

And likewise Basil,

> For of the Father, Son, and Holy Spirit there is the same nature and one Godhead.[87]

For them the divine three share the one being (*ousia*), yet they are eternally three *hypostases*. The *hypostases* can be distinguished but not separated, differentiated but not divided. Sharing the one being (*ousia*), the three *hypostases* interpenetrate one another and may be conceived of as united in the most intimate personal communion (*koinonia*) and mutual self-giving. On this last matter developing Athanasius' idea of coinherence, they insist that each *hypostasis* inheres in the other two (cf. Jn 10:30, 38; 14:11; 17:21).

Also like Athanasius, the Cappadocians not only teach that all three persons are one in being, but also that they work/function/operate as one. Oneness in being implied for them oneness in action and vice versa. They oppose the teaching of Eunomius, who clearly distinguished between divine being or essence and activity or function (*energeia*). Eunomius, says Ayres, was "at pains to argue that activity is not

in *The Trinity, An Interdisciplinary Symposium*, eds. S. T. Davis, D. Kendall, and G. O'Collins (New York: Oxford, 1999), 123–44; and Ayres, *Nicaea*, 344–59.

[82] Gregory of Nazianzus, "On the Holy Spirit," in *NPNF* 7:14 (p. 322).

[83] Gregory of Nazianzus, "On the Arrival of the Egyptians," in *NPNF* 7:9 (p. 336).

[84] Gregory of Nazianzus, "Oration on Holy Baptism," in *NPNF* 7:41 (p. 375). See also "On the Holy Spirit," in *NPNF* 7:40.41 (p. 375).

[85] Gregory of Nyssa, "On the Holy Trinity," in *NPNF* 5 (p. 329).

[86] Gregory of Nyssa, "On 'Not Three Gods,'" in *NPNF* 5 (p. 331).

[87] Basil, "Letters," in *NPNF* 8:110.4 (p. 250).

coterminous with essence."[88] In reply, the Cappadocians with one voice argue that divine being and work/operations/function cannot be separated. Basil writes,

> We perceive the operation of Father, Son and Holy Spirit to be one and the same, in no respect showing difference or variation; from this identity of operation we necessarily infer the unity of nature.[89]

And,

> The work of the Father is not separate or distinct from the work of the Son; whatever the Son sees the Father doing ... that the Son does likewise.[90]

Gregory of Nyssa makes the same point.

> In the case of the divine nature we do not similarly learn that the Father does anything by himself in which the Son does not work conjointly, or again that the Son has any special operation apart from the Holy Spirit.[91]

> We understand that the operation of the Father, the Son and the Holy Spirit is one, differing or varying in nothing, the oneness of their nature must needs be inferred from the identity of their operations.[92]

None of the Cappadocians will allow any separation or division in being and work/function between the persons of the Trinity, but they all believed that something distinct is contributed to every divine action by each person. There is an order (*taxis*) in trinitarian operations that in no way impacted on their equality. Basil says,

> And in creation think first, I pray thee, of the original cause of all things that are made, the Father, of the creative cause, the Son, and of the perfecting cause, the Holy Spirit.[93]

Basil immediately adds that this orderly way of working is freely willed by the Father and by the Son. There is no compulsion or imperfection in divine simplicity.[94]
Gregory of Nyssa writes,

> In every operation which extends from God to the creation, and is named according to our variable conceptions of it, has its origin from the Father, and proceeds through the Son, and is perfected by the Spirit.[95]

---

[88] Ayres, *Nicaea*, 148.

[89] Basil, "Letters," in *NPNF* 8:189 (p. 231).

[90] Basil, "On the Spirit," in *NPNF* 8:19 (p. 13). In this instance I follow the translation given by D. Anderson, *St. Basil the Great on the Holy Spirit* (New York: St. Vladimir's, 1980), 39.

[91] Gregory of Nyssa, "Not Three Gods," in *NPNF* 5 (p. 334).

[92] Gregory of Nyssa, "On the Holy Spirit" in *NPNF* 5 (p. 328).

[93] Basil, "On the Spirit," in *NPNF* 8:16.38 (p. 23).

[94] On this point see Ayres, *Nicaea*, 208.

[95] Gregory of Nyssa, "On 'Not Three Gods,'" in *NPNF* 5 (p. 334).

In speaking in this manner the Cappadocians allow for an "order" in the operations or works of the three *hypostases*, but one that does not imply a hierarchy in being, function, or authority. Robert W. Jenson says the great achievement of the Cappadocians was to conceptualize the ordering of the three *hypostases* not hierarchically as Origen had done, but horizontally.[96] The Roman Catholic theologian William J. Hill makes virtually the same point. He argues that the Cappadocians affirmed order within the Trinity without sub-ordering.[97]

For the Cappadocians the Father, Son, and Holy Spirit are differentiated by their differing origins and thus differing relations and nothing else.[98] For them differentiating the persons did not in any way suggest the subordination of the Son or the Spirit. It is true that they spoke of the Father as the "sole source" or "sole origin" (*monarche*) of the being of the Son and the Spirit. In their thinking this did not imply any subordination whatsoever, for the three *hypostases* shared in the one being of the Godhead; each interpenetrated the other, and they always work as one. In other words, for them derivation of being did not imply any diminution of being or authority. In making the Father the *arche*/origin of the being of the Son and the Spirit, many Western theologians think a conceptual weakness is inherent in the Cappadocian doctrine of the Trinity.[99] A certain priority is given to the Father. To simply deny that the *monarche* of the Father envisages the Son and the Spirit standing "below" the Father does not solve the problem. Eastern Orthodox theologians generally endorse the *monarche* of the Father, denying it implies any hint of subordinationism. Nevertheless in recent times, as an outcome of ecumenical dialogue, some of them have begun speaking, as Athanasius did, of the divine Trinity as the *arche*.[100] Like most contemporary theologians they want to completely exclude subordinationism.

It is to be emphasized that the Cappadocians' motive for insisting on the *monarche* of the Father was not to subordinate the second and third persons in any way. They are emphatic on this point. Basil says,

---

[96] Robert W. Jenson, *The Triune Identity: God According to the Gospel* (Philadelphia: Fortress, 1982), 106.

[97] William J. Hill, *The Three-Personed God: The Trinity as a Mystery of Salvation* (Washington, D.C.: Catholic University of America Press, 1982), 278–79. Similarly, Gerald O'Collins, *The Tripersonal God: Understanding and Interpreting the Trinity* (Mahwah, N.J.: Paulist, 1999), 134.

[98] Later when we discuss how orthodoxy has differentiated the divine three, we will see that they do recognize other secondary differences, but here we note that Gregory of Nyssa says explicitly that we recognize "differences only in respect to unoriginateness." "Against Eunomius," in *NPNF* 5:1.33 (p. 78).

[99] Prestige, *God in Patristic Thought*, 249; Edmund Fortman, *The Triune God* (Grand Rapids, Mich.: Baker, 1972), 282; Pannenberg, *Systematic Theology*, vol. 1, 279–80; T. F. Torrance, *Trinitarian Faith*, 241.

[100] See T. F. Torrance, *Trinitarian Perspectives: Towards Doctrinal Agreement* (Edinburgh: T&T Clark, 1994), 115–43; and my *The Trinity*, 100.

Those who teach subordinationism, and talk about First, Second and Third, ought to recognize they are introducing erroneous Greek polytheism into pure Christian theology ... subordination cannot be used to describe persons who share the same nature.[101]

Gregory of Nyssa adds,

We do not know of any difference by way of superiority and inferiority in attributes which express our conceptions of the divine nature.[102]

Gregory of Nazianzus is even more emphatic. Speaking against the teaching of the long-dead Arius, he says,

For he did not honor the Father, by dishonoring his Offspring with his unequal degrees of Godhead. But we recognize one glory of the Father, the equality of the Only-begotten; and one glory of the Son and the Spirit. And we hold that to subordinate any of the three, is to destroy the whole.[103]

The one Godhead and power found in the three in unity, and comprising the three separately, not unequal in substance or natures, neither increased or diminished by superiorities or inferiorities; in every respect equal, in every respect the same.[104]

The Cappadocians and Bishop John Zizioulas

At this point it is appropriate to make a brief mention of the interpretation of Cappadocian trinitarian teaching given by John Zizioulas, the Greek Orthodox theologian and metropolitan of Pergamon. In his important book *Being As Communion*,[105] Bishop Zizioulas claims to be restating the teaching of the Cappadocians, who he says recognized for the first time that: (1) divine being is communal, (2) the *hypostases* are to be understood as divine persons, and (3) divine unity only can be maintained if the Father is recognized as the *Monarche* of the Son and the Spirit. It is hard to check his conclusions by referring to the Cappadocians because he seldom cites the great Greek fathers. He argues mainly by assertion. Ayres puts the point bluntly, saying his proposals lack evidence.[106] What would seem to be the case is that he is arguing for a

---

[101]Basil, "On the Spirit," in *NPNF* 8:47 (p. 30). Again for clarity of wording I have followed Anderson's translation, 75.

[102]Gregory of Nyssa, "On the Holy Trinity," in *NPNF* 5 (p. 327).

[103]Gregory of Nazianzus, "The Panegyric on St. Basil," in *NPNF* 7:30 (p. 405).

[104]Gregory of Nazianzus, "Oration on Holy Baptism," in *NPNF* 7:40.41 (p. 375).

[105]John Zizioulas, *Being As Communion* (London: Darton, Longman and Todd, 1985). See also his "The Doctrine of the Holy Trinity: The Significance of the Cappadocian Contribution," in *Trinitarian Theology Today*, ed. C. Schwobel (Edinburgh: T&T Clark, 1995), 40–60.

[106]Ayres, *Nicaea*, 313.

position he embraces personally and then looks back 1600 years to find support for it in the Cappadocian Fathers.[107] Although he is not the first to speak of divine being as communal, his brilliant exposition of this idea has gained wide support.[108] His case that the Cappadocians were the first to think of the divine three as persons is the most doubtful of his propositions. The Western theologian, Tertullian, deserves this honor more than the Cappadocians.[109] Ayres argues that the Cappadocians were not interested in developing "an ontology of divine personhood."[110] It is, however, his thesis that the person of the Father must be understood as the *Monarche* (sole source) of the Son and the Spirit that has divided opinion most of all. This idea is definitely taught by the Cappadocians, but whether or not they give it the prominence and dogmatic importance that Zizioulas gives it, and whether or not it is a good point to ground trinitarian relations, are matters much debated.

John Wilks argues that for the Cappadocians the one divine *ousia* is the unifying principle in the Godhead, not the *monarche* of the Father.[111] He also notes that Gregory of Nazianzus was not without his reservations about thinking of the person of the Father as the *arche* of the Son and the Spirit lest it should suggest their subordination.[112] Thomas F. Torrance also opposes Zizioulas' thesis that the great fourth-century Greek theologians uniformly taught the *monarche* of the Father, and thus it is to be embraced today.[113] Beginning with Gregory of Nazianzus' comment just mentioned, which he takes as the apex of Cappadocian thinking on this matter, and appealing to Athanasius, Epiphanius, and Cyril, he argues the Eastern tradition makes divine being in communion the *monarche* of the persons of the Trinity, not the person of the Father.[114] Alan J. Torrance, in his important discussion of Zizioulas' work, also finds wanting his arguments that the *monarche* of the Father has to be upheld. He asks whether or not the Greek bishop is "consistent with himself." If divine being is eternally communal, how, he asks, can the Trinity be derived "from a causal act of

---

[107]See L. Turcescu, " 'Persons' versus 'Individual' and Other Misreadings of Gregory of Nyssa," *Modern Theology* 18, no. 4 (2002): 527–39.

[108]On the evolution of this insight see A. J. Torrance, *Persons in Communion: An Essay on Trinitarian Description and Human Participation* (Edinburgh: T&T Clark, 1996).

[109]This is not to say that Bishop Zizioulas does not contribute helpfully to the quest to understand personhood. It is, however, doubtful that his ideas come from the Cappadocians. They seem more like twentieth-century ideas. See Turcescu, "Persons," 527–39.

[110]Ayres, *Nicaea*, 280, cf. 395–96.

[111]John Wilks, "The Trinitarian Ontology of John Zizioulas," *Vox Evangelica* 25, no. 1 (1995): 69–73.

[112]Ibid., 73. On Gregory see *NPNF* 7:5.43 (p. 376).

[113]This debate is clearly set out in R. Del Colle, " 'Persons' and 'Being' in John Zizioulas, Trinitarian Theology: Conversations with Thomas Torrance and Thomas Aquinas," *Scottish Journal of Theology* 54, no. 1 (2001): 70–86.

[114]T. F. Torrance, *The Christian Doctrine of God*, 175–85.

the Father" alone?[115] Finally, we mention the fact that many Western theologians are critical of the thesis that the Father should be thought of as *Monarche* of the being of the Son and the Spirit, because logically it could imply subordinationism.[116] Colin Gunton is sympathetic to Zizioulas' work, but he argues the Greek bishop needs to give more weight to the *homoousian* principle to avoid tritheism.[117]

The Creed of Nicea and the Nicene Creed

Soon after his conquest of the eastern part of the Roman Empire, the Emperor Constantine called an ecumenical council, primarily to deal with the divisions caused by Arius' teaching. The council convened on June 19, 325, in the city of Nicea, now Isnik, Turkey. About 300 bishops came. A creed with four anti-Arian anathemas attached was accepted and signed by all but two of the bishops.

It declares that the Son is

> begotten as only begotten of the Father; that is of the substance (*ousia*) of the Father, God of God, Light of Light, true God of true God, begotten not made; consubstantial (*homoousios*) with the Father, through whom all things came into existence ... who for us men and for our salvation came down and was incarnate and became man, suffered and rose again.[118]

In affirming that the Son is "God of God, Light of Light, true God of true God,"[119] who is "consubstantial with the Father," the bishops at Nicea endorse both divine differentiation and divine unity. What the Father is so too is the Son. In affirming that the Son "for us men [meaning men and women] and for our salvation came down and was incarnate and became man [meaning human] and suffered ...," the temporal subordination of the Son is also endorsed. In juxtaposing these two truths—the Son is "true God" and he "became man and suffered"—the bishops at Nicea agreed that the *temporal* subordination of the Son to the Father within the economy of salvation did not entail the subordination of the Son in the *eternal* or immanent Trinity.

T. F. Torrance holds that "an absolutely fundamental step" was made in the Christian understanding of God when the words "one in being with the Father" (*homoousios*

---

[115] Alan Torrance, *Persons in Communion*, 292.

[116] So Prestige, *God in Patristic Thought*, 249; Pannenberg, *Systematic Theology*, vol. 1, 279–80; T. F. Torrance, *The Trinitarian Faith*, 241; Fortman, *The Triune God*, 282, etc.

[117] Colin Gunton, *The Promise of Trinitarian Theology* (Edinburgh: T&T Clark, 1991), 167.

[118] The full text in Greek and English is given in J. N. D. Kelly, *Early Christian Creeds* (London: Longman, Green, 1950), 215–16. Hanson, *The Search*, 163, gives a slightly different English translation. In the above quote I follow Hanson.

[119] As noted earlier these words are included not to speak of derivation in being but of unity of being. This is the "X from X" argument.

to Patri) were included in this creed. It was, he says, "a turning point of far-reaching consequences."[120] These words "clearly asserted not only that there is no division between the being of the Son and the being of the Father, but also that there is no division between the acts of the Son and the acts of the Father."[121] Thus the Father and the Son are both associated with the work of creation in this creed. If the Father and the Son are one in being and act, then the idea that the Son is eternally set under the Father, ontologically or functionally, is categorically excluded. When two people are true equals, the permanent and necessary subordination of one party to the other in being, function, or authority is excluded on principle.

David Cunningham says the Council of Nicea intentionally excluded all expressions of subordinationism known at that time. "In order to rule out Arianism and other forms of subordinationism, the Nicene Council rejected a whole variety of attempts to place the three in hierarchical order—logical, causal, temporal, or otherwise. The Council's clarity on this point is especially visible in the Nicene anathemas, which claim that there was no time when the Word was not. And to make it clear that the begetting of the Son need not imply temporal order, the Creed states that this begetting takes place eternally. Nor is there any logical hierarchy among the Three; they all imply one another and are dependent on one another, so that no one of them can be understood in a position of primacy over the others."[122]

At the council of Constantinople in 381, the "faith of Nicea" was reaffirmed in a creed with different wording at key points and with an additional clause spelling out the full divinity of the Holy Spirit. This is the so-called "Nicene Creed," which is used in Western and Eastern churches today.[123] It is technically designated "the Nicene-Constantinopolitan Creed." This creed was ratified again at the Council of Chalcedon in 451. The wording of the Creed of Nicea and the Nicene Creed of 381 is not identical, but the theology of the two creeds is the same. In both creeds the Son of God is confessed as "of one substance or being (homoousious) with the Father," and as coming down from heaven "for us and our salvation." Once these two truths were established as theological principles, they then became hermeneutical principles.

---

[120]T. F. Torrance, The Trinitarian Faith, 144. On the significance and implications of the inclusion of these words in both the creed of Nicea and the Nicene-Constantinopolitan Creed see the full discussion in Torrance, ibid., 132–45.

[121]Ibid., 137.

[122]David Cunningham, These Three Are One: The Practice of Trinitarian Theology (London: Blackwell, 1998), 112.

[123]With one notable exception. The Nicene Creed speaks of the Spirit as "proceeding from the Father." At the third council of Toledo in 589 the words "and the Son" were added by the mainly Western bishops present. In Latin this is one word, Filioque. The Eastern Orthodox Churches have never accepted this addition and say the creed without it. See further my The Trinity, 50–51.

Those who confess Christ in these words are agreeing that these two clauses accurately encapsulate what the Bible as a whole teaches about the eternal oneness in being of the Father and the Son and of the Son's voluntary and temporal subordination — his coming down from heaven for our salvation. This confession then becomes for them an interpretative guide in the understanding of individual passages in Scripture that could be read to deny either of these basic truths.

We thus conclude that those who speak today of the *eternal* subordination of the Son in being, or function, or authority not only contradict the theology of the Nicene Creed, but also the interpretive principles it enshrines. In failing to note the hermeneutical guidance the Nicene Creed offers, they wrongly conclude that texts which speak of the temporal subordination and obedience of the incarnate Son define his eternal status and role. Thus no matter how many texts they quote in support of their case, this creed judges their efforts to be mistaken. They have failed to grasp what Athanasius calls "the scope of Scripture," by which he means the overall drift or the theological center of Scripture.

Augustine

Augustine brings the pro-Nicene case against subordinationism to its conclusion.[124] Every theological student should be obligated to read and carefully note his classic study *The Trinity*.[125] His theological brilliance is seen in how he develops the trinitarian tradition he has inherited by answering the questions the doctrine of the Trinity raises in three complementary ways. First of all, with Scripture as his starting point, Augustine develops his doctrine of the Trinity from an economic perspective — from what is revealed in God's unfolding revelation of himself in history and in Scripture. However, Augustine is conscious that an economic approach to the doctrine of the Trinity is inadequate on its own. He realizes that the theologian also has to speak of the triune God as he is in himself, what we call today "the immanent Trinity." So second, Augustine makes deductions about the immanent Trinity building on what is clearly revealed in Scripture and from what he thinks are trajectories given in Scripture. Third, in books 8 to 15 in *The Trinity*, Augustine moves beyond Scripture, building on the insights of Gregory of Nyssa[126] to meditate on the complexities of human consciousness, where he finds vestiges of the triune being of God. On this last matter Kelly says, "[His goal] is not so much to demonstrate that God is Trinity (in his view revelation provides ample assurance of this)

---

[124] Ayres, *Nicaea*, 364–84, makes a very good case for accepting that Augustine stands squarely in the pro-Nicene tradition.

[125] Augustine, *The Trinity*, trans. Edmund Hill (Brooklyn: New City Press, 1991). All references to *De Trinitate* (*The Trinity*) are from this translation.

[126] Ayres, *Nicea*, 291.

as to deepen our understanding of the mystery of the absolute oneness and yet real distinctions of the Three."[127]

Augustine's primary aim is to develop the catholic doctrine of the Trinity on the basis of scriptural teaching, but he is aware that "the heretics try to defend their false and misleading opinions from these very Scriptures"[128] and that there are seeming "contradictions"[129] and "multifarious diversity" in Scripture.[130] So he makes his first objective the developing of a number of what he calls "canonical rules"[131] for reading Scripture aright. The most important of these is that all texts that speak of Christ as equal in divinity, majesty, and authority with the Father refer to him "in the form of God"—his eternal divine nature—and all texts that speak of his human limitations, subordination, or obedience refer exclusively to him in "the form of a servant," as the incarnate Son.[132] This hermeneutical rule he found spelled out in Php 2:4–11, a text to which he repeatedly returns. A second rule is that texts that speak of the Son doing the Father's will, or judging on behalf of the Father, or of his "begetting" and "sending," "mark him neither as less nor equal, but only intimate that he is from the Father."[133] A third rule is that the God of the Bible should not be defined "in bodily terms."[134] Like Athanasius, Augustine sees clearly that biblical language is, to use later terms, analogical and metaphorical. Human words such as *father*, *son*, and *sending* are thus not to be understood univocally when applied to God.

He begins his exposition of the Trinity in these words:

> The purpose of all Catholic commentators I have been able to read on the divine books of both Testaments, who have written before me on the Trinity which God is, has been to teach that according to the Scriptures Father Son and Holy Spirit in the inseparable equality of one substance present a divine unity; and therefore there are not three Gods but one God: although indeed the Father has begotten the Son, and therefore he who is Father is not the Son; and the Son is begotten by the Father, and therefore he who is the Son is not the Father; and the Holy Spirit is neither the Father nor the Son, but only the Spirit of the Father and the Son, himself co-equal to the Father and the Son, and belonging to the threefold unity.

> It was not, however, the same three (their teaching continues) that was born of the virgin Mary, crucified and buried under Pontius Pilate, rose again

---

[127]Kelly, *Early Christian Doctrines*, 276.
[128]Augustine, *The Trinity*, 1.1.6 (p. 69).
[129]Ibid., 1.4.22 (p. 82).
[130]Ibid., 2, prologue 1 (p. 97).
[131]Ibid., 2.1.2 (p. 98).
[132]Ibid., 1.3ff. (pp. 74ff.), 2.1.2–3 (pp. 98–99).
[133]Ibid., 2.1.3 (p. 98).
[134]Ibid., 1.1.1 (p. 65).

on the third day and ascended into heaven, but the Son alone. Nor was it this same three that came upon Jesus in the form of a dove at his baptism … but the Holy Spirit alone. Nor was it the same three that spoke from heaven, "You are my Son" … but it was the Father's voice alone addressing the Son. This also is my faith inasmuch as it is the Catholic faith.[135]

On reading this passage I find myself asking, could a better brief summary be given of the doctrine of the Trinity? Here the unequivocal unity of the divine three and their differentiation is emphatically affirmed in the light of revelation. In this passage it is implied that the one substance is nothing other than the divine three, and in other writings Augustine makes this point explicit. In his letter to "Consentius, his most beloved brother,"[136] he first of all denies that the one substance is as it were a "fourth person." It is rather, he says, "what is common to all as the divinity of all and in all."[137] And then later he adds, "The Father, Son and Holy Spirit are the Trinity."[138]

What the divine three should be called is a question that Augustine recognizes is very difficult.[139] No human word is adequate, and yet a word is needed. "So that we are not simply reduced to silence when we are asked three what,"[140] he argues that the word *person* (Latin *persona*) may be used so that it is possible to speak of one God and at the same time of the three "persons," Father, Son, and Spirit, who are the one God, not three Gods.

Augustine does not think that the theological quest has been completed when Scripture has been understood correctly. There are still questions that Scripture does not directly answer. Attempts at answering these questions can be made by considering where Scripture is pointing, by drawing on the tradition, and by the use of good reasoning. What Augustine clearly sees is that an adequate doctrine of the Trinity has to make deductions about the immanent Trinity—God as he is in himself. On this matter he makes many advances. First of all he endorses the Western trinitarian tradition's basic premise, namely that the divine three are inseparably one because they are one substance (Latin *substantia*). From this premise it follows that whatever is said of God in unity may be said of the three divine persons separately. Thus all three have the same attributes. All three are "great, good, [and] omnipotent."[141] Furthermore, because the three persons are one in substance, it follows that their work

---

[135]Ibid., 1.2.7 (p. 69).

[136]*Saint Augustine Letters*, vol. 2 (Letters 88–120), trans. Sister Wilfred Parsons (Washington, D.C.: Catholic University of America Press, 1953), 300–317. On this matter see further Ayres, *Nicaea*, 375–78.

[137]Ibid., 306.

[138]Ibid., 310.

[139]Augustine, *The Trinity*, 7.3.7 (p. 224).

[140]Ibid., 7.3.11 (pp. 228–29).

[141]Ibid., 5.3.12 (p. 197), 5.2.9 (p. 195).

in the world is also one. He says, "The Trinity works inseparably in everything that God works."[142] Particular works may be "appropriated" to each person (e.g. creation to the Father, redemption to the Son, and sanctification to the Spirit), but always the divine three work as one.[143] They operate in perfect unison and harmony. And finally, this "inseparable unity" means that the divine persons have only one will. "The Father and the Son have but one will and are indivisible in their workings."[144] In Augustine's theology of the Trinity it is simply not possible to separate essence and work, being and function, in the divine life. What God does speaks of who God is; and to be person specific, what the Son does speaks of who the Son is.

With his stress on the unity and equality of the three divine persons, Augustine had to differentiate the divine persons unambiguously and carefully to avoid any hint of modalism. The Father is distinguished as Father because he "begets" the Son; the Son is distinguished because as the Son he is "begotten"; the Spirit is distinguished from the Father and the Son because he is "bestowed" by them.[145] In a subsequent chapter we will discuss divine differentiation in more detail. But before leaving this matter, it is to be noted that Augustine thinks that alongside the term *begotten* the term *sent* also distinguishes the Father and the Son.[146] He never questions the fact that the Bible speaks of the Father sending the Son: what he questions is the meaning or force of the word *sent* when used of God. He will agree that sending and being sent differentiate the Father and the Son, not that they subordinate the Son to the Father, as the Arians argued.[147]

> If, however, the reason why the Son is said to have been sent by the Father is simply that one is the Father and the other the Son, then there is nothing at all to stop us believing that the Son is equal to the Father.[148]

> For the Son is from the Father, not the Father from the Son ... not in virtue of some disparity of power or substance or anything in him that was not equal to the Father.[149]

At this point I say no more on Augustine's treatment of the biblical idea that the Father sends the Son. It will be discussed more fully in a later chapter.

---

[142] Ibid., 1.2.8 (p. 70); cf. 2.1.3 (p. 99).

[143] Ayres, *Nicaea*, 296–300, cogently argues that it was the Cappadocians who first developed the doctrine of appropriations and Augustine simply built on their work.

[144] Augustine, *The Trinity*, 2.2.8 (p. 103).

[145] Ibid., 5.1ff. (pp. 190ff.).

[146] Ibid., 2.2.7 (p. 102).

[147] Augustine stresses that differentiation does not imply inequality, ibid., 4.5.26–29 (pp. 171–74). See also 4.5.32 (p. 176), 5.3.13–14 (p. 198).

[148] Ibid., 4.5.2 (p. 172). Similarly 4.5.32 (p. 176).

[149] Ibid., 4.5.2 (p. 172).

Next we make a brief comment on Augustine and the Spirit. He thought of the Holy Spirit as the mutual love of the Father and the Son and as the communal bond that unites them. This meant that for him the Holy Spirit could not be the Spirit of just one of them but rather of the two in relationship. This theological insight he found taught in Scripture. He noted that the Bible spoke of the Holy Spirit as both the Spirit of the Son and the Spirit of the Father.[150] This led to a tension in his thinking on the Trinity which is not resolved. Three ideas bear on him: (1) what he finds in Scripture; (2) the idea that the Father is the *monarche* of the Son and the Spirit, which is in the tradition he has received from Hilary of Poitiers and the Cappadocians, and (3) his belief that all thinking about the Trinity should begin with the one substance of the divine three. It is thus of little surprise that the couple of comments he makes on the *monarche* of the Father are not altogether logically consistent or clear. First he says, "We must confess that the Father and the Son are the origin (*principium*) of the Holy Spirit; not two origins (*non duo principia*), but just as Father and Son are one God ... so with reference to the Holy Spirit they are one *origin* (*unum principium*)."[151] Then second, "The Father is called the one from whom the Word is born and from whom the Holy Spirit principally (*principaliter*) proceeds. I added 'principally' (*principaliter*), because we have found the Holy Spirit also proceeds from the Son."[152]

In Augustine the emphasis falls on the one triune substance or being of God and thus the inseparable unity of Father, Son, and Spirit. With this starting point there can be no subordination whatsoever in the Trinity. All three persons, he says, "share the inseparable equality of one substance present in divine unity"[153] and, "In God therefore, when the equal Son cleaves to the equal Father, or the equal Holy Spirit to the Father and the Son, God is not made bigger than each of them singly, because there is no possibility of his perfection growing."[154] Kelly's conclusion is that for Augustine, "The unity of the Trinity is set squarely in the foreground, subordinationism of every kind being rigorously excluded."[155]

The Filoque

In the light of Augustine's understanding of the procession of the Spirit, it is not surprising that in 589 at the third Council of Toledo the words "and the Son" (these

---

[150]Ibid., 5.3.12 (p. 197).

[151]Ibid., 5.3.15 (p. 199). On the difference in meaning of the Latin term *principium* and the Greek term *monarche*, see the note on this in Augustine, "On the Trinity" in *NPNF* 3:95n. 5.

[152]Ibid., 15.29 (p. 419). And in 4.5.32 (p. 177) he says, "The Father is the source and origin of all deity" (*Propter principii commendationem*).

[153]Ibid., 1.2.7 (p. 69).

[154]Ibid., 6.2.9 (p. 211).

[155]Kelly, *Early Christian Doctrines*, 273.

three English words translate one Latin word, *Filioque*) were added to the Nicene Creed, which had until that time spoken of the Spirit as proceeding solely "from the Father." This reflected a growing divide between Eastern and Western theologians. The latter generally believe this addition safeguarded the vital truth established in the Nicene Creed: the Father and the Son are inseparably one, and it disallowed any disjunction between the Son and the Spirit that would be contrary to Scripture where the Spirit can be called either "the Spirit of God" or "the Spirit of Jesus" (Ac 16:7; cf. Ro 8:9; Gal 4:6). This addition was not intended to subordinate the Spirit to the Father and the Son, but it must be admitted that the Eastern Orthodox objection that it does just this, at least conceptually, cannot be ignored. The traditional Eastern approach has been to argue that only if the Father is conceived of as the *monarche* (sole-source) of the Son and the Spirit can divine unity be preserved. Although Eastern theologians insist that the Father, Son, and Spirit each share the one divine being, thereby excluding subordinationism, many Western theologians have thought that making the Father the sole source of the being of the Son and the Spirit conceptually implies the subordination of the Son and the Spirit.

Neither the Western nor the Eastern way of conceiving of the procession of the Spirit can be considered satisfactory. In an eternally coequal Trinity, Alasdair Heron argues, to subdivide the Godhead into "'two here' and 'one there,' or 'two of this sort,' and 'one of that'" is untenable.[156] Neither view, he says, is "adequately trinitarian, both reflect a double rather than a triple pattern."[157] And he adds, "Neither approach is easily reconcilable with the history of Christ and the Spirit as presented in the New Testament."[158] Many suggest that the answer is to speak of the Spirit proceeding from the Father *through* the Son, but some think this hierarchically orders the Trinity.[159] In his extended discussion of this issue, Robert Letham argues the best solution is to speak of the Spirit proceeding *from the Father in the Son*.[160]

Yves Congar, writing in 1983, is of the opinion that "there is no chance" that in the foreseeable future this division between Eastern and Western Christians can be resolved.[161] However, in 1991 a surprising development occurred. The Orthodox Church and the Reformed Churches issued a joint statement declaring that they had

---

[156]Alasdair Heron, *The Holy Spirit* (Philadelphia: Westminster, 1983), 177.

[157]Ibid.

[158]Ibid.

[159]So Letham, *The Holy Trinity*, 219.

[160]Ibid. For a helpful, more nuanced suggestion see T. Smail, "The Holy Spirit in the Holy Trinity" in *Nicene Christianity: The Future for a New Ecumenism*, ed. Christopher Seitz (Grand Rapids, Mich.: Brazos, 2001), 149–65.

[161]Yves Congar, *I Believe in the Holy Spirit: The River of Life Flows in the East and the West*, vol. 3 (London: G. Chapman, 1983), 201. His whole discussion on this matter on pp. 19–201 is well worth reading.

come to a common mind on the doctrine of the Trinity and of the *Filoque* clause in particular. They had agreed that the *Monarche* is the divine triune Being, not the person of the Father. I quote a key section: "The perfect simplicity and indivisibility of God in his Triune Being mean the *Arche* (*arche*) or *Monarchia* (*monarchia*) cannot be limited to one Person, as Gregory the Theologian pointed out. While there are inviolable distinctions within the Holy Trinity, this does not detract from the truth that the whole Being of God belongs to all of them as it belongs to each of them, and thus does not detract from the truth that the Monarchy is One and indivisible, the Trinity in Unity and the Unity in Trinity whole Being of God."[162]

In this understanding of the *Monarche* the statement adds, "There are no degrees of deity in the Holy Trinity, as implied in a distinction between the underived Deity of the Father and the derived Deity of the Son and the Spirit. Any notion of subordination is completely ruled out."[163]

Thomas Torrance more than anyone else was instrumental in this historic breakthrough, and now only time will tell if it wins over theologians from both East and West.[164] This model, it is to be noted, overcomes the inherent problems in both the traditional Western and Eastern approaches that Alasdair Heron raises.

The Athanasian Creed

After Augustine's death, his teaching on the Trinity was encapsulated in the so-called Athanasian Creed (that would be better called Augustine's Creed).[165] This creed claims to give "the catholic faith" that needs to be believed to be saved. Roman Catholics, Anglicans, and Lutherans among others endorse this creed, giving it the same authority as the Apostles' and Nicene creeds. The Athanasian Creed stresses the unity of the Trinity and the equality of the persons. I think it settles every issue in contention in this debate.

- Modalism and tritheism are excluded absolutely. There is one God and three persons. "We worship one God ... neither confounding the persons: nor dividing the substance." "So the Father is God, the Son is God and the Holy Spirit is God. And yet there are not three Gods but one."

---

[162]Quoted from T. F. Torrance, *The Christian Doctrine of God*, 185. For more detail on this joint statement, see also T. F. Torrance, "Agreed Statement on the Holy Trinity," *Trinitarian Perspectives*, 115–22.

[163]Ibid.

[164]Thomas Torrance's exposition of this position should be mandatory reading for all students of the doctrine of the Trinity. See his *The Christian Doctrine of God*, 180–93.

[165]It is admitted, nevertheless, that there is wording in this creed, mainly on Christology, that reflects a period after his death. See J. N. D. Kelly, *The Athanasian Creed* (London: Adam and Charles Black, 1964).

- The Father is given no priority. "Such as the Father is, such is the Son and such is the Holy Spirit." This is the first of many statements seeking to exclude subordinationism in any form.
- The Father is not the source of the being of the Son or the Spirit. This creed does not make the Father the *monarche* of the Son and the Spirit. The Spirit proceeds from the Father and the Son.
- No subordination in the *being* of the Son or the Spirit is allowed. The substance/being of God is one.
- No subordination in authority whatsoever is allowed. All three persons are said to be equally "almighty" and "Lord."
- The persons are differentiated by only one thing besides their personal identities: the Father is "unbegotten," the Son is "begotten," and the Spirit is "proceeding." This creed and the tradition do not allow that differentiation implies subordination in any form.
- In this Trinity "none is before or after another" (no hierarchical ordering) and "none is less than another" (no eternal subordination); all three are "co-eternal" and "co-equal."
- The Son is "only inferior to the Father as touching his manhood." As touching his "Godhead," he is "equal to the Father."

A comment on this last clause is needed. First, it is noted that in the authoritative original Latin, the word translated "inferior" is *minor*, which can be accurately translated as inferior, less than, or subordinated. Second, these words do not indicate that the Son, because he continues as God and man after his resurrection, is subordinated in the eternal or immanent Trinity, as some of my evangelical friends maintain. After his resurrection, the apostles are agreed, Christ rules as the sovereign, omnipotent Lord. This clause is to be interpreted in the light of Augustine's formulation of the doctrine of the Trinity, even if the wording used is not his.[166] For Augustine, Christ is equal to the Father "in the form of God" and less than, or inferior to, the Father in "the form of man," by which he means eternally equal and unqualified God in relation to the Father and the Spirit, temporally subordinated in his free decision to become man. His proof of this distinction is always Php 2:6–7, which limits the Son's subordination to the time of his earthly ministry. After going to the cross he is raised as Lord: all earthly limitations are left behind. He continues as God and man in the one person, but in his exaltation his humanity is glorified and he is given a "spiritual body" (1 Co 15:42–49). Following Calvin, later Reformed theologians clarify matters by making a contrast between the Son of God as man in the state of humiliation and the Son of God as man in the state of exaltation. J. N. D. Kelly says this clause is

---

[166]Kelly, *The Athanasian Creed*, 80.

"patently anti-Arian."[167] I thus conclude it speaks against the eternal subordination of the Son in any way whatsoever.

A more explicit repudiation of the *eternal* subordination of the Son in being, function, or authority than given in the Athanasian Creed is hard to imagine. The onetime Oxford professor Leonard Hodgson says the Athanasian Creed is the only one of the ancient creeds "that explicitly and unequivocally states the full Christian doctrine of God," and this creed, he adds, "express[es] rejection ... of all subordinationism."[168] Similarly, Kelly, another Oxford professor, says in the Athanasian Creed "the dominant idea [is] the perfect equality of the three persons."[169] Thus to confess this creed is to confess a rejection of any form of subordinationism and the belief that this is what the Bible teaches when read correctly.

Thomas Aquinas: A Brief Comment

Thomas Aquinas in the thirteenth century restated and developed Augustine's doctrine of the Trinity. Like Augustine, he began with and emphasized the unity of God before he discussed the distinction of the persons. With his stress on the divine unity of the Godhead, it is inconceivable for him that the Son and the Spirit might be subordinate in any way. Thomas lived in a patriarchal culture, and he endorses hierarchical ordering among heavenly beings and human beings, but when it comes to the Trinity he is countercultural. He wrote, "For among divine persons there is a kind of natural order but no hierarchic order."[170] Roman Catholic theologians have consistently followed him, totally rejecting subordinationism.

John Calvin

Calvin has no separate section on God. His chapter on the Trinity is his doctrine of God.[171] For him the God of Christian revelation is triune and the doctrine of the Trinity is "the most important doctrine of our religion."[172] In these two insights he anticipates the creative contribution of Barth to trinitarian theology in the mid-twentieth century. Foreshadowing contemporary practice, he eclectically draws on the best of the so-called Eastern and Western trinitarian traditions,[173] seeking always

---

[167]Ibid.

[168]Leonard Hodgson, *The Doctrine of the Trinity* (London: Nisbet, 1955), 102.

[169]Kelly, *Athanasian Creed*, 79.

[170]Thomas Aquinas, *Summa Theologiae*, 1.108.1 (p. 125).

[171]John Calvin, *Institutes of the Christian Religion*, vol. 1, ed. John T. Neill, trans. Ford Lewis Battles (London: SCM, 1960), chapter 13 (pp. 120–59).

[172]Quote taken from J. Bonnet's translation, *Letters of John Calvin*, vol. 1 (Philadelphia: Presbyterian Board of Publication, no date), letter 15.

[173]However, Richard H. Muller, *The Triunity of God*, vol. 4, *Post-Reformation Reformed Dogmatics* (Grand Rapids, Mich.: Baker, 2003), 72–73, argues that Calvin predominantly reflects the "Western" tradition.

to be faithful to the formulations of this doctrine as it had been passed on. However, as the Bible is his primary authority, he is not adverse to modifying terminology or explanations found in the tradition so that the Scriptures determine the theology he enunciates.

He soon discovered that appealing to the Bible did not silence his subordinationist opponents, who also appealed to Scripture, quoting texts that seemed to support their position. Like Athanasius and Augustine before him, he concluded that a theologically based hermeneutic was needed to read the Bible correctly, and like them he found this spelled out in Php 2:4–11. He returns to this text time and time again.[174] Here he sees the Scriptures teaching that in becoming man the Son willingly and freely chose to subordinate himself for our salvation. He took "the form of a slave ... and became obedient to the point of death." On this basis Calvin insists, like Athanasius and Augustine, that all texts that speak of the frailty, subordination, and obedience of the Son refer only to his incarnate existence. Eternally the Son is equal in divinity, majesty, and authority with the Father and the Spirit. He writes, "Laying aside the splendour of majesty, he showed himself obedient to his Father (cf. Phil. 2:8). Having completed this subjection, 'he was at last crowned with glory and honour' (Heb. 2:9) and exalted to the highest Lordship that before him 'every knee should bow' (Phil. 2:10)."[175]

Calvin begins his study of the Trinity with a discussion of what to call "the three." He is aware that some have objected to using the term *person*. For this reason he allows that the Greek equivalent word, *hypostasis*, or its Latin translation, *subsistentia* ("subsistence") may be used as alternatives. How the term *person* is understood, however, is for Calvin the key issue. His definition is given in a carefully worded paragraph.

> "Person," therefore, I call a "subsistence" in God's essence, which while related to the others, is distinguished by an incommunicable quality. By the term "subsistence" we would understand something different from "essence." For if the Word were simply God, and yet possessed no other characteristic mark, John would have wrongly have said that the Word was always with God (John 1:1). When immediately after he adds that the Word was also God himself, he recalls us to the essence as a unity. But because he could not be with God without residing in the Father, hence emerges the idea of a subsistence, which even though it has been joined with the essence by a common bond, and cannot be separated from it, yet has a special mark whereby it is distinguished from it.[176]

---

[174] Calvin, *Institutes*, 1.13.11 (p. 135), 24 (p. 152), 26 (p. 155), 2.11.12 (p. 461), 2.13.2, 3 (p. 476), 2.14.3 (p. 485), 2.16.5 (p. 508), 2.16.15 (p. 524).
[175] Ibid., 2.14.3 (p. 485).
[176] Ibid., 1.13.6 (p. 128).

In this important paragraph Calvin makes three matters explicit. First, the word *person* when used in trinitarian discourse is to be defined as a "subsistence in God's essence or being." Second, each of the three in their individual subsistence is to be distinguished from the others. It is important to note that what differentiates them as Father, Son, and Holy Spirit, Calvin says, is an "incommunicable quality." What this is he does not say, because we presume he recognizes that the Scriptures do not answer this question, but whatever it is, it is unique to each. Third, the three subsistences share one divine being or essence. In making these points Calvin excludes modalism, tritheism, and subordinationism all at the same time. The persons are distinguished, the one being of God is affirmed, and the equality of the three is established by stressing that they all share in the one divine essence or being. "Hence," he says, "it is quite clear that in God's essence reside three persons in whom one God is known."[177]

Time and time again Calvin warns against dividing the one Godhead. He allows only for "a distinction not a division" between the three. He writes, "Let us not then be led to imagine a Trinity of persons that keeps our thoughts distracted and does not at once lead them back to that unity."[178] His stress on the divine unity naturally leads him to endorse the doctrine of *perichoresis*, although he does not use this term. He writes, "The Father is wholly in the Son, the Son wholly in the Father, even as he himself declares: 'I am in the Father, and the Father is in me' (John 14:10)."[179] Torrance notes that Calvin has his own telling expression to speak of this profound unity of the three persons. It is the Latin term, "*in solidium*."[180]

Calvin gives four arguments based on Scripture for the full divinity of the Son: (1) He is the eternal Word which "abides everlastingly one and the same with God, and is God himself"[181]; (2) he is frequently called "the Lord," the very title also given to God, the Father; (3) he is said to do things that are the prerogatives of God alone (save, create, heal, raises the dead, etc.); and (4) to him we address our prayers and offer our worship. He deploys basically the same arguments to establish the deity of the Spirit.

When thinking of the person of Christ Calvin primarily thinks of him as the Mediator.[182] This is the Messiah's distinctive "office." Stephen Edmondson argues that when Calvin speaks of Christ's "office" he means in modern terms his "function" or "role."[183] His "office," "function," or "role" are simply a reflection of who

---

[177]Ibid., 1.13.16 (p. 140).

[178]Ibid., 1.13.17 (p. 141).

[179]Ibid., 1.13.19 (p. 143).

[180]Thomas Torrance, "Calvin's Doctrine," in *Trinitarian Perspectives: Towards Doctrinal Agreement* (Edinburgh: T & T Clark, 1994), 73.

[181]Calvin, *Institutes*, 1.13.7 (p. 130).

[182]Stephen Edmondson, *Calvin's Christology* (Cambridge: Cambridge University Press, 2004), 47. See the key section in Calvin's *Institutes*, 2.12.1–7.

[183]Ibid., 185–88.

Christ is. He functions as the Mediator because he *is* the Mediator. There can be for Calvin no separation between person and office or being and role, Edmonson says: "Christ does not merely play the part of the Mediator for Calvin: he is the Mediator, and this office or role has its particular color and shape in so far as it is personned by Christ. It is not insignificant to Calvin's understanding of Christ's office that the one who mediates God's wisdom and truth is, himself, in his divinity, the very presence of that Wisdom and Truth, only veiled in human nature so that we might receive it."[184]

The title *mediator* for Calvin does not indicate that Christ stands somewhere between humankind and God, that he is a subordinated mediator. As the Mediator he has to be man and God, but this in no way lessens his divine majesty, power, and authority. Edmondson says that for Calvin Christ the Mediator is "God in all of God's inscrutability and with all of God's privileges or attributes.... For Christ to be anything less would mean for him not to be really God at all."[185]

In arguing for the full divinity of the Son, Calvin reasons that because Christ does what only God can do he must be fully God, one in being with the Father. His works reflect his divine being, and the reverse, his divine being is reflected in his works. On this premise he explicitly speaks of the "deeds" Christ does as "the function of the Creator alone."[186] It is his view that the Father and Son work as one. He says that the Son "was constantly at work with the Father from the very beginning of the world."[187] In this argument Calvin is indicating that he believes unity of being necessitates unity in action and authority. Who the divine three *are*, and what they *do*, cannot be divided in any way. Torrance says, "Having shown that there is a oneness in being between the incarnate Son and the Father, Calvin goes on to show that there is also a oneness in agency and power between them."[188]

Thus Calvin never suggests that in their work/operations/functions/roles the Son and/or the Holy Spirit are eternally subordinated to the Father, or differentiated from the Father by what they do—just the opposite. The Father, Son, and Spirit are one in being, action, and authority. In his commentary on John he says, "We must therefore believe that there is a unity between the Father and the Son so that they have

---

[184]Ibid., 189.

[185]Ibid., 208. Calvin actually opposes those who argue that it is Christ as man who is the Mediator, quoting 1Ti 2:5 in support. See Edmondson, *Calvin's Christology*, 14–39. In the *Institutes*, 2.12.14 (p. 465), Calvin says Paul speaks of the Mediator as "the man Christ Jesus" because he wants his readers to realize that the Mediator is "one of ourselves." He is compassionate. Calvin then goes on to emphasize that the Mediator is both fully man and fully God. He must be both to fulfill this office or role.

[186]Calvin, *Institutes*, 1.13.12 (p. 136).

[187]Ibid., 1.13.7 (p. 130). Italics added.

[188]Torrance, "Calvin's Doctrine," 52.

nothing separate from each other."[189] For this reason, in contrast to many modern-day conservative evangelicals, Calvin never depicts the Father as being at the top of a chain of command as if in eternity he directs and the Son obeys. Such an idea would be totally alien to everything he believed about the Trinity.

Nevertheless, like Athanasius and the Cappadocians, Calvin accepts there is an "order" or structuring in how the three persons operate and relate to each other, but nothing that he says on this matter suggests that he thought this operational order implied hierarchical ordering in the eternal or immanent Trinity, and much would suggest he wanted to exclude this idea.[190] In approaching the matter of order in the Godhead, he admits hesitation lest he be misunderstood or give rise to error. "It is not fitting to suppress *the distinction* that we observe to be expressed in Scripture. It is this: to the Father is attributed the beginning of activity, and the fountain and wellspring of all things; to the Son, wisdom, counsel and the order and disposition of all things; but to the Spirit is assigned the power and efficacy of that activity. Indeed, although the eternity of the Father is also the eternity of the Son and the Spirit, since God could never exist apart from his wisdom and power, *and we must not seek in eternity a before or after,* nevertheless the observance of this *order* is not meaningless or superfluous, when the Father is thought of as first, then from him the Son and finally from both the Spirit."[191]

In this comment on order reflecting Basil's teaching,[192] Calvin first of all excludes hierarchical ordering in the eternal or immanent Trinity by saying there can be "*in eternity* no before or after" within the Godhead. Then second he intimates that this order applies only to what is revealed in the economy. It is what is seen and observed. In this order the Father as the creator is rightly thought of as "first."

For Calvin divine equality and operational order are not contradictory ideas. "But because the peculiar qualities in the persons carry an *order* within them, e.g., in

---

[189]John Calvin, *The Gospel According to St. John* (Edinburgh: Oliver and Boyd, 1959), 2, 141.

[190]Muller, *The Triunity of God*, 80, seems to me to be confused on this matter, if not mistaken. He says, "Calvin certainly allowed some subordination in the order of the persons—but order only, as indicated by the generation of the Son from the Father ... but he adamantly denied any subordination of divinity or essence." If he simply means that Calvin spoke of the Father as initiating the work undertaken by the Son through the Spirit there is no problem, but why use the word *subordination*? It seems, however, he does not have this in mind, because he appeals to the "generation of the Son from the Father" as proof of this subordination in order. The problem with this is that Calvin opposes the idea that the Father is the source of the Son's being or divinity—something Muller himself notes on p. 81 and pp. 324–25. On Calvin's teaching on the eternal generation of the Son see chapter 6 following. On p. 84 Muller then says Calvin accepted "a subordination" "in the order of the procession and operation of the persons." However, as we have just shown, Calvin did not subordinate the Son and the Spirit in operations. Muller returns to this matter again in a very brief comment on p. 324.

[191]Calvin, *Institutes*, 1.13.18 (p. 143).

[192]So Torrance, "Calvin's Doctrine of the Trinity," in *Trinitarian Perspectives*, 56.

the Father is the beginning and the source, so often as mention is made of the Father and the Son together, or the Spirit, the name of God is peculiarly applied to the Father. In this way, unity of essence is retained, and a reasoned *order* is kept, which yet takes nothing away from the deity of the Son and the Spirit."[193]

Thomas Torrance, commenting on Calvin on divine order, says, "[For him order] has to do not with status but with position, not with substance but with form, and not with power but with sequence. There is no difference between them [the divine three] in respect to being, power, or majesty, for each considered in himself is the one God who has his Being from himself alone. They are fully equal, for the whole Being (*tota essentia*) and the total nature (*tota natura*) of the one God is in each person."[194]

In dealing with the few biblical texts that can be read to imply the eternal subordination of the Son, Calvin determines to let tradition rule his interpretative decisions.[195] Like Athanasius and Augustine, he will not concede an interpretation of any text that might suggest a diminution in the eternal divinity, majesty, or authority of the Son. Passages where the Son is depicted as being subordinated or inferior to the Father Calvin reads as speaking only of the incarnational work of the Son.[196] He interprets them economically and soteriologically, not ontologically. Furthermore, he emphatically refuses to read back into the immanent or eternal Trinity the subordination of the Son seen in the incarnation. I give two examples where we can see Calvin's commitment to the tradition controlling his exegesis.

In commenting on Jn 14:28, "My Father is greater than I," which he maintains is often "twisted in various ways"[197] by those who want to "prove" that the Son is in some way eternally subordinated to the Father, he says:

> He [Jesus] places the Father in the higher rank, seeing the bright perfection of splendour that appears in heaven differs from that measure of glory which was seen in him when he was clothed in flesh.[198]

> Christ is here not drawing a comparison between the divinity of the Father and of himself, nor between his own human nature and the divine essence of the

---

[193]Calvin, *Institutes*, 1.13.20 (p. 144). Italics added.

[194]Torrance, "Calvin's Doctrine," 71–72.

[195]Robert Reymond, *A New Systematic Theology of the Christian Faith*, 2d ed. (Nashville: Nelson, 1998), 317–42, is of a different opinion. He argues that at points Calvin actually breaks with the Nicene tradition. In reply see Paul Owen, "Calvin and Catholic Trinitarianism: An Examination of Robert Reymond's Understanding of the Trinity and His Appeal to John Calvin," *Calvin Theological Journal* 35, no. 2 (2000): 262–82.

[196]Calvin, *Institutes*, 1.13.26 (p. 155).

[197]Calvin, *The Gospel According to John, Chapters 11 to 21*, trans. T. H. L. Parker (Grand Rapids, Mich.: Eerdmans, 1961), 89.

[198]Calvin, *Institutes*, 1.13.26 (p. 155).

Father, but rather between his present state and his heavenly glory to which he was shortly to be received.[199]

In contemporary conservative evangelical subordinationism, Paul's comment that God is "the head of Christ" (1Co 11:3) is a key text. It is read to teach that the Father *eternally* rules over the Son. Calvin asks, What "preeminence" do these words give to the Father in relation to the Son?

> The answer is, since he has made himself subject to the Father in our flesh, for, apart from that, being of one essence with the Father, he is equal with him. Let us bear in mind, therefore, that this is said about Christ the mediator. My point is that he is inferior to the Father because he has clothed himself with our nature, so that he might be the first born among many brothers.[200]

For Calvin the Father is only "the head" of Christ during the time Christ "made himself subject to the Father" by taking "our flesh." In his eternal being and role he is one with the Father. The great Reformer does not see in this comment any hint that the Father eternally rules over the Son.

How Calvin deals with the problematic idea that the Father is the *monarche* (sole origin), or the beginning, or the *principium* of the Son (and the Spirit) is significant.[201] Like Augustine, he argues that when the Son is thought of apart from the Father, he "exists of himself."[202] His divinity is not derived from another, and he is his own beginning (*arche*). However, when we think of the Son in relation to the Father, he is the Son *of* the Father, just as the Father is the Father *of* the Son, and these relational distinctions can never change. Calvin puts his case in this way:

> Christ with respect to himself is called God; with respect to the Father, Son. Again, the Father with respect to himself is called God; with respect to the Son, Father. In so far as he is called Father with respect to the Son, he is not the Son; in so far as he is called the Son with respect to the Father he is not the Father; in so far as he is called both Father with respect to himself, and Son with respect to himself, he is the same God. Therefore when we speak simply of the Son without regard to the Father, we well and properly declare him to be of himself; and for this reason we call him the *sole beginning*. But when we mark the relation that he has with the Father, we rightly make the Father the *beginning* of the Son.[203]

---

[199]Calvin, *The Gospel of John*, 90.

[200]John Calvin, *The First Epistle of Paul the Apostle to the Corinthians*, trans. John Frazer (Grand Rapids, Mich.: Eerdmans, 1960), 229.

[201]For what follows see Calvin, *Institutes*, 1.13.19 (the paragraph at the top of page 144), 1.13.23 (p. 149), and 1.13.25 (p. 154).

[202]Ibid., 1.13.25 (p. 154).

[203]Ibid., 1.3.19 (p. 144). Italics added. See also 1.13.23 (p. 149), 1.13.25 (p. 153).

Following this argument he then vehemently attacks those who argue that the deity of the Son and the Spirit are *derived* from God the Father as if he were "the sole God" who infused into them his own deity. He gives more space to rejecting derivative subordinationism than any other topic he deals with in his section on the Trinity. To suggest that God the Father is the "essence giver" or the sole source of deity, he says, is to "cast the Son down."[204] The Father, the Son, and the Spirit are emphatically differentiated by Calvin but not on the basis of differing degrees of deity, or differing work, or differing authority. For him the Father is eternally the Father and not the Son, and the Son and the Spirit are eternally themselves and no other.[205] Difference does not imply subordination.

As we conclude this outline of Calvin's doctrine of the Trinity, we are left wondering how so many evangelicals can claim that Calvin is an advocate of the eternal subordination of the Son in being, function, or authority. Nothing would seem further from the truth. It must be presumed that those who make this claim have either not read Calvin closely, or they have not understood him, or they are being disingenuous. Warfield and Torrance in their scholarly studies of Calvin's doctrine of the Trinity are agreed that the great reformer is opposed to subordinationism in any form. Warfield argues that Calvin wrote seeking the "elimination of the last remnants of subordinationism,"[206] being consistently in "inexpugnable opposition to subordinationists of all types."[207] As far as Torrance is concerned, Calvin "leaves no room for any element of subordinationism."[208]

Reformation Confessions

All of the Reformation confessions of faith seek to exclude tritheism, modalism, and subordinationism, but as these three errors were rejected by the Catholic Church and by the Nicene and Athanasian Creeds, what they say on the Trinity is usually brief and to the point. God is one divine essence or substance in three persons who are to be distinguished but not divided, being "equal in power and alike eternal."[209] A lengthier section on the Trinity is found in the Belgic Confession of 1561. Here we

---

[204]Ibid., 1.13.23 (p. 149). See also 1.13.25 (p. 154) for similar ideas.

[205]In chapter 6 following, how Calvin differentiates the divine three will be explored in more detail.

[206]B. B. Warfield, "Calvin's Doctrine of the Trinity," in *Calvin and Augustine* (Philadelphia: Presbyterian and Reformed, 1956), 230.

[207]Ibid., 251.

[208]Torrance, "Calvin's Doctrine of the Trinity," 66.

[209]So *The Augsburg Confession*, art. 1; *The Tetrapolitan Confession*, 1530, art. 2; *The First Confession of Basel*, 1534, art. 1; *The First Helvetic Confession of Faith*, 1536, art. 6; *The Confession of Faith Used by the English Congregation in Geneva*, 1556, art. 1; *The French Confession of Faith*, 1559, art. 6; *The Scots Confession*, 1560, art. 1; *The Thirty-Nine Articles of Religion*, 1563, art. 1.

are told that within the Trinity, "all three are co-eternal and co-essential. There is neither first nor last; for they are all three one, in truth, in power, in goodness, and in mercy" (art. 8). Then follow three more clauses giving first scriptural proofs for this doctrine of the Trinity and then what is to be believed about Jesus Christ. He is the "true, eternal, and almighty God, whom we evoke, worship and serve," and then a clause entitled on the Holy Spirit, "the true and eternal God." The Second Helvetic Confession of 1566, "the most widely received among Reformed Confessions,"[210] composed by Heinrich Bullinger, likewise expands on the brief paragraph on the Trinity found in most reformation confessions of faith. This confession opposes the "blasphemies" of those who teach that any person within the Trinity is "subservient or subordinate ... unequal in it, are greater or less ... (or) different with respect to character or will." The term *subservient* condemns those who teach that the Son must always obey the Father as a servant (i.e. he is eternally subordinate in work/role/function/operations), while the term *subordinate* condemns those who teach the Son is subordinate in being/essence/substance/nature.

Like the Nicene and Athanasian Creeds, the Reformation confessions of faith exclude subordinationism in any form. They are doctrinal statements outlining reformation trinitarian orthodoxy and rulings on how the Bible should be read by those who would claim to stand in the Reformation tradition.

And Finally, the Present

An important part of the case made for the eternal subordination of the Son by my debating opponents is the claim that what "we" teach the great theologians of the past taught and most contemporary theologians endorse today. We have seen the historical claim is false; now we consider contemporary support for this claim without going into any detail.[211] It has already been noted that from the time of Calvin until late in the twentieth century, most Protestant theologians lost interest in the doctrine of the Trinity, as did most Roman Catholic theologians. The tendency was to treat the Trinity as a formal doctrine that needed to be outlined and then left to one side. I called this earlier the time of exile for the doctrine of the Trinity. In this period, this doctrine was often inadequately expounded, and subordinationism was all too often uncritically accepted.

It is very different today. From the 1960s onwards there has been a steady flow of well-informed, scholarly studies on the Trinity, and as I pointed out in the first

---

[210]So A. C. Cochrane, *Reformed Confessions of the 16th Century* (London: SCM, 1966), 220. He gives the English translation of both the Belgic and Second Helvetic Confessions.

[211]It would take another chapter to go into detail on what exactly each of the more important contemporary trinitarian theologians taught. For detail readers should consult one or more of the many excellent recent introductions to this doctrine.

chapter of this book, one of the most important emphases has been a rejection of subordinationism in any form. I have read all the contemporary books on the Trinity on the shelves of the university library I use, as well as other books on this topic I have borrowed elsewhere or bought, including all the conservative evangelical works that endorse the eternal subordination of the Son. I have not found a Roman Catholic theologian who gives any support to the idea that the Son is eternally subordinated in any way, and only rarely a mainline Protestant who explores this possibility. Arthur Wainwright[212] and Colin Gunton[213] are the best examples of exceptions to the general rule, but both of them only open up the matter tentatively, admitting that they are questioning the tradition. It is true that Barth and those who follow him speak of the Son as Lord *and* servant, but they never let go of this dialectic.[214] The Son of God is never for Barth the subordinated Son *simpliciter*.

Many of the best introductions to the doctrine of the Trinity are written by Roman Catholics. They seldom say anything on the eternal subordination of the Son or hierarchical ordering in the Trinity after the time of the Arian disputes, because for them subordinationism in any form is a heresy excluded by the creeds and their doctrinal tradition. Of those who do discuss the error of subordinationism as an ongoing problem, I found Edmund Fortman had the most to say on this matter and was most aware of its insidious nature. This erudite Catholic theologian is adamant that to eternally subordinate the Son in any way is a grave theological error.[215]

Post-1970s' evangelical theologians who have written on the Trinity and are not preoccupied with the permanent subordination of women do not endorse the eternal subordination of the Son. However, they seldom delve into this issue, because like the Roman Catholic scholars just mentioned, they consider subordinationism and hierarchical ordering in the Trinity a heresy proscribed by the creeds and confessions. The

---

[212]Arthur W. Wainwright, *The Trinity in the New Testament* (London: SPCK, 1962). Wainwright's book is an important study on what the Bible says on the Trinity. As an exegete he notes that some sayings in the Gospel could imply the Son's subordination (p. 179), and he finds similar texts in Paul, especially 1Co 15:24–28 (p. 187). However, later he says these texts do not teach "subordinationism" (p. 194). It is also to be noted that alongside his few comments on texts that can be read to subordinate the Son, he says far more on texts and passages that indicate that Father and Son are coequal God. Wainwright published in 1962 and thus has no knowledge of the modern renaissance in trinitarian theology and its insights.

[213]Most of what Gunton says on the Trinity is perfectly orthodox, but early in his career as a disciple of Barth he speaks of the Son as Lord and servant. Later in his career as a professional theologian, he begins to question historic orthodoxy's stress on the coequality of the persons. In the concluding chapter of this book, I end with a postscript in which I discuss Gunton's views

[214]On Barth and his disciples, see the concluding chapter of this book.

[215]Edmund Fortman, *The Triune God*, 56–57, 61, 62, 68, 106, 122, 123, 140, 141, 150, 152, 263, 280.

specific doctrine of the *eternal role or functional subordination of the Son* is not mentioned, either because they are unaware that some evangelicals are teaching this or because they do not want to enter this contentious territory. Thus the excellent introductions to the doctrine of the Trinity by Christopher Kaiser,[216] Charles Sherlock,[217] Gerald Bray,[218] Roger Olson and Christopher Hall,[219] and Stanley Grenz[220] are of one mind: the Bible and creedal orthodoxy disallow any suggestion that the Son or the Spirit are eternally subordinated to the Father. Thomas F. Torrance, who also stands in the evangelical tradition broadly defined, is implacably opposed to any suggestion that the Son is subordinated in any way in the immanent or eternal Trinity.[221] The respected conservative evangelical systematic theologian Millard Erickson has written the only general introduction to the doctrine of the Trinity that specifically opposes the novel thesis that the Son of God can be eternally subordinated in role or function without implying his ontological subordination or inferiority. He says, "A temporal, functional subordination without inferiority of essence seems possible, but not an eternal subordination. And to speak of the superiority of the Father to the Son while denying the inferiority of the Son to the Father must be contradictory."[222]

Erickson embraces what is called "a social doctrine of the Trinity," speaking of "three centers of consciousness" in the Trinity, and an egalitarian model, speaking of the "mutual submission" of the divine persons. For him, "The Trinity is a communion of three persons, three centers of consciousness, who exist and always have existed in union with one another and in dependence on one another … Each is essential to the life of the others, and to the life of the Trinity. They are bound to one another in love, *agape* love, which therefore unites them in the closest and most intimate of relationships. This unselfish, *agape* love makes each more concerned for the other than for himself. There is therefore a mutual submission of each to each of the others and a mutual glorifying of one another. There is complete equality of the three."[223]

First we found that the great theologians of the past, the creeds, and the Reformation confessions gave no support to the idea that the Son of God is eternally

---

[216]Christopher Kaiser, *The Doctrine of God* (London: Marshall, Morgan and Scott, 1982).

[217]Charles Sherlock, *God on the Inside* (Canberra, Aust.: Acorn, 1991).

[218]Gerald Bray, *The Doctrine of God* (London: Inter-Varsity, 1993).

[219]Roger E. Olson and Christopher A. Hall, *The Trinity* (Grand Rapids, Mich.: Eerdmans, 2002).

[220]Stanley J. Grenz, *Rediscovering the Triune God: The Trinity in Contemporary Theology* (Minneapolis: Fortress, 2004).

[221]See Torrance's books *The Trinitarian Faith* and *The Christian Doctrine of God*.

[222]Millard Erickson, *God in Three Persons: A Contemporary Interpretation of the Trinity* (Grand Rapids, Mich.: Baker, 1995), 309.

[223]Ibid., 331.

subordinate to the Father; indeed they passionately opposed this teaching. Now we have seen that contemporary theologians, including most evangelical ones, are totally opposed to the idea that the Son of God is eternally subordinated to the Father. The doctrine of an eternally subordinated Son in function and authority is an idiosyncratic and dangerous doctrine found today only in the writings of evangelicals committed to the permanent subordination of women.

Back to the Beginning

At the commencement of this chapter I said we were asking five questions of the tradition. We have found that with one voice our historical sources have answered with a firm *no* to each question.

1. No, the Son is not in any way less than, inferior to, or eternally subordinated to the Father. The Father, Son, and Spirit are one in being, work, and authority.

2. No, the Father, Son, and Spirit are not ordered hierarchically in being, function, or authority. There is an order in how the divine three are revealed and how they operate in the world, but this is a disposition, not a sub-ordering.

3. No, we cannot allow any division to be made between the one being/essence/nature/substance of the divine three and what they do—their works/operations/functions/roles. They are one in person and work, being and function. Who they are and what they do is one.

4. No, we cannot allow any division or separation to be made between what the Father does and what the Son does. They do different things but they are never divided in their operations/works/functions. Father, Son, and Spirit always work inseparably and in unity.

5. No, speaking of the Son as "begotten of the Father," or of the Father as the *monarche* (sole source) of the person of the Son and the Spirit, or confessing that the Son is "God from God, Light from Light, true God from true God" (the Nicene Creed) do not suggest that the Son is dependent on the Father for his divinity, being, or authority, or that he is eternally subordinated to the Father. The Father, Son, and Spirit are "coeternal," "coequal," and alike omnipotent God.

THE FATHER AND THE SON DIVIDED OR UNDIVIDED IN POWER AND AUTHORITY

We now come to the most fundamental and distinctive element in the contemporary evangelical doctrine of the Trinity that I am disputing: the eternal subordination of the Son in authority. Professor Wayne Grudem is emphatic that this idea stands right at the heart of his understanding of the Trinity. It is his view that the Father has "the role of commanding, directing, and sending," and the Son the role of "obeying, going as the Father sends, and revealing God to us."[1] It is differing authority, he says, that primarily distinguishes the divine persons. He writes, "Authority and submission between the Father and the Son ... and the Holy Spirit, *is the fundamental difference* between the persons of the Trinity."[2] And again, "If we did not have such differences in authority in the relationships among the members of the Trinity, then we would not know of any differences at all."[3] There is for him nothing more important than this authority structure in the Trinity and between men and women. It is "the *most fundamental* aspect of interpersonal relationships in the entire universe."[4]

---

[1] Wayne Grudem, *Systematic Theology: An Introduction to Biblical Doctrine* (Grand Rapids, Mich.: Zondervan, 1995), 250.

[2] Wayne Grudem, ed., *Biblical Foundations for Manhood and Womanhood* (Wheaton, Ill.: Crossways, 2002), 31.

[3] Wayne Grudem, *Evangelical Feminism and Biblical Truth* (Sisters, Ore.: Multnomah, 2004), 433.

[4] Ibid., 429. Italics added.

The 1999 *Sydney Anglican Diocesan Doctrine Commission Report*, "The Doctrine of the Trinity and Its Bearing on the Relationship of Men and Women,"[5] also makes the eternal subordination of the Son in authority the most fundamental issue. The whole document is predicated on the premise that the Father is (authoritatively) "head" over the Son just as husbands in the home and men in the church are (authoritatively) "head" over women. In this report the eternal subordination of the Son in authority is predicated on the differences in the being or nature of the person of the Son, not simply in differing roles or functions, and it is said to be involuntary. The authors write, "The Son's obedience to the Father arises from the *very nature of his being as Son. His freedom consists in doing what is natural to him, which is to submit to his Father ... he is incapable of doing other than the Father's will*."[6] His obedience to the Father is not "voluntary, temporary, and personal."[7] Rather it reflects "the *essence* of the eternal relationship between them."[8]

Robert Doyle, a key contributor to this report, writing in 2004 is still arguing for "the priority of the Father" in authority in the Godhead. He designates the Father the "eternal Monarch" or sole ruler and says the Son defines himself "in subordination to that monarchy."[9] The American evangelical theologian Bruce Ware is of the same opinion. In rejecting the egalitarian case that the Son is only subordinated in authority to the Father in taking the form of a servant and in becoming man, he says, "An eternal relationship of authority and obedience is grounded in the eternal, immanent, inner-trinitarian relations of Father, Son, and Holy Spirit."[10] Then later he adds, "The authority-obedience relation of Father and Son in the immanent Trinity is *mandatory* if we are to account for God the Father's purposes to elect and save."[11]

Robert Letham in his book *The Holy Trinity in Scripture, History, Theology, and Worship* more carefully words his case, but he too makes the eternal obedience of the Son to the Father basic to his doctrine of the Trinity.[12] He does not adopt the language of "role" and "function," and he rejects that the divine Father-Son

---

[5] This document is quoted in full in my book *The Trinity and Subordinationism* (Westmont, Ill.: InterVarsity, 2002), 122–37. For the original see *Year Book of the Diocese of Sydney* (Sydney, NSW: Diocesan Registry, 2000), 538–50.

[6] Par. 18. Italics added.

[7] Par. 32, 33.

[8] Ibid. Italics added.

[9] Robert Doyle, "Are We Heretics? A Review of *The Trinity and Subordinationism* by Kevin Giles," *The Briefing* (April 2004): 13.

[10] Bruce Ware, "Tampering with the Trinity: Does the Son Submit to the Father?" in *Biblical Foundations for Manhood and Womanhood*, ed. Wayne Grudem (Wheaton, Ill.: Crossway, 2002), 242.

[11] Ibid., 250. Italics added.

[12] Robert Letham, *The Holy Trinity in Scripture, History, Theology, and Worship* (Phillipsburg, N.J.: P&R, 2004).

relationship should be defined in terms of the human father-son relationship.[13] However, on the absolutely central issue in this debate he is convinced that the Son is eternally set under the Father's authority.[14] "The Son submits in eternity to the Father." "Being God he serves the Father."[15] "His human obedience reflects his divine submission."[16] Letham says this does not imply hierarchical ordering, which he recognizes is an Arian error, but his denial would seem to be without substance. If the Son is eternally set under the authority of the Father, and the Spirit eternally set under the Father and the Son, then this is hierarchical ordering. In support of his case he quotes Barth. Barth does speak of the obedience of the Son as God, but as I will show later, the obedient Christ for Barth is God identified with man.[17] What is more, for Barth the divine Son is always both Lord and servant at one and the same time. The other argument Letham uses to make his case for the eternal submission of the Son is his human nature. He reasons that if Christ was subordinated as man, as all agree, he must be eternally subordinated, because he continues to be man after his resurrection. It is accepted, of course, that Christ continues as God and man (1Co 15:49; 1Ti 2:5–6). What is not accepted is that this indicates that he is eternally subordinated in authority to the Father. In the resurrection he is exalted to the highest place to reign as the omnipotent Lord.[18] All the limitations that his taking on human flesh entailed are left behind (1Co 15:42–50). He is no longer God and man in the state of humiliation. He is now God and man in the state of exaltation. After his resurrection he is unambiguously revealed as equal God in all majesty, glory, and authority. As such he is not eternally subordinated or submissive to the Father, with whom he is one.

Similarly, the English evangelical theologian Thomas Smail in his book *Like Father, Like Son* distinguishes and divides the Father and the Son on the basis of differing authority. He says, "The distinctive function of the Father"[19] is his "initiating sovereignty."[20] He is the "protype of leadership."[21] The Son's self-defining characteristic is his "attentive responsiveness."[22] Obedience to the Father is what is "proper to his Sonship."[23] He sums up his position in these words: "The Father sovereignly initiates,

---

[13] Ibid., 398.

[14] Ibid., 392–404.

[15] Ibid., 402.

[16] Ibid., 403.

[17] See the concluding chapter on Barth.

[18] Louis Berkhof, *Systematic Theology* (London: Banner of Truth, 1958), 344.

[19] Thomas Smail, *Like Father, Like Son* (Milton Keyes, Bucks.: Paternoster, 2005), 159.

[20] Ibid., 103.

[21] Ibid., 161.

[22] Ibid., 104–5.

[23] Ibid., 105.

the Son obediently executes."[24] The title of Smail's book, *Like Father, Like Son*, captures accurately orthodoxy. The Son is "like"[25] the Father in all things, except that he is the Son and not the Father. However, Smail's primary thesis directly contradicts orthodoxy on this critical and fundamental matter. For him, and all others who argue for the eternal subordination or submission of the Son, the Son is *unlike* the Father in authority.

What these evangelicals are seeking to support by arguing that the Son eternally obeys the Father is the authority of husbands in the home and men in the church. They want us to believe that the Son of God obeys the Father like women should obey the men set over them by God. For this reason we are constantly told "the priority of the Father" must be upheld. Every conservative evangelical article or book arguing for the eternal obedience of the Son has this agenda dictating how the doctrine of the Trinity is to be understood.

The Supporting Evidence

Two arguments are commonly used to give credence to this idea, one analogical in nature and one textual. First, appeal is made to the human father-son relationship. In the earthly sphere, we are told, human fathers have authority over sons. It is the same in the heavenly sphere; the divine Father has authority over the Son. Wayne Grudem writes, "God the Father has always been the Father and has always related to the Son as a father relates to his son." "The [divine] Father has greater authority. He has a leadership role among all the members of the Trinity that the Son and the Holy Spirit do not have."[26] Bruce Ware similarly says, "Clearly, a central part of the notion of father is that of fatherly authority."[27] This indicates, he says, that within the immanent Trinity there is "an eternal relationship of authority and obedience." The Father has authority over the Son.[28] Likewise, the Australian evangelical theologian Robert Doyle argues that the divine Father must rule over the Son because he is a father. Human fathers command; sons obey. He writes, "The Father is a real father and the triune Son a real son. Neither names are metaphorical."[29] This reasoning leads to what Daniel Doriani calls "the family order/church order argument."[30] God the Father's authority typifies

---

[24] Ibid., 107.

[25] In this usage I take the word *like* to mean "alike," virtually identical although differentiated as Father and Son. I assume the book title is supposed to reflect the words of the Athanasian Creed, "Such as the Father is, such is the Son."

[26] Grudem, *Systematic Theology*, 459.

[27] Ware, "Tampering with the Trinity," 245.

[28] Ibid., 242.

[29] Doyle, "Are We Heretics?" 14.

[30] In A. Kostenberger, T. Schreiner, and H. Scott Baldwin eds., *Women in the Church* (Grand Rapids, Mich.: Baker, 1995), 260.

the kind of leadership expected of men in the home and the church. As plausible as this analogical appeal to human relationships to explain divine relationships may sound to those who advocate the eternal subordination of the Son of God in authority, it sets human experience over biblical revelation. Divine relations are defined in terms of human experience rather than on what Scripture reveals.

Human language is never adequate to speak about God, but this is all we have. It has long been recognized that the words we humans use of God are metaphorical or analogical in nature. Our language can capture accurately something of the triune Christian God, yet it never captures fully the reality to which it points. For this reason our words used of God should never be taken literally, as if every aspect of a human word applied to God. The words most relevant for this study, *father* and *son*, are classic examples of what we are talking about. In using the terms *father* and *son*, Scripture tells us the first two persons of the Trinity are *in some ways like* human fathers and sons. Yet it is obvious that in some ways the divine Father and Son are unlike human fathers and sons. The divine Father has no father and most theologians would say he is asexual, to mention only two matters that distinguish him from all human fathers. Likewise the divine Son has no son(s) and never can, and he is designated Lord (master, king) in the same way as the Father. What is implied when the Bible speaks of the divine "Father" and "Son" only the Bible can tell us, not human experience. In our study of Scripture, we found that in the New Testament these two terms spoke predominantly of the intimacy, mutuality, and love between the Father and the Son and of the Son's dignity and royal rule. In what follows in this chapter, we will consider how the best of theologians from the past have understood the Father-Son relationship.

The second way support is found for the idea that the Father eternally rules over the Son is by appeal to a particular interpretation of 1Co 11:3. How this text should be translated is fundamental to how it is understood. I give the rendering found in *Today's New International Version.*[31] "The head of every man is Christ, and the head of the woman is man, and the head of Christ is God." In our study of biblical teaching we considered what Paul might have been wanting to say in this perplexing comment and concluded from the context that he was not speaking of a hierarchy in authority with the Father ruling over the Son, the Son over men, and men over women, as my debating opponents want us to believe.[32] Rather, he was speaking of three differentiated relationships in which in each case one party could be considered the *kephale*—and in this context this Greek word does not mean "head over" or "authority over." Here

---

[31] *Today's New International Version* (Grand Rapids, Mich.: Zondervan, 2002).
[32] For our exegetical treatment of this text see chapter 2.

it is also to be remembered that the predominant way the Son is depicted after the resurrection is as "Lord," never as the obedient servant. Moreover, Paul twice speaks of the resurrected Christ as "head over all things" (Eph 1:22; Col 2:10).

One Question Only

In this chapter only one question is before us. Does the tradition indicate that the best of theologians from the past and today and the creeds and Reformation confessions teach that the Father and the Son are *eternally differentiated and divided by power and authority*? Are we to believe that orthodoxy thinks of the divine Father as the supreme monarch who commands and the Son, like all sons, is the one who must obey? Is the Trinity to be understood as a threefold hierarchy in which there are descending degrees of power and authority?

All those with whom I am debating claim that their doctrine of the Trinity in which the Father rules and the Son obeys is exactly what the creeds and the great theologians of the past teach, and I am the one "tampering" with the historic doctrine of the Trinity. In the last chapter we examined their claim that the Son is eternally subordinated in function to the Father and found it wanting. Neither the Bible nor the tradition give this idea any support. Indeed, both speak clearly against it. Now we will examine their claim that the church has always believed that the Father is eternally set over the Son in authority. The Father rules; the Son obeys.

The Tradition

Monarchianism

In the second and third centuries the primary concern of Christian theologians when speaking of the Trinity was to safeguard the unity of God. In this context the word *monarchy* (Gk *monarchia*) came into prominence. Literally, the word means "sole rule" (*mon* = one, *archy* = rule or authority), but it was understood more as a metaphor for kingship and monotheism.[33] The term was introduced into Christian theology by the Apologists to repudiate any suggestion that they were polytheists because they spoke of Father, Son, and Spirit as God.[34] There was only one divine ruler, they argued, even if there is a triad. How God could be one and three was never satisfactorily explained by the Apologists. Tertullian was the first to attempt a solution. In his treatise *Against Praxeas*, who believed there was only one God who revealed himself in three modes or ways (an error later called modalism), Tertullian argued that the one God shared his rule with his Son and the Spirit without ever compromising his unity. He says, "I am sure that *monarchia* (or monarchy) has no other meaning than

---

[33] George Leonard Prestige, *God in Patristic Thought* (London: SPCK, 1959), 94.
[34] Justin, *Dialogue*, 1.3; Tatian, *To the Greeks*, 14.1; Theophilus, *To Autolycus*, 2.4, 2.35, 2.38.

single and individual rule."[35] Nevertheless, he adds, the rule or monarchy of the one God does not exclude the idea that this rule can be shared with others, especially with a Son. "I contend no dominion so belongs to one only, as his own, or is in such a sense singular, or is in such a sense a monarchy [Lat. *Monarchiam*], as not also to be administered through other persons most closely connected with it, and whom itself has provided as officials to itself. If moreover, there be a son belonging to him whose monarchy [Lat. *Monarchia*] it is, it does not forthwith become divided and cease to be a monarchy."[36]

What is of special interest to us is that despite this argument Tertullian did not distinguish the power and authority of the Father, the Son, and the Spirit in the exercise of this rule. He goes on to say that the Son is a "sharer" in this dominion since it is "equally his"; the two "are inseparable"; and the Son and the Spirit are the "instruments of his might, nay his power itself and the entire system of his monarchy."[37]

The Arian Heresy

Arius was quite convinced that the Son is eternally set under the Father's authority. The Son must do as the Father commands. For Arius and all who in the fourth century were called Arians, God the Father was an unoriginated Monad, and for this reason the Son and the Spirit were radically different and unlike him. They could be spoken of as "God" but not in the same sense as the Father. On this basis the Arians taught that the Father and the Son (in the early stage of the debate it was these two divine persons who were always in focus) were of different being and authority. That Arius ontologically subordinated the Son to the Father is well known. What is less well known and adequately recognized is that he and all the Arians also subordinated the Son in authority. Richard Hanson in his monumental study of Arianism says the Arians consistently taught that the Son "does the Father's will and exhibits *obedience and subordination* to the Father, and adores and praises the Father, *not only in his earthly ministry but in Heaven*."[38]

In their innovative study *Early Arianism*, Robert Gregg and Dennis Groh also point out that the eternal obedience of the Son was a primary element in Arian theology.[39]

---

[35] Tertullian, *Against Praxeas*, in *The Ante-Nicene Fathers*, vol. 3, *Latin Christianity: Its Founder, Tertullian*, ed. J. Donaldson (Grand Rapids, Mich.: Eerdmans, 1973), 1.3 (p. 599).

[36] Ibid.

[37] Ibid.

[38] R. P. C. Hanson, *The Search for the Christian Doctrine of God: The Arian Controversy, 318–381* (Grand Rapids, Mich.: Baker, 2005), 103. Italics added.

[39] Robert Gregg and Dennis Groh, *Early Arianism: A View of Salvation* (Philadelphia: Fortress, 1981). What is distinctive to his book is the thesis that the early Arians (principally Arius, Asterius the Sophist, and Eusebius of Nicomedia) were more concerned about how salvation was achieved by Christ than with the being of Christ the Son of God.

They say, "At *the center* of Arian theology was a redeemer obedient to his Father's will, whose life of virtue modeled perfect creaturehood and hence a path of salvation for all Christians."[40] And for "Arius and his fellow thinkers ... the Father and the Son relationship [was] a relationship in which the former was prior, superior, and dominant.... Conceived relationally rather than ontologically [it] was marked by dependence rather than co-equality."[41]

What authority the Son had was of a "derivative character."[42] The supreme Father gave it to him: "The derivative character of the power and authority manifest in Jesus' ministry was traced by Arian exegetes from a series of biblical texts which spoke of the things bestowed on him by the Father."[43] Thus, "the savior who the early Arians discovered in Scripture and promulgated in their writings was never far from an obedient servant who followed God's commands."[44]

What completely surprised me in reading this book was that the way Gregg and Groh described the essence of Arianism is almost identical to how contemporary evangelicals depict the divine Father-Son relationship. The Father is prior and supreme. He rules over the Son. Any authority the Son has is derived from the Father.

Athanasius

In contrast to Arius and my evangelical debating opponents, Athanasius will not allow any disjunction or separation between the Father and the Son in being, work, *or authority*. The God of the Bible, he holds, is not a monad who has a subordinate Son. He is for all eternity a triad of inseparable and equal divine persons. He writes, "The faith of Christians acknowledges the blessed Triad as unalterable and perfect and ever what it was."[45] He stresses repeatedly that the Father and the Son are eternally correlated or paired. "We may neither say that God [the Father] was ever without his Word, nor that the Son was ever non-existent."[46] Because the Son and Father are inseparably one God, Athanasius asks the Arians, "Must not he who is perfect be equal to God?"[47] He of course believes only an affirmative answer is possible. Athanasius' tenacious belief that the Father and the Son cannot be divided or separated in any way leads him to repeatedly lay down, as already noted, what I call the Athanasian

---

[40] Ibid., x, italics added.

[41] Ibid., 91.

[42] Ibid., 6.

[43] Ibid., 91. For this Arian argument and Athanasius' reply, see Athanasius, "Discourses," in *The Nicene and Post-Nicene Fathers of the Christian Church* (henceforth *NPNF*), eds. Philip Schaff and Henry Wace (Grand Rapids, Mich.: Eerdmans, 1971), 4:3.36 (p. 413) .

[44] Ibid., 24.

[45] Athanasius, "Discourses," in *NPNF* 4:1.18 (p. 317).

[46] Ibid., 1.19 (p. 317).

[47] Ibid., 1.10 (p. 327).

"rule": "The same things are said of the Son which are said of the Father, except for calling him Father."[48]

From this it follows that Athanasius cannot allow that the Son is eternally set under the Father in authority. Whatever his personal failings may have been as a man, as a theologian the logic and consistency of his reasoning is without fault. At no point at any time does he waver from his belief that the Father and the Son are inseparably one in being, work/function, *and authority*. All his efforts are put to refuting the Arian arguments that seek to radically differentiate the Father and the Son by depicting him as less in deity and authority. To argue that Athanasius teaches the "monarchy" (sole rule) of the Father and the eternal subordination in authority of the Son, thereby dividing the Father and the Son, is quite mistaken. Nothing could be further from the truth. However, the Australian theologians Mark Baddeley and Robert Doyle both argue just this. Baddeley says for Athanasius "Fatherhood and authority" and "Sonship and obedience" asymmetrically differentiate the divine persons.[49] Doyle similarly holds that Athanasius taught that the Father alone is the eternal "monarch," or ruler over all. The Son defines himself "in subordination to that monarchy."[50] The *monarchy* or sole rule of the Father, Doyle argues, is basic to Athanasius' understanding of divine Fatherhood. I am not convinced. In every case where Athanasius speaks of God the Father ruling, the Son is ruling with him. The Father and his *Logos* or Wisdom rule conjointly.[51] When we consider Athanasius' use of the particular Greek word *monarchia*, Doyle's thesis completely collapses. According to Muller's concordance,[52] Athanasius uses the Greek word *monarchia* only four times, and none of them indicate that he ever thought of the Father ruling alone, let alone ruling over the Son. In the first usage Athanasius is quoting Bishop Dionysius with approval for repudiating those who "divide" "the divine monarchy" which is "a Triad" for all eternity.[53] In the fourth "Discourse Against the Arians," probably not written by Athanasius, yet reflecting

---

[48] Athanasius, "Discourses," in *NPNF* 4:3.4 (p. 395), 3.5 (p. 395), 3.6 (p. 396); Athanasius, "The Councils," in *NPNF* 4:3.49 twice (p. 476).

[49] Mark Baddeley, "The Trinity and Subordinationism," *Reformed Theological Review* 63, no. 1 (2004): 13. In support of his ideas Baddeley quotes from Athanasius, "Four Discourses Against the Arians," in *NPNF* 4:2.3–4 (pp. 334–35), where the great Alexandrian bishop says all fathers have authority over their sons. Sadly he did not read on. Next Athanasius argues that this human idea does not apply to the Son of God. He says in 2.15.14 (p. 355) that although the Son "took a servant's form, yet the assumption of the flesh did not make a servant of the Word, who was by nature Lord."

[50] Doyle, "Are We Heretics?" 13.

[51] Athanasius, "Against the Heathen," in *NPNF* 4:40.2, 4, 5 (p. 24), "On Luke 10:22," in *NPNF* 4:1–6 (pp. 87–90), and "Defense of the Nicene Council," in *NPNF* 4:30 (p. 171).

[52] G. Muller, *Lexicon Athanasianum* (Berlin: de Gruyter, 1953), col. 921.

[53] Athanasius, "Defense of the Nicene Definition," in *NPNF* 4:5.26 (p. 167).

his teaching,[54] the point is reiterated. There can only be "monarchy," one rule, and it includes the Father and the Son: "So the Father and the Son are two, yet the Monad of the Godhead is indivisible and inseparable. And thus too we preserve one beginning (Gk *Arche)* of Godhead and not two beginnings, whence there is strictly a monarchy (Gk *Monarchia)*."[55]

The only two other uses of this word in Athanasius' writings appear in the text of a discursive confession circulated by *Homoean* Arians that he quotes at some length. First he quotes them as saying that they reject Marcellus of Ancyra's teaching denying the eternal existence of the Son "on the pretence of supporting the divine monarchy."[56] Then later he quotes their confession that says that although the Father and the Son are God, it is to be understood that "the Father alone being head over the whole universe wholly and over the Son himself, and the Son subordinated to the Father … such is the divine monarchy towards Christ."[57] In both these examples of the use of the Greek word *monarchia*, referring to the sole rule of the Father, Athanasius is quoting from those he thinks are guilty of "blasphemy" and of falling into "the Arian heresy."[58] What Athanasius cites as erroneous teaching, the sole rule of the Father and thus the rule of the Father over the Son, Doyle claims Athanasius teaches.

For Athanasius the Son's incarnation did not involve any diminution of his divinity or authority, but it did involve him in becoming a servant and in being "obedient to the point of death, even death on a cross." He writes, "For though the Word existing in the form of God took a servant's form, yet the assumption of the flesh did not make a servant of the Word, who was by nature Lord."[59]

In their quest to make God the Father preeminent, true God alone, all the fourth-century Arians developed arguments for the Son's subordination in work and authority. Many of these arguments depended on appeal to human relationships and on the presumption that human language used of God is to be taken literally. Thus, as we have already noted, the Arians made much of the fact that the Bible speaks of a "Father" and a "Son." On the basis of how these terms are used in human speech, they concluded that the Son must have been brought into existence in time like all sons, and like all sons be set under his Father's authority. In book 1 of his "Discourses Against the Arians," a good example of how Athanasius replied to such reasoning is found. To the assertion by Athanasius that the Son is in all things one with the Father, the Arians countered

---

[54] Hanson, *The Search*, 418.

[55] Athanasius, "Discourses," in *NPNF* 4:4.1 (p. 433). It is generally thought that the fourth discourse reflects Athanasius' ideas but he did not write it.

[56] Athanasius, "Councils of Ariminum and Seleucia," in *NPNF* 4:26 (p. 463).

[57] Ibid. (p. 464).

[58] Ibid., 4 (p. 452).

[59] Ibid., 2.14 (p. 355), 2.50 (p. 375).

by saying, "If the Son is the Father's offspring and image, and is like in all things to the Father, then it necessarily holds that as he [the Son] is begotten, so he begets, and he too becomes a father."[60] "Authors of blasphemy," Athanasius exclaims. "Sooner than confess that the Son is the Father's image they [the Arians] conceive material and earthly ideas concerning the Father."[61] Athanasius agrees that the Son may be said to be "begotten of the Father," but he will not allow that this terminology suggests that the Father is greater or more powerful than the Son. Rather he insists that all the attributes of the Father—"eternal, immortal, powerful, light, king, sovereign, God, Lord, creator, maker"—belong to the Son as well, so that "He who has seen the Son has seen the Father."[62] For Athanasius the Scriptures indicate that the Father and the Son are one in being, inseparable in operations, and indivisible in power and authority. To argue otherwise, he believes, is to build one's ideas of God on earthbound human family relations, as Arius did,[63] Athanasius held that this practice resulted in a "doctrine alien to the divine oracles."[64] By depicting God in human terms, he concludes, the Arians fell into idolatry. "Wherefore when the Arians have these speculations and views, do they not rank themselves with the Gentiles? For they too, as these, worship the creature rather than God the creator of all."[65] For Athanasius the binding rule is, "If God be not as a man, as he is not, we must not impute to him the attributes of man."[66]

Towards the end of his third "Discourse Against the Arians," we find a long section in which Athanasius argues against another variant of this kind of reasoning.[67] Apparently the early Arians held that the Son was created by the will of the Father like all human sons. On this premise the Son is dependent on the Father for his existence, subordinated to the Father, and created in time. What the Arians wanted to uphold, Gregg and Groh say, is "the derivative character of the power and authority" of the Son of God.[68] Athanasius in reply writes, "For he who says, 'The Son came to be at the divine will,' has the same meaning as another who says, 'Once he was not,' and 'He is a creature.'"[69] The idea that the Son came into being by divine "will and pleasure" Athanasius finds nowhere in Scripture and much to

---

[60] Ibid., 1.21 (p. 318).

[61] Ibid.

[62] Ibid.

[63] He pours scorn on their reasoning. "If then God be a man, let him also become a parent as a man, so that his Son should become a father of another." Ibid., 1.21 (p. 319).

[64] Ibid., 1.10 (p. 312).

[65] Ibid., 3.16 (p. 402).

[66] Ibid., 1.21 (p. 319).

[67] Ibid., 3.58–67 (pp. 425–31).

[68] Gregg and Groh, *Early Arianism*, 91.

[69] Athanasius, "Discourses," in *NPNF* 4:3.59 (p. 426).

the contrary,[70] and he says it suggests that the Son is created by God the Father, and thus there are two Gods, a greater and a lesser—"polytheism" in other words.[71] In the context of this discussion Athanasius says the Son is not *of* the will of the Father; rather "he is himself the Father's living counsel (*patros agathon boulema*), and power and framer of things that seemed good to the Father."[72] Alvyn Pettersen commenting on these words says that for Athanasius, "The Logos *is* the Father's will, and is not the consequence of the Father's will."[73] Earlier in his second "Discourse," in introducing the problems inherent in the Arian idea that the Son is dependent on the Father's will, Athanasius expands on this comment. First he says that through the Son "creation comes to be" and then "if he [the Son or Logos] has the power of will, and his will is effective, and suffices for consistence of things that come to be, and his Word is effective, and a framer, that Word must surely be the will of the Father, and an essential energy."[74] Athanasius does not exactly say the Father and the Son have one will, but this is the logic of his reasoning.[75] What the Father wills the Son wills. In his third "Discourse," Athanasius challenges another related Arian argument. Apparently in reply to Athanasius' insistence on the unity in being and work of the Father and the Son, the Arians argued that the Son is only one with the Father in the sense that he does the will of God perfectly. To reason this way is "unseemly and irrational," says Athanasius. "The sun and the moon and the stars ... are obedient to their maker," but none of these are called "the only-begotten Son and Word and Wisdom."[76]

Athanasius is particularly emphatic that the Father and the Son share the divine attributes equally. They are not separated or divided in any way. Thus he says,

> The Father is eternal, immortal, powerful, light, king, sovereign, God, Lord, creator, and maker. These attributes must be in the image ... the Son.... If the Son be not all this ... he is not a true image of the Father.[77]

> He is himself the Father's power and wisdom.[78]

> The attributes of the Father [are] spoken of the Son.[79]

---

[70] Ibid., 3.59–61 (p. 426–27).

[71] Ibid., 3.64 (p. 429).

[72] Ibid.

[73] Alvyn Pettersen, *Athanasius* (New York: Morehouse, 1996), 172.

[74] Athanasius, "Discourses," in *NPNF* 4:2.2 (p. 349). See also for the same idea 2.31 (p. 365).

[75] Lewis Ayres, *Nicaea and Its Legacy: An Approach to Fourth-Century Trinitarian Theology* (New York: Oxford, 2005), 114.

[76] Athanasius, "Discourses," in *NPNF* 4:3.13 (p. 401).

[77] Ibid., 1.21 (p. 318).

[78] Ibid., 3.1 (p. 394).

[79] Ibid., 3.5 (p. 395).

Peter Widdicombe says that for Athanasius, "The Son possesses the divine attributes (things) in the same way as the Father possesses them, because he is the proper offspring of the Father's being. He possesses them not in a transferred sense, but fully and properly."[80]

Athanasius specifically affirms that the Father and the Son are equally omnipotent. Speaking of the Son he says,

[He] is seated upon the same throne as the Father.[81]

He is Lord and King everlasting.[82]

For he ever was and is Lord and sovereign of all, being like in all things to the Father.[83]

He is Lord of all because he is one with the Father's Lordship.[84]

Athanasius discusses Jesus' prayer in the Garden of Gethsemane a number of times because the Arians argued that here Jesus involuntarily submitted to the Father's will. Athanasius holds that the tension seen in the prayer is between the human and the divine wills in the one Christ, and the human will gladly and freely accepts the divine will. He says, "these affections," alluding to Jesus' emotions as he prayed, "may be acknowledged as, not proper to the very Word by nature, but proper by nature to the very flesh."[85] I can find in Athanasius' writings no discussion of Heb 5:8 that speaks of the Son learning obedience, but he does discuss in some detail Lk 2:52, a passage that speaks of the child Jesus being "obedient" to his parents and "growing in wisdom and stature." These words, Athanasius argues, apply solely to Christ's human nature. He says it is foolishness to think the Son who is "ever in the Father," and "equal to God" could learn anything. He asks how could "Wisdom advance in wisdom?" And then answering his own rhetorical question he says, "To men belongs advance."[86]

The evidence is compelling. For Athanasius the Father and the Son are one in being, inseparable in work/operations/functions, and indivisible in power and

---

[80] Peter Widdicombe, *The Fatherhood of God from Origen to Athanasius* (Oxford: Clarendon, 1994), 204. Several times in quotes from Athanasius the word *properly* (Gk *idios*) has appeared. This is an important and much-used term in his writings. He uses it to underline the coessential unity of the Father and the Son. On this term see Widdicombe, *The Fatherhood of God*, 193–203; and Pettersen, *Athanasius*, 145–46.

[81] Athanasius, "Discourses," in *NPNF* 4:1.61 (p. 341).

[82] Ibid., 2.13 (p. 355).

[83] Ibid., 2.18 (p. 357).

[84] Ibid., 3.64 (p. 429).

[85] Ibid., 3.34 (p. 412); see also 3.26 (p. 408), 3.54 (p. 423), 3.56–57 (p. 424).

[86] Ibid., 3.50 (p. 421); see also 3:27 (p. 408).

authority. He totally rejects all the Arian arguments so similar to ones used by many conservative evangelicals today. He will not allow that the Son derives his being or authority from the Father, that the Son is eternally set under the Father's authority, that the Son is differentiated from the Father because the Father is he who commands and the Son is he who obeys, and that the Father and the Son are differentiated by their work or roles. For him there can be no separation or division between the Father and the Son in being, work, will, or authority.

The Cappadocians

The obedience of Christ is a major theme in the voluminous writings of the Cappadocians. It is clear why this is so. Eunomius, the Cappadocians' arch neo-Arian opponent, subordinated the Son in being, origination, *and authority* to the Father. In his *Confession of Faith* that he sent to the emperor Theodosius in 383, Eunomius professes,

> We believe in the one and only true God ..., he has no sharer of his Godhead nor participator of his glory *nor joint possessor of his authority* nor consort of the throne of his kingdom, for he is one and sole God almighty....
>
> And we believe in the Son of God ... He is *obedient* in creating and giving being to things that exist, *obedient* in all his administration, not having received his being Son or God because of his *obedience*, but from his being Son and being generated as only-begotten God, being *obedient* in words, *obedient* in acts ...[87]

Like the early Arians Athanasius opposed, Eunomius emphasized the human traits of Christ seen in the incarnation. These, he believed, indicated the eternal subordinate status of the Son in eternity. Gregory of Nazianzus more than once lists the "expressions" of his humanity quoted *ad nauseam* by Eunomius. They are given as allusions to the passages or teaching Eunomius quoted in evidence: "My God and your God, or greater or created, or made or sanctified; add if you like *servant and obedient*, and gave and learnt and was commanded and was sent, can do nothing of himself, either say or judge, or give or will. And further to these—his ignorance, subjection, prayer, asking, increase being made perfect ..."[88]

In their reply to Eunomius' teaching, the Cappadocians offer a threefold response. First of all, like Athanasius they make a clear distinction between the Son of God as God and the Son of God in the incarnation. They argue that the limitations the Son embraced in becoming incarnate in no way impinge on his divine status as equal with

---

[87] The reconstituted text in full is given in Hanson, *The Search*, 619–21. I have simply quoted the relevant sections from the text he gives. Italics added.

[88] Gregory Nazianus, "The Theological Orations," in *NPNF* 7:3.17 (p. 307). See for similar comments, ibid., 4.6 (p. 311). Italics added.

God the Father. Gregory of Nyssa writes, "We recognize two things in Christ, one divine, the other human (the divine by nature, but the human in the incarnation, we accordingly claim for the Godhead that which is eternal, and that which is created we ascribe to his human nature)."[89] In his "Against Eunomius" he adds, "By his partaking of creation he also partook of servitude. And him who is in servitude you will surely invest with the servant's form."[90] Second, the Cappadocians argue that the incarnate Son was representative man.[91] His obedience countered the disobedience of Adam that had brought ruin to the human race. Gregory of Nyssa in answering Eunomius points out that "the mighty Paul" says "he became obedient (Php 2:8) ... to accomplish the mystery of redemption by the cross, who had emptied himself by assuming the likeness and fashion of a man ... healing the disobedience of men by his own obedience."[92] In reply to the claim that Jesus is forever the servant of God the Father, Gregory Nazianzus writes, "In truth he was in servitude to flesh and to birth and to the condition of our life with a view to our liberation."[93] Then countering Eunomius' interpretation of the words from the epistle to the Hebrews, "he [the Son] learnt obedience," which Eunomius took to mean, the Son's "obedience is part of his nature [it is] impossible for him not to be obedient," Gregory replies that the Son "became obedient ... by becoming for our sakes flesh, a servant and a curse, and sin." He did so according to "his free will." Then noting that Christ goes voluntarily by his own choice to the cross (Jn 10:18) he adds, "Even in the time of his passion he is not separated from his authority; where can heresy possibly discern the subordination to authority of the King of Glory?"[94] To this we can add the words of Gregory of Nazianzus: "In his character as the Word he is neither obedient nor disobedient. For such expressions belong to servants, and inferiors.... In character of the form of a servant, he condescends to his fellow servants."[95]

And third, the Cappadocians argue that the Son's obedience was not compulsory submission to the will of the Father, but rather a coincidence of willing. What the Father wills and what the Son wills are always one. In reply to those who make much of the Son going, speaking, and doing as the Father wills, Basil argues that the Son's "will is connected in indissoluble union with the Father. Do not let us then understand by what is called a 'commandment' a peremptory mandate delivered by

---

[89] Gregory of Nyssa, "On the Faith: To Simplicius," in *NPNF* 5 (p. 337).

[90] Ibid., 6.4 (p. 187). For similar comments see Basil, "Letters," in *NPNF* 8:261.2 (p. 300).

[91] As Gregory of Nazianzus says explicitly. See "Theological Orations," in *NPNF* 7:4.5 (p. 311).

[92] Gregory of Nyssa, "Against Eunomius," in *NPNF* 5:2.11 (p. 121). See also Basil, "Letters," in *NPNF* 8:261.2 (p. 300).

[93] Gregory Nazianzus, "Theological Orations," in *NPNF* 7:4.3 (p. 310).

[94] Ibid., 4.6 (p. 311).

[95] Ibid.

organs of speech, and giving orders to the Son, as to a subordinate, concerning what he ought to do. Let us rather in a sense befitting the Godhead, perceive the transmission of will, like the reflection of an object in a mirror, passing without note of time from Father to Son."[96]

Similarly, Gregory of Nyssa writes, there is "no divergence of will between the Father and the Son."[97] "If the Father wills anything, the Son who is in the Father knows the Father's will, or rather he is the Father's will."[98] Or to quote Gregory Nazianzus, "We have one Godhead so we have one will."[99]

In reply to Eunomius' confession that the Father has no "joint possessor of his authority or consort of the throne of his kingdom," Gregory of Nyssa has much to say. He assails Eunomius for severing "the only begotten from the Godhead," denying him "the prerogatives of deity" and breaching the divine unity. Gregory's view is that the Scriptures teach that "the Father, the Son, and the Holy Spirit are alike in a position of power to do what they will." And the Son "has all things that the Father himself has, and is possessor of all his power, not that this right is transferred from the Father to the Son, but that it at once remains in the Father and resides in the Son. For he is manifestly in the Father with all his own might."[100] "For we do not know of any difference by way of superiority and inferiority in attributes."[101]

The Cappadocians, like Athanasius, are very conscious of the limitations of human language used of God. Eunomius, like the early Arians, argued that the Father's superiority and the Son's subordination were indicated by the terms *begotten*, *Father*, and *Son*, which he understood literally. Gregory of Nazianzus emphatically rules out of court the possibility of discovering anything about God by building on human language and analogies. He says, "I have been unable to discover anything on earth with which to compare the Godhead."[102] When it comes to the name *Father* he says, "Father is not a name neither of an essence or an action, most clever sirs. But it is the name of a relation in which the Father stands to the Son, and the Son to the Father.... [These names] denote an identity of nature."[103] And of the Son he says, "In my opinion he is called Son because he is identical with the Father in essence."[104]

---

[96] Basil, "On the Spirit," in *NPNF* 8:8.20 (p. 14).
[97] Gregory of Nyssa, "Answer to Eunomius," in *NPNF* 5:2 (p. 272).
[98] Ibid.
[99] Gregory Nazianzus, "Theological Orations," in *NPNF* 7:4.12 (p. 314).
[100] Gregory of Nyssa, "Against Eunomius," in *NPNF* 5:2.6 (p. 107).
[101] Gregory of Nyssa, "On the Holy Trinity," in *NPNF* 5 (p. 327).
[102] Gregory of Nazianzus, "The Fourth Theological Oration," in *NPNF* 7:31 (p. 328).
[103] Gregory of Nazianzus, "The Third Theological Oration," in *NPNF* 7:16 (p. 307). See also the lengthy discussion on the meaning of the title *Father* by Gregory of Nyssa, "Against Eunomius," in *NPNF* 5:37–38 (pp. 85–92).
[104] Gregory of Nazianzus, "The Fourth Theological Discourse," in *NPNF* 7:20 (p. 316).

Basil writing on the term *begotten* says, "Let us not fall into the material sense of the relations. For the substance was not separated from the Father and bestowed on the Son ... the mode of begetting is ineffable and inconceivable by human thought."[105] Gregory of Nyssa likewise dismisses the Arians "who confirm their idle notions about the deity by illustrations from the circumstances of ordinary life."[106]

Eunomius' attempt to explain God in human categories by likening the Son to a servant who only has delegated authority particularly angered Gregory of Nyssa. Eunomius first pointed out that, "In a wealthy establishment one may see the more active and devoted servant set over his fellow servants by the command of his master, and so invested with superiority over others in the same rank and station."[107] Then he said, "Transfer this notion to the doctrines concerning the Godhead, so that the Only-begotten God, though subject to the sovereignty of his superior, is in no way hindered by the authority of his sovereign in the direction of those inferior to him."[108]

This reasoning, Gregory holds, only leads to "heresy." The triune Godhead is "simple, uncompounded and indivisible." If the Father is "Lord," so too is the Son. It is not possible for them to have "contrary attributes." Setting the Son under the Father's authority in this way, Gregory says, leads to idolatry: "He who affirms the Only-begotten to be a slave, makes him out by so saying to be a fellow servant with himself: and hence will of necessity ... worship himself instead of God. For if he sees in himself slavery, and the object of his worship also in slavery, he of course looks at himself, seeing the whole of himself in that which he worships."[109]

Because the Cappadocians cannot allow human language used of God to be taken literally, they never suggest that the name *Father* implies authority over the Son. Their constant teaching, as we have seen, is that the Father and the Son have the same divine attributes, most importantly omnipotence. They are indivisible in power and authority. Michel Barnes says that all the pro-Nicene theologians of the second half of the fourth century held that "the Father and the Son have the one power [because] they have one and the same nature."[110]

---

[105]Basil, "Letters," in *NPNF* 8:52.3 (p. 156). See similarly Gregory of Nazianzus, "The Third Theological Oration," in *NPNF* 7:5 (p. 302).

[106]Gregory of Nyssa, "Against Eunomius," in *NPNF* 5:10.4 (p. 227).

[107]Ibid. (p. 226).

[108]Ibid.

[109]Ibid. (p. 227).

[110]Michel Barnes, *The Power of God: Dunamis in Gregory of Nyssa's Trinitarian Theology* (Washington, D.C.: Catholic University of America Press, 2001), 13. In this detailed and careful study Barnes notes that Athanasius frequently identifies Jesus, the Son of God, or Logos as "the power of God," citing 1Co 1:24. In the Cappadocians, particularly Gregory of Nyssa, he sees development. Unity of being and operations implies unity in power. The triune God can even be defined as the one power.

The much-quoted text in the contemporary debate, 1Co 11:3, which is supposed to parallel and endorse the authoritative "headship" of the divine Father and men, plays little part in the historic trinitarian debates, although it is referred to occasionally for various reasons.[111] Basil has the most significant comment, which is worth quoting in full: "If 'the head of man is Christ, and the head of Christ is God,' and man is not of one substance with Christ, who is God (for man is not God), but Christ is of one substance with God (for he is God), therefore God is not the head of Christ, in the same sense as Christ is the head of man. The natures of creatures and the creative Godhead do not exactly coincide. God is head of Christ as Father; Christ is head of us as Maker."[112]

His interpretation assumes that speaking of the Father as the *kephale*/head of the Son means something very different from speaking of Christ as the *kephale*/head of man. We may assume he would follow the same rule in the third pairing, "man is the

---

[111] At the proofreading stage of this book, another Moore College lecturer went into print advocating hierarchical ordering in the Trinity and in the male-female relationship. See Peter G. Bolt, "Three Heads in the Divine Order: The Early Church Fathers and 1 Corinthians 11.3," *Reformed Theological Review* 64, no. 3 (December 2005), 147–61. I agree with Bolt that in v. 3c God/*theos* refers to God the Father, who is to be eternally and irreversibly differentiated from God the Son. I disagree with his unsupported assertion that the Greek word *kephale* in this verse implies "rule, authority, subjection, obedience, under, below" (p. 159), for reasons I give in chapter 3 of this book. Bolt helpfully tracks down all the references to 1Co 11:3c — "God is the *kephale* of Christ" — in the patristic sources. He concludes that "the Fathers" interpret these words "hierarchically." God the Father is eternally set over God the Son in authority. Origen certainly can be quoted to support hierarchical ordering in the Trinity, but we see Bolt's subordinationist spectacles distorting the evidence when he reads Origen's words "unceasingly 'the Father is in the Son, as the Son is in the Father' (cf. Jn 14:10) unceasingly" to refer to the Son's eternal (*unceasing*) subordination (p. 148). It is obvious that for Origen what is "unceasing" is the mutual indwelling. Irenaeus and Tertullian do use this text to give preeminence to the Father, which is what we would expect because for them God the Father, a monad, is God in a unique sense. The other quotes Bolt accumulates on close inspection do not unambiguously substantiate his thesis, and in the case of Didymus the Blind, Basil, Ambrose, and Augustine (cf. Hill, *The Trinity*, 6.10, p. 212), they speak against his theses. Eusebius of Caesarea, whom Bolt also quotes in support, was not an unambiguous supporter of the Nicene faith. He also quotes two anathemas of the Council of Sirmium quoted by Hilary, not mentioning that these are Arian statements. Hilary is not always as clear or strong on key issues as Athanasius, the Cappadocians, and Augustine, but he called "blasphemy" what this council decreed. What is completely missing from this essay is how a hierarchical reading of 1Co 11:3c could be harmonized with the primary New Testament confession, "Jesus is Lord," and the unified voice of the orthodox tradition that the three divine persons are indivisible in power and authority, alike in an unqualified way, omnipotent God.

[112] This quote is cited in the "Prolegomena" to St. Basil's writings in *NPNF* 8:xl, but there is some debate as to whether or not Basil actually wrote these words. They are, however, a reflection of pro-Nicene orthodoxy and as such they are relevant to our study.

head of woman."[113] The other thing to be noted is that Basil in neither pairing sees the *kephale*/head imagery suggesting "authority over." In the first pair he mentions he says the word *kephale* implies a Father-Son relationship, in the second, Christ and man, a Creator-creature relationship.

Gregory of Nazianzus sums up why the Cappadocians so vehemently opposed the Arians: "[They] did not honor the Father by dishonoring his Offspring with his unequal degrees of Godhead. But we recognize one glory of the Father, the equality of the Only-begotten; and one glory of the Son and the Spirit. And we hold that to subordinate any of the three is to destroy the whole."[114]

For the Cappadocians the divine three are united in being, work, authority, and will. The Son is not subordinated to the Father in power or authority. He is Lord. To quote Gregory of Nazianzus again: "To us there is one God, for the Godhead is one ... though we believe in three persons. For one is not more and another less God; nor is one before or after another; nor are they divided in will or parted in power."[115]

Like Athanasius, the Cappadocian Fathers hold that the Father and the Son (and the Spirit) are one in being, inseparable in work/operations/function, and indivisible in power and authority.

Augustine

Augustine likewise gives no support whatsoever to the idea that Christ is eternally set under the Father's authority. This is not an issue he focuses on, but his emphasis on the "inseparable equality" of the divine three, his insistence that the work of the Father and the work of the Son are one, and the comments he makes on the specific issue leave no doubt as to where he stands on this matter. He is implacably against subordinating the Son to the Father in any way.

As has already been noted, Augustine like Athanasius is particularly keen to first establish how the Scriptures are to be read correctly—"canonically" is his word. His first rule of interpretation is that all texts that speak of the Son's divinity, majesty, and authority speak of him "in the form of God," and all texts that speak of his dependence on and obedience to the Father, or of his frailty, speak of him "in the form of a servant," in his temporal state as the incarnate Son.[116] This rule on its own, he recognized, was not sufficient to give a consistent reading of Scripture. It did not explain the texts that spoke of the Son and the Spirit being "sent." These the Arians quoted

---

[113] It is to be noted that "Basil" does not follow Paul's pairing order. In 1Co 11:3 the threefold pairing is Christ-man, man-woman, God-Christ.

[114] Gregory of Nazianzus, "The Panegyric on St. Basil," in *NPNF* 7:30 (p. 405).

[115] Gregory of Nazianzus, "On the Holy Spirit," in *NPNF* 7:14 (p. 322).

[116] Augustine, *The Trinity*, trans. Edmund Hill (Brooklyn: New City Press, 1991), 1.14–21 (pp. 74–84). All references to *De Trinitate* (*The Trinity*) are to this translation.

to prove that the Son and the Spirit are subject to the Father's directions. He says, "in error" they presume, "the one who sends is greater than the one sent."[117]

In a reply to such reasoning Augustine argues that sending does not necessarily entail subservience: only that the one sent comes "from" the sender. He thus concludes that just as the terms *unbegotten* and *begotten* differentiate the Father and the Son, while not suggesting any eternal subordination, so too do the terms *sending* and *being sent*.[118] What Augustine has seen clearly is that human terms such as *begetting* and *sending* when used of divine persons do not necessarily have the same content as they do in everyday speech. It would be a grave error to think that because the Bible speaks of the Father sending and the Son being sent, a division of wills or superiority or inferiority is envisaged. The Father and the Son have one will, and they are inseparably one in deity, majesty, and authority. On the basis of this reasoning Augustine formulates a second rule of interpretation. Texts that speak of the Son's sending by the Father do not teach that "the Son is less than the Father, but that he is from the Father. This does not imply any dearth of equality, but only his birth in eternity."[119] Earlier he says such texts "mark him neither as less nor equal, but only intimate that he is from the Father."[120] But this is not the end of the matter for Augustine. He then asks, "What can really be meant by this sending of the Son, or of the Holy Spirit?"[121] His reply is that this *sending* refers to the temporal *mission* of the Son and the Spirit seen in history, to be distinguished from the *begetting* of the Son and the *procession* of the Spirit hidden from human eyes, which speak of their *eternal generation*.

Augustine's recognition of the fact that all human language used of God is analogical is not paralleled by many contemporary evangelicals. Thus they want us to believe, unlike Augustine, that the language of sending indicates that the divine Father has authority over the divine Son like husbands have over wives and men over women in the church. Professor Bruce Ware gives a classic example of such reasoning. Choosing Augustine of all people as proof of his thesis that historic orthodoxy teaches that the Son is eternally set under the Father's authority, he argues that this great Latin-speaking theologian "affirmed the distinction of persons is constituted precisely by the differing relations among them, in part manifested by the inherent authority of the Father and the inherent submission of the Son."[122] In support he quotes a paragraph from Hill's translation of *The Trinity* on the sending of the Son by the Father.[123]

---

[117] Ibid., 2.7 (p. 101). The issue of what the sending of the Son entails is of great importance to Augustine, and he returns to this topic repeatedly in *The Trinity*.

[118] Ibid., 4.29 (p. 174).

[119] Ibid., 2.3 (p. 99).

[120] Ibid. (p. 98).

[121] Ibid., 2.8 (p. 102).

[122] Ware, "Tampering with the Trinity," in *Biblical Foundations*, 246.

[123] Augustine, *The Trinity*, 4.27 (p. 172).

The strange thing is that the passage he quotes denies the very thing he is asserting. In this paragraph Augustine says that when the Bible speaks of the Father sending and the Son as sent "there is nothing [in these words] to stop us believing that the Son is equal to the Father and consubstantial and co-eternal.... One is not greater and the other less, but because one is the Father and the other Son: one is the begetter, the other the begotten; the first is the one from whom the sent one is; the other is the one who is from the sender. For the Son is from the Father, not the Father from the Son." As I read this quote it seems to me it is emphatically denying what Bruce Ware is affirming. Augustine is insisting on the complete equality of the persons and on their irreversible distinctions. The Father and the Son are one in substance, inseparable in operations, indivisible in power and authority, but the Father is not the Son and never can be, and the Son is not the Father and never can be. For Augustine divine differentiation does not imply the Son or the Spirit's subordination in any way.

An important text for all the fourth-century Arians was 1Co 15:24–28. It was read (as it is often read today) to teach that at the end Christ will be placed under the Father's authority and rule. Augustine found this text difficult, but as he wants to be true to Scripture he has to find an interpretation that does not contradict the catholic faith as it has been handed down to him, or other parts of Scripture that speak of the eternal rule of the Son. His treatment of the passage is convoluted and difficult.[124] His interpretation is governed by three beliefs he held firmly, each of which he found clearly taught in Scripture: (1) the Father and Son are inseparable in their being and work; (2) the Son reveals the Father; and (3) the humanity of the Son reveals as well as conceals the Father in all his glory. On this basis he argues that the handing over of rule alludes to when the Son "brings believers to a direct contemplation of God the Father."[125] This does not involve depriving the Son of anything, since the Father and the Son are forever one, but it does indicate a change. No longer will believers see the Father only through the Son clothed in human flesh. They will contemplate him directly. At this time Augustine believed "every creature" will be made subject to God, "including even the creature in which the Son of God became the Son of man, for in this created form the Son himself shall also be made subject to the one who subjected all things to him, that God may be all in all (1Co 15:28)."[126] For Augustine "God" is the triune God: there is no other God.

In Augustine's "model" of the Trinity the Father, the Son, and the Spirit can never be set in opposition or divided in being, work, *or authority*. Given the premise that the divine three are "equal and indivisible" in substance and divinity, it follows that they must be "equal and indivisible" in activity and attributes. He reasons this

---

[124]See ibid., 1.15–21 and 1.28 (pp. 75–81 and p. 87).
[125]Ibid., 1.16 (p. 76).
[126]Ibid., 1.28 (p. 87).

way because in the Bible what God does indicates who God is. Quite explicitly he speaks of the unity of work and will of the divine three. He says, "The Trinity works inseparably in everything that God works,"[127] and "The Father and the Son have but one will and are indivisible in their workings."[128] Furthermore, the divine three are one in their attributes. He writes, "The Father is almighty, the Son is almighty, the Holy Spirit is almighty; yet there are not three almighties but one almighty ... so whatever God is called with reference to self both is said three times over about each of the persons, Father, Son and Holy Spirit, and at the same time is said in the singular and not the plural about the Trinity. As it is not one thing for God to be and another for him to be great, but being is for him the same thing as being great."[129] It is thus of no surprise to find that nowhere in Augustine's writings do we find him speaking of the Son being subject to the Father's will, or of the Father commanding and the Son obeying. Such ideas are completely excluded by his doctrine of the Trinity.

However, Augustine does speak of the temporal obedience of Christ in reference to his death on the cross. In an important section of *The Trinity*, Augustine returns to the matter of the Son's sending and asks yet again, "Why does the Bible speak of the Son as sent by the Father?"[130] This time he concludes that sending implies a purpose. People are sent on a mission to accomplish something. His reply is that the Son was sent and took human flesh so that he might be the mediator between God and humankind. His mission was to win our salvation by reversing the disobedience of Adam. He quotes Paul, "As by one man came death so by one man there might come the resurrection of the dead (1Co 15:21)."[131] Repeatedly he speaks of Christ going to the cross willingly and voluntarily. He says it was necessary that our condemnation achieved by Adam "should be undone by the death of the just man issuing from voluntary freedom and mercy."[132] Later he adds, "As he was able not to die if he did not wish to, it follows since he did die it was because he wished to."[133] In all this Augustine closely follows Paul. Jesus is the second Adam, the perfectly obedient person, who wins our salvation on the cross and then is raised to rule in majesty and authority— mission accomplished! He writes, "And what greater example of obedience could be given to us ... than God the Son obeying God the Father *even to death on the cross* (Php 2:8)? Where could the reward of

---

[127]Ibid., 1.8 (p. 70); cf. 2.3 (p. 99).

[128]Ibid., 2.9 (p. 103).

[129]Ibid., 5.9 (p. 195). In 3.12 (p. 197) he gives two lists of attributes shared by the divine three.

[130]I refer to book 4 (pp. 152–77). Augustine's argument is not easy to follow, and Hill's explanation is very helpful (pp. 147–51).

[131]Ibid., 4.3.15 (p. 163).

[132]Ibid., 4.4 (p. 155).

[133]Ibid., 4.17 (p. 165).

obedience be shown to better advantage than in the flesh of such a mediator when it rose to eternal life."[134]

Throughout his writings on the Trinity Augustine is perfectly consistent. In the eternal Trinity the Father, the Son, and the Holy Spirit are "one and indivisible" in being, work, authority, and will, yet in becoming man the Son voluntarily made himself "less than" the Father by taking the form of a servant. This did not involve the giving up of his divinity or divine attributes, but it did involve him as man in humble service, obedience to the Father, and death on the cross. Thus he says the New Testament "presents him [the Son] not in divine strength in which he is equal to the Father, but in human weakness through which he was crucified."[135]

Professor Lewis Ayres argues that Augustine stands squarely in the pro-Nicene tradition. Central to this tradition is the confession that the triune God of biblical revelation is one in being, function, *and authority*. Ayres says, "Fundamental to all pro-Nicene theologies" is the belief "that God is one power, glory, majesty and rule.... the assertion that God is a unity in these respects is universal."[136]

The Athanasian Creed

In the so-called Athanasian Creed composed in about 500, what is basically Augustine's teaching on the Trinity is identified as "the catholic faith." In this creed the unity of the divine Trinity is to the fore, and any suggestion that the Son or Spirit is subordinated in being or authority is unambiguously excluded. Three clauses specifically deny that the Son is less than the Father in authority. "So likewise the Father is almighty, the Son almighty, and the Holy Spirit almighty. And yet there are not three almighties but one almighty." "So likewise the Father is Lord, the Son is Lord and the Holy Spirit is Lord. And yet not three Lords but one Lord." "In this Trinity none is greater or less than another ... all are co-equal." The only difference between the members of the Trinity allowed is that of differing origination, and this does not in any way imply subordination in being, work, or authority. Nothing could be plainer. The Athanasian Creed is emphatic. The Father, Son, and Spirit are "co-eternal" and "co-equal" God, and as such are indivisible in power and authority.

The Roman Catholic Church, the Anglican Church, and the Lutheran Church among others endorse this creed as a doctrinal norm. Its teaching not only prescribes what is to be believed; it also prescribes how the Bible is to be read by those who confess this creed. This statement of faith sums up what the church believes the Bible teaches on the Trinity and the incarnation.

---

[134]Ibid., 13.5.22 (p. 361). See also Augustine, "On Forgiveness of Sins and Baptism," in *NPNF*, 5.16, 17, 18 (p. 21).

[135]Augustine, *The Trinity*, 1.1.3 (p. 67).

[136]Ayres, *Nicaea*, 279.

Calvin

On reading Calvin's discussion on the Trinity in the *Institutes*, his emphasis on the unity of God[137] and on the full divinity of Christ cannot be missed. These two motifs dominate, and there is a reason for this. Throughout his ministry in Geneva, Calvin was battling subordinationists of various kinds,[138] the most dangerous he thought were what I have called elsewhere "derivative subordinationists."[139] Their concern was to give preeminence and priority to the Father by making him "the essence giver,"[140] "as if he were the deifier of the Son."[141] Calvin reasoned that if the Father and the Son were divided in this way "we definitely cast the Son down."[142] We imply that he is not in any substantive sense equal to God. In reply he argues that since the Father and the Son are one in being they are one in divinity, and thus one in power. The Son is as much God in the fullest sense of this term as is the Father. To be God is to be omnipotent.

In arguing for the full divinity of Christ, one of Calvin's most important arguments is that Christ "functions" as God. He says "the divinity of Christ is demonstrated by his works,"[143] and his works all depict him as omnipotent God. He governs "the universe with providence and power" (Heb 1:13), he regulates "all things by the command of his own power," and his deeds are "the *function* of the Creator alone."[144] Calvin holds that in forgiving sins, Christ "possesses not the administration merely but the actual power of the remission of sins."[145] Likewise in healing the sick and raising the dead "he [Christ] showed forth his *own power*." He was "the real author of the miracles."[146] In appealing to the Old Testament he says, "Christ is brought forward by Isaiah both as God and as adorned with the highest power, which is the characteristic mark of the one true God."[147] He is to be identified with "true Jehovah."[148] Later in specifically combating derivative subordinationism he says, "Whatever is of God is

---

[137]In the next chapter we discuss Calvin's stress on divine unity.

[138]The best summary of all this is found in Philip Walker Butin, *Revelation, Redemption and Response: Calvin's Trinitarian Understanding of the Divine-Human Relationship* (New York: Oxford, 1995), 25–38. See also B. B. Warfield, "Calvin's Doctrine of the Trinity" in *Calvin and Augustine* (Philadelphia: Presbyterian and Reformed, 1956), 207ff.

[139]Kevin Giles, *The Trinity and Subordinationism* (Downers Grove, Ill.: InterVarsity, 2002), 64–69.

[140]Calvin, *Institutes*, 1.13.23 (p. 149).

[141]Ibid., 1.13.24 (p. 152).

[142]Ibid., 1.13.27 (p. 149).

[143]Ibid., 2.13.12 (p. 135).

[144]Ibid., 1.13.12 (p. 136). Italics added.

[145]Ibid.

[146]Ibid. Italics added.

[147]Ibid., 1.13.9 (p. 131).

[148]Ibid., 1.13.9 (p. 132).

attributed to Christ." He rules "in majesty as King and Judge."[149] The Father, Son, and Spirit created in "common" and "common also [is] the authority to command."[150] It is beyond dispute. For Calvin, the Father, Son, and Spirit are inseparable in work or function and indivisible in authority and power. Thomas Torrance says that for Calvin there is "oneness in agency and power" between the divine three and "an inseparable relation between what he [the Son] does and what God [the Father] does."[151]

Calvin primarily thinks of Christ as the Mediator.[152] This is the Messiah's distinctive office or role. He *is* the Mediator and he *functions* as the Mediator. His being and role are one.[153] The title for Calvin did not indicate that Christ stands somewhere between humankind and God: he is a subordinated mediator. No, for Calvin Christ the Mediator is God in all his majesty, power, and authority. As the Mediator he took human flesh and was obedient as the second Adam, but he never relinquished any of his prerogatives as omnipotent God.[154] In his office or role as the Mediator, he is for Calvin at one and the same time prophet, king, and priest. As prophet he reveals the Father to us, as King he reigns as Lord, and as priest he reconciles us to the Father.[155] Edmondson, speaking Calvin's understanding of the Mediator's work as king says, "Christ, as Lord, exercises God's power and authority over the Church, and his lordship, thereby, entails his roles as both the Church's protector and its master."[156]

When Calvin comes to think of the Son in relation to the Father, he is quite clear that the Son is to be differentiated from the Father in respect to person; he is the Son *of* the Father, but he will not allow that he may be differentiated from the Father in respect to his being. The divine three share without distinction the one being. So he can speak of Christ as "self-existence" God (Gk *autoousia*, Lat. *aseity*). He writes, "We confess that the Son since he is God, exists of himself."[157] Towards the end of his life when he was challenged on this teaching by the pastors in Neuchâtel, Calvin went a step further, speaking of Christ as *autotheos* (God of himself).[158] At this point it becomes clear why Calvin is so insistent that Christ exercises the power and authority of God in his own right. He has seen that if the divine three are one in being, they

---

[149]Ibid., 1.13.24 (p. 152).

[150]Ibid. (p. 153).

[151]Thomas Torrance, "Calvin's Doctrine of the Trinity," in *Trinitarian Perspectives* (Edinburgh: T&T Clark, 1994), 52.

[152]Stephen Edmondson, *Calvin's Christology* (Cambridge: Cambridge University Press, 2004), 47.

[153]Ibid., 185–87.

[154]Calvin, *Institutes*, 2.12.3 (p. 466).

[155]Ibid., 2.15.1–6 (pp. 494–503).

[156]Edmondson, *Calvin's Christology*, 124.

[157]Calvin, *Institutes*, 1.13.25 (p. 154).

[158]See further, Warfield, "Calvin's Doctrine of the Trinity," 233–37; Letham, *The Holy Trinity*, 256–57.

are one in divinity; and if one in divinity, they are one in power and authority. They are alike omnipotent. In regard to being or power they cannot be differentiated. Gerald Bray sees the logic of Calvin's position with absolute clarity: "By saying that each person of the Trinity is *autotheos*, Calvin has ensured that the relations between them must be voluntary, since no one person can claim the authority to impose his will on the others. But this freedom can never imply contradiction or lead to anarchy, because in God there is but a single will, which is governed by the operation of his perfect love."[159]

Immediately following his rejection of derivative subordinationism, a matter he gives more space to than anything else in his exposition of the doctrine of the Trinity, Calvin has a section entitled, "The subordination of the incarnate Word to the Father is no counter evidence."[160] Like Athansisus and Augustine, he will not allow that the subordination seen in the incarnation in any way suggests that the Son is subordinated in relation to the Father in the immanent Trinity. In this section he appeals to Php 2:4–11, a text he returns to time and time again. Here he sees the Scriptures teaching that in becoming incarnate the Son willingly and freely chose to be subordinate for the salvation of men and women. He took "the form of a slave ... and became obedient to the point of death." On this basis Calvin teaches, along with Athanasius and Augustine, that all texts that speak of the frailty, subordination, and obedience of the Son refer solely to his incarnate existence. As the divine Son he is equal in divinity, majesty, *and authority* with the Father and the Spirit.

Later in discussing the person and work of Christ he notes that in Php 2:8 Paul quite specifically speaks of the Son's "obedience" as one of the human traits that his "voluntary" emptying of himself involved. He writes, "Laying aside the splendor of majesty, he showed himself obedient to the Father (cf. Php 2:8). Having completed his subjection, 'he was at last crowned with glory and honour' (Heb 2:9) and exalted to the highest Lordship that before him 'every knee should bow' (Php 2:10)."[161]

Then in the next sub-section of the *Institutes* while speaking of the salvific work of the Son, he returns to the matter of his obedience. Here he points out that the Son had to be obedient if he were to be the second Adam. To make his point he asks, "How has Christ abolished sin, banished the separation between us and God and acquired righteousness to render God favorable and kindly towards us? To this we can in general reply that he has achieved this for us by the whole course of his obedience. This is proved by Paul's testimony: 'As by one man's disobedience many were made sinners, so by one man's obedience we are made righteous' (Ro 5:19)."[162]

---

[159]Gerald Bray, *The Doctrine of God* (London: Inter-Varsity, 1993), 204.
[160]Calvin, *Institutes*, 1.13.26 (p. 154).
[161]Ibid., 2.14.3 (p. 485).
[162]Ibid., 2.16.5 (p. 507).

He then adds, "His willing obedience is the important thing because a sacrifice not offered voluntarily would not have furthered righteousness."[163] E. D. Willis in his exposition of Calvin's Christology concludes that for the great Reformer, "The full humanity is absolutely indispensable because it constitutes the instrument of Christ's redemptive obedience. What is saving in Christ's teaching, miracles, and death is not simply that they occurred, but they occurred voluntarily. The heart of the reconstituting act is the free obedience of the second Adam, which displaces the willful disobedience of the first Adam."[164]

Calvin's exegesis of 1Co 15:24−28, which speaks of the Son handing over his rule to God, is significant. He writes,

> Surely the Kingdom of the Son of God had no beginning and will have no end. But even as he lay concealed under the lowliness of flesh and "emptied himself, taking the form of a servant" (Php 2:7), laying aside the splendor of majesty, he showed himself obedient to his Father (cf. Php 2:8). Having completed this subjection, 'he was at last crowned with glory and honor" (Heb 2:9), and exalted to the highest lordship that before him "every knee should bow" (Php 2:10). So then will he yield to the Father his name and crown of glory, and whatever he has received from the Father, that "God may be all in all" (1Co 15:28). For what purpose were power and Lordship given to Christ, unless that by his hand the Father might govern us. In this sense also Christ is said to be seated at the right hand of the Father (cf. Mk 16:19; Ro 8:34). Yet this but for a time, until we enjoy the direct vision of the Godhead. Here we cannot excuse the error of the ancient writers who pay no attention to the person of the mediator, obscure the real meaning of almost all the teaching one reads in the Gospel of John and entangle themselves in many snares. Let this, then, be our key to right understanding: those things which apply to the office of the Mediator are not spoken of simply either of the divine nature or of the human. Until he comes forth as judge of the world Christ will therefore reign, joining us to the Father as the measure of our weakness permits. But when as partakers in heavenly glory we shall see God as he is, Christ having then been discharged the office of Mediator, will cease to be the ambassador of his Father and will be satisfied with that glory which he enjoyed before the creation of the world.... Then he returns the lordship to his Father so that—far from diminishing his own majesty—it may shine all the more brightly.[165]

---

[163]Ibid.

[164]E. D. Willis, *Calvin's Catholic Christology* (Leiden: Brill, 1966), 84. See also Paul Van Buren, *Christ in Our Place* (Grand Rapids, Mich.: Eerdmans, 1957), 38. He says, "We cannot speak of the obedience of Christ in Calvin's theology without speaking of the strong emphasis he puts on the idea that this obedience was performed in Christ's human nature only." See also pp. 23−40 where he develops this theme. For a virtually identical conclusion see also Robert A. Peterson, *Calvin and the Atonement* (Ross-shire, UK: Mentor, 1999), 61−68.

[165]Calvin, *Institutes*, 2.14.3 (p. 485).

Calvin makes Php 2:4–11 the "key" to understanding this perplexing passage. The Son is forever omnipotent God, but just as he willingly humbled himself in the incarnation, so he will willingly hand over his rule as the Mediator at the end of time. At that point the rule of Christ as the Mediator of redemption will cease.[166] When Christ has no further soteriological work to accomplish, he relinquishes his ruling work to the Father. In doing this Calvin does not say Christ gives up his humanity, or his personal identity as the Son, or his equality with the Father and the Spirit, or his power and authority. In this change Christ is in no way diminished; indeed Calvin believed his majesty will "shine all the more brightly." At that time, Calvin believes, we will enjoy "a direct vision of the [triune] Godhead." For Calvin the Godhead is eternally triune and can never be otherwise.

The evidence is unambiguous. For Calvin the Son is equal God without any caveats. His power and authority is inherently his as true God. The Father, Son, and Spirit are alike omnipotent. The Son's subordination and obedience is limited to the incarnation. His choice to take human flesh for our salvation necessitated this. His last act of obedience was the cross (Php 2:8). From then on he rules as Lord and head over all until the consummation of all things when he willingly gives back direct rule to the Father with whom he is joined with the Holy Spirit for all eternity. In his discussion on the person and work of Christ in the *Institutes*, Calvin contrasts what he calls "the time of his humiliation"[167] during his incarnate ministry in the form of a servant on earth, with the time of his exaltation after the resurrection when he reigns as Lord in majesty and power.[168] Thus for Calvin to read back into the exalted status what Scripture explicitly limits to the Son's humbled status in the incarnation is a grave error.

In summing up Calvin's contribution to trinitarian theology, Thomas Torrance says that as far as Calvin was concerned, "There is no difference between them [the divine three] in respect to Being, power, or majesty, for each considered in himself is the one God who has his being from himself alone. They are fully equal ..."[169] "He leaves no room for any element of subordinationism in his doctrine of the Trinity."[170]

---

[166]On Calvin's understanding of this passage and on the views of others see J. F. Jensen, "1 Cor. 15:24–28 and the Future of Jesus Christ," *Scottish Journal of Theology* 40 (1987): 543–70.

[167]Calvin, *Institutes*, 2.11.12 (p. 461).

[168]On this basis Reformed theologians developed their Christology speaking of the two states of Christ, his humiliated state in the incarnation and his exalted state after the resurrection.

[169]Torrance, "Calvin's Doctrine," 72.

[170]Ibid., 66.

The Confessions

Not surprisingly the Second Helvetic Confession of 1566, composed by Calvin's friend, Heinrich Bullinger, condemns the "blasphemies" of those who teach that any person within the Trinity is eternally "subservient or subordinate ... unequal in it, are greater or less, ... or different with respect to character or *will*." The term *subservient* specifically rejects the idea that the Son is like a servant set under the Father's authority; the term *subordinate* rejects the idea that the Son is less in being than the Father. This confession is widely acclaimed as the best summary of Reformed theology from the sixteenth century.

Robert Doyle, in his very critical review of my book *The Trinity and Subordinationism*, claims that I have misread the teaching of this confession by quoting it "out of context" and "omitting several important words."[171] What he means by these two comments escapes me. Is my failure not to have given the confession in full? He then adds a third criticism. I have not acknowledged that this confession not only distinguishes the persons but also speaks of an "order without inequality." As I unequivocally accept order in the Trinity, simply denying this involves hierarchical ordering, this comment is perplexing at first thought. It seems to criticize me for what I endorse. What Doyle fails to make clear in this article is that for him the word *order* means by definition "hierarchical order," or sub-ordering.[172] Here is where we differ. I hold that to *eternally* sub-order the Son to the Father in being, function, or authority indicates "inequality." It is to break with the tradition. Doyle is of the opposite opinion. He thinks divine equality and the sub-ordering in function and authority of the Son can be embraced without the one contradicting the other, and this is the tradition. I, however, still think the Second Helvetic Confession excludes what Doyle is teaching. This confession rightly affirms divine distinctions *and* order in the Trinity and rightly excludes inequality or sub-ordering in being, function, *or authority*. The Son is neither eternally "subordinate" nor "subservient" to the Father.

As an Anglican, like Doyle, Baddeley, and all the Sydney Doctrine Commission members, I was particularly interested to note that the first article of the "39 Articles of Religion" defines the triune God as "three persons, of one substance, power, and eternity." To teach that the Son is less in power than the Father, in terms of this

---

[171]I have already quoted several times from Doyle's article, "Are We Heretics?" published in the April 2004 edition of *The Briefing*. Readers of this article are referred to a longer version on *Briefings Web Extra*. Doyle's comments on my appeal to the Helvetic Confession are only found in this longer version. See http://www.matthiasmedia.com.au/briefing/webextra/apr04_giles.html, 7.

[172]Robert Doyle, "God in Feminist Critique," *Reformed Theological Review* 52, no. 1 (1993), 21; and "Sexuality, Personhood, and the Image of God," in *Personhood, Sexuality, and Ministry*, ed. B. Webb (Sydney, Aust.: Lancer, 1987), 43–46.

debate, "subordinated in authority," would be to deny that the Father and the Son are one in power, what all Anglicans are supposed to believe. The Augsburg Confession likewise speaks of the three divine persons as "equal in power" (article 1), and the Westminster Confession says they are of one "power" (2.3). This information should be of particular interest to Lutherans and Presbyterians respectively.

Twentieth-Century Breaks with the Tradition

To conclude this chapter, I want to alert my readers to the fact that two of the most important contributors to the twentieth-century renaissance in trinitarian theology break with the way the tradition, and I believe the Bible, speak of the obedience of Christ. What they say on this matter is innovative and exploratory.

1. Karl Barth

Some of my critics have been quick to point out that possibly the greatest theologian of the twentieth century, Karl Barth, repeatedly speaks of the obedience of Christ as God. They say to me, if Barth teaches this, then we cannot be wrong. Because it is very important to me to be fair and open to all the evidence, I have carefully examined this claim in a separate concluding chapter. What I found by reading Barth is that while he does break with the tradition by speaking of Christ as subordinate, obedient, and suffering *as God*, he never lets go of the belief that Christ is also at the same time Lord. For him the Son is never the subordinated, suffering, obedient Son *simpliciter*. He is always *both* Lord and servant. He is at one and the same time the sovereign electing God, eternally one in power and authority with the Father and the Spirit, and the subordinated, obedient, suffering Son, God identified with man for all eternity. Evangelicals who appeal to Barth in support for their doctrine of the eternal subordination of the Son in authority miss this dialectic in Barth's christological trinitarianism.

2. Wolfhart Pannenberg

Pannenberg also thinks that Christ's obedience is not to be limited to the incarnation, or to be understood simply as a consequence of him taking human flesh (the incarnation). His agenda is broad in scope.[173] He sets out to restate the doctrine of the Trinity while seeking to avoid the errors of tritheism, subordinationism, and modalism that the traditional formulation of the doctrine rightly rejected. Instead of differentiating the persons primarily on the basis of origination, Pannenberg differentiates them by

---

[173]I make no attempt to outline in any detail Pannenberg's doctrine of the Trinity. Most of the contemporary introductory studies on the doctrine of the Trinity provide this. Stanley J. Grenz, *Rediscovering the Triune God: The Trinity in Contemporary Theology* (Minneapolis: Fortress, 2004), 88–106, gives a very good summary.

their mutual dependence on one another—one cannot exist alone or without the others. For him self-differentiation always involves dependence. The term *person* is a correlative concept. Personhood is found in the self-giving of oneself to another whereby one's identity is established by the other. This leads him to speak of the Son subjecting himself to the Father and the Spirit subjecting himself to the Son and the Father.[174] However, he then immediately goes on to speak of the Father subjecting himself to the Son and Spirit,[175] which, he says, discloses the "mutuality in their relationships."[176] For Pannenberg this "mutuality" is seen most clearly in the handing over and handing back of the rule of the universe. Following Easter, the Father gives all rule to the Son, and at the end the Son gives rule back to the Father (1Co 15:28).[177]

Pannenberg's reconceptualization of the doctrine of the Trinity is imaginative and evocative. It demands a hearing, but as it radically breaks with the tradition, it must be considered exploratory. For contemporary evangelicals who believe in the eternal subordination of the Son in authority to the Father, Pannenberg's conception of the divine persons counts against their case. On his view of the Trinity, the logical conclusion would be that the Father and the Son are mutually subordinate to one another, and this would suggest that this is the ideal for the man-woman relationship (cf. Eph 5:21)!

Theological Postscript

Before leaving the question before us in this chapter, two insurmountable theological problems face those who want to argue that the Son of God is eternally set under the Father's authority.

First of all, the assertion that the Father rules over the Son indicates that it is believed that the Father has greater authority and power than the Son. He reigns over all, including the Son as a monarch. He is the one in charge. This teaching cuts right across the universally held belief that the Father, Son, and Spirit are indivisibly omnipotent—all-powerful. I have not found a hint in any book discussing the attributes of God that the power or authority of the divine persons can be distinguished. One of the most important facets of the Christian definition of the triune God is his omnipotence. Not to be omnipotent would mean not to be God. Thus in orthodoxy the divine three are thought of as indivisible in power and authority because they are indivisibly God. To suggest that the Son is eternally less in power and authority than the Father is to suggest that the Son is less fully God than the Father—what all the Arians taught.

---

[174]Wolfhart Pannenberg, *Systematic Theology*, vol. 1 (Grand Rapids, Mich.: Eerdmans, 1991), 308–13, 321.
[175]Ibid., 313–414, 322.
[176]Ibid., 313.
[177]Ibid., 312–13.

Second, the language of commanding and obeying implies that the parties involved each have their own will. The Son and the Spirit must each submit their will to the Father's will. The illustration given is that just as wives need to submit to the authority of their husband, so must the Son to the Father. It is of course accepted that husbands and wives each have their own will, but orthodoxy absolutely rejects the possibility that the divine three each have their own will. It is agreed that in the incarnation Jesus of Nazareth had a human will as a full human being and that he needed to bring this into harmony with the divine will. We see this struggle most profoundly in the Garden of Gethsemane on the night of his betrayal. It is because he is perfectly obedient *as man* that he fulfills the Mosaic law perfectly and can undo the disobedience of the first Adam, thereby winning our salvation. However, in relations between the divine Father, Son, and Spirit, perfect harmony prevails. They are one in mind and will. The idea that each divine person has his own will and the Son in particular is called to submit his will to that of the Father's will implies tritheism. To argue that the Son can do no other than obey, as the Sydney theologians do, means that he is not free and thus his actions are not obedience. He is a robot. On the Grudem model the Son is depicted like a liberated wife who should obey her "head"; on the Sydney model the Son is depicted like a completely submissive wife who can only do as her "head" commands! Tragically, these self-serving models of the Trinity contradict the model of the Trinity the Bible implies and orthodoxy has made explicit—of three divine "persons" united in being, power, love, and self-giving, having one will in all things.

Conclusion

In the historical sources that have just been surveyed, we see the obedience of Christ being discussed both christologically and soteriologically, as it is in the New Testament. From a christological perspective, the incarnate Christ's will to do his Father's will is indicative of the perfect harmony of mind and will between the Father and the Son.[178] It speaks of a coincidence of willing or of a unity of will. From a soteriological perspective, Christ's obedience is understood in reference to his work as the obedient second Adam, representative humankind, who perfectly does the will of God and thereby wins our salvation. The cross is the culmination of his work as the incarnate obedient Son. In his resurrection he is raised to rule as Lord. In both perspectives it is recognized that the incarnation necessitated the divine Son of God taking the form of a servant, but orthodoxy insists that he never ceased to be God and thus never gave up the power and authority that are intrinsically his as true God.

---

[178]The Synoptic Gospels make it plain that the incarnate Christ has both a human will and a divine will. This is somewhat less clear in John's gospel, as we noted in our chapter on biblical teaching.

The idea that the Father rules supreme and the Son is eternally subordinated in authority to the Father as an obedient servant was normative for historic fourth century "Arianism" in its various forms. Athanasius was quick to see that this model of the Trinity called into question that the divine three were *one being*. It divided and separated the one Godhead, setting in juxtaposition the Father and the Son. In answer to the Arians, Athanasius, the Cappadocian Fathers, and Augustine insist that the Son is "true God from true God," one in being, work/function, and authority with the Father, and that the Father and the Son have one will. To quote Professor Ayres's words again, "It is fundamental to all Pro-Nicene theologies that God is one power, glory, majesty and rule, Godhead essence and nature."[179] Calvin in the sixteenth century was exactly of the same opinion.

In answer to the question, "Are the Father, Son, and Spirit divided in power and authority?" the Bible and the tradition with one voice answer with a resounding *no*. The Father, the Son, and the Spirit are one in being, "coequal" God, and therefore indivisible in power and authority.

---

[179] Ayres, *Nicea*, 271.

CHAPTER

DIFFERENTIATING THE TRINITARIAN PERSONS

In the last chapter I focused on what I believe is the central issue in the contemporary evangelical doctrine of the eternal subordination of God the Son to God the Father: the Son's subordination in *authority*. I argued that this not only implies the Son's ontological and personal subordination but also suggests tritheism: the divine persons each have their own will. This means they are not truly one. Now I come to what those who espouse this position want us to believe is the central issue. It is the eternal *differentiation* of the Father and the Son. Just as men and women are differentiated, we are told, so too are the Father and the Son. No issue is more important to those against whom I am arguing than differentiating the Father and the Son and men and women. They tell us that if sexual differentiation is not stressed, then sexual equivalence follows,[1] and if divine differences are not stressed, modalism follows.

Evidence to substantiate what has just been said can be found in virtually every evangelical book advocating the eternal subordination of the Son. Professor Wayne Grudem in his *Systematic Theology* says, if we do not have "subordination then there is no inherent difference in the way the three divine persons relate to one another, and consequently we do not have three distinct persons."[2] In his later book *Evangelical Feminism*, he adds, "The differences in authority among the Father, Son, and Holy

---

[1] For documentation on this side of the issue see my book *The Trinity and Subordinationism* (Westmont, Ill.: InterVarsity, 2002), 183–87.

[2] Wayne Grudem, *Systematic Theology: An Introduction to Biblical Doctrine* (Grand Rapids, Mich.: Zondervan, 1995), 251.

Spirit are the *only* interpersonal differences that the Bible indicates that exist *eternally* among the members of the Godhead."[3] And, "if we did not have such differences in authority in relationships among the members of the Trinity, then we would not know of any differences at all."[4] Should anyone object to this reasoning either in relation to women or the divine Son, arguing that neither women nor the Son are *permanently* subordinated, the reply is made, "You are denying difference." So Robert Letham, writing in the *Westminster Theological Journal*, says, if the Son is not eternally subordinated to the Father, "then we are left with modalism."[5] Later in his book *The Holy Trinity* he adds that a "feminized doctrine of God" that tends to eliminate "the submission of the Son to the Father" results in "a thorough going homogenization of the [divine] persons in fully mutual relations."[6]

In the *Sydney Doctrine Commission Report* we are told, "The egalitarian case [re: women] ... logically leads to a claim for undifferentiated equality in relation to the three [divine] persons."[7] English evangelical Thomas Smail follows the same line of reasoning.[8] He argues that there is a growing tendency driven by "egalitarian and feminist ideologies"[9] to minimize or deny divine and male-female differentiation. This he believes must of necessity lead to the errors of modalism[10] and "undifferentiated sameness."[11]

All this sounds very strange to someone well read in trinitarian theology, or cognizant of contemporary women's studies. Who is not differentiating the Father and the Son or men and women? I have challenged my debating opponents for years in public forums and in international publications to give me one example of a Roman Catholic, or mainline Protestant, or evangelical theologian who has denied human or divine differentiation, and not a single example has been forthcoming. All that they can say is, well, if you deny that women or the divine Son are permanently subordinated, then you must be denying difference. For me to affirm vehemently that I embrace differentiation apart from subordination does not register with them.

What then is the issue? It is not differentiation as such. It is the idea that differentiation must be predicated on superordination and subordination. My debating oppo-

---

[3] Wayne Grudem, *Evangelical Feminism and Biblical Truth* (Sisters, Ore.: Multnomah, 2004), 433. Italics added.

[4] Ibid.

[5] Robert Letham, "The Man-Woman Debate: Theological Comment," *Westminster Theological Journal* 52 (1990): 69.

[6] Robert Letham, *The Holy Trinity in Scripture, History, Theology, and Worship* (Phillipsburg, N.J.: P & R, 2004), 392.

[7] Par. 44, cf. pars. 30, 31.

[8] Thomas Smail, *Like Father, Like Son* (Milton Keynes, Bucks.: Paternoster, 2005).

[9] Ibid., 240.

[10] Ibid., 78–80.

[11] Ibid., 250.

nents believe that unless the divine Son is subordinated in authority to the Father and women to men, differentiation cannot be upheld. The right to rule or the exclusion from rule differentiates the persons and defines their personal identity—their being. So entrenched in the minds of those I am debating against is the idea that difference can only be upheld if one party in these two relationships is subordinated in authority that if I or anyone else denies the permanent subordination of women in authority, or the eternal subordination of the Son in authority, then it is taken that difference itself is being denied.

The idea that the differing authority of the Father and the Son is the most important differentiating characteristic in the divine Father-Son relationship unites all contemporary evangelicals who speak of the eternal subordination or submission of the Son. They are of one mind on this matter. There are two sides to their case: (1) differentiation implies by necessity the subordination of one party, and (2) if subordination in authority is not endorsed, differentiation cannot be maintained, and in the case of the Trinity, modalism must result. Neither argument has any force whatsoever. Differentiation and equality are not mutually exclusive concepts. Two "persons," divine or human, can be equal in authority and do the same things and yet be differentiated. Thus historic orthodoxy has been able to make both the equality and the differentiation of the Father, Son, and Spirit absolutes without allowing one to eclipse the other. The truth is no one is denying divine or male-female differentiation. This constant assertion that egalitarians are doing this is disingenuous. *The dispute is about whether the Son of God is eternally subordinated to the Father and whether women are permanently subordinated to men.*

The question therefore before us in this chapter is not whether the Father, Son, and Spirit are eternally and indelibly differentiated. Absolutely no orthodox theologian denies this, and I certainly do not. In my reading I have found no one denying divine differentiation or even suggesting it. The question is thus, *how* can the Father, Son, and Spirit be differentiated without falling into the errors of modalism, subordinationism, or tritheism?

The Word *Difference*

From what has just been said, it is obvious that we have a problem in communication once the word *difference* appears. For one side this word implies and necessitates subordination in authority. Thus if subordination in authority is denied, then it is understood that difference itself has been denied. For the other side the word *difference* means "not the same," "not identical," "other than," "distinguished from." It does not mean or imply subordination, and no dictionary gives the word this meaning. A dog and a cat are very different creatures, yet their differences do not determine which should exercise authority over the other. Size and aggression determine who rules when a cat and a dog cross paths. A Chinese person is different from a Polynesian person, but this says nothing about who should be in charge if they worked together. The examples could be multiplied. The word *difference* in everyday usage does not imply or necessitate the subordination of one party. What is more, difference and equality can be correlated. People and things can be equal in some or many ways and different in others. Chinese people and Polynesian people are fellow human beings made in the image and likeness of God; they are equal in the most profound ways, yet they can be differentiated.

In the opening chapter of this book, I explained how this special use of the word *difference* emerged in evangelical circles. I briefly reiterate the facts. When in the 1970s it could no longer be claimed that women are "inferior" to men, as virtually everyone had said until this time, evangelicals determined to maintain the subordination of women began saying, "We believe men and women are equal; they simply have different roles." This sounded perfectly acceptable to modern ears. However, once unpacked, what we have here is deliberately obfuscating language. The *only* difference that is ever in mind is who is in charge and who is set under them. Men's "role" is to lead, women's is to obey. Absolutely basic to this position is the idea that the man-woman relationship was hierarchically ordered in creation and thus it is God's ideal for all time in every culture. From this it follows, despite the strident denials by my debating opponents, that women are not equal with men in any substantive way. They are not simply functionally subordinated, they *are* the subordinated sex, and this can never change. Sadly this ideologically driven rewording of the case for the subordination of women was then used to reword and reformulate the doctrine of the Trinity so that then appeal could be made to the Trinity to support the permanent subordination of women. We were told the Father and the Son are equals; they simply have differing roles. Just as women are permanently set under men in authority, so too is the Son eternally set under the Father in authority — this is historic orthodoxy. In these parallel arguments for the subordination of women and the Son of God the word *difference* bears the meaning "subordinate."

This special usage of the word *difference* must be brought out in the open because it profoundly confuses the debate among evangelicals over the doctrine of the Trinity. In historic orthodoxy affirmations about the difference between the divine persons allude solely to the fact that the divine three are eternally distinct "persons." They never imply subordination of one or more of the persons. When the great theologians of the past and the creeds and Reformation confessions speak of divine differentiation, they are saying the divine three cannot be identified. They are one in divinity, being, work, majesty, and authority, but not one and the same. The Father is eternally the Father, the Son is eternally the Son, and the Spirit is eternally the Spirit. Evangelicals committed to the eternal subordination of the Son, in contrast, read every comment in the church fathers and the creeds and confessions that speak of divine differentiation as speaking of the Son (and the Spirit's) subordination. Thus when they see Athanasius, the Cappadocians, or Augustine saying the Father is "unbegotten" and the Son "begotten," or the Father "sends" and the Son "is sent," and these distinctions cannot be reversed, or the Father is the Father and not the Son, they think these differences set the Father over the Son. For them differentiation presupposes hierarchical ordering in the immanent Trinity. As long as this word *difference* has one meaning for one side and another meaning for the other side, communication is impossible. I ask my debating opponents to justify their claim that the word *difference* implies and necessitates subordination, or to abandon this idea.

I also ask them to abandon altogether their argument that differentiating the divine persons or the sexes is the key matter that divides evangelicals today. It is not. Both sides in this debate without exception endorses divine and sexual differentiation. It is my case that evangelicals committed to the eternal subordination of the Son have only made difference the central issue because it sounds plausible and positive to say, "We are upholding divine and sexual differentiation; the other side is not." It is not so easy to be completely open and to say, "What we want to maintain above all else is that men should permanently rule over women, just as the Father eternally rules over the Son."

The import of these contrasting affirmations that the three divine persons are "equal and different" must be spelled out. Historic orthodoxy takes "equal and different" to mean that the Father, Son, and Spirit are coequal in every significant way, yet they are not to be identified. The divine persons are differentiated not by any deficit in the Son or the Spirit, but by the fact that one is eternally the Father and another the Son and another the Spirit; they have differing origination and thus differing relations (the Father is the Father of the Son, the Son is the Son of the Father, the Spirit proceeds from the Father, or the Father and the Son).[12] This stands in contrast to the contemporary evangelical opinion that "equal and different" means that while the divine persons are all truly God, equal in divinity, the Son and the Spirit are not the Father's equal in power and authority—and this difference in authority is grounded in who they are, their identity as the Son and the Spirit. Differentiation is predicated on an eternal personal subordination in authority. This means that divine differentiation is based on a deficit in the Son and the Spirit. The Son (and the Spirit but it is only the Son that is in focus) is less than or inferior to the Father in authority. He is not really coequal in "the most fundamental"[13] divine attribute, omnipotence.

---

[12] See Gerald O'Collins, *The Tripersonal God: Understanding and Interpreting the Trinity* (Mahwah, N.J.: Paulist, 1999), 178–79.

[13] Gerald Bray, *The Doctrine of God* (London: Inter-Varsity, 1993), 103.

Subordinationism and Tritheism

From what has just been said, it is obvious that this conservative evangelical emphasis on divine differentiation predicated on an eternal deficit in authority in the Son has ontological implications. The Son *is* the subordinated Son; he does not simply function subordinately or freely chose subordination for a period of time. His subordination is eternal, and it defines his person. This teaching also has dire consequences for divine unity and simplicity. In the previous chapter we made the point that if the Son must eternally obey the Father, this presupposes that the divine persons each have their own will. Three separate wills imply three *separate and divided* persons, and this is classic tritheism. Emphasizing divine differentiation exacerbates this problem. When the differences between the divine three are brought to the foreground, divine unity is eclipsed. We see this in the literature produced by those who speak of the eternal subordination of the Son. Comments on divine unity are seldom found and ones on divine equality with any substance are even more rare. Apart from affirmations that all three persons are divine, all the emphasis falls on their differentiation. The end result is the persons of the Trinity are divided and separated. In this contemporary conservative evangelical doctrine of the Trinity, first divine equality is sacrificed, and then divine unity is sacrificed.

Most evangelicals who argue for the eternal subordination of the Son want to limit this to an eternal subordination in function and authority. They say they embrace ontological equality. I have pointed out repeatedly in reply that this argument is untenable. If the Son is *eternally* set under the Father in function and authority, if this is what differentiates the two, then they are not equals in any substantive way. The Son does not simply function subordinately; he *is* the subordinated Son. His subordination defines his person. Many of the more informed evangelical theologians committed to the eternal subordination of the Son recognize this with absolute clarity. Thus the evangelical theologians on the 1999 Sydney Doctrine Commission argue that the differences between the divine persons reflect "differences of being" among the divine persons.[14] It is in their "nature" or "very person" that the divine three are differentiated. In reply to my earlier book *The Trinity and Subordinationism*, in which I highlighted this ontological differing of the divine persons, Robert Doyle, a key contributor to the 1999 *Sydney Doctrine Report*, says using terms "like, 'essence,' 'being,' and 'eternal nature' in talking about who they [the divine three] are in their differences is close to inescapable."[15] John Frame, the American conservative Reformed theologian, is of the same mind. He says the subordination of the Son and the Spirit is

---

[14] Par. 25. Cf. pars. 17, 18, 20, 21, 22, 24, 32, 33.

[15] Robert Doyle, "Are We Heretics? A Review of *The Trinity and Subordinationism* by Kevin Giles," *The Briefing* (April 2004): 17.

not "merely economic, for it has to do with *the eternal nature* of the persons, *the personal properties* that distinguish each one from the others."[16] In even more explicit terms, John Dahms, writing in the *Journal of the Evangelical Theological Society*, speaks of "the ontological basis for the dissimilarity of the Father and the Son."[17]

Unity Before Differentiation

In stark contrast to the contemporary evangelical emphasis and preoccupation with divine differentiation, historic orthodoxy with one voice, at least until very recently,[18] has emphasized divine unity, simplicity, and equality. Putting the emphasis on divine differentiation was one of the hallmarks of Arianism. In his definitive study of the fourth-century Arian debates, *Nicaea and Its Legacy*, Professor Lewis Ayres speaks of "four theological trajectories" that divided the opposing parties.[19] The first of these, he says, is that one side emphasized "the difference between Father and Son," and the other side the unity and equality of the Father and the Son.[20] Those who emphasized difference were the so-called "fourth-century Arians."[21] Those who emphasized unity and equality without in any way denying divine differentiation were "the pro-Nicenes." For them the divine persons were one in being, work, and authority. Again it would seem that contemporary evangelicals who emphasize divine differentiation stand closer to Arianism than historic orthodoxy.

While reading Thomas Aquinas on the Trinity, I was fascinated to note that he went so far as to oppose the use of the word *difference* in reference to the divine persons. He writes, "We must not, in speaking of God, use the words 'diversity' and 'difference' lest we should compromise the unity of nature; we can, however, use the word 'distinction' on account of relative opposition. Thus if we come across a reference to diversity or difference of persons in any authoritative text, we take it to mean 'distinction.' "[22]

---

[16]John Frame, *The Doctrine of God: A Theology of Lordship* (Phillipsburg, N.J.: P&R, 2002), 723. Italics added. To be quite fair, both the *Sydney Doctrine Report* and John Frame have many comments alongside such quotes that are orthodox. This does not excuse what they say in error.

[17]John Dahms, "The Generation of the Son," *Journal of the Evangelical Theological Society* 32, no. 4 (1989): 497.

[18]I allude to the contemporary interest in what is called "the social model of the Trinity," which has already been discussed and to which I will return at the end of this chapter.

[19]Lewis Ayres, *Nicaea and Its Legacy: An Approach to Fourth-Century Trinitarian Theology* (New York: Oxford, 2005), 41.

[20]Ibid., 42–43. This is a topic to which Ayres repeatedly returns. See also pp. 80, 115, 159, 199, 245, etc.

[21]Ibid., 42.

[22]Thomas Aquinas, *Summa Theologiae*, vol. 6, trans. C. Velecky (London: Blackfriars, 1963), 89.

With these introductory matters outlined, we now turn to see what Athanasius, the Cappadocian Fathers, Augustine, Calvin, and the creeds and Reformation confessions say on divine unity and divine differentiation. In this discussion I show first that in the historic tradition the emphasis falls on divine unity and equality; and, second, that when it speaks of divine differentiation, it is never predicated on differing work/function or authority between the divine three.

Differentiating the Persons in Different Periods

Before entering into the details of what various theologians have said and thought on trinitarian unity and differentiation, it is important to point out that before the Council of Nicea in 325 the church fathers who wrote on the Trinity had one agenda and after Nicea another. Before the council, the main concern of the Apologists and Tertullian was to explain how the Father, Son, and Spirit could be one and yet differentiated without falling into the error of tritheism. In the immediate period before the council and following the council the main agenda for Bishop Alexander of Alexandria (d. 328), Athanasius, the Cappadocian Fathers, and other pro-Nicene theologians was to explain how the Father, Son, and Spirit could be one and yet eternally differentiated without falling into the error of subordinationism. Naturally these contrasting concerns lead to differing theological outcomes.

Theologians before Nicea

The first to attempt to explain how there could be one God differentiated as three persons, Father, Son, and Holy Spirit, was made by the "Apologists," ardent mono-theists, who assumed that the one true God, God the Father, was a monad.[23] Their challenge was to explain how the Son in particular, but also the Holy Spirit, might be thought of as God as well. They differ in some details, but all of them identify Jesus with the *Logos* ("The Word" or "Reason" of the one true God) who was made manifest in creation and became incarnate in Jesus of Nazareth. They found the Stoic distinction between the *Logos endiathetos* (the immanent Word) and the *Logos prophorikos* (the expressed Word) particularly helpful in making their case. The Apologists confess God as a Father, Son, and Spirit but have little to say about the Holy Spirit. They succeed in safeguarding the *monarchy* (the sole rule) of the Father by making the Son and the Spirit creatures brought forth in time to do the sole Monad's will. However, in setting such a sharp division between the Father and the Son and the Spirit, they could not avoid subordinating the Son and the Spirit.

Irenaeus was deeply indebted to the Apologists, although he was much more of a biblical theologian. His monumental five books, *Against Heresies*, preeminently

---

[23] *The Ante-Nicene Fathers*, vol. 1, *The Apostolic Fathers, Justin Martyr, Irenaeus*, eds. Alexander Roberts and James Donaldson (Grand Rapids, Mich.: Eerdmans, 1973).

addresses the Gnostics. He too begins his thinking about the Trinity, believing that "the one true God" is God the Father and Jesus is his *Logos*. He writes, "He [the Father] is the creator, he is Lord of all, and there is no one beside him, or above him — nor is there a second God — He is the Father of our Lord Jesus Christ: through his Word, who is his Son through him he is revealed and manifested."[24]

This passage hints at what we see more clearly elsewhere in his writings. The Father is differentiated from the Son and the Spirit because the Father is God in the ultimate sense and because the Son and the Spirit have differing works or functions to accomplish for the Father. He progresses past the Apologists, but he is still a second-century theologian who thinks of God the Father as a monad who becomes a triad and sees no problem in differentiating the Son and the Spirit by making them the subordinate agents of the Father in the world.

Wolfhart Pannenberg holds that the chief merit of the *Logos* Christology was that "it asserted the differentiation of Father and Son within the Godhead."[25] However, he adds, "The dogmatic weakness of the *Logos* Christology is that the *Logos* is seen as going forth from God as a being subordinate in rank in comparison to the Father who has no beginning."[26] Edmund Hill commends Justin and Irenaeus for affirming the real distinction between the Father and the Son, but for him the key problem is that this distinction is grounded in "differing functions or roles" in creation and redemption. The *Logos* is simply the "operative principle in the divine order."[27] In this pre-Nicene "model" of the Trinity, differentiation is unambiguously affirmed, but the Son and the Spirit are not coequal God.

Tertullian

With Tertullian the discussion on what the Bible teaches about the three divine persons takes another turn. In writing on the Trinity, Tertullian's main purpose is to refute Praxeas, a Christian teacher who came to Rome from Asia Minor and with others taught that there was only one God who is revealed in three successive modes or ways. This error became known as Monarchianism in the West and Sabellianism in the East. It was predicated on strict monotheism. Modalism, as this error later became known as, allowed for no differences in the eternal or immanent Trinity, only differing roles or functions in the economy. Because there is only one God who appears in three different roles, no subordination is possible. Tertullian

---

[24] Ibid., "Irenaeus Against Heresies," 2.30.9 (p. 406).

[25] Wolfhart Pannenberg, *Jesus: God and Man* (Philadelphia: Westminster, 1964), 160, 163.

[26] Ibid., 164.

[27] Edmund Hill, *The Mystery of the Trinity* (London: Chapman, 1985), 49. Exactly the same criticism is made by William J. Hill, *The Three-Personed God: The Trinity as a Mystery of Salvation* (Washington, D.C.: Catholic University of America Press, 1982), 33.

inveighed against this teaching, expressing alarm at its popularity among ordinary believers.[28]

Tertullian immediately saw that this teaching completely undermined the personal distinctions within the Godhead so clearly affirmed in Scripture. His main emphasis therefore in writing is to prove that in the one God three distinct "persons" coexist. Beginning with the premise adopted by the Apologists and Irenaeus that God the Father is the one true God, the *Monarchia*, Tertullian seeks to explain how the Son and the Spirit as distinct persons may also be understood to be God. All that *monarchia* means, he says, is rule by one person. It does not disallow the monarch sharing his rule with others, especially with a son. For Tertullian the word *economy* (Gk *oikonomia*, Lat. *dispensatio, dispositio*) refers to how the one God, the monarch, becomes three. He says we "believe there is one only God, but under the following dispensation, or *oikonomia*, as it is called, this one only God has also a Son, his Word, who proceeded from himself, by whom all things were made."[29] The two main problems with this explanation of the Trinity are, first, that the triune nature of God is not eternal and constitutive—the one God becomes three in time—and second, it results in the subordination of the Son and the Spirit. The Father alone is God in his own right; the Son and the Spirit are less than the Father. So Tertullian speaks of the Son as "second" and the Spirit as "third" "from God," or "in degree."[30]

Tertullian must be commended for routing modalism and avoiding tritheism by appeal to the monarchy of the Father, but in stressing the distinctions between the Father and the Son and the Spirit he is not able to affirm an eternally coequal Trinity. The emphasis on the distinctions of the divine three persons creates a disjunction and separation between them. His attempt to explain how the one God could be three persons by focusing on the divine economy alone was the problem. It was a valiant attempt to take seriously what was revealed in Scripture and history about the Father, Son, and Spirit, but it did not facilitate "seeing" the deeper theological and conceptual issues that would lead later catholic theologians to insist on the eternal trinitarian nature of the Christian God, and on the equality in being, work/function, and rule/authority of the three divine persons. Tertullian rightly stressed the differences between each of the divine persons but failed to recognize that the God revealed in Scripture is an eternal Trinity of three coequal persons who are eternally one in being, inseparable in their work, and indivisible in power and authority.

---

[28] Tertullian, "Against Praxeas," in *The Ante-Nicene Fathers*, vol. 3, *Latin Christianity: Its Founder, Tertullian*, eds. Alexander Roberts and James Donaldson (Grand Rapids, Mich.: Eerdmans, 1973), chapter 2 (p. 598).

[29] Ibid., chapter 2 (p. 598).

[30] Ibid., chapter 4 (p. 599), chapter 7 twice (p. 602), chapter 8 (p. 603), chapter 9 (p. 604), chapter 13 (p. 608).

Arius

A little more than a hundred years later, the issue of the differentiation of the persons of the Trinity came to the fore again, this time starting a heated theological conflict that lasted for most of the fourth century and tore the church apart. It all began in about 319 when Arius, an Alexandrian presbyter, began stressing the difference between the Father and the Son. Right at the heart of Arius' teaching was ontological subordinationism, and this presupposed a radical distinction between the Father and the Son. For Arius the Father was unoriginated, the Son originated in time, a creature. He was not of the same being as the Father, and for this reason, he did not have the same power and authority as the Father, nor was he able to do the works the Father did. He was truly *different* from the Father.

As far as Arius' writings go, we have no more than three letters, a few fragments, and possibly a quotation from his *Thalia*.[31] Most of our information on what he taught comes from the writings of his opponents, especially from the pen of Athanasius, his bitterest foe. From Arius' own pen we know he believed that God the Father, who he liked to call "the Unbegotten," was a "monad" who is "prior to everything, . . . unlike the Son who is not unbegotten, nor any part of the Unbegotten . . . |who| before he was begotten and created, or determined or established, did not exist." These quotes show how Arius saw a great crevasse between the one true God and the Son. Athanasius says that the Arians believed that the Son "has nothing proper to God in proper subsistence, he is not equal, nor one in essence with him." "God is wise, he [the Son] is the teacher of wisdom." "The Father is more glorious than the other [the Son]." "The Son is created and exists at the will of the Father." The Son does not fully know the Father, "it is impossible for him to investigate the Father who is by himself."[32] In Athanasius' version of the letter Arius wrote to Alexander his bishop, the emphasis falls on the uniqueness of the Father. Arius writes, "We acknowledge *one* God, *alone* ingenerate, *alone* everlasting, *alone* unbegotten, *alone* true, *alone* having immortality, *alone* wise, *alone* good, *alone* sovereign . . ." To this he adds, the Father "is above him [the Son], as being his God and before him."[33] Athanasius summarized Arius' position in this way: "The essences of the Father and the Son and the Holy Spirit are separate in nature and estranged and disconnected, and alien, and without participation of each other;

---

[31] See in more detail R. P. C. Hanson, *The Search for the Christian Doctrine of God: The Arian Controversy, 318–381* (Grand Rapids, Mich.: Baker, 2005), 5–6. The quotes from Arius' own writings are taken from Hanson's translations of these texts.

[32] Athanasius, "The Councils of Ariminum and Seleucia," in *The Nicene and Post Nicene Fathers of the Christian Church* (henceforth *NPNF*), ed. Philip Schaff and Henry Wace (Grand Rapids, Mich.: Eerdmans, 1971), 4:15 (p. 457).

[33] Ibid., 16 (p. 458). Italics added.

and in his own words, 'utterly unlike from each other in essence and glory unto infinity.' "[34]

The differences between the Father and the Son could not be more sharply drawn. Professor Jaroslav Pelikan argues that in the end Arianism was a form of polytheism or tritheism[35] — a point Athanasius himself made.[36] It implied a "plurality" of separate divine beings.

Athanasius

Arius' main agenda was to separate and differentiate the Father and the Son in every possible way. Athanasius' main agenda in reply was to stress the "inseparable unity" of the Father and the Son in every possible way. Athanasius knew well of the danger of Sabellianism, but he was never going to fall into this error because his most fundamental belief was that the God of Christian revelation is eternally triune and can never be otherwise. He never confuses or conflates the Father, the Son, or the Spirit, but differentiating the persons was not his primary concern. It was always the unity in being, work, and authority of the Father and the Son.

What Athanasius wants to avoid at any cost is a separation or disjunction between the divine persons. He constantly and emphatically stresses the unity and coequality of the Father and the Son, or of the three persons of the Trinity.

> There is an eternal and one Godhead in a Triad and there is one glory of the holy Triad.[37]

> There is but one form of Godhead, which is also in the Word; and one God the Father existing by himself according as he is above all, and appearing in the Son according as he pervades all things, and in the Spirit according as in him he acts in all things through the Word. For thus we confess God to be one through the Triad.[38]

> The Son's Godhead is the Father's Godhead, and thus the Father in the Son exercise his providence over all things.[39]

> The Father and the Son are two, yet the monad of the Godhead is indivisible and inseparable.[40]

---

[34] Athanasius, "Discourses," in *NPNF* 4:1.6 (p. 309).

[35] Jaroslav Pelikan, *The Christian Tradition: A History of the Development of Doctrine*, vol. 1, *The Emergence of the Catholic Tradition (100–600)* (Chicago: University of Chicago Press, 1971), 200.

[36] Athanasius, "Discourses," in *NPNF* 4:3.15 (p. 402).

[37] Ibid., 1.18 (p. 316–17).

[38] Ibid., 3.15.9 (p. 402).

[39] Ibid., 3.36 (p. 414).

[40] Ibid., 4.1 (p. 433).

Possibly the text Athanasius quotes the most is, "The Father and I are one" (Jn 10:30; cf. 17:21, 22), with a close second being, "Whoever has seen me has seen the Father" (Jn 14:9).

For him the unity of the three divine persons was so profound that it implied their coinherence. Building on the words of Jn 14:11, "I am in the Father and the Father in me," a text he constantly quotes, he reasoned that at all times there is a complete mutual indwelling in which each person, while remaining what he is by himself as Father, Son, or Holy Spirit, is wholly in the others as the others are wholly in him. Thus he writes, "For where the Father is there is the Son,"[41] and "the Son is in the Father ... because the whole being of the Son is proper to the Father's essence."[42]

It is thus of no surprise in the light of all this to find Athanasius repeatedly saying, "The same things are said of the Son, which are said of the Father, except calling him Father."[43] This I call "Athanasius' rule" to direct all thinking about the Father-Son relationship.

How then did Athanasius distinguish the divine three, or in particular the Father and the Son, to avoid any hint of modalism, or as he names it Sabellianism? We have seen in earlier chapters that he did not distinguish them in being, work, authority, or will. On these things they are inseparably one. He uses a number of strategies. One of his less profound arguments is simply to pour scorn on Sabellianism as an "absurdity" for suggesting that the "same becomes at one time Father, at another his own Son."[44] More important is his argument that the names *Father* and *Son* designate eternal and unchangeable distinctions within the Triad. He says, "The Father is ever Father and never could become Son, so the Son is ever Son and never could become Father."[45] Athanasius never questions the differences between the Father and the Son, because the Father and the Son are clearly distinguished in Scripture and Scripture is his ultimate authority. When the Arians pointed to texts that could be read to suggest that the Son's authority was derived authority given by the Father,[46] Athanasius replies that the texts quoted reflected the fact that the Son is to be differentiated from the Father, not subordinated in authority to the Father. He says texts like "'was given to me,' and 'I received,' and 'were delivered to me,' only show that he is not the Father, but the Father's Word ... [they do not] impair the Godhead of the Son, but rather show

---

[41] Ibid., 2.41 (p. 370).

[42] Ibid., 3.3 (p. 395).

[43] Ibid., 3.4 (p. 395); cf. 3.1 (p. 394), 3.5 (p. 395), 3.6 (p. 396), 4.3 (p. 434), "Councils of Ariminum and Seleucia," in *NPNF* 4:49 (p. 476, lines 3 and 4 and lines 66–67), "On Luke 10:22," in *NPNF* 4:3 and 4 (pp. 88–89).

[44] Ibid., 3.4 (p. 395); cf. 3.36 (p. 413), 4.2 (p. 432), 4.12 (p. 437), etc.

[45] Ibid., 1.22 (p. 319); cf. 3.36 (p. 413).

[46] So Robert Gregg and Dennis Groh, *Early Arianism: A View of Salvation* (Philadelphia: Fortress, 1981), 91.

him to be truly Son."[47] And for Athanasius sonship does not imply subordination. It speaks rather of equality, agency, and intimacy.

It is, however, differing origination that is for him the most important distinguishing mark. The Son is "begotten," the Father "unbegotten." He was not the first to use these terms to differentiate the Father and the Son, but he came to embrace them in the context of his heated dispute with the early Arians. They equated the terms "begotten" (*gennetos*) and "created" (*genetos*), which in Greek happen to have only one consonant to distinguish the two words. Athanasius takes no objection to their argument that the Father is different from the Son in that he is "unbegotten" and the Son is "begotten." The words *begotten* or *offspring* are for Athanasius helpful words to use of the Father-Son relationship because they "signify a Son. And beholding the Son we see the Father."[48]

The terms *unbegotten* and *begotten* for Athanasius certainly differentiate the Father and the Son, allowing for no confusion of the persons, but for him these terms speak more of the inseparable unity of the Father and the Son and of the intimacy of their relationship than anything else. The fact that the Son is begotten of the Father indicates for Athanasius that the Son is one in being with the Father, and the terms *father* and *son* imply a loving, intimate father-son relationship. Athanasius never explicitly says that differing origination implies differing relations, as later theologians would do, but in understanding the term *begotten* as indicative of the Father-Son relationship, he paved the way for this later important insight. Pannenberg says that for Athanasius, "The unity of the Son with the Father was set on a different foundation from that of relation of origin, namely on the logic of the relation posited when we call God 'Father.' "[49]

For Athanasius *ousia* (being/substance) is what makes God God, and all three divine persons share this one *ousia*. For this reason he accepts and then later strongly argues for the use of the term *homoousios* enshrined in the creed of Nicea to define the profound unity of the Father and Son. In reply to those who objected to the term *homoousios*, seeing in it the danger of modalism which collapsed the distinctions within the Godhead, Athanasius argued that the term spoke both of the unity of being of the one God who is eternally a Triad, and of the eternal distinctions of the three persons — only differing things or persons can be said to be *homoousios*.[50] Until the later part of his life he did not use the term *hypostasis* to designate the divine three. It was only at a church council in 362 he convened and chaired in Alexandria, of which

---

[47] Athanasius, "Discourses," in *NPNF* 4:3.36 (p. 413).

[48] Ibid., 1.16 (p. 316).

[49] Wolfhart Pannenberg, *Systematic Theology*, vol. 1, trans. Geoffrey Bromley (Grand Rapids, Mich.: Eerdmans, 1991), 278.

[50] J. N. D. Kelly, *Early Christian Doctrines*, 5th ed. (London: Adam and Charles Black, 1977), 254.

he gives an account in his "Synodal Letter to the People of Antioch,"[51] that he agreed to the formula "one *ousia*, three *hypostases*." George Prestige says from this time it was accepted that, "While *hypostasis* lays stress on concrete independence, *ousia* lays it on intrinsic constitution ... the one word denotes God as manifest, the other connotes God as being.... Athanasius taught that in God one and the same identical 'substance' or object, *without any division, substitution, or differentiation of content* is permanently present in three distinct objective forms."[52]

Athanasius does not differentiate the persons on the basis of differing functions or authority, let alone being, and yet he allows for a constant pattern or order in how the divine three operate or work. Nothing in God for Athanasius is random or arbitrary. Like on so many things, he was the first to recognize that the Bible indicates that each divine person has his distinct contribution to make to every common work that they do. So he says, "Through the Son does the Father create,"[53] "he works through the Son,"[54] and he "speaks through the Son."[55] In The *Letters of St. Athanasius Concerning the Holy Spirit*, this motif is given full trinitarian expression. "The Father does all things *through* the Word *in* the Holy Spirit. Thus the unity of the Holy Triad is preserved."[56] In these words Athanasius acknowledges that how the divine persons work also distinguishes them without any suggestion of the subordination of any of the divine three.

The inseparable unity in being, work, and authority of the Triad for Athanasius is beyond dispute or refutation. We must give him full marks for resoundingly repudiating all the Arian arguments that would radically differentiate the Father and the Son by subordinating the Son in being, function, and authority. There is no question that what he stresses is divine unity, equality, and simplicity. Nevertheless, he is adamant that the Father, Son, and Spirit are eternally differentiated and cannot be confused or identified, but this is a secondary issue in all his writings.[57] Nowhere at any point do we find him suggesting that divine differentiation implies or necessitates the subordination of the Son or the Spirit. Indeed he repeatedly rejects this idea.

---

[51] Athanasius, "Synodal Letter to the People of Antioch," in *NPNF* 4:4 (pp. 483–86).

[52] George Leonard Prestige, *God in Patristic Thought* (London: SPCK, 1959), xxix, see also 86–190. Italics added. See further on this T. F. Torrance, *The Trinitarian Faith: The Evangelical Theology of the Ancient Catholic Church* (Edinburgh: T&T Clark, 1993), 310–11 and *The Christian Doctrine of God: One Being Three Persons* (Edinburgh: T&T Clark, 1996), 104, 128. On Athanasius' use of the terms *ousia* and *hypostasis*, Hanson, *The Search*, 444–45, gives a somewhat different interpretation of the development in Athanasius' thinking and usage.

[53] Athanasius, "Discourses," in *NPNF* 4:2.4 (p. 370).

[54] Ibid.

[55] Ibid., 4:3.14 (p. 412).

[56] Athanasius, *The Letters of Saint Athanasius Concerning the Holy Spirit*, trans. C. R. B. Shapland (London: Epworth, 1951), 1.28 (p. 135).

[57] More than one scholar has argued that Athanasius borders on modalism, but with Ayres, *Nicaea*, 238, I have no sympathy with that argument.

When Stephen Kovach and Peter Schemm claim that differentiation for Athanasius indicates that he believed in an eternal "order of subordination" in the Trinity, they are totally mistaken.[58]

The Cappadocian Fathers

Like Athanasius, the Cappadocian Fathers' main agenda was to absolutely repudiate the idea that the Son was to be radically differentiated from the Father. Their principal adversary was Eunomius, who more consistently and with more philosophically based arguments differentiated the divine three more than Arius and the early Arians had done. In his "Confession," Eunomius begins with the belief that God is a monad who cannot share with any other his "being" (*ousia*), "glory," or "authority" — "he is one and sole God almighty." In contrast to the Father, the Son is "the first born of all creation, ... not uncreated," "not to be measured in rank along with him who generated him nor in any point to the Father's *ousia*," "obedient in words and obedient in acts." "After him we believe in the *Paraclete*, the Spirit of truth ... who came into existence by means of the sole God, through the Only-begotten, wholly subordinated. He is not to be reckoned beside or along with the Father ... nor to be put on equality with the Son."[59]

In reply to this radical differentiation of the divine Father from the Son and the Spirit, which led the Neo-Arians to hierarchically order the persons of the Trinity in descending degrees of being, glory, and authority, the Cappadocians like Athanasius conceive of God, not as a monad who is different from the Son and the Spirit, but as one Godhead who is eternally a triad of equal "persons." The unity of the triune God, not the differences between the divine three, is always to the fore in the Cappadocians' thought. Gregory of Nyssa says,

> Since we cannot find any diversity in their nature, we not unreasonably define the Holy Trinity to be of one Godhead.[60]

> We say that the Godhead of the Father and of the Son and of the Holy Spirit is one, and yet we forbid men to say, "There are three Gods."[61]

Basil is of the same mind.

> For of the Father, Son and Holy Spirit there is the same nature and one Godhead.[62]

---

[58] Stephen Kovach and Peter Schemm, "A Defense of the Doctrine of the Eternal Subordination of the Son," *Journal of the Evangelical Theological Society* (1999): p. 465 on the Nicene Fathers; p. 466 on Athanasius.

[59] Hanson, *The Search*, 620–21, gives the full text of Eunomius' confession of faith.

[60] Gregory of Nyssa, "On the Holy Trinity," in *NPNF* 5 (p. 329).

[61] Gregory of Nyssa, "On 'Not Three Gods,'" in *NPNF* 5 (p. 331).

[62] Basil, "Letters," in *NPNF* 8:110.4 (p. 250).

But it is Gregory Nazianzus that we find the strongest statements on divine unity. For example he says,

> To us there is one God for the Godhead is one ... though we believe in three persons.[63]

And,

> No sooner do I conceive of the One than I am illumined by the splendor of the Three; no sooner do I distinguish them than I am carried back to the One. When I think of any One of the Three I think of him as the whole ... I cannot grasp the greatness of that One so as to attribute a greater greatness to the rest. When I contemplate the Three together, I see but one torch, and I cannot divide or measure out the Undivided Light.[64]

And,

> To us there is one God, for the Godhead is one, and all that proceeds from him is referred to one, although we believe in three persons. For one is not more and another less God; nor is one before and another after; nor are they divided in will or parted in power.[65]

The divine three cannot be divided, the Cappadocians agree, because they share the one *ousia* and they interpenetrate one another in perfect personal communion (*koinonia*). It was Basil in his celebrated book *On the Holy Spirit* who first gave prominence to the conception of the Trinity as a *koinonia*, or communion of persons. He emphatically declared, "The union consists in the communion (*koinonia*) of the Godhead,"[66] and from creation we learn of "the communion (*koinonia*) of the Spirit with the Father and the Son."[67] So he concludes, "In all things the Holy Spirit is inseparable and wholly incapable of being parted from the Father and the Son."[68] Later in one of his letters he wrote, "In Father, Son, and Holy Spirit ... is seen a certain communion (*koinonia*) indissoluble and continuous,"[69] adding some lines later, "it is in no wise possible to entertain the idea of severance or division, in such a way that the Son should be thought of apart from the Father or the Spirit."[70]

For the Cappadocians the term *ousia* designated what was one in God, and *hypostases* what was three in God. In this usage *hypostasis* came to mean "person of the

---

[63] Gregory Nazianzus, "On the Holy Spirit," in *NPNF* 7:15 (p. 322).
[64] Gregory Nazianzus, "Orations on Holy Baptism," in *NPNF* 7:41 (p. 375).
[65] Gregory Nazianzus, "On the Holy Spirit," in *NPNF* 7:14 (p. 322).
[66] Basil, "On the Spirit," *NPNF* 18.45 (p. 28).
[67] Ibid., 37 (p. 23).
[68] Ibid.
[69] Basil, "Letters," in *NPNF* 8:38.4 (p. 139).
[70] Ibid., 38.4 (p. 139).

Trinity."[71] These terminological distinctions in no way challenged the inseparable unity of the one Godhead. For the Cappadocians the persons may be distinguished but not divided. So Basil writes, "For all things that are the Father's are beheld in the Son, and all things that are the Son's are the Father's; because the whole Son is in the Father and he has all the Father in himself. Thus the *hypostasis* of the Son becomes as it were the form and face of the knowledge of the Father, and the *hypostasis* of the Father is known in the form of the Son."[72]

Because Eunomius held that the Son did not share the one *ousia* of the Father, it followed that he did not have the same power and authority as the Father, and thus his works were not equal with the Father's works. In other words, he differentiated the Father and the Son in particular on the basis of what they did, or as we might say their functions and authority. Gregory of Nyssa quotes Eunomius as saying, "Their differences amount to that existing between their works."[73] I take these words to mean from the context that Eunomius taught that the differences in work between the Father and the Son were a clear indication of their differences in being. The Cappadocians give considerable time to arguing just the opposite. The works of the Son — raising the dead, forgiving sins, offering salvation, healing the sick — indicate that Father, Son, and Spirit operate/work/function as one. Basil writes, "The work of the Father is not separate or distinct from the work of the Son.'"[74] Gregory of Nyssa makes the same point.

> But in the case of the divine nature we do not learn that the Father does anything by himself in which the Son does not work conjointly, or again that the Son has any special operation apart from the Holy Spirit.[75]

> We understand that the operation of the Father, the Son and the Holy Spirit is one, differing or varying in nothing, [thus] the oneness of their nature must needs be inferred from the identity of their operations.[76]

In reply to Eunomius' "Confession" that the Father has no "joint possessor of his authority or consort of the throne of his kingdom," Gregory of Nyssa assails him for severing "the only begotten from the Godhead," denying him "the prerogatives of deity" and breaching the divine unity. Gregory's view is that the Scriptures teach

---

[71] Hanson, *The Search*, 691.

[72] Basil, "Letters," in *NPNF* 8:38.8 (p. 141). Some think Gregory of Nyssa may have written this letter.

[73] Gregory of Nyssa, "Against Eunomius," in *NPNF* 5:1.24 (p. 65). See also 1.27 for a similar quote from Eunomius and a similar reply from Gregory.

[74] Basil, "Letters," *NPNF* 8:19 (p. 13). In this instance I follow the translation given by D. Anderson, *St. Basil the Great on the Holy Spirit* (New York: St. Vladimir's, 1980), 39.

[75] Gregory of Nyssa, "On 'Not Three Gods,'" in *NPNF* 5 (p. 334).

[76] Gregory of Nyssa, "On the Holy Spirit," in *NPNF* 5, (p. 328).

that "the Father, the Son, and the Holy Spirit are alike in a position of power to do what they will." The Son "has all things that the Father himself has, and is possessor of all his power, not that this right is transferred from the Father to the Son, but that it at once remains in the Father and resides in the Son. For he who is in the Father is manifestly in the Father with all his own might."[77] Thus he says, "We do not know of any difference by way of superiority and inferiority in attributes."[78] And, "Simplicity in the case of the Holy Trinity admits to no degrees."[79]

The Cappadocians speak of the Father as the *arche*/source of the Son and the Spirit because they think this safeguards the unity of the Godhead. Their view is that if the Son and the Spirit share in the one *ousia* of the Father, there can be no subordination or disjunction between the divine three. For them derivation of being did not entail diminution in being or authority, because all three shared the same divine being identically. Gregory of Nazianzus, however, could see the pitfalls in thinking of the Father as the *arche*/source of the Son and the Spirit and warned of its dangers. He said, "I am afraid to use the word origin (*arche*), lest I should make him the origin of inferiors, and thus insult him by precedence of honor. For the lowering of those who are from him is no glory to the source ... For in the consubstantial persons there is nothing greater or less in point of substance."[80]

More than anyone else, Gregory Nazianzus' theology impacted on those who gathered at the Council of Constantinople in 381. In his famous "Five Theological Orations" delivered in Constantinople before the Council and in his presidential oration delivered to those assembled, he was able to spell out his well-thought-out theology of the Trinity. It is thus not surprising that in the creed finally agreed to, which we know today as the Nicene Creed, the idea that the Father is the *monarche* (sole source) of the Son does not appear. Some have suggested that in the creed the words "God from God, light from light, true God from true God" teach that the Son derives his divinity or being from the Father, but this was not the intent of the authors. These words are to be understood as "the X from X argument." The compilers of the creed wanted people to believe that the Son is true God, just as much as the Father is true God. He is "one in being with the Father." Nevertheless, in its 381 form this creed did say that the Spirit "proceeds from the Father," and not as we confess in the West today, "from the Father and the Son."[81]

How then do the Cappadocians differentiate the divine three? They reject differentiating the persons by when each was created (all are eternal), or in being (all

---

[77] Gregory of Nyssa, "Against Eunomius," in *NPNF* 5:2.6 (p. 107).

[78] Gregory of Nyssa, "On the Holy Trinity," in *NPNF* 5 (p. 327).

[79] Gregory of Nyssa, "Against Eunomius," in *NPNF* 5:1.19 (p. 57).

[80] Gregory of Nazianzus, "Theological Orations," in *NPNF* 7:5.43 (p. 376).

[81] See my earlier discussion in chapter 4 on how these words were added.

have the one *ousia*), or in authority (all have the same attributes and power), or in work/function (they work as one), or by numbering (what Basil calls "subnumeration"),[82] or by hierarchical ordering. Gregory of Nyssa says we recognize differences between Father, Son, and Spirit "only in respect of originateness,"[83] and although this is unquestionably the Cappadocians' primary distinguishing mark, they also differ the persons terminologically and allow for a difference in operational order.

Basil speaks of the particular originating characteristics of the three *hypostases* as "paternity" (*patrotes*), "sonship" (*huiotes*), and "sanctifying power" (*hagiastike dunamis*).[84] The other Cappadocians define the originating characteristics as "unbegotten" (*agennetos*), "begotten" (*gennetos*), and "proceeding" (*ekporeutai* cf. Jn 1:14; 15:26). One of their number, Gregory Nazianzus, however, took differing origination one step further. He argued that what makes the divine persons distinct from each other, and not just nominally distinct, was their mutual and exclusive relationships, which are expressed by their proper names that indicate their relationships of origin. The name *Father* expresses a relationship having its correlative *Son*, and the name *Son* expresses a relationship that has its correlative *Father*. These relationships can never change: they are essential to the person. So Gregory writes, "Father is not a name of either an essence (*ousia*) or of an action, most clever sirs [the Arians]. It is the name of a relation (*schlesis*) in which the Father stands to the Son, and the Son to the Father."[85]

Eternal differentiation in relationships of origin indicates nonidentity. The Father is always the Father of the Son, he begets the Son, the Son is always the Son of the Father, he is begotten, and the Spirit proceeds from the Father. These relataions are nonrevisable and eternal. Differentiation in origin, or in irreversible relations, or nonidentity never indicates subordination for any of the Cappadocians.

Apparently one of Eunomius' arguments was that *only* the Son of God could become incarnate, because sons always assumed subordinate tasks.[86] This same argument is found in evangelical literature today. In reply Gregory of Nazianzus says,

> We assert there is nothing lacking—for God has no deficiency. But the difference of manifestation, if I may so express myself, or rather of their mutual relations one to another, has caused the difference of their names. For indeed it

---

[82] They are all wary of referring to the divine persons as "first," "second," and "third," but at times do this mainly for stylistic reasons. Basil, however, specifically attacks this practice in his work on the Holy Spirit. He rejects what is translated as "subnumeration." See Basil, "On the Holy Spirit," in *NPNF* 8:41–42 (pp. 26–27).

[83] Gregory of Nyssa, "Against Eunomius," in *NPNF* 5:1.33 (p. 78).

[84] Basil, "Letters," in *NPNF* 8:214.4 (p. 254).

[85] Gregory Nazianzus, "Second Theological Oration," in *NPNF* 7:29.16 (p. 307).

[86] Doyle, "Are We Heretics?" 15, and Mark Baddeley, "The Trinity and Subordinationism," *Reformed Theological Review* 63, no. 1 (2004): 7, say quite explicitly that only the eternally subordinated Son who is by nature a servant could become incarnate.

is not some deficiency in the Son which prevents his being Father (for Sonship is not a deficiency), and yet he is not Father. According to this line of argument there must be some deficiency in the Father in respect to him not being Son. For the Father is not Son, and yet this is not due to either deficiency or subjection of essence: but by the fact of being unbegotten or begotten, or proceeding has given the name of Father to the first, of the Son to the second, and of the third, him of whom we are speaking, of the Holy Spirit, that the distinctions of the three persons may be preserved.[87]

Once the Cappadocians embraced the *homoousian* principle, the hierarchical ordering of the *hypostases* was excluded absolutely. The divine three are one in being. Nevertheless, all of them speak of an order (*taxis*) in divine operations which in no way impacts on their equality, yet it distinguishes them. Basil says, "And in creation think first, I pray thee, of the original cause of all things that are made, the Father, of the creative cause, the Son, and of the perfecting cause, the Spirit."[88]

Gregory of Nyssa writes, "In the case of the divine nature we do not learn that the Father does anything by himself in which the Son does not work conjointly, or again that the Son has any special operation apart from the Holy Spirit; but in every operation which extends from God to the creation, and is named according to our variable conceptions of it, has its origin from the Father, and proceeds through the Son, and is perfected by the Spirit."[89]

Here it must be noted that the word *order* in English and the word *taxis* in Greek do not necessarily mean hierarchical order. This is clearly understood by the Cappadocians, as these two passages show and from what we have seen of their teaching on the divine persons given above. The point is, however, made explicit by Basil. In discussing the divine dignity of the Spirit, he completely rejects the idea that the Spirit is sub-ordered under the Father and the Son. His scriptural proof is the three-fold baptismal formula given at the end of Matthew's Gospel: "The words of baptism are the same, and they declare that the relation of the Spirit to the Son equals that of the Son with the Father ... Their names are mentioned in one and the same series, how can we speak of numbering with or under?... How dare anyone say the Spirit is subordinate. It is nothing but Greek sophistry to speak of inferior essences, degrees of rank, or subordination expressed with numbers [in the Trinity]."[90] And, "Those who teach subordinationism, and talk about First, Second and Third, ought to recognize

---

[87] Gregory of Nazianzus, "Fifth Theological Oration: On the Holy Spirit," in *NPNF* 7:9 (p. 320).

[88] Basil, "On the Spirit," in *NPNF* 8:16.38 (p. 23).

[89] Gregory of Nyssa, "On 'Not Three Gods,'" in *NPNF* 5 (p. 334).

[90] Basil, "On the Spirit," in *NPNF* 8:43 (p. 27). Words quoted from Anderson, *St. Basil the Great*, 70.

they are introducing erroneous Greek polytheism into pure Christian theology ... subordination cannot be used to describe persons who share the same nature."[91]

Robert W. Jenson says the great achievement of the Cappadocian Fathers was to conceptualize the *order* of the three divine *hypostases* (persons) not hierarchically as Origen had done but horizontally.[92]

Stephen Kovach and Peter Schemm in their article "A Defense of the Doctrine of the Eternal Subordination of the Son" in the *Journal of the Evangelical Theological Society* come to the opposite conclusions. They argue that the Cappadocians differentiate the divine persons on the basis of differing authority and hierarchically order the divine persons. Neither assertion is true. They make Gregory of Nazianzus the representative Cappadocian theologian, claiming that he unambiguously "speaks of an [hierarchical] order and ranking" in the Godhead.[93] Two quotations are given as proof, but neither supports this contention. In the first,[94] taken from his "Oration on the Holy Spirit" where in seeking to explain Jn 14:28, "the Father is greater than I," Gregory says the Father is "greater" only in the sense that he is the origin of the Son. He then adds that he says this with caution, for the Father and the Son are "equals" and "I am afraid to use the word origin, lest I should make him [the Father] the origin of inferiors."[95] Immediately before this quote he stresses the unity of the three[96] and then says, "No, my friends, there is nothing servile in the Trinity."[97] How Kovach and Schemm can find hierarchical "order and ranking in the Godhead" in this quote read in context completely escapes me. The second quote given by them as proof of the eternal subordination in authority of the Son is even less consequential.[98] It is simply an affirmation of the non-identity of the Father, Son, and Spirit. What Gregory calls a "difference in manifestation ... or rather their mutual relations."[99] "We assert," he adds, "there is nothing lacking [in any divine person] ... for God has no deficiency."[100]

---

[91] Basil, "On the Spirit," in *NPNF* 8:47 (p. 30). Again for clarity of wording I have followed Anderson, *St. Basil the Great*, 75.

[92] Robert Jenson, *The Triune Identity: God According to the Gospel* (Philadelphia: Fortress, 1982), 106.

[93] Kovach and Schemm, "A Defense of the Doctrine," 469. I have added the word *hierarchical* because it cannot be denied that for these two authors the term *order* means hierarchical order. So they speak of an "order and ranking" in the Trinity and on page 465 "an order of subordination."

[94] Ibid., 467.

[95] Gregory of Nazianzus, "Oration on the Holy Spirit," in *NPNF* 7:43 (p. 375).

[96] Ibid., 41 (p. 375).

[97] Ibid., 42 (p. 375).

[98] Kovach and Schemm, "A Defense of the Doctrine," 468.

[99] Gregory of Nazianzus, "Fifth Theological Oration: On the Holy Spirit," in *NPNF* 7:7 (p. 320).

[100] Ibid., 9 (p. 320).

Kovach and Schemm's reading of the Cappadocians in general and Gregory Nazianzus in particular is mistaken. For none of the Cappadocians does function or authority differentiate the divine persons, nor does order imply sub-ordering.

Augustine

The teaching of Scripture is Augustine's chief concern in chapters one to four of his famous book *The Trinity*. He begins writing, he says, on the premise that the Scriptures speak of a God who is eternally triune, inseparably one yet differentiated as Father, Son, and Holy Spirit. In regard to divine unity and equality no catholic theologian could be more emphatic than Augustine. He never tires of speaking of "the inseparable equality" of Father, Son, and Spirit. He says, "In God therefore, when the equal Son cleaves to the equal Father, or the equal Holy Spirit to the Father and the Son, God is not made bigger than each of them singly, because there is no possibility of perfection growing."[101]

Whatever is affirmed of God in unity is affirmed equally of each of the three persons separately. Thus the three divine persons have the same attributes. All three are "great, good, (and) omnipotent."[102] And he insists that they always work as one and have one will. He says, "The Father and the Son have but one will and are indivisible in their workings."[103] Kelly's conclusion is that for Augustine, "The unity of the Trinity is set squarely in the foreground."[104]

When it comes to differentiating the persons Augustine is also unambiguous. He deals with this matter in a number of ways. First of all, like Athanasius and the Cappadocians, he argues the persons are not to be confused, because each has his own unchanging and unchangeable identity. "The Father is not the Son, and the Son is not the Father, and the Holy Spirit ... is neither the Father nor the Son."[105] Next he differentiates them on their differing origins. The Father is "unbegotten," or "begets the Son"; the Son is "begotten"; and the Spirit is "bestowed by" or "proceeds from" them.[106] This differing origination, he insists, belongs to eternity. Thus he makes a distinction between the eternal *procession* of the Son and the Spirit and the temporal *mission* of the Son and the Spirit in history.[107] On this basis it is absolutely clear that God is eternally triune by his very nature or essence, not just in the economy (God's unfolding work in history), as the Apologists, Irenaeus, and Tertullian had suggested.

---

[101]Augustine, *The Trinity*, trans. Edmund Hill (Brooklyn: New City Press, 1991), 6.9 (p. 211). All references to *De Trinitate* (*The Trinity*) are from this translation.

[102]Ibid., 5.12 (p. 197), 5.9 (p. 195).

[103]Ibid., 2.8 (p. 103).

[104]Kelly, *Early Christian Doctrines*, 273.

[105]Ibid., 1.10 (p. 196).

[106]Ibid., 4.27 (p. 172), 4.29 (p. 174), 5.8 (p. 193), 5.15 (p. 199), 15.47 (p. 432).

[107]This is a matter he returns to repeatedly. For one extended discussion see 4.25ff. (pp. 171ff.).

As we have seen in our discussion on the obedience of Christ, the fact that the New Testament speaks of the Father sending and of the Son as sent is of considerable interest to Augustine, because the Arians argued these ideas set the Son under the authority of the Father. Augustine first of all argues that not too much should be made of the comments that the Son is sent by the Father because this is simply human language. It should not be taken to imply superiority and inferiority in the Trinity, because this may be suggested in human speech. In contrast to any two humans, Augustine points out, "the sender and the sent [are one] because the Father and the Son are one."[108] Augustine accepts without reserve that this language differentiates the Father and the Son, and that it reflects an economic or revelational order that cannot be reversed, but he cannot accept the Arian claim that it eternally subordinates the Son, or that it breaches divine unity. "The reason why the Son is said to have been sent by the Father is simply that the one is the Father and the other the Son, then there is nothing at all to stop us believing that the Son is equal to the Father and consubstantial and coeternal, and yet that the Son is sent by the Father. Not because one is greater and the other less, but because one is the Father and the other the Son; one is the begetter, the other begotten ... for the Son is from the Father not the Father from the Son."[109]

Augustine tells us that "the Arians" put to the orthodox a "cunning dilemma." They asked whether the distinctions in the Godhead, according to Aristotelian categories, were to be understood as "substance" or "accidents." "Substance" for Aristotle is what makes something or someone what it is. It does not change. "Accidents," on the other hand, are what is external to the substance, and they can change. Augustine cannot allow that the differing origins refer only to accidents in God, because nothing is secondary and changing in God. And he cannot concede that they are substance, because this would mean that the three divine persons were independent of one another, which would lead to tritheism. Augustine's solution is to argue that the divine three are differentiated neither by substance nor accidents but by "relation," a third Aristotelian category. Unbegotten, begetting, and proceeding (or being bestowed) indicate three unchanging relations in the sense that whatever each of them is, he is in relation to one or both of the others, and this can never change. To solve the problem that the name *Holy Spirit* does not suggest a relationship, he designates the Spirit "Gift," which implies a relationship with the Giver. By differentiating the divine three principally on the basis of their relationships with each other, Augustine builds on the ideas of Gregory Nazianzus. Differentiation for Augustine does not in any way breach divine unity. "It does not follow," he says, that "because the Father

---

[108]Ibid., 4.29 (p. 174).
[109]Ibid., 4.27 (p. 172).

is not the Son nor the Son the Father, or one is unbegotten, the other begotten, that therefore they are not one being; for these names only declare their relationships."[110] And it should be noted that for Augustine unity of being always envisages unity of action/function and authority. He writes, "Just as the Father, Son, and Holy Spirit are inseparable, so do they work inseparably."[111] This is the unified opinion of all the pro-Nicene theologians. The Father, Son, and Spirit are one in being, inseparable in operations, and indivisible in power and authority.

Augustine closes off the last avenue that would allow for any dividing of the divine persons, or the subordinating of the Son and the Spirit by what later Latin theologians would call "the doctrine of appropriation," an idea first seen in the Cappadocians, especially Gregory of Nyssa.[112] Because for Augustine the one and the same "substance" is shared by the three divine persons, whatever can be said of one can be said of the three. This means that no act of God relating to human beings can be said to be the work of the Father, Son, or Spirit *alone*. Nevertheless, he recognizes that in Scripture certain actions are ascribed to the Father or the Son or the Spirit, and so they are rightly appropriated to one or another of the divine three. So creation is ascribed to the Father because he is the originator of all, the incarnation to the Word because revelation comes through the Word, and love to the Holy Spirit because he is the gift of the love between the Father and the Son.[113] Professor Ayres says the doctrine of "appropriation is for pro-Nicene [theologians] an important habit of Christian speech because it is central to Scripture's own speech about the divine persons."[114]

From this you would think no one would appeal to Augustine for proof that historical orthodoxy differentiates the divine persons by dividing them in function and authority. Surprisingly this is not the case. In the contemporary evangelical literature advocating the eternal subordination of the Son, Augustine is often quoted as differentiating the Father and the Son by setting the Son under the Father in function and authority. Stephen Kovach, for example, says that while Augustine emphasizes "the unity of the Trinity," he also affirms "the Nicene view of the eternal subordination of the Son by teaching that the Son is subordinate to the Father as to the person and relationship (not essence or dignity)."[115] In more detail Professor Bruce Ware argues that

---

[110]Ibid., 7.3 (p. 221).

[111]Ibid., 1.7 (p. 70), 2.9 (p. 103).

[112]Ayres, *Nicaea*, 296–300.

[113]This is discussed mainly in books 6 and 7 but see also 2.9 and 2.18. Augustine's reasoning on this matter is disjointed and hard to follow.

[114]Ayres, *Nicaea*, 297. See his excellent discussion of this whole matter on pp. 296–300.

[115]Stephen Kovach, "The Eternal Subordination of the Son: An Apologetic Against Evangelical Feminism," *Journal of Biblical Manhood and Womanhood* 3, no. 2 (1996): 4. Writing later in conjunction with Peter Schemm he says much the same thing. See Kovach and Schemm, "A Defense of the Doctrine," 468–69.

Augustine holds to both "the essential equality of the three trinitarian persons" and eternal differentiation based on the "inherent authority of the Father and the inherent submission of the Son."[116] In support, he quotes a paragraph from Hill's translation of *The Trinity* on the sending of the Son. In this paragraph, which we discussed above, Augustine argues that when the Bible speaks of the Father sending and the Son as sent "there is nothing [in these words] to stop us believing that the Son is equal to the Father and consubstantial and co-eternal.... One is not greater and the other less, but because one is the Father and the other Son: one is the begetter, the other the begotten; the first is the one from whom the sent one is; the other is the one who is from the sender. For the Son is from the Father, not the Father from the Son."[117] As I read this quote, it seems to me Augustine is emphatically denying what Bruce Ware is affirming. Augustine is insisting on the inseparable equality of the persons and on their irreversible distinctions. In Australia, Robert Doyle likewise thinks Augustine's comments on the sending of the Son by the Father not only differentiate the Father and the Son but also subordinate the Son in authority.[118]

The Athanasian Creed

In the so-called Athanasian Creed what Augustine taught on the Trinity is identified with "the catholic faith" and made necessary for salvation. In this creed the unity of the divine three is stressed, as is their equality.

> The Godhead of the Father, of the Son, and the Holy Spirit is all one: the glory equal, the majesty co-eternal.
> Such as the Father is, such is the Son, such is the Holy Spirit.
> The Father is almighty, the Son is almighty, the Holy Spirit is almighty....
> The Father is Lord, the Son is Lord: and the Holy Spirit is Lord....
> In this Trinity none is before or after [no hierarchical ordering], none is greater or less than another [no subordination in authority]. But the whole three persons are co-eternal and co-equal [no temporal or ontological subordination].

Only in one matter are the divine three said to differ.

> The Father is made of none: neither created nor begotten.
> The Son is of the Father alone: not made, nor created, but begotten.
> The Holy Spirit is of the Father and the Son: neither made, nor created, nor begotten, but proceeding.

---

[116] Bruce Ware, "Tampering with the Trinity: Does the Son Submit to the Father?" in *Biblical Foundations for Manhood and Womanhood*, ed. Wayne Grudem (Wheaton, Ill.: Crossway, 2002), 246.

[117] Augustine, *The Trinity*, 4.27 (p. 172).

[118] Doyle, "Are We Heretics?" 14.

Differing origination alone distinguishes the coequal persons. It is thus hard to believe that a group of evangelical theologians on a church doctrinal commission could come to the conclusion that "the Athanasian Creed while strongly affirming the equality of the persons, makes these *differences of being* most clear," and then the words from the creed on differentiation just quoted are given as proof! The equality of the Son spoken of in this creed, we are then told, "is a derived equality. With the second and third persons, the *mode of derivation* and their *relationship of being* is distinct."[119] How this can be claimed simply escapes me. To speak of "differences in being" and of differing "relationships of being" directly contradicts what the Athanasian Creed (and the Nicene Creed) make central: the Father and the Son are *one in being or substance.* The claim that the Athanasian Creed teaches that the Son's being is *derived* from the Father is also to be rejected. This creed does not say the Son and the Spirit "derive" their divinity, or their being, or their substance, from the Father. It says that the "Son is *of* the Father" and "the Spirit is *of* the Father and the Son." A doctrine of the *monarche* of the Father is not found in the Athanasian Creed. The fact that some evangelicals can find in this creed the eternal subordination of the Son in function and authority, and for some being as well, suggests an agenda other than understanding the words as given. If I wanted to write a document that absolutely excluded the idea that the Son of God is eternally subordinated to the Father, without conflating the persons, I could not do it better than the Athanasian Creed.

This stress on the unity and coequality of the divine persons seen in the Athanasian Creed reached its theological zenith at the Council of Florence (1438–45). At this time Anselm's "rule" that "in God everything is one except where there is relative opposition" was made Catholic dogma.[120] Rahner tells us these words mean that "the Father, Son and Spirit are identical with the one Godhead and are 'relatively' distinct from one another. The three as distinct are constituted *only* by their relatedness to one another."[121]

Calvin

Calvin follows in the steps of the pro-Nicene theologians first by making divine unity the primary and most important issue in the construing of the doctrine of the Trinity, and second by allowing only for distinctions in the Godhead, not division

---

[119] *Sydney Anglican Diocesan Doctrine Commission Report,* "The Doctrine of the Trinity and Its Bearing on the Relationship of Men and Women," (1999), par. 25.

[120] Quoted in Karl Rahner, *The Trinity* (New York: Herder & Herder, 1997), 72. For a slightly different worded translation of the Latin and a short discussion on this "rule" see Edmund Fortman, *The Triune God* (Grand Rapids, Mich.: Baker, 1972), 226–27.

[121] Rahner, *The Trinity,* 72. Italics added.

or separation. The following quote substantiates what I have just said. In approaching the question of the "threeness" in God, Calvin says, "Again Scripture sets forth a distinction of the Father from the Word, and the Word from the Spirit. Yet the greatness of the mystery warns us how much reverence and sobriety we ought to use in investigating this. And that passage in Gregory of Nazianzus vastly delights me: 'I cannot think on the one without quickly being encircled by the splendor of the three, nor can I discern the three without being straightway carried back to the one.' Let us not, then, be led to imagine a trinity of persons that keeps our thoughts distracted and does not at once lead back to that unity. Indeed, the words 'Father,' 'Son,' and 'Spirit' imply a real distinction—not division."[122]

Calvin allows that the word *person* is an acceptable way to designate the divine three as are its synonyms, the Greek word *hypostasis* and the Latin word *subsistentia*. These synonyms, he adds, are to be distinguished from the term *essence* that designates what is one in God and common to all the three divine persons. Calvin defines the term *person* "as a subsistence in God's essence, which while related to the others, is distinguished by an *incommunicable quality*."[123] He then says, "Now of the three subsistences I say that each one, while related to the others, is distinguished by *a special quality* ... [that] I maintain to be incommunicable because whatever is attributed to the Father as a *distinguishing mark*, cannot agree with, or be transferred to the Son."[124]

What the "incommunicable quality," "special quality," or "distinguishing mark" of each person is Calvin never tells us, presumably because it is not defined in Scripture. All he wants to affirm is that the three persons are differentiated, and what is distinctive to each cannot be transferred to another.

He must face, however, the problem of how the divine three are distinguished, although he admits he is reluctant to delve into this mystery. First he notes that in the Gospels the Son is depicted as distinct from the Father in that he is "begotten" and "sent by the Father"; and it is he who dies on the cross and not the Father. The Spirit is likewise differentiated because he is said to proceed from the Father and because Jesus calls him "another" (Jn 14:16).[125] In the following paragraph in the *Institutes* (1.13.18) Calvin seeks to go deeper as he explores what these differences might entail. Again he begins by stressing the limits of human reason and language to deal with these issues. Then following in the steps of the Cappadocians, he distinguishes the divine three by the way they consistently operate in a complementary and ordered manner: "To the Father is attributed the beginning of activity, and to the fountain and wellspring of

---

[122]John Calvin, *Institutes of the Christian Religion*, ed. John T. Neill, trans. Ford Lewis Battles (London: SCM, 1960), 1.13.17 (pp. 141–42).

[123]Ibid., 1.13.6 (p. 128). The discussion on the term *person* begins in 1.13.2 (p. 122).

[124]Ibid., 1.13.6 (p. 128). Italics added.

[125]Ibid., 1.13.17 (p. 142).

all things; to the Son wisdom, counsel and the ordered disposition of all things; but to the Spirit is assigned the power and efficiency of that activity."[126]

Nevertheless, he adds, with the divine persons "we must not seek in eternity a before or after"—so he excludes eternal hierarchical ordering in the eternal or immanent Trinity. This operational "order" for him speaks of how the divine three are revealed in history and to the human mind—it is restricted to the economy.[127] It is an "observed order." "When the Father is thought of as first, then from him the Son, and then finally from both the Spirit ... [this is how] the mind of each human being is naturally inclined to think of God."[128] Torrance says this order for Calvin has to do "not with status but with position, not with substance but with form, and not with power but with sequence."[129]

Calvin then progresses immediately to stress once again divine unity and equality: "This distinction is so far from contravening the utter simple unity of God as to permit us to prove from it that the Son is one God with the Father because he shares with the Father one and the same Spirit, and that the Spirit is not something other than the Father and different from the Son. For in each *hypostasis* the whole divine nature is understood, with this qualification—that to each belongs his own peculiar quality. The Father is wholly in the Son, the Son is wholly in the Father, even as he himself declares: 'I am in the Father and the Father in me' (Jn 14:10)."[130] In this quote stressing divine unity, simplicity, and equality, Calvin acknowledges that each divine person is distinguished by "his own peculiar quality," but again he does not tell us what this is. He is content to affirm distinction without speculating on what exactly this involves.

This immediately leads him to discuss a conflict in "the opinions of the ancients" as to whether or not "the Father is the beginning of the Son," or that "the Son has both divinity and essence from himself and thus has no one beginning from the Father."[131] Appealing to Augustine he concludes, "Christ with respect to himself is called God; with respect to the Father, Son. Again, the Father with respect to himself is called God; with respect to the Son, Father. In so far as he is called Father with respect to the Son, he is not the Son; in so far as he is called the Son with respect to the Father, he is not the Father; in so far as he is called both Father with respect to himself, and Son with respect to himself, he is the same God. Therefore when we

---

[126]Ibid., 1.13.18 (p. 142).

[127]Thomas Torrance, "Calvin's Doctrine of the Trinity," in *Trinitarian Perspectives* (Edinburgh: T&T Clark, 1994), 71.

[128]Calvin, *Institutes*, 1.13.18 (p. 143), 1.13.20 (p. 144).

[129]Torrance, "Calvin's Doctrine," 71–72.

[130]Calvin, *Institutes*, 1.13.19 (p. 143).

[131]Ibid., 1.13.19 (pp. 143–44).

speak simply of the Son without regard to the Father, we well and properly declare him to be of himself; and for this reason we call him the *sole beginning*. But when we mark the relation that he has with the Father, we rightly make the Father the *beginning* of the Son."[132]

Calvin's argument is that Jesus is rightly called "the Son" in relation to the Father. He is the Son *of* the Father just as the Father is identified as the Father *of* the Son. However, when Jesus is thought of without regard to the Father, "we well and properly declared him to be of himself: for this reason we call him the sole beginning."[133] Later he returns to this matter and denounces those who suggest that the Father is "truly and properly the sole God, [who] in forming the Son and the Spirit, infused into them his own deity."[134] He warns against "certain rascals" who teach just this, maintaining that "if we consider no one but the Father to be God, we definitely cast down the Son in rank."[135] "Therefore," he says, "whenever mention is made of deity, we ought by no means to admit any antithesis between Son and Father."[136] What Calvin is opposing in this paragraph and in paragraph 1.13.19 is "derivative subordinationism" — the idea that the primary difference between the Father and the Son and the Spirit is that the second and third members of the Trinity derive their existence, deity, and authority from the Father. For Calvin all three persons of the Trinity are God in an absolute sense for all eternity (*autotheos*). Derivative subordinationism for him is a very dangerous heresy. He gives more space to opposing this error than any other matter.[137] Gerald Bray says that in insisting that the Son is *autotheos* Calvin completely excluded "any hint of causality latent in the terms 'generation' and 'procession.'"[138]

For Calvin differing origination, or differing relations of origin, are not seen as the most basic and important way to differentiate the divine persons. In the early sections of his discussion on the Trinity he mentions in passing a couple of times that the Son is "begotten" of the Father, but it is only in his lengthy refutation of derivative subordination that he takes up this matter with theological intent. As he draws to a conclusion his extended critique of the idea that the Father is "the deifier of the Son," he says, "We teach from the Scriptures that God is one in essence, and hence that the essence both of the Son and of the Spirit is *unbegotten*; but inasmuch as the Father is first in order, and from himself begot his Wisdom, as has just been said, he is

---

[132]Ibid., 1.13.19 (p. 144). Italics added. See also 1.13.23 (p. 149), 1.13.25 (p. 153).
[133]Ibid., 1.13.20 (p. 144).
[134]Ibid., 1.13.23 (p. 149).
[135]Ibid.
[136]Ibid.
[137]Ibid., 1.13.19 (p. 144), 1.13.23, 24, 25, 26 (pp. 149–56).
[138]Bray, *The Doctrine of God*, 204.

rightly deemed the beginning and fountainhead of the whole of divinity. Thus God without particularization is *unbegotten*; and the Father also in respect to his person is *unbegotten*."[139]

Here Calvin again returns to his characteristic emphasis. The Son is in his own right God in the fullest sense (*autotheos*), yet in relation to the Father he is the Son *of* the Father. On this basis he concludes that the Father and the Son in their shared and united divine essence are both "unbegotten." Only in so far as the Son and the Father are distinguished as persons may we think of the Father as "unbegotten" and the Son as "begotten." In the above quote Calvin gives a carefully circumscribed priority to the Father, designating him as "the fountainhead of all deity," but in doing so does not suggest any subordination in being, work, or authority in the Son (or the Spirit).

Calvin — like Athanasius, the Cappadocians, and Augustine — places greatest stress on divine unity, simplicity, and equality, but he does unambiguously distinguish the persons. However, he is so guarded in what he concedes and makes so many qualifications that in the end we do not have much content. So we note that,

1. He says each person has a distinctive "incommunicable quality," a "distinguishing mark," and a "special quality" that differentiates one from another, but he never tells us what this is.
2. He follows Scripture, noting that each divine person does certain things that the others are not said to do, but then he has them working in unison and allows no separation between the work of the Father or the Son or the Spirit.
3. He speaks of a given operational order among the three, but he does not allow this to be a hierarchical order. In this order of functioning one divine person is never separated, or divided from, or set over another.
4. He says the Father may be thought of by frail human minds as "first," the "beginning of [divine] activity," and the "fountainhead of deity." However, he also insists that all three divine persons are eternal: none is chronologically first; all are equal in power and authority; all three always work inseparably as one, and the Son is God in his own right (*autotheos*). As such he is his own sole beginning (*monarche*); his divinity is not derived from the Father.
5. And he holds that whatever distinctions there may be in the divine three they must not contravene "the utterly simple unity of God."[140] The Father, the Son, and the Spirit all share eternally the same divinity, majesty, and authority.

---

[139]Calvin, *Institutes*, 1.13.25 (p. 153). Italics added.
[140]Ibid., 1.13.19 (p. 143).

Warfield in his lengthy study of Calvin's doctrine of the Trinity is also of the opinion that Calvin gives primary place to the unity and equality of the divine persons. He says, "[Calvin] conceives more clearly and applies more purely than ever had been previously done the principle of equalization in his thought on the relation of the persons to one another, and therefore as we have already hinted, marks an epoch in the history of the doctrine of the Trinity."[141] And "the principle of his construction of the trinitarian distinctions is equalization rather than subordination."[142]

However, it is Thomas Torrance who reaches the most relevant conclusion for this chapter. He says that for Calvin, "there is no difference between them [the divine three] in respect to being, power, or majesty, for each considered in himself is the one God.... they are fully equal."[143]

Karl Barth

Barth also places most stress on divine unity, simplicity, and equality. On reading volume 1.1 of Barth's *Dogmatics*, his emphasis on the unity of God cannot be missed. So emphatic is he on divine unity that he can speak of the Father, Son, and Spirit as the "one God in threefold repetition."[144] Because he believes the word *person* necessarily implies three centers of consciousness, something that would undermine the unity of the Christian God, Barth chooses rather to speak of a "mode or way of being" (German *Seinsweisen*) to designate the divine three.[145] For Barth these three *modes or ways of being* can never be separated. They work as one, and they have the same divine attributes. So he says, "No attribute, no act of God is not in the same way the attribute or act of the Father, the Son, and the Spirit."[146] Subordinationism in all forms is excluded. "Father, Son, and Spirit are the one, single, and equal God."[147] To suggest that the Son is less than the Father in any way is a denial that he is the one Lord. Barth grounds divine differentiation primarily on differing origination, never on differing authority. To confess that Jesus is eternally begotten of the Father "emphasizes the oneness, which means the exclusiveness and uniqueness of the revelation and reconciliation enacted in Jesus Christ."[148] Because he is begotten before all time, he is not a creature; "he is God himself," "light of light, very God of very

---

[141] B. B. Warfield, "Calvin's Doctrine of the Trinity," in B. B. Warfield, *Calvin and Augustine* (Philadelphia: Presbyterian and Reformed, 1956), 230.

[142] Ibid.

[143] Torrance, "Calvin's Doctrine," 72.

[144] Karl Barth, *Church Dogmatics* (Edinburgh: T&T Clark, 1975), 1.1 (p. 350).

[145] Ibid., 359.

[146] Ibid., 362.

[147] Ibid., 381. Those tempted to believe in the eternal subordination of the Son should read this page carefully.

[148] Ibid., 424.

God." This wording indicates "distinction and unity in God."[149] To say more than this, Barth concludes, is impossible, for the language of "begetting" is metaphorical: "The natural character of the metaphor of begetting makes it clear at the outset that in all that is said about Father and Son in description of the two modes of being in God we have a frail and contestable figure of speech. We denote God in this way but we do not grasp him."[150]

Thus for Barth the language of "begetting" says as much about the unity and equality of the divine Father and Son as it does about their differences. Indeed, this metaphor for Barth underlines that in Christ we meet the one true God, not one who is other than the Father in divinity, majesty, or authority.

After Barth

Karl Rahner, the Roman Catholic theologian who did so much to revive theological reflection on the Trinity among Roman Catholics, similarly emphasizes divine unity, simplicity, and equality in his writings on the Trinity. In the next chapter I will outline in more detail his thinking on the Trinity. However, in the innumerable books on the Trinity that have followed the pioneering work of Barth and Rahner, the predominant emphasis, as I noted in chapter one, has been on a more plural view of God.[151] David Cunningham puts it this way, "Recent trinitarian theology has emphasized the relational focus of the doctrine. God is not simply a solitary entity, nor three individual 'somethings,' but a complex network of relations."[152] The inspiration for this has been the work of the Cappadocian Fathers who were the first to depict the one God of Christian revelation in fully relational and communal terms.[153] In its more conservative form of this model of the Trinity, divine unity is rightly stressed, but the unity of the Godhead is understood strictly in communal terms. Thomas F. Torrance gives classic expression to this position when he speaks of the Christian God as "the fullness of Personal being in himself, indeed as himself a transcendent *Communion of Persons,* for the three divine persons, Father, Son and Holy Spirit *are* the one God. With God, Being and Communion are one and the same."[154]

---

[149]Ibid., 428.

[150]Ibid., 431.

[151]For more on this see Stanley J. Grenz, *Rediscovering the Triune God: The Trinity in Contemporary Theology* (Minneapolis: Fortress, 2004), 117–62.

[152]David Cunningham, *These Three Are One: The Practice of Trinitarian Theology* (London: Blackwell, 1998), 20.

[153]See further Grenz, *Rediscovering the Triune God,* 117–62.

[154]Torrance, *The Christian Doctrine of God,* 104. Another excellent exposition of this position is found in Alan Torrance, *Persons in Communion: An Essay on Trinitarian Description and Human Participation* (Edinburgh: T&T Clark, 1996).

In the more radical form of this model of the Trinity, divine differentiation is so stressed that divine unity is threatened.[155] Jürgen Moltmann gives classic expression to this position. The Trinity, he says, is "three Persons—one family,"[156] or "three subjects, Father, Son, and Spirit" who conjointly work in the world.[157] Speaking of the death of Christ he says, "On the cross the Father and the Son are so deeply separated that their relationship breaks off."[158] In this so-called "social model," we often are told that in the Trinity there are three centers of consciousness and each divine person submits to the others.[159] I find these two ideas very problematic. I think that perfect communal unity implies that God is of one mind and will. The Father and the Son certainly glorify one another, love one another, and work as one, but I find nowhere in Scripture the idea of mutual subordination. Human beings should rightly submit to one another (Eph 5:21), but to suggest this is how the coequal divine persons should relate is to read into trinitarian relations realities from this fallen world. If the divine persons eternally coexist in perfect communion and self-giving love, they must be always of one mind and will.

Although in this model of the Trinity in its "weak" and "strong" form divine differentiation comes to the fore, the subordination of the Son and/or the Spirit is never envisaged. The emphasis falls squarely on the equality of the divine persons. The persons are united in the most profound unity of love and self-giving: none is before or after, greater or less than another. Mainline theologians who argue for a fully communal model of the Trinity as far as I know without exception are opposed to subordinationism in any form. The conservative evangelical theologian Millard Erickson, who fully endorses a social doctrine of the Trinity, speaks of "the complete equality of the three."[160]

Wolfhart Pannenberg

Pannenberg is one of the leading exponents of this more plural model of the Trinity. He begins his exposition of the doctrine of the Trinity in his *Systematic Theology* by addressing the basic problem of divine unity and divine differentiation.[161] He commends Athanasius and the Cappadocians for recognizing that the persons of the

---

[155]See Robert Letham, *The Holy Trinity in Scripture, History, Theology, and Worship* (Phillipsburg, N.J.: P&R, 2004), 307–9.

[156]Jürgen Moltmann, *The Trinity and the Kingdom* (New York: Harper and Row, 1981), 199.

[157]Ibid., 156.

[158]Ibid., 82.

[159]Even the conservative evangelical Millard Erickson, *God in Three Persons: A Contemporary Interpretation of the Trinity* (Grand Rapids, Mich.: Baker, 1995), 333, adopts this language.

[160]Ibid., 33.

[161]Wolfhart Pannenberg, *Systematic Theology*, vol. 1 (Grand Rapids, Mich.: Eerdmans, 1991), 271–80.

Trinity are primarily differentiated by their relations and united in their operations. The Cappadocians' error, he argues, was to seek also to ground divine unity and differentiation in the Father as "the source and principle of deity."[162] Both the idea that the Father is the *monarche* of the Son and the Spirit and that the Son is "eternally begotten" and the Spirit "eternally proceeds," he believes, undermine the "mutuality" and "reciprocity" basic to the divine unity.[163] To overcome this problem he argues that the unity and distinctions within the Godhead should be grounded on the dependence of each divine person on the others—one cannot exist alone or without the others.[164] This leads him in the end to define divine unity and differentiation entirely in communal terms. "The [divine] persons simply are what they are in their relations to one another, which both distinguish them from one another and brings them into communion with one another."[165]

Distinguishing the Divine "Persons"

It is now time to begin bringing into focus what we have learned about divine unity and differentiation. The Bible would suggest that personal identity is what primarily and indelibly distinguishes the divine three. The Father is the Father and not the Son or the Spirit, the Son is the Son and not the Father or the Spirit, and the Spirit is the Spirit and not the Father and the Son, yet they are never divided or separated. They are, as Basil argued, united in the most perfect and intimate communion. Differing origination or differing relations of origin are simply attempts to explain these personal and eternal distinctions within the one God.

The distinguishing of the Father and the Son on the basis that one is "unbegotten" and the other "begotten" is not directly taught in Scripture, although the idea can be inferred from Scripture.[166] Nevertheless the idea that the Son is eternally

---

[162]Ibid., 279.

[163]Ibid., 312–13. See the fuller explanation of all this at the end of the previous chapter.

[164]Ibid., 313–414, 322.

[165]Ibid., 320.

[166]In the history of trinitarian thinking, differentiating the Father, Son, and Spirit on the basis of *origination* has been very important, but biblical support is not strong. The *temporal* incarnational sending or mission of the Son and the post-Easter sending or mission of the Spirit is well-attested in Scripture. In John's gospel, Jesus is said forty-one times to be sent by the Father. Likewise the Spirit is once said to be sent by the Father (Jn 14:26), once by the Son "from the Father" (Jn 15:26), and once by the Son (Jn 16:7). *The eternal procession* of the Spirit does not seem to be mentioned at all in Scripture. Twice in Hebrews Jesus is designated the "begotten Son" (*gennao*) (Heb 1:5; 5:5; cf. Ac 13:33) in quotes from Ps 2:7, but it would seem the author of the epistle to the Hebrews is pointing to his royal dignity as the Son of God, not speaking of his eternal generation or temporal mission. In the Authorized Version translation of the Johannine writings, Jesus is said to be "the only begotten Son" a number of times (Jn 1:14, 18; 3:16, 18; 1Jn 4:9), but etymologically the Greek adjective *monogenes* is related to *ginomai*, "to become," not *gennao*, "to beget." Some evangelical theologians have

begotten, or as Augustine said, eternally generated, has proved to be a helpful theological way to speak of the divine Father-Son relationship. This idea was developed
by the pro-Nicene theologians to exclude the temporal subordination of the Son; to
differentiate the Father and Son without any hint of the subordination of the Son, and
to underline that the differences between the Father and the Son are to be understood
primarily in terms of intimate, loving, and coequal relationships. I therefore cannot
agree with Grudem when he argues that the idea of the Son's eternal begetting or
generation be removed "from modern theological formulations" of the Trinity.[167] To
reject a theological idea enshrined in the creeds and confessions seeking to replace it
with another idea—the eternal subordination of the Son in authority—as the primary basis for divine differentiation, with no historical support at all, or any theological merit, is doctrinally dangerous.

The most basic premise of orthodoxy is that divine unity and the eternal distinctions of Father, Son, and Spirit are both absolutes. God is both one and three. As Alan
Torrance puts it, "The doctrine of the Trinity demands a conception of the triune
persons which integrates their distinctness and particularity, on the one hand, and
their radical union and communion on the other."[168] What is surprising is that in the
tradition, at least until very recently, it is divine unity that is characteristically stressed.
The pro-Nicene theologians, the later Athanasian Creed, Aquinas, Calvin, Barth,
Rahner, and most Roman Catholic theologians today emphasize the unity, simplicity, and equality of the divine three. As important as divine differentiation is, it is
given less attention. They have done this to exclude subordinationism, the perennial
heresy. In the fourth century it was the Arians who stressed divine differentiation,
speaking of the Son as differentiated from the Father in being, work, and authority.
In placing all of the *emphasis* on divine differentiation so as to eclipse divine unity
and coequality, my evangelical debating opponents are closer to the Arians than to
the historic tradition.

One of the important contributions to trinitarian theology made by theologians
in the last thirty years has been the recognition that this emphasis on the divine unity
and how it is conceptualized in the so-called Western tradition is deficient. In its

---

concluded that because the actual term *begetting* to speak of Christ's eternal generation has
little biblical support it should be abandoned. So Grudem, *Systematic Theology*, appendix 6
only in post 2000 printings, 1233–34; John S. Feinberg, *No One Like Him: Foundations of
an Evangelical Theology* (Wheaton, Ill.: Crossway, 2001), 489–92; Robert Reymond, *A New
Systematic Theology of the Christian Faith*, 2d ed. (Nashville: Nelson, 1998), 324–30; Donald
MacLeod, *The Person of Christ* (Westmont, Ill.: InterVarsity, 1998), 71–74, 131–35. However, Frame, *The Doctrine of God*, 711–12 and Letham, *The Holy Trinity*, 384–89, argue for
accepting the term *begotten* to differentiate the Father and the Son.

[167] Grudem, *Systematic Theology*, post 2000 editions, 1234.

[168] Torrance, *Persons in Communion*, 281–82.

place a "communal" or "social" model of the Trinity has been advocated and widely endorsed. In this approach the unity of God is not found in "one divine substance," a very abstract and unitary idea, but in the most profound community of love and self-giving imaginable that characterizes the inner life of the divine persons. I confess that I think when worded carefully this is an important corrective to "the unity model." It seems to me it captures more accurately how the Bible speaks of the unity of the Father, Son, and Spirit. Its danger is that pushed too far it seems to infer tritheism. This debate reminds us that all theological work on the Trinity has to affirm unequivocally both divine unity and divine differentiation. This communal model of divine life is, however, of no help to my debating opponents. As far as I can see, every contemporary advocate of a more communal model of the Trinity emphasizes the equality of the divine three. The premise is that perfect communion necessitates personal equality.

Conclusion

The question we have been considering in this chapter is not, Are the Father, Son, and Spirit eternally and indelibly differentiated? With one voice every orthodox theologian past and present affirms this. Rather we have been asking, Can the claim made by so many contemporary evangelicals that the Father and the Son (the Spirit is hardly ever mentioned) are differentiated *primarily if not exclusively* by differing functions and authority be endorsed? From our survey of the historical sources, we have found no support at all for this idea and much to the contrary. It would seem to differentiate the divine persons on the premise that they are divided in what they do and divided in power and authority breaches both divine unity and the *homoousian* principle. It is a denial of historic orthodoxy. The constantly expressed assertion by conservative evangelicals that unless the subordination of the Son in authority is upheld divine differentiation cannot be maintained is simply confused thinking at best and special pleading at worst. Not one of the great theologians of the past, the creeds, or Reformation confessions, and not one contemporary mainline theologian even hints at such an idea.

THE ECONOMIC AND IMMANENT TRINITY: CORRESPONDENCE YES, IDENTITY NO

Central to the perennial debate as to whether the Son of God is eternally subordinated to the Father is the question, Is the subordination of the incarnate Son seen on earth, which none dispute, indicative of his subordination to the Father in heaven? Or to put the question in the technical language of the theologians, Is the subordination seen in the economic Trinity a revelation of what is true in the eternal or immanent Trinity? Those who believe the Son is eternally subordinated to the Father argue that what is revealed in the incarnation reveals what is forever true. On earth Jesus was subordinated to the Father and obedient to him, and this tells us that he is subordinated and obedient to the Father in heaven. In contrast, those who are adamantly opposed to the eternal subordination of the Son argue that the subordination seen in the incarnation does not reveal the Son's eternal relationship with the Father in heaven. In taking human flesh the Son of God freely subordinated himself for our salvation, but he never ceased to be God in all glory, majesty, and power. In Jesus of Nazareth we do not have a revelation of the Son as he is in heaven with the Father and the Spirit but a revelation of God in the flesh, God in *kenotic* form, self-subordinated God. In the contemporary sharp and painful division among evangelicals over the Trinity this question takes us right to the heart of the dispute. No other issue is more important. In this debate one side points to the Gospel texts that speak of the Son as sent by the Father, doing the Father's will, and praying to the Father as proof that the Son is eternally subordinated to the Father. The other side points to Paul's words that speak of Christ as equal God yet freely subordinating himself for our salvation (Php 2:5–11) as proof that the Son's subordination is temporal and voluntary. Who is right? My debating opponents are convinced their case is compelling.

Robert Letham in making his case for the eternal subordination of the Son in the *Westminster Theological Journal* says that subordination and obedience seen in the Son's relationship with the Father on earth makes known "in human history … realities inherent in God eternally." He thus concludes, "the revelation of the economic Trinity truly indicates the ontological Trinity."[1] If the Son is subordinated to the Father on earth and must obey him, he must be subordinated in heaven. Similarly, John Dahms writing in the *Journal of the Evangelical Theological Society* asks, "Is the subordination [seen in the incarnation] merely economic, as many affirm?" To which he replies, "I submit that it is essential and eternal."[2]

Similar ideas appear in Scott Horrell's 2004 article also in the *Journal of the Evangelical Theological Society*.[3] He says, "The purpose of this paper is to contribute to how we think about God by tightening the relationship between the economic and the immanent images of the Trinity."[4] Noting the many texts in the Gospels that speak of the subordination of the incarnate Son, he concludes, "The hierarchy of the economic Trinity appears largely inviolable in the Bible itself"[5] If this is the case, he reasons, then the Son must be subordinated in heaven because the economic Trinity is to be identified with the immanent Trinity.

Wayne Grudem also embraces this position. He argues that the subordination and obedience of the Son to the Father seen in his earthly life should be read into trinitarian relations before and after the incarnation.[6] He says, "The egalitarian claim that the Son's subordination to the Father was only for his time on earth is surely incorrect."[7] What was true in the incarnation tells us what is true before Christ became incarnate and after his resurrection: he is subordinated in authority to the Father. Grudem identifies the economic Trinity and the immanent Trinity. For him the economic Trinity is the eternal or immanent Trinity without any caveats whatsoever.

The Sydney Doctrinal Commission is of the same mind. In their 1999 statement

---

[1] Robert Letham, "The Man-Woman Debate: Theological Comment," *Westminster Theological Journal* 52 (1990), 68.

[2] John Dahms, "The Subordination of the Son," *Journal of the Evangelical Theological Society* 37, no. 3 (1994), 351.

[3] Scott Horrell, "Toward a Biblical Model of the Social Trinity," *Journal of the Evangelical Theological Society* 47, no. 3 (2004): 399–421.

[4] Ibid., 399.

[5] Ibid., 415.

[6] Wayne Grudem, *Evangelical Feminism and Biblical Truth* (Sisters, Ore.: Multnomah, 2004), 406–13.

[7] Ibid., 407.

of faith endorsed by the synod the question is asked, "Whether the subordination [of the Son] is true of the inner, eternal relations of the essential Trinity, or only in the outworkings of salvation?" In reply the authors insist on the former. They say, "According to Scripture, the submission of Christ does not express a temporary and arbitrary arrangement, *but the very nature of God in himself.*"[8] The subordination of the Son seen in the incarnation reflects what is true in the immanent Trinity.

The Australian evangelical theologian Robert Doyle, a member of the commission that drew up the above statement on the Trinity, also argues that the subordination seen in the incarnation is to be read back into the immanent Trinity. It is his view that since Jesus is set under the Father in the economy of salvation he must be subordinated in eternity. The Son's relationship with his Father in the immanent Trinity, he argues, cannot be other than what is revealed in history. He appeals to Barth and Rahner in particular for support of his opinion but holds that this is what the great church fathers also believed.[9] He writes, "The methodological point made by Barth, which is also that of Athanasius and Rahner (amongst others), is that unless the ordering in the relations [he means "sub-ordering"] we see in the economy actually witness to the relations in the immanent Trinity then we are not in touch with God himself [in the incarnate Son]."[10] In the preceding paragraph to the one just quoted, Doyle claims that Augustine taught that the "economic subordination" of the Son speaks "of the eternal relations, not just the one substance."

Mark Baddeley—his colleague at Moore Theological College, Sydney—follows him. He too thinks both Barth and Rahner rightly read back into the immanent Trinity the economic subordination of the Son seen in the incarnation, and that this is historic orthodoxy.[11] He says that Barth rejects a "purely economic subordination as modalism,"[12] teaching rather "the subordination of the Son to the Father within

---

[8] *Sydney Anglican Diocesan Doctrine Commission Report*, "The Doctrine of the Trinity and Its Bearing on the Relationship of Men and Women," par. 21. Italics added.

[9] Robert Doyle, "Are We Heretics? A Review of *The Trinity and Subordinationism* by Kevin Giles," *The Briefing* (April 2004): 11–18.

[10] Ibid., 15.

[11] Mark Baddeley, "The Trinity and Subordinationism," *Reformed Theological Review* 63, no. 1 (2004): 9. Mark Baddeley asked me to submit anything to him that mentioned his work. I gladly sent him this chapter and the one on Barth. I made the few corrections he suggested. I am pleased to admit as he asked me to do that my thinking has developed on what I said in my earlier book. If my thinking had not developed after all this work, I would be very sad. I do not concede, however, that I have radically changed my mind on anything substantial, as he seems to think. The basic thesis of my earlier work on the Trinity was that to eternally subordinate the Son in function and authority is a form of the error of subordinationism, and this is still the central thesis of this book. I am also still of the opinion that Barth and Rahner do not teach the eternal subordination of the Son in function and authority.

[12] Ibid., 4, 6.

the immanent Trinity."[13] In reference to Rahner he says his "maxim [i.e. his rule] teaches that the incarnation reveals the divine nature."[14] This means he believes that Jesus' subordination seen in the incarnation is indicative of his subordinate divine nature in time and eternity.

In Great Britain Thomas Smail adopts the same position in his little paperback, *The Forgotten Father.*[15] He first speaks of the subordination and obedience seen in the incarnate Christ and then concludes that, "If what Christ is on earth is what the Son is eternally with the Father then we must see this functional subordination as being within the very being of God's own life."[16] Note what he says: the functional subordination of the Son is to be read back into "the *very being* of God's own life." What the Son does on earth, without any qualifications, discloses his subordinate being in heaven.

Quotations could be multiplied, but I think the point has been established. The contemporary conservative evangelical case for the eternal subordination of the Son is built on the premise that what is true in the incarnation, often called "the economy of salvation," must be true in the eternal or immanent Trinity. The temporal reveals the eternal. If the Son is subordinated on earth and must do as the Father commands, he must be subordinated in heaven and have to do as the Father commands for all eternity. Before we clarify the terminology and respond to this common evangelical teaching, one other thing should be noted. What these evangelicals are arguing perfectly matches how the fourth-century Arians argued. Catherine LaCugna says, "Arius concluded that the subordination of Christ to God according to the economy (*kat 'oikonomian*) implied subordination at the level of God's being (*kata theologian*). In this respect at least Arius assumed a strict correspondence between *oikonomia and theologia.*"[17]

This chapter is in three sections, all related to what has just been said. First I explain how the economic–immanent Trinity distinction arose and what these and other related technical expressions mean. The best way to do this, I concluded, was to outline how the terms in question were first used in the early church. Second, I move to the twentieth century to explore the economic–immanent Trinity divide, which has been one of the most discussed topics in works on the Trinity in the last thirty years. This matter must be discussed in this book because, as we have just shown, evangelicals are sharply divided over the implications of believing that the

---

[13] Ibid., 4.
[14] Ibid., 7.
[15] Thomas Smail, *The Forgotten Father* (London: Hodder and Stoughton, 1980).
[16] Ibid., 120.
[17] Catherine LaCugna, *God for Us* (San Francisco: HarperSanFrancisco, 1991), 35.

economic Trinity reveals the immanent Trinity. Third, I will ask if Karl Rahner, who more than anyone else has brought the economic–immanent Trinity distinction onto center stage, is a supporter of the eternal subordination of the Son in function and authority, as many conservative evangelicals claim.

I. Technical Terms and Expressions as They Were First Used

Theology (Gk theologia)

Today the word *theology* is used either inclusively of the academic study of the Bible, biblical languages, church history, etc., that usually leads to a degree called a "theology degree," or more exclusively of one part of this study called "systematic theology" or "doctrine," which covers the central truths of Christianity.[18] The earliest Christian usage of this word was, however, much more restrictive. The etymology of the word determined its meaning. "Theo-logy" was the science or study of God. Athanasius uses the word to mean either accurate knowledge of God or quite specifically the triune God.[19] Similarly, the Cappadocians use the word *theologia*/theology to refer to the triune God as he is in himself.[20]

Economy (Gk oikonomia)

The Greek noun *oikonomia* is a combination of the words for house and law, literally meaning the law or rule of the household. In everyday speech it was used of the administration and management of a household, or the overseeing of a task according to a plan or design. So in 1Co 4:1 Paul calls Apollos, Cephas, and himself "servants of Christ and stewards (*oikonomoi*) of God's mysteries" (cf. 1Co 9:17; Col 1:25), and in Eph 1:10 he speaks of God's economy (*oikonomia*) "for the fullness of time, to gather up all things in [Christ]" (cf. Eph 3:9). In this second example, God's eternal plan for the redemption of the world now made known in Christ is called God's *oikonomia*. This plan is initiated by God the Father, achieved by God the Son, and realized in the life of the believer through God the Spirit (Eph 1:14).

Irenaeus over a century later first saw the profound significance of what Paul says in Ephesians about salvation being brought about through the outworking of a divine plan involving the three persons of the Trinity. Building on this idea he says,

---

[18] See further on these terms LaCugna, *God for Us*, 22–30.

[19] Athanasius, "Discourses," in *The Nicene and Post-Nicene Fathers of the Christian Church* (henceforth *NPNF*), ed. Philip Schaff and Henry Wace (Grand Rapids, Mich.: Eerdmans, 1971), 4:1.18 (p. 317) (twice). See also *The Letters of Saint Athanasius Concerning the Holy Spirit*, trans. C. R. B. Shapland (London: Epworth, 1951), 1.2 (p. 63), 1.6 (p. 73). Reference to the Greek is needed to find these uses. In the first instance Shapland translates *theologia* as "doctrine" and in the second as "knowledge of God."

[20] See also on this *NPNF* 8:7 note 2 and *NPNF* 7:326 note *d*.

"Thus therefore was God revealed; for God the Father is shown forth through all these operations (*oikonomia*), the Son indeed working, and the Spirit ministering, while the Father was approving, and man's salvation was accomplished."[21] In this usage the word *oikonomia* refers to God's orderly way of achieving the salvation of men and women.[22]

In Tertullian the Greek word *oikonomia* (Latin *dispensatio, dispositio*) is used in a different way. His basic premise was that there is one God, the monarch, or sole ruler of the universe. The word *economy* is used to explain how the one God becomes three. He says we "believe there is one only God, but under the following dispensation, or *oikonomia*, as it is called, this one only God has also a Son, his Word, who proceeded from himself, by whom all things were made."[23] In this usage the word *economy* refers to how the one God, a monad, can have a Son, or when the Spirit comes into focus, how the monad can become a trinity. Because Tertullian thought God's work in history fully explained the Trinity, he did not distinguish between what we now call today the economic and immanent Trinity. He thought that what God revealed in history fully defined the triune God apart from history. Thus for him the Father, Son, and Spirit were not eternally a trinity of distinct persons; they become a trinity in space and time.

Athanasius and the Cappadocians use the term in yet another way. For them *oikonomia* refers to the revelation of God in the incarnate Christ for our salvation. What they had to explain is how the incarnate Son who shows all the frailties of human existence can be in fact God in the fullest sense of the word. The Arians believed that because Jesus hungered, got thirsty, tired, suffered, and was obedient to the Father, he was less than God in his eternal being. In reply Athanasius makes a distinction between the Son or Logos as eternal God and the Son or Logos as incarnate God. He argues that all the human characteristics seen in the incarnate Son were limited to his flesh. They did not apply to his divinity. It is in this context that he uses the word *oikonomia* to speak of "The Word's visitation in the flesh."[24] In this usage the term *economy* refers to the Logos incarnate in Jesus of Nazareth. Its counterpart in Athanasius is the term *theo-logy* (Gk *theologia*), which for him as we have already noted alludes to either accurate knowledge of God or the eternal

---

[21] Irenaeus, *The Ante Nicene Fathers* (henceforth *ANF*), eds. Alexander Roberts and James Donaldson, 4:20.6 (p. 489).

[22] Irenaeus uses this term 120 times, of which 33 refer to the Gnostic ordering of the *pleroma*. On this see further Eric Osborn, *The Emergence of Christian Theology* (Cambridge: Cambridge University Press, 1993), 134–37.

[23] *ANF*, "Against Praxeas," chapter 2 (p. 598).

[24] Athanasius, "Discourses," in *NPNF* 4:1.59 (p. 340), 1.64 (p. 343), 2.12 (p. 354), 2.45 (p. 372), 2.76 (p. 389). See also for a clear example *The Letters of St. Athanasius Concerning the Holy Spirit*, 2–3, 7 (p. 164).

Trinity. The Cappadocians use these two terms in much the same way. For them the term *oikonomia* most commonly signifies the incarnation. Basil says that no one will err if they understand Christ's ignorance was limited "to the economy."[25] Similarly Gregory of Nazianzus distinguishes between the Son's divine nature and his *oikonomia*, translated as his "human nature."[26] Again in the Cappadocians the *oikonomia* is contrasted with *theologia*. So Basil warns against "heeding the theology but neglecting the economy."[27]

Thus to sum up, in Athanasius and the Cappadocians the term theology/*theologia* usually refers to God as he is in himself apart from history, or more specifically to God the eternal Trinity. Economy/*oikonomia*, on the other hand, is used to refer to God's revelation of himself in the incarnate Christ. For them Christ was subordinated in the economy of salvation but not as God (*theologia*). The *oikonomia* revealed the *theologia*, but the two were not to be identified. They clearly distinguish between the *oikonomia* and the *theologia*, because although they believe that after the resurrection the Son reigns as God and man, they will not ascribe to his exalted state any of the limitations of his incarnate state. He is for them after his resurrection and exaltation the reigning Lord in all majesty, glory, and authority.[28]

Immanent

The term *immanent* in theological texts usually refers to God's presence in this world as contrasted with his transcendence. The idea is that although God is separate from the world, he is in the world. In this usage *immanent* means "present" or

---

[25] Basil, "Letters," in *NPNF* 8:236.1 (p. 276), 8.3 (p. 117).

[26] Gregory of Nazianzus, "The Fourth Theological Oration," in *NPNF* 7:29.18 (p. 308).

[27] Basil, "Letters," in *NPNF* 8:8.3 (p. 117). See also Gregory of Nazianzus, "The Panegyric on St. Basil," in *NPNF* 7:43.68–69 (pp. 418–19) and "On the Holy Spirit," in *NPNF* 7:26 (p. 326).

[28] Athanasius held that in the economy we see the Son with all the limitations the taking of human flesh involved, not the eternal Son as God without the limitations of fleshly existence. He will not allow that the "properties of the flesh ... such as to hunger, to thirst, to suffer, to weary and the like," may be ascribed to the divine Word ("Four Discourses," in *NPNF* 4:3.31 [p. 410]. Cf. 3.16 [p. 402]). In answering his opponents who appeal to texts that speak of Christ's human frailties and obedience to prove he is subordinate in the *theologia* (i.e., eternally subordinate) he says, "Cease then, O abhorred of God, and degrade not the Word, nor detract from his Godhead, which is the Father's, ... For these belong not to the Word, as the Word, but are proper to men" (*NPNF* 4:3.41 [p. 416], 3.55 [p. 423]). The binding rule for Athansius is, "If God be not as a man, as he is not, we must not impute to him the attributes of man" (*NPNF* 4:3.41 [p. 416], 3.55 [p. 423]). The Cappadocians have exactly the same doctrine. Gregory of Nyssa writes, "We recognize two things in Christ, one divine, the other human (the divine by nature, but the human in the incarnation, we accordingly claim for the Godhead that which is eternal, and that which is created we ascribe to his human nature)" ("On the Faith: To Simplicius," in *NPNF* 5 [p. 337]).

"indwelling." In the expression, "the immanent Trinity," the idea of presence is still close at hand but not in relation to the world. The immanent Trinity is God present to himself, God in his own inner life (Latin *in se*). In other words, the immanent Trinity is the transcendent Trinity, the triune God as he is even if there were no created world. In this usage the word *immanent* means "inherent in." The idea is that God is inherently triune.[29] The argument that a distinction should be made between the triune God as he is in himself apart from history and the triune God as he is revealed in history and Scripture did not arise until the eighteenth century, and the use of the term "immanent Trinity" to designate the former came even later.[30] Because the meaning of the word *immanent* when used of the Trinity is not immediately obvious, some theologians prefer alternatives such as "the eternal Trinity," "the ontological Trinity," "the transcendental Trinity," or "the essential Trinity."

Before we leave this section, a comment on the Latin terms often used as equivalents is given. The economic Trinity can be equated with the Latin term God *ad extra* — God acting in the world in history, or God *pro nobis* — "God for us." The immanent Trinity, on the other hand, can be equated with the Latin God *in se* — God in himself, or God *ad intra* — God on the inside, or the triune God inwardly.

Having clarified the meaning of these important terms and distinctions, we now turn to see how they have been developed and used in the renaissance of trinitarian theology in the twentieth century. The question of how a doctrine of the Trinity is to be formulated and on what basis suddenly and forcibly came onto center stage with the publication of Karl Barth's epoch-making volume one of his *Church Dogmatics*, first published in German in 1932, and first translated into English in 1936. Building on Barth's work, Karl Rahner raises the same questions for Roman Catholics in a short study on the Trinity first published in German in 1967, which appeared in English translation in 1970 entitled *The Trinity*. Sometimes Rahner stands close to Barth in what he says; at other times he stands far away. Because it was Rahner who began the debate on the relationship between the economic and immanent Trinity, although Barth made this distinction, we begin with him.

---

[29] I follow LaCugna's explanation in *God for Us*, 211–12. For a less plausible explanation see H. Blocher, "Immanence and Transcendence in Trinitarian Theology," in *The Trinity in a Pluralistic Age: Theological Essays on Culture and Religion*, ed. Kevin Vanhoozer (Grand Rapids, Mich.: Eerdmans, 1997), 104.

[30] Wolfhart Pannenberg, *Systematic Theology*, vol. 1 (Grand Rapids, Mich.: Eerdmans, 1991), 291 and note 111; Stanley J. Grenz, *Rediscovering the Triune God: The Trinity in Contemporary Theology* (Minneapolis: Fortress, 2004), 58. Michel Rene Barnes, "De Regnon Reconsidered," *Augustinian Studies* 26 (1995): 55–71 makes the most serious effort to pinpoint the origins of this distinction but leaves many questions unanswered.

II. The Economic–Immanent Trinity Distinction in the Twentieth Century

Karl Rahner

Karl Rahner more than anyone else has made the economic–immanent Trinity distinction one of the most discussed topics in books on the Trinity in the past thirty years. He is widely thought of as one of the most influential Roman Catholic theologians of the twentieth century. In opening any of Rahner's writings, an evangelical is immediately surprised by the paucity of scriptural references, especially if one has read Barth.[31] This alerts us to the fact that Rahner is a philosophical theologian. He theologizes not primarily by appeal to Scripture and how this has been understood by the best of theologians from the past but primarily on the basis of a philosophical position that may be called "transcendental anthropology." This presupposes that human beings as embodied spiritual beings can comprehend God who is spirit through reflecting on human experience.[32] This means for him that our knowledge of God is not mediated exclusively by an encounter with Jesus Christ. It also comes, he says, through an "unthematic and anonymous" experience of God.[33] In arguing that divine revelation is not given exclusively in Christ, Rahner opts for a position that Barth totally rejects.

Rahner never wrote a definitive study on the Trinity.[34] He has only left us with a few exploratory essays and his small but highly influential book *The Trinity*, published in English in 1970.[35] As a result, students of Rahner seeking to establish his views on the Trinity are often left frustrated, wishing he had explained himself better.[36] He begins his most important contribution, *The Trinity*, by criticizing the scholastic doctrine of the Trinity. He believes the most significant turn in the wrong direction was made when Aquinas discussed *De Deo Uno* (the one God) before *De Deo Trino* (the triune God), as if the trinitarian nature of God was something secondary. This

---

[31] A notable exception to this is seen in Rahner's essay *"Theos in the New Testament," Theological Investigations*, vol. 1 (London: Darton, Longman and Todd, 1961), 79–148.

[32] This very brief comment on Rahner's methodology lacks nuance and precision because of its brevity, but without going into detail I cannot avoid that problem. In more detail see Karl-Heinz Weger, *Karl Rahner: An Introduction to His Theology* (New York: Seabury, 1980); Karen Kilby, *Karl Rahner* (London: Fount, 1997); Paul Molnar, *Divine Freedom and the Doctrine of the Immanent Trinity* (Edinburgh: T&T Clark, 2003), 181–92.

[33] Karl Rahner, *Foundations of Christian Faith: An Introduction to the Idea of Christianity* (London: Darton Longman and Todd, 1978), 21.

[34] In his essay, "The Mystery of the Trinity," *Theological Investigations* 16 (1979): 256, Rahner says he regrets that he is now too old to write a comprehensive systematic work on the Trinity.

[35] Karl Rahner, *The Trinity*, trans. J. Donceel (London: Burns and Oates, 1970).

[36] Neil Ormerod, "Wrestling with Rahner on the Trinity," *Irish Theological Quarterly* 66, no. 3 (2003): 213–27.

led to abstract rationalistic discussions about the being and attributes of God that refer "hardly at all to salvation history."[37] In this approach the immanent Trinity becomes the focus of scholarly theological reflection, and the economic Trinity is eclipsed. To overcome this error, Rahner argues that the doctrine of the Trinity should be grounded in what is revealed in salvation history, that is, in "the economy." In arguing this point he enunciates the principle that is now known as Rahner's rule: *"The 'economic' Trinity is the 'immanent' Trinity and the 'immanent' Trinity is the 'economic' Trinity."*[38]

If Rahner is asserting that all that we can know about the triune God is given in his unfolding revelation of himself in history and Scripture, then none should dissent from his rule. Indeed, every theologian should embrace this methodological principle, because it enunciates the right epistemological foundation for constructing a theology of the Trinity. So Yves Congar says, "If it is merely a question of the knowledge we have of the Tri-unity of God there is no real problem."[39] The problem is that Rahner's rule is, to quote Walter Kasper, "susceptible of several meanings and open to various misrepresentations."[40]

Fred Sanders argues that this ambiguity arises because Rahner himself is ambivalent.[41] At times it seems he is trying to push the immanent Trinity out of the picture so that the economic Trinity takes center stage. At other times he seems to be wanting to anchor the economic Trinity in the transcendent primal ground of the immanent Trinity.[42] Not surprisingly interpreters of Rahner's rule can be divided into two categories according to their understanding of the "is" in Rahner's rule. The first category Fred Sanders calls "radicalizers." The implication of Rahner's rule is for them that all that we have is the economic Trinity. He lists Piet Schoonenberg, Hans Kung, Jürgen Moltmann, Wolfhart Pannenberg, Robert Jenson, and Catherine Mowry LaCugna as taking this position. The second category he calls "restricters" because they want to restrict the implications of Rahner's rule. For them the economic Trinity must not be allowed to eclipse the immanent Trinity. In this category

---

[37] Karl Rahner, *The Trinity* (New York: Herder & Herder, 1997), 17–18.

[38] Ibid., 22, 34.

[39] Yves Congar, *I Believe in the Holy Spirit: The River of Life Flows in the East and the West*, vol. 3 (London: G. Chapman, 1983), 3, 12.

[40] Walter Kasper, *The God of Jesus Christ* (London: SCM, 1983), 275. For the interpretative options see Randal Rauser, "Rahner's Rule: An Emperor without Clothes?" *International Journal of Systematic Theology* 7, no. 1 (2005): 81–94.

[41] Fred Sanders, *The Image of the Immanent Trinity: Rahner's Rule and the Theological Interpretation of Scripture* (New York: Peter Lang, 2005). Sander's book is the most detailed study of Rahner's rule available. It only came to me as I was polishing up my manuscript, so I have not utilized it as fully as it deserves.

[42] Ibid., 81–94.

he lists Yves Congar, Walter Kasper, Hans Urs von Balthasar, Thomas F. Torrance, and Paul Molnar.[43] Sanders describes himself as a "restricter," arguing that the distinction between the economic and immanent Trinity is best captured by speaking of the economic Trinity as "the image" of the immanent Trinity.[44]

The Roman Catholic theologian Yves Congar was one of the first to try to unravel what Rahner meant and to warn that his rule could be read to discount the importance and primacy of the immanent Trinity. Thus he rejects the reading of Rahner's rule to mean that God's revelation of himself in history (the economic Trinity) definitively reveals God as he is in himself apart from history (the immanent Trinity). He asks, "Can the free mystery of the economy and the necessary mystery of the Tri-unity of God be identified?"[45] He answers that this is not possible, because such an equation would make God dependent on his historical manifestation. It would limit God's freedom to be God. He writes, "As the fathers who combated Arianism said, even if God's creatures did not exist God would still be a trinity of Father, Son, and Holy Spirit, since creation is an act of free will."[46]

Next, Congar seeks to exclude the possibility of reading Rahner's rule to imply that in history, and particularly in the incarnation, God reveals himself exactly as he is apart from history. It is his view that Rahner does not make clear that all divine revelation is accommodated to human capacities. He says God's "self-communication takes place in the economy in accordance with the rule of 'condescension,' 'humiliation,' ministry, and 'kenosis.' We have therefore to recognize that there is a distance between the economic revealed Trinity and the eternal Trinity."[47] Rahner's rule rightly reminds us that God is not other than his revelation of himself in history, but from this it does not necessarily follow that this historical revelation comprehensively reveals the triune God as he is apart from history. Bruno Forte, a Roman Catholic professor of systematic theology at Naples University, makes the same point in a pithy maxim: "Correspondence cannot be conceived as identity. The economy cannot exhaust God's depth."[48]

Like Congar, Walter Kasper endorses what he takes to be the core truth in Rahner's rule, namely what God reveals of himself in history truly reveals God as he is apart from history, and this historical revelation is the only source of our knowledge of God. What he wants to exclude, like Congar, is the idea that the economic and immanent Trinity can be completely equated like the symbols in "the formula A = A." To avoid

---

[43] Ibid., 6–7.
[44] Ibid., 7.
[45] Congar, *I Believe*, 13.
[46] Ibid.
[47] Ibid., 15.
[48] Bruno Forte, *The Trinity as History: Saga of the Christian God* (New York: Alba, 1989), 11.

such a deduction he rephrases Rahner's rule as follows: "In the economic self-communication the intra-trinitarian self-communication is present in the world in a new way, namely under the veil of historical works, signs, and actions, and ultimately in the figure of the man Jesus of Nazareth. The need is to maintain not only the *kenotic* character of the economic Trinity but also its character of graciousness and freedom in relation to the immanent Trinity and thus to do justice to the immanent mystery of God in (not behind) his one self-revelation."[49]

In this restatement of Rahner's rule, the possibility of limiting God's freedom to be God by making it necessary for him to reveal himself, or the possibility of reading back into the immanent or eternal Trinity the subordination seen in the incarnation, is excluded. The danger that both Congar and Kasper see so clearly in Rahner's rule is it could be taken to suggest that the economic Trinity *is* the immanent Trinity; that is, there is nothing other than what is revealed. It is not just correspondence he is talking about but complete identity. God in himself is fully revealed in historical revelation: God as man in the flesh reveals God as he is in eternity apart from human flesh. Rahner is speaking not about epistemology but ontology. The economic Trinity *is* the immanent Trinity. This possible way of understanding Rahner's rule introduces us to the work of Catherine LaCugna, our first representative of a "radicalizer" who reads Rahner in just this way, arguing that the economic Trinity is the immanent Trinity.

Catherine LaCugna

LaCugna's 1991 book *God for Us* is a warm-hearted exposition of the Trinity with a specific agenda. She says she writes to remind the church that the "doctrine of the Trinity is ... not teaching about the abstract nature of God ... but teaching about God's life with us and our life with each other."[50] On this basis she develops the unifying theme of her book, namely that from the time of Athanasius onwards a growing tendency can be seen, culminating in Aquinas, to think of the doctrine of the Trinity as an exposition of the inner life of the triune God in eternity. In this process she says the immanent Trinity eclipsed the economic Trinity.

Her solution to this problem is to limit all discussion about the Trinity to "the economy of salvation (*oikonomia*), in the self-communication of God in the person of Christ and the activity of the Holy Spirit."[51] She advocates abandoning the "misleading terms, economic and immanent Trinity,"[52] and the distinction to which they allude. These terms erroneously suggest that there is some reality other than the God

---

[49] Kasper, *The God*, 276.
[50] LaCugna, *God for Us*, 1.
[51] Ibid., 2.
[52] Ibid., 223.

revealed in Jesus Christ and the Spirit. She writes, "If God is truly *self*-communicating then we do know the essence (personal existence) of God: we know God as he truly is, in the mediation of God's self-revelation in Christ and the Spirit."[53] Instead of speaking of the economic and immanent Trinity, she argues for a return to the terms *oikonomia* (economy*)* and *theologia* (theology*)*, first paired as we have seen by Athanasius and the Cappadocians. For her the term *oikonomia* should not be understood to refer to the Trinity *ad extra*, but to what is revealed in Jesus Christ, and *theologia* "not to the Trinity *in se* but much more modestly and simply *to* the mystery of God."[54] In reply we must ask, Does what is revealed in the incarnation tell us all that is revealed of the triune God? I think not. The Scriptures frequently speak separately of the Father and the Spirit as distinct divine and omnipotent "persons," and say things about Christ that transcend what is revealed in the incarnation. For example, before he became man, Christ existed with and as God (Jn 1:1), and was equal to God (Php 2:6), and after the incarnation he was raised to reign as Lord. LaCugna's definition of the term *theologia* is also problematic. For her this term does not refer to God as he is in himself, as it does in Athanasius and the Cappadocians, but only to what can be known in experience and as such is a "mystery." In this definition she would seem to leave in doubt the objective reality of God and again discount biblical revelation as a source of our knowledge of God.

In objecting to the eclipse of the economic Trinity in traditional Catholic theology, LaCugna does the opposite. She eclipses the immanent Trinity. In doing this she limits God's right to be God. The only God left is the God revealed in the incarnation, or as she sometimes says, in the experience of salvation. If it were not for redemption, God would not be triune. In this claim she interprets Rahner's rule in exactly the way that Congar and Kasper reject. "The economic Trinity *is* the immanent Trinity." There is no other.

If LaCugna followed the logic of her basic thesis, it is hard to see how she can avoid subordinationism. In the *oikonomia* Christ is set under the Father and obeys him. If there is nothing other than the *oikonomia*, then Christ must be eternally subordinated to the Father. This she cannot allow. She is totally opposed to subordinationism. She excludes this error not by juxtaposing the Son of God in the form of man and in the form of God, as Athanasius and Augustine did, but by arguing that the Trinity is by definition a communion of coequal persons.[55] For her the *mon-arche* is the divine tri-une God. On this premise one divine person cannot be thought of as ruling over the others as the monarch. Monarchy is shared equally. This leads her to see the Trinity as a charter for human liberation. She writes, "The *arche* of God understood

---

[53] Ibid., 229.
[54] Ibid., 223.
[55] Ibid., 388–400.

from within a properly trinitarian theology, excludes every kind of subordinationism among persons, every kind of predetermined role, every kind of reduction of persons to uniformity.... any theological justification of hierarchy among persons also vitiates the truth of our salvation through Christ."[56]

Much of what LaCugna says on the Trinity is faith inspiring, helpful, and informative, but because of the problems in her work which I have outlined and other problems I have not mentioned,[57] her book has met with a very mixed reception.[58]

Moltmann, Pannenberg, Jenson, and Peters

Jürgen Moltmann,[59] Wolfhart Pannenberg,[60] Robert Jenson,[61] and Ted Peters[62] are also "radicalizers" of Rahner's rule but in a very different way than Catherine LaCugna. They want to make God dependent on history in becoming what he will be eschatologically on the last day.[63] The logic of Rahner's rule is, they argue, that the immanent Trinity should not be thought of as a transcendent and otherworldly static reality that is only revealed imperfectly in this world. Pannenberg, who would seem to be the most careful in developing this eschatological transformation of Rahner's rule, says, "By the creation of the world and the sending of his Son and Spirit to work in it, he [the Father] has made himself dependent upon the course of history."[64] In this revolutionary way of thinking of God there is a blurring of the distinctions between the immanent and economic Trinity, between God as he is in himself and events in history. Again the immanent Trinity is eclipsed by the economic Trinity.

I do not intend to say more on this eschatological interpretation of Rahner's rule because it would demand many pages to fairly outline the thought of each theologian

---

[56] Ibid., 400.

[57] One of these is the interpretations she gives of the writings of her key debating partners, Athanasius, the Cappadocians, Augustine, Gregory Palamas, and Aquinas. Some of these are disputed.

[58] For a positive appraisal of her work see E. T. Groppe, "Catherine Mowry LaCugna's Contribution to Trinitarian Theology," *Theological Studies* 63 (2002): 730–63. And for a highly critical appraisal see Molnar, *Divine Freedom*, 3–6, 127–40.

[59] We see his thinking on this matter developing over the years. Jürgen Moltmann, *The Trinity and the Kingdom* (New York: Harper and Row, 1981), I think expresses his position on this matter most fully.

[60] Pannenberg, *Systematic Theology*, vol. 1, 327–36.

[61] Again his thinking on this matter developed over the years. See in particular Robert Jenson, *The Triune Identity: God According to the Gospel* (Philadelphia: Fortress, 1982).

[62] Ted Peters, *God as Trinity: Relationality and Temporality in Divine Life* (Louisville: Westminster, 1993), especially pp. 128–75.

[63] The best summary of the respective positions of the first three theologians on this specific matter is given by Sanders, *The Image*, 83–112. He does not list Peters in this grouping or discuss his work in any detail.

[64] Pannenberg, *Systematic Theology*, vol. 1, 329.

on this matter and because what they say on this does not bear directly on the issues with which this book is concerned. None of them give any support at all to the idea that because the Son is subordinated in the economy he is eternally subordinated in the immanent Trinity. Indeed, Moltmann polemicizes against hierarchical ordering in any form.[65] I include this short comment simply to make readers aware of another way of taking Rahner's rule.

The Economic Trinity Should Not Eclipse or Be Identified with the Immanent Trinity

In reply to the "radicalizers" who would give primacy to the economic Trinity, I want to argue that the immanent Trinity must be given, might we say, a life of its own. God is triune even if he had not created the world or the Son had become incarnate. The Triune God is the Lord of history. Events in this world do not prescribe his being, or his tri-unity, or indicate that the Father is eternally set over the Son in authority. It is true that all we know of the immanent Trinity is given in revelation, but revelation does not and cannot fully reveal God to human minds. As a "restricter" I take Rahner's rule to speak of a correlation between the economic and immanent Trinity, not identification. The limitations the Son gladly assumed for our salvation in becoming man must not be read back into the immanent Trinity. In taking this approach I follow in the steps of Athanasius and the Cappadocian Fathers from the early church and Congar and Kasper from our own time, and many others.

Basic to the position I am taking is the premise that the revelation of economic Trinity is far more than the incarnation. I want to make the point that the triune God reveals himself in history from the creation to the consummation: from the book of Genesis to the book of Revelation. If the economic Trinity is limited to what is revealed in the incarnation, then the eternal subordination of the Son to the Father naturally follows. Jesus is subordinated on earth, and thus he must be subordinated in heaven. To counter this line of reasoning, I argue that the incarnation is not the totality of what is revealed of God, Father, Son, and Spirit in the Bible. Even in reference to the Son alone, the Bible says far more about him than that he took flesh, assuming the form of a servant. He is also spoken of as true God and as such the co-creator and the Lord who reigns supreme.

In arguing that the economic Trinity must not be allowed to eclipse the immanent Trinity, I follow Cornelius Van Til and Barth, who wrote before Rahner; Torrance, who wants to balance what Rahner says; and Molnar, who writes in direct opposition to Rahner.

---

[65] For a helpful summary of Moltmann's views on the Trinity see Grenz, *Rediscovering the Triune God*, 73–88.

Cornelius Van Til

In American conservative Reformed circles, Cornelius Van Til is a theological giant. For him the doctrine of the Trinity "is the heart of Christianity." No other doctrine is more important.[66] He presupposed as a philosophical given that the one and the many, the unity and the diversity, the oneness and the threeness, in the Christian God are "equally ultimate."[67] For him both divine coequality and eternal differentiation are absolutes. "The three persons of the Trinity are co-substantial; not one is derived in his substance from either or both of the others. Yet there are three distinct persons in this unity; the diversity and the identity are equally underived."[68] Subordinationism for him is the error of a reading back into the immanent or eternal Trinity the temporal subordination of the incarnate Son, of merging "the temporal in a correlative union with the eternal."[69] Indeed he argues, "All heresies with respect to the Trinity can be reduced to one great heresy of mixing the eternal and the temporal."[70]

From this it is of no surprise to discover that time and time again he insists that the immanent or eternal Trinity be given priority over the economic Trinity. He says we must always think first "of the ontological Trinity before we think of the economical Trinity."[71] He makes the same point when he says, "The internal relation of the persons in the Godhead is prior to and independent of, the relation of the Godhead to the created universe."[72] He agrees that in his human nature Christ was temporally subordinated to the Father, but he insists that Scripture makes it plain that as the second person of the eternal Trinity he continued to share "in the incommunicable attributes of the Godhead."[73] As the eternal divine Son, he was not subordinated to the divine Father in being, function, or authority. "The eternal and the temporal were not confused."[74] This must be so, he says, because "the eternal must always remain independent of and prior to the temporal."[75] He thus concludes that

---

[66] Cornelius Van Til, *The Defense of the Faith* (Philadelphia: Presbyterian and Reformed, 1967), 12, 25.

[67] Ibid., 25.

[68] Ibid., 12.

[69] Cornelius Van Til, *An Introduction to Systematic Theology* (Philadelphia: Presbyterian and Reformed, 1955), 233–34.

[70] Ibid., 234.

[71] Van Til, *Defense*, 16.

[72] Van Til, *An Introduction*, 234.

[73] Van Til, *Defense*, 16.

[74] Van Til, *An Introduction*, 235.

[75] Van Til, *Defense*, 17. In *An Introduction*, 231, he says much the same thing when he writes, "The Trinity as it exists in itself, apart from its relation to the created universe, is self complete, involving as it does the equal ultimacy of unity and plurality."

"a consistent biblical doctrine of the Trinity would imply the complete rejection of all subordinationism."[76]

There is much in Van Till that should give contemporary evangelical subordinationists food for thought. In opposition to them, he rejects that what is seen in the incarnation in the temporal sphere defines what is true of the Son in the eternal sphere and thus that the Son is eternally subordinated to the Father. However, in giving absolute priority to the immanent Trinity over the economic Trinity, he falls into the error of Catholic scholasticism that Rahner's rule at its most basic level seeks to correct. How is it possible, we may ask, to think "first" of the immanent Trinity if it is the economic Trinity that reveals the immanent Trinity?

John Frame, who is a sympathetic but not uncritical disciple of Van Til, more carefully expresses his position. He says, "I believe, however, that it is too much to say with Rahner that the 'economic' Trinity is the 'immanent' Trinity and the 'immanent' Trinity is the 'economic' Trinity. There is a difference between what God is necessarily and what he freely chooses to do in his plan for creation."[77]

Karl Barth

Barth bases his doctrine of the Trinity on divine revelation, not the words of revelation given in the Bible.[78] It is his argument that God does not impart information about himself; he imparts himself in threefold form as Revealer (the Father), as Revelation (the Son), and as Revealedness (the Spirit).[79] He insists that there is no other route to knowing God, let alone discovering that he is triune. This leads him to assert that what is revealed in history in Revelation, that is Jesus Christ, reveals what is true in eternity: "We have consistently followed the rule, which we regard as basic, that statements about the divine modes of being antecedently in themselves cannot be different in content from those that are being made about the reality in revelation. All our statements concerning what is called the immanent Trinity have been reached simply as confirmation or underlinings or materially as the indisputable premise of the economic Trinity ... the reality of God which encounters us in his revelation is his reality in all the depths of eternity."[80]

And similarly, "We have to say that, as Christ is in revelation, so He is antecedently in Himself. Thus He is antecedently in Himself light of light, very God of very

---

[76] Cornelius Van Til, *A Christian Theory of Knowledge* (Philadelphia: Presbyterian and Reformed, 1969), 104.

[77] John Frame, *The Doctrine of God: A Theology of Lordship* (Phillipsburg, N.Y.: P&R, 2002), 706–7.

[78] Barth's theology will be expounded and explained more fully in the next chapter.

[79] Karl Barth, *Church Dogmatics* (Edinburgh: T&T Clark, 1975), 1.1, 295–333.

[80] Ibid., 1.1, 479.

God, the begotten of God, and not His creature. We have to take revelation with such utter seriousness that in it as God's act we must directly see God's being too."[81]

Conservative evangelicals committed to the idea that the Son is eternally subordinated to the Father think that such "antecedent" statements in Barth indicate he thought that just as Jesus was subordinated in the incarnation so he is subordinated in heaven. Barth in fact is arguing in exactly the opposite way. He is saying that just as Christ is fully God in eternity so he is in revelation. In Christ we do not see subordinated God other than God the Father in being, work, or authority. We see God. Jesus Christ is God without any caveats. To understand Barth, his most fundamental premise must be firmly grasped: Jesus Christ reveals God.

Barth embraces the Chalcedonian confession that Jesus Christ is fully God and fully man (human) in the one person, yet because he believes the divine must always triumph over the human, he consistently speaks of Christ simply as "God." The man Jesus in his being repeats and reflects the inner being or essence of God. "If he [the Son] reveals God, then irrespective of His creaturehood He Himself has to be God. And since this is a case of either/or, He has to be full and true God without reduction or limitation, without more or less. Any such restriction would not merely weaken His deity; it would deny it. To confess Him as the revelation of His Father is to confess Him as essentially equal in deity with this Father of His."[82]

Even at the cross we see "the one true God": "The one true God being Himself the subject of the act of atonement in such a way that His presence and action as the Reconciler of the world coincide and are indeed identical with the existence of the humiliated and lowly and obedient man Jesus of Nazareth. He acts as the Reconciler in that—as the true God identical with this man—He humbles himself and becomes lowly and obedient. He becomes and is this without being in contradiction to his divine nature."[83]

From what has been said so far, it could be thought that Barth believed that in the incarnation God is perfectly revealed in Christ, or more generally that the economic Trinity reveals the immanent Trinity, but this is not the case. Barth in fact argues for a "deliberate and sharp distinction" between what is revealed in Jesus Christ, "God for us," and God as he is in himself, between the economic Trinity and the immanent Trinity. He says it is "absolutely essential that along with older theology we make a deliberate and sharp distinction between the Trinity of God as we may know it in the Word of God revealed, written and proclaimed, and God's immanent Trinity, i.e., between 'God in himself' and 'God for us,' between the 'eternal history of God' and his temporal acts."[84]

---

[81] Ibid., 4.1, 428.
[82] Ibid., 1.1, 406.
[83] Ibid., 4.1, 199. See also 130.
[84] Ibid., 1.1, 172.

Again agreeing with Chalcedon, Barth accepts that the incarnate Christ is one person, but he does not allow that the flesh assumed by Christ reveals God. It is his view that what is "creaturely" in the incarnate Christ must not be read back into the immanent Trinity. God taking flesh is an act in history, but God does not become what he is through historical events. So he writes, "The Word is what He is even before and apart from His being flesh."[85] For Barth the immanent Trinity is for ever what it is apart from history: the incarnation does not effect or indicate a change in the triune God. In seeking to explain how Christ can be eternally God and man and yet become incarnate in a point of time in world history, Barth appeals to the important old distinction between the *Logos asarkos* (the Logos without flesh) and *the Logos ensarkos* (the Logos in the flesh).[86] The Son is forever God and man, but only for a limited period was he man in the flesh as Jesus of Nazareth.

What Barth cannot allow is that Jesus' incarnate life as such discloses his divinity. He can even say, "The form of God's Word, then, is in fact the form of the cosmos which stands in contradiction to God."[87] In the "unveiling" of revelation there is also a "veiling," he repeatedly says.[88] He can even speak in stark and provocative language of the humanity of Christ "concealing" his divinity.[89] He writes, "He makes Himself known to us, but in the means and sign which He uses to be known by us, He makes Himself foreign and improper to Himself ... in revealing Himself in this way, He also conceals himself."[90]

Thus it is of no surprise to find him saying, "The Godhead is not so immanent in Christ's humanity, that it does not also remain transcendent to it."[91] To hold otherwise, he believes, would blur the distinction between events in God himself and events in human history and suggest that the human limitations of the incarnate Christ, what is "creaturely," be read back into the immanent Trinity. Ultimately, however, Barth makes this "sharp distinction" between the economic and immanent Trinity to preserve God's freedom—possibly his most basic concern. For him God is eternally triune, not just triune in creation and reconciliation, and Christ is forever sovereign God.

Thomas F. Torrance

Torrance stands very close to Barth in his understanding of the relationship between the economic and immanent Trinity. On the one hand he stresses that the economic

---

[85] Ibid., 1.2, 136.
[86] On this topic see ibid., 1.2, 168ff.; 3.1, 54; 3.2, 65ff., 147ff.; 4.1, 52.
[87] Ibid., 1.1, 166. On this theme see ibid., 1.1, 163–66, 323–34 and 2.1, 287.
[88] Ibid., 1.1, 165–66, 316–26.
[89] Ibid., 1.1, 165, 316, 321, 323.
[90] Ibid., 2.1, 55.
[91] Ibid., 1.1, 323.

Trinity reveals all that we know of the immanent Trinity, or as he calls it, "the onto-logical Trinity." For this reason they should not be held apart or divided. He writes, "The economic Trinity and the ontological Trinity overlap one another and belong to one another, and can no more be separated than the Act of God can be separated from his Being or his Being from his Act."[92]

Torrance wants to underline that what God is towards us in his saving work in the world he is in himself. He is not other than he reveals himself. There is an "indis-soluble connection"[93] between what is revealed and what is true in eternity—between the economic and immanent Trinity.

However, Torrance cannot allow that the economic and ontological Trinity be identified. He says we must speak of both of "the distinction and of the oneness between the economic and the ontological Trinity."[94] He makes this point because he absolutely rejects that the subordination seen in the work of redemption be ascribed to the Son in the ontological Trinity. He says we are not to "read back into God what is human and finite."[95] The human is of the essence of the revelation given but not its substance. He says, "Since God makes himself known to us within the modalities of our creaturely and human reality (as in the incarnation), there is an inevitable and proper element of anthropomorphism in our human knowledge of God." This makes it all the more imperative for us, however, to distinguish what is properly anthropo-morphic and what is improperly anthropomorphic in our knowledge of him.... This applies above all, of course, to our use of the terms 'father' and 'son.' "[96]

Torrance is adamant that the voluntary subordination and obedience of the Son seen in the incarnation and the titles *Father* and *Son* reveal something true of the triune God and of the divine Father-Son relationship. What he wants to exclude is the reading back into the immanent Trinity anything from the strictures of historical revelation, or the content of words used in reference to human relationships, or the voluntary and temporal subordination of the Son in the incarnation for our salvation. For him the *homoousian* principle excludes any suggestion that the Father and the Son are separated in divinity, being, majesty, work/function, or authority. The Father and the Son are one in being and act and can never be otherwise.[97] The economic Trin-ity reveals the immanent Trinity, but what takes place in history does not prescribe God's being or triune relations apart from history nor exhaustively reveal the triune

---

[92] T. F. Torrance, *The Christian Doctrine of God: One Being Three Persons* (Edinburgh: T&T Clark, 1996), 8. See also p. 95 for a similar categorical statement on this connection.

[93] Ibid., 95.

[94] Ibid., 30. See for an almost identical comment p. 97.

[95] Ibid., 99.

[96] Ibid., 99–101.

[97] Ibid.

God as he is in himself. What is creaturely in Christ is not to be read back into the immanent Trinity.

Paul Molnar

To complete this discussion on the immanent–economic Trinity distinction in modern theology Paul Molnar's book *Divine Freedom and the Doctrine of the Immanent Trinity*, published in 2003, must be mentioned. He writes "to articulate a contemporary doctrine of the immanent Trinity" in a period when many theologians today "polemicize against such a doctrine" or simply pay lip service to it.[98] Only a robust doctrine of the immanent Trinity, he argues, preserves "God's freedom and distinction from creation."[99] His quest is to discover how first we may "avoid both separating and confusing the immanent Trinity and economic Trinity and adhere to the economic Trinity for our information about the immanent Trinity."[100] And second, speak "accurately of God's Fatherhood and Sonship, and about God's relationality and temporality without projecting our limited human relations of fatherhood and sonship and created temporality into the divine life," thus compromising God's sovereignty and freedom.[101] For Molnar, like Barth, God's freedom is the primary issue. Only a strong doctrine of the immanent Trinity allows God the freedom to exist as Father, Son, and Spirit apart from creation and redemption, apart from human history, and apart from human experience.

He accepts that we can only know God through the categories of human experience open to us, but he wants to insist that nothing within human experience or human relationships prescribe who God is in himself or explains eternal trinitarian relations. We only know God through grace and faith. From this we immediately see that Molnar stands close to Barth and far from Rahner, LaCugna, and the theological liberal tradition. Indeed he thinks these two theologians and others he names have led the church down the wrong path. By defining God from human experience, they have undermined the majesty of the triune God as he is, and the freedom of God to be God.[102] In the end the goal of such theology, he says, is not to say who God is but "to make the Trinity a doctrine which is alive so that it reflects our experience of faith and incorporates relationality and temporality into the divine life."[103]

For Molnar, Barth more than any other modern theologian has rightly grasped the *how* and the *what* of trinitarian theology. He makes revelation the sole basis for

---

[98] Molnar, *Divine Freedom*, x.
[99] Ibid.
[100] Ibid.
[101] Ibid.
[102] Ibid., 1–25.
[103] Ibid., 163.

knowing God and Jesus Christ the locus of this revelation. In Jesus the Father is "reiterated." A failure to recognize Jesus' full deity and Lordship means a failure to recognize God as he is. Nevertheless, for Barth Jesus' humanity conceals as well as reveals. The revelation of the Father in the Son is given by grace through faith.[104] Neither in regard to God's revelation in Christ, nor in God's revelation of himself in creation and consummation, can there be a blurring of the distinction between events in history and God as he is in himself. For Barth, Molnar says, "God exists eternally as the Father, Son, and Holy Spirit and would so exist even if there had been no creation, reconciliation, or redemption."[105] Thus along with Barth, Molnar makes the immanent Trinity the indispensable foundation of the economic Trinity. The economic Trinity, God *ad extra*, reveals the immanent Trinity, God *in se*, but for God to be God and thus free, these historical events cannot simply be identified with God as he is in himself apart from history. He thus endorses Barth's determination to make "a deliberate and sharp distinction" between the economic and immanent Trinity.[106]

Molnar takes no prisoners along the way. He is convinced that both Catholic and Protestant theological liberals are in error. They depict God in human categories and define divine triune relations according to human relations, thereby making the Creator in the image of the creature. Molnar was completely unaware[107] that this is also what many contemporary evangelicals have done by redefining the Father-Son relation in terms of what they would like the man-woman relationship to be. Paradoxically, this means that at this point modern liberalism and the more socially and theologically conservative evangelicals fall into the same error.

Back to the Bible

It would seem that today most evangelicals who have thought about the Trinity would accept that the notional and theological distinction between the economic and the immanent Trinity is a helpful one. First of all, it is a reminder that what is revealed by God in the Bible gives us trustworthy knowledge of the triune God as he is in himself. God is not other than his revelation. And second, that even if God had not created the world or come to humanity to save, he would still be triune. It is not revelation that makes God triune. God is free to be God. What divides evangelicals today on the economic–immanent Trinity issue is whether the subordination of the Son seen in the incarnation is to be read back into the immanent Trinity. Behind this question lies another. Is the revelation of the Son given in the incarnation definitive of his person and power apart from history?

---

[104]Ibid., 27–43.
[105]Ibid., 63.
[106]Ibid., 197, 235, 64.
[107]So he told me in correspondence.

No ones denies that in the incarnation the Son was subordinated and obedient as man to the Father. If the economic Trinity is defined as what is revealed in the economy of salvation, and it is held that the economic Trinity *is* the eternal or immanent Trinity, then it follows (1) there is hierarchical ordering in the eternal Trinity, (2) the Son is eternally subordinated to the Father in function and authority, and (3) my debating opponents are right. The economic Trinity, however, cannot be limited to what is revealed in the incarnation. The economic Trinity is by definition the revealed Trinity, the revelation to human beings on earth of the Father, Son, and Spirit. This revelation is given in Scripture in its totality, not just in the Synoptic Gospels.[108]

The revelation of the eternal Son of God cannot be limited to what is revealed in the incarnation, because this is not all that is revealed of the Son in Scripture. In the Bible we also learn of his preexistence as equal God and present reign as Lord. Long ago Athanasius pointed out that there is a "double account" of the Savior in Scripture: one of him as he is as God and one as he is as God incarnate. The Synoptic Gospels concentrate on the latter. They show Jesus as fully human, praying to his Father in heaven, tiring, suffering, and dying. The other "account" speaks of Christ as he is eternally apart from the subordination assumed in the incarnation. From this latter perspective John says of Christ, "In the beginning the Word was with God and the Word was God.... All things came into being through him" (Jn 1:1–2), and he records Jesus as frequently calling himself "I am," God the Father's own self-designation in the Old Testament. Paul similarly says, "He [Christ] is the image of the invisible God ... in him all things in heaven and earth were created ... he himself is before all things, and in him all things hold together ... in him the fullness of God was pleased to dwell" (Col 1:15–19). And he frequently calls the resurrected Jesus "the Lord," the title used of God by the Greek translators of the Hebrew Scriptures. Then we have the words of the writer of the epistle to the Hebrews, "He [Christ] is the reflection of God's glory and the exact imprint of God's very being" (Heb 1:3). Texts belonging to this "account" led the fourth-century opponents of Arianism to speak of Christ as *one in being*, work, and authority with the Father. These comments on the divine side of the "double account" do not tell us all that we might like to know of Jesus in relation to the Father, but they certainly presuppose a doctrine of a coequal immanent Trinity. They complement what is revealed in the incarnation taken in isolation. Or to put it another way, they give the divine side of the double account. Any adequate and accurate doctrine of the Trinity must embrace these two perspectives given in Scripture. One must not be allowed to eclipse the other. The

---

[108]I of course do not deny "general revelation," but I would deny this is saving revelation or that it gives us accurate knowledge of God.

Father is revealed in the incarnate subordinated Son who anticipates the Spirit, but the triune God apart from history is not exhaustively revealed in all his majesty, glory, and power by the incarnation and subsequent giving of the Spirit to all who believe.

I thus argue that a fully biblical doctrine of God must take into account all that is said of the Father, Son, and Spirit throughout the Bible and that the revelation of God in Christ must not be limited to what is revealed in the incarnate Christ. God is revealed in Jesus Christ, because Christ is God, but in the incarnate Christ we see God in human flesh, in self-emptied or kenotic revelation, in the form of a servant. After his resurrection he continues to be fully God and fully man, but in his exaltation to rule as Lord, his unqualified divinity, glory, and authority are unveiled.[109]

To Sum Up on the Economic-Immanent Trinity Debate

What we have discovered is that the distinction between the economic and immanent Trinity comes relatively late in the historical development of the doctrine of the Trinity, but it is anticipated by what has just been called the "double account" of the Savior and by the pro-Nicene fathers' distinction between *theologia*, understood as either God as he is, or the triune nature of God, and *oikonomia*, understood as God's revelation of himself in the incarnation of the Son. There are of course not two trinities. This notional and theological distinction between the immanent and economic Trinity is simply a reminder that while there is a correlation between the triune God as he reveals of himself in time and space and as he is in eternity, the latter does not exhaust the former. There is correspondence but not identity. The triune God is not other than he reveals himself, but historical revelation never captures fully the divine reality. For this reason it is necessary and imperative that we do not read back the Son's subordination in the economy of salvation into the eternal or immanent Trinity.

III. Does Karl Rahner Teach the Eternal Subordination of the Son?

Evangelicals, as we have noted, have found a number of things in Rahner's writings that lead them to believe that he embraced the eternal subordination of the Son in a way very similar to them. The first and most important, they say, is that he equates the economic and immanent Trinity. This means that because the Son is subordinated in the economy, he must be subordinated eternally. We have just examined this argument and found it wanting. Now in this final section of this chapter we consider

---

[109]Louis Berkhof, *Systematic Theology* (London: Banner of Truth, 1958), 344.

specific teaching in Rahner's writings that has been taken by some evangelicals to indicate he believed in the eternal subordination of the Son.

First we examine the claim that Rahner believed in a hierarchically ordered Trinity where the Son is set under the Father. I find no support for this thesis at all and much to the contrary. For Rahner the economic Trinity is the "self-communication" of the Father in the Son and through the Spirit in salvation history, beginning with creation and ending in the consummation.[110] It is, as he says explicitly, "the Trinity *ad extra*."[111] The mission of the Son, an event in history, reveals that God is not abstractly unitary and that the Father and the Son are to be differentiated. But what the incarnation is above all else is God communicating himself. Jesus is not the Father, but he is not other than the Father. He writes, "The one God communicates himself in absolute self-utterance and an absolute donation of love. Here is the absolute mystery revealed only to us in Christ: God's self-communication is truly a *self*-communication."[112]

Rahner emphatically underlines both unity and distinction in the Godhead: "We must say that the Father, Son, and Spirit are identical with the one godhead and are 'relatively' distinct from one another. The three as distinct are constituted only by their relatedness to one another, so the axiom which asserts identity of the essences and the distinction of the three may also be formulated (as Anselm was first to do and as done by the Council of Florence) as follows: in God everything is one except where there is relative opposition."[113]

The divine three are "identical with the one Godhead" and "relatively distinct from one another." It is their differing relations with one another that constitute the distinctions. Rahner definitely does not predicate divine differentiation on differing functions/operations or authority. He writes, "The divine persons cannot be divided from one another in being or in operation, and form only one principle of action *ad extra*."[114] For him the divine three are in their unity and distinction all "omnipotent."[115]

These quotes give no support to the suggestion that Rahner taught the eternal subordination of the Son. Rather they indicate that he believed in a coequal Trinity. For him the Son is nothing less than the "self-communication" of the Father. However, Rahner's decision to identity God as the Father and make him the *monarche* of

---

[110] Rahner, *The Trinity*, 23, 27, 36, 37, 82, 83, etc.

[111] Karl Rahner, "Trinity, Divine" in *Sacramentum Mundi: An Encyclopaedia of Theology*, vol. 6, eds. K. Rahner, C. Ernst, K. Smyth (London: Burns and Oates, 1970), 300.

[112] Rahner, *The Trinity*, 36.

[113] Ibid., 72.

[114] Rahner, "Trinity, Divine," *Sacramentum Mundi*, 295.

[115] Ibid., 297.

the Son and the Spirit, following the Cappadocians, has been thought by some scholars to open the door to subordinationism.[116] William J. Hill[117] and Joseph DiNoia,[118] both highly respected Catholic theologians, and John Thompson,[119] a well-informed Protestant scholar, make this charge. Depicting the Father as the *monarche* of the Son and the Spirit does not necessarily lead to subordinationism, as the Cappadocian theology proves. This charge is simply a warning that this "model" of the Trinity can easily lead to subordinationism and often has by making the Father God in a unique sense. William Hill says, "Rahner himself is fully alert to the cryptic subordinationism towards which the logic of his trinitarianism tends at this point in its development and is quick to repudiate any such implications."[120]

Rather than leaning towards subordinationism, the more general opinion is that Rahner leans a little towards modalism, the error that excludes all forms of subordinationism. In modalism the divine three are eternally one without distinctions in the immanent Trinity. Rahner may speak of the divine "persons" as "three distinct manners of subsisting," but he is not a modalist. The divine three are for him eternally differentiated. Nevertheless, the informed Catholic theologian William Hill calls Rahner's model of the Trinity, "Modal Trinitarianism."[121] By this he is in effect saying that Rahner stresses divine unity more than divine differentiation. My conservative evangelical debating opponents do exactly the opposite. On this matter they and Rahner are to be contrasted rather than compared.

Rahner's Christology

Rahner's doctrine of the Trinity is perfectly orthodox, but this is not to say that at times his Christology is not without problems. Just as there is ambivalence in his understanding of the relationship between the immanent and economic Trinity, so too there is ambivalence in his Christology.[122] At times he asserts that the incarnate Christ is the "self-communication" of God, unlike what we are, and at other times

---

[116] In his essay "*Theos* in the New Testament" (*Theological Investigations*, vol. 1, 146), Rahner writes, "*O Theos* in the language of the New Testament signifies the Father ... the concrete, individual uninterchangeable Person ... who is in fact the Father, not the single divine nature that is seen subsisting in three hypostases, but the concrete Person who possesses the divine nature unoriginately."

[117] William J. Hill, *The Three-Personed God: The Trinity as a Mystery of Salvation* (Washington, D.C.: Catholic University of America Press, 1982), 143.

[118] John DiNoia, "Karl Rahner," in *The Modern Theologians: An Introduction to Christian Theology in the Twentieth Century*, vol. 1, ed. David Ford (Oxford: Blackwell, 1996), 189, 197.

[119] Joseph Thompson, *Modern Trinitarian Perspectives* (New York: Oxford, 1994), 28.

[120] Hill, *Three-Personed God*, 113.

[121] Ibid., 145.

[122] See further on this Bruce Marshall, *Christology in Conflict: The Identity of the Saviour in Rahner and Barth* (London: Blackwell, 1987), 40–60.

that the incarnate Christ is what we all are, only more so. In tension he develops "a Christology from above" (Christ is God come down to earth) and "a Christology from below" (Christ was the most godly of men taken up into the Godhead) without ever seeking to reconcile the two. As a consequence his Christology is seemingly contradictory.

In his "Christology from above" Rahner allows for no distinction between the eternal *Logos* and the incarnate *Logos*.[123] He thinks of the *Logos* deifying the human nature. He says, "The human nature is not a mask (the *prosopon*) assumed from without, from behind which the Logos hides to act things out in the world. From the start it is the constitutive real symbol of the Logos himself."[124]

With this in mind he speaks of "the Son as the 'absolute bringer of salvation' and as self-communication of the Father."[125] In the Son, he says, "the Father, his will, his salvation, his pardon, his kingdom 'are there' in absolute and final proximity."[126]

The description of the Son as the "self-communication" of the Father is unquestionably Rahner's primary and dominant way of thinking of the Son.[127] It emphatically distinguishes the Father from the Son, but it does not imply that he is in some way set apart from the Father in divinity, being, or authority. Rather, these words make the Son the one who reveals the Father both in majesty as the ultimate ruler and in all lowliness as the one who goes to the cross. If this were not the case, Rahner says, "God's communication would be basically Arian."[128]

At times, however, Rahner opts for what is called "a Christology from below." He thus can speak of Christ as a man fully possessed by the Logos. He is the true man standing before God who lives the life of perfect obedience. Patrick Burke says that for Rahner, "In the Logos' unity with man is created the perfect human response to the divine self-communication. Jesus freely gives his humanity into the divine mystery so as to receive everything from it and therefore man, the *potentia obedientialis*, is absolutely filled by him."[129]

In reasoning this way Burke believes Rahner introduces an "Arian tendency."[130] Christ is understood as the greatest of creatures in a special relationship with God,

---

[123]In *The Trinity*, 33, Rahner says, "The Logos with God and the Logos with us, the immanent and the economic Logos, are strictly the same."

[124]Ibid., 33. In more detail see Karl Rahner, "The Theology of the Symbol," *Theological Investigations* 4 (1966): 221–52.

[125]Rahner, *The Trinity*, 63.

[126]Ibid.

[127]See particularly ibid., pp. 83–99, where Rahner makes it clear that the Son being the Father's "self-communication" is his primary emphasis.

[128]Ibid., 38.

[129]Patrick Burke, *Reinterpreting Rahner: A Critical Study of His Major Themes* (New York: Fordham University Press), 136.

[130]Ibid., 155.

but not God in the absolute sense of this word. Paul Molnar in his discussion of this same matter uses a much better and more accurate designation. Taking over Barth's categories, he argues that Rahner exhibits "a form of Ebionite Christology."[131] Christ is the exceptional man God deifies.

There is a "liberal" or "Ebionite" tendency in Rahner's Christology, but to suggest that his doctrine of the Trinity envisages the eternal "functional subordination in some form"[132] of the Son in authority is to be rejected. Mark Baddeley thinks he finds Rahner teaching just this in one paragraph in his book *The Trinity*. The dozens of paragraphs that suggest the opposite are ignored. These are the words Baddeley quotes in support of his case. "May we really say without more ado that from the concept Son of the synoptic Jesus we must eliminate his obedience to the Father, his adoration, his submission to the Father's unfathomable will? For we eliminate them when we explain this kind of behavior in him only through the hypostatic union as such. They are then properties of the Son, but not constitutive moments of his sonship."[133]

It is possible to read these words as Baddeley interprets them, if they are divorced from their context. However, read in context this interpretation seems very unlikely or impossible. Rahner at this point in his book is seeking to pinpoint what differentiates the Father and the Son. Rahner first argues that Jesus' own self-consciousness as the Son of the Father is a "dangerous" basis for distinguishing the Son as the Son in distinction to the Father. A better option, he believes, is to ground it in the reality of the incarnation. The Son's obedience, adoration, and submission to the Father seen in the Synoptic Gospels defines what it meant to be the incarnate Son. His temporal submission to the Father were "constituent moments of his sonship."[134] They were what the Son did in taking on flesh for our salvation. They are not simply limited to our reflections of his human nature. The Son of God truly became man, taking the form of a servant, and went to the cross in obedience to win our salvation. The Son did these things, not the Father or the Spirit.

That Rahner is not suggesting the eternal subordination of the Son is made crystal clear in the immediately following paragraph where he defines the Son "as the 'Absolute Bringer of Salvation' and as a self-communication of the Father." In the Son, he says, the Father is there "in absolute and final proximity"[135] It thus seems to me that what Rahner is arguing in these few pages in his book *The Trinity* is that the

---

[131]Molnar, *Divine Freedom*, 113. The Ebionites were an early Jewish Christian sect that thought of Jesus Christ as a godly man who was deified by a special endowment to the Spirit. They were the first to teach a "Christology from below."

[132]Baddeley, "The Trinity and Subordinationism," 9.

[133]Rahner, *The Trinity*, 62–63.

[134]Ibid., 63.

[135]Ibid.

Son must be differentiated from the Father, and the incarnation unambiguously does this. Nevertheless, in the Son we do not see eternally subordinated God other than the Father. We see the Father himself in the incarnate and temporally subordinated Son. To quote him again: "The Son is the economic (historical) self-communication of the Father."[136]

Only the Logos or the Son Could Become Incarnate

One argument Rahner develops in his book *The Trinity* is that of the three divine persons only the Son or Logos could have become incarnate. Evangelicals committed to the eternal subordination of the Son similarly believe that only the Son could have become incarnate and taken the form of a servant. On seeing this argument in Rahner for the necessity for the Logos to be the one incarnated, my evangelical friends have concluded that like them he is arguing that the Son had to become incarnate because he is subordinated God. He does as the Father commands. This in fact is not Rahner's argument at all. The idea of *necessity* is the only thing common to both.

Rahner begins his case by rightly pointing out that in the incarnation it is not "God in general" who is revealed, but rather the Father through the Son. It was the Logos who took human flesh. The Son or Logos is not the Father, but the "Father's self-expression to the world ... implying an 'inner' differentiation in God himself." If this were not the case, Rahner says, "then the fact of the incarnation of the *Logos* reveals properly nothing about the *Logos himself*, that is about his own relative specific features within divinity. For in this event the incarnation means for us practically only the experience that God in general is a person."[137]

Rahner makes an important point. In the incarnation it is the Son of God or Logos who becomes man to reveal the Father. John the evangelist teaches this very thing when he records Jesus as saying, "No one has ever seen God. It is God the only Son who is close to the Father's heart, who has made him known" (Jn 1:18). It thus follows that in our attempts to articulate a doctrine of the Trinity the divine person should not be confused at any time or in any way. The Father is the Father and not the Son, the Son is the Son and not the Father or the Spirit, and the Spirit is the Spirit, not the Father or the Son.

Rahner then goes on to argue that the Son or Logos had to be the one who became incarnate. His argument for the *necessity* of the *Logos* becoming incarnate is that the *Logos* by definition is God in communication. The Father could not become incarnate because he is the invisible God and cannot be otherwise.[138] In making this argument Rahner is rejecting the scholastic position given classic expression by

---

[136]Ibid.
[137]Rahner, *The Trinity*, 28.
[138]Ibid.

Aquinas that any of the divine three persons could have taken human flesh.[139] Aquinas insists that as the power or authority of each divine person is the same, although their personal properties are distinct, human nature could have been assumed by "the Father or the Holy Spirit, even as it did unite to the Son."[140] Indeed, Aquinas asks, Would it have been better if the Father had become incarnate? "By the Son's becoming man, many have been held back from a true knowledge of God, for they referred to the Son himself those things said in his humanity. Arius, for example, held for an inequality of persons because of the text, *The Father is greater than I.* This error would not have cropped up if the Father had become incarnate, for no one would think of the Father as less than the Son. It seems therefore preferable for the Father instead of the Son to become incarnate."[141]

Having asked this daring question and opened up the idea that perhaps it would have been better if the Father had become incarnate, Aquinas draws back. He agrees that it was completely "appropriate" that the Son become incarnate because in him God's wisdom and power are revealed (1Co 1:24).[142]

It is of course true that it was the Son or Logos who became man, and no other divine "person," but to say that the Logos by *necessity* had to be the one who became man would seem to limit the freedom of God and contravene Paul, who in Php 2:4–11 depicts Christ as equal God yet freely and voluntarily choosing to become man, take the form of a servant, and die on the cross. It is not by necessity that he lays aside his majesty and authority to become man but by a free sovereign decision. Rahner makes his case by calling the Son the *Logos.* This title defines the Son as God in communication, but is this title intrinsic to the second person of the Trinity, or is he given this title because this is the work he did?

The late nineteenth-century conservative evangelical B. B. Warfield, in his essay "The Biblical Doctrine of the Trinity," objects to the idea that the Son by necessity had to be the one who became incarnate. He wants to highlight the voluntary nature of the work of the Son. He speaks of the divine persons coming to an "agreement" as to who should become incarnate.[143] I always get a picture in my mind when I read this passage of the divine three drawing straws and for this reason feel uneasy with it. It seems to suggest tritheism. John Frame takes a very similar position but with more

---

[139]Aquinas, *Summa Theologica*, trans. R. J. Hennessey (London: Blackfriars, 1976), 48, 3a,Q1–3 (pp. 35–86).

[140]Ibid., 99.

[141]Ibid., 3a.Q3.8 (p. 111).

[142]Ibid. Supplementary reasons are given in 3a.Q3.8 (p. 113).

[143]B. B. Warfield, *Biblical Foundations* (Grand Rapids: Eerdmans, 1958), 111. In this language he reflects the seventeenth century idea of "a covenant of redemption" made between the Father and the Son as to who would become man to save the human race. See Barth, *Church Dogmatics*, 4.1, 65.

circumspect wording. He argues, "that the Son, rather than the Father or the Spirit, became incarnate, was a decision made freely by the persons of the Trinity, but not an arbitrary one."[144] Conservative evangelicals committed to the eternal subordination of the Son have generally not followed Warfield on this matter. Like Rahner they have tended to argue for the *necessity* of the Son becoming incarnate, not because he is the Logos, but because he is the Son. As the Son he is subordinated and obedient to the Father just as every human son is subordinated and obedient to his father. If one divine person had to be commanded by the Father to go, assume human flesh, and do the work of a servant, it had to be the Son.

Wayne Grudem puts this position very clearly in his *Systematic Theology*. He says that what eternally distinguishes the Father and the Son is their differing "roles," by which he means in plain speak, their differing authority. If one divine person had to step down from the glories of heaven it had to be the Son. The "role" that defines the Son as the Son is that of "obeying [and] going as the Father sends." In contrast the "role" that defines the Father as the divine Father is "commanding, directing and sending."[145] Jesus Christ is literally a son, and sons do as they are told by their father. Subordination to the Father is what is distinctive about Christ in history and eternity.[146]

Bruce Ware makes a similar point in seeking to refute those who speak of a coequal Trinity. He says the Son's eternal subordinate relationship with the Father necessitates that he and no other be the one to become incarnate.

> The egalitarian denial of any eternal submission of the Son to the Father makes it impossible to answer the question why it was that the "Son" and not the "Father" or the "Spirit" was sent to become incarnate.
>
> ... In their [i.e. the egalitarian] understanding, nothing *in God* grounds the Son being the Son of the Father, and since every aspect of the Son's submission to the Father is divorced altogether from any *eternal relation* that exists between the Father and the Son, there is simply no reason why the *Father* should send the *Son* ... it appears that the egalitarian view would permit "any one of the three persons" to become incarnate.[147]

Robert Letham likewise argues that there must be a reason why the Son and not the Father or the Spirit became incarnate. It is, he concludes, because the Son is

---

[144]Frame, *The Doctrine of God*, 706.

[145]Wayne Grudem, *Systematic Theology: An Introduction to Biblical Doctrine* (Grand Rapids, Mich.: Zondervan, 1995), 250.

[146]The comprehensive nature of this subordination is spelled out at length in Grudem's later book, *Evangelical Feminism*, 406–15.

[147]Bruce Ware, "How Shall We Think about the Trinity?" in *God Under Fire: Modern Theology Reinvents God*, eds. Douglas S. Huffman and Eric L. Johnson (Grand Rapids, Mich.: Zondervan, 2002), 275. Italics and internal quotation marks inserted by Ware.

eternally set under the Father's authority.[148] The Son's obedience is predicated on "his eternal condition" as the Son.[149]

My Australian debating opponents explicitly appeal to Karl Rahner in support of the idea that the Son has to be the one who takes the form of a servant and becomes incarnate. Robert Doyle says, "Rahner strongly insists that ... what happened in the economy of salvation is rooted in the differentiation of the three persons."[150] He then says, again mentioning Rahner, "that unless the ordering in relations we see in the economy actually witnesses to the relations in the immanent Trinity, then we are not in fact in touch with God himself."[151] Elsewhere Doyle says he believes "order means hierarchy."[152] Mark Baddeley likewise appeals to Rahner in arguing that "there is a connection between being the Son and being incarnate." There is something "that made it uniquely appropriate for the Son to be incarnate."[153] He is the eternally subordinated Son who must obey his Father.

Before continuing it is important to make clear what these evangelicals are arguing. Their case is that the eternal subordination and obedience of the Son *defines who he is*. The Father is defined by his commanding role, the Son by his subordinate and obedient role. The ontological implications cannot be missed. The Son does not simply function subordinately; he *is* in his person subordinated, and this can never change. Subordination prescribes his *being*. For this reason, the Son has to be the one to take the form of a servant and die on the cross. He must be subordinated as the Son because human sons are subordinated in authority to their father. Not the Bible but human experience proves the point wanting to be made.

Just as Rahner's argument for the *necessity* of *the Logos* becoming incarnate fails to convince, so too does the conservative evangelical argument for the *necessity* of *the Son* becoming incarnate. Both predetermine the answer wanted by the titles they selectively use. For Rahner only the Logos could become man, because only the Logos is God in communication. For my evangelical debating opponents only the Son could become incarnate, because sons by definition are subordinated to their fathers. If they took Rahner's preferred title *Logos*, or the title *Lord* preferred by New Testament writers, this argument would collapse. It would be seen to be special pleading. Behind the evangelical case lies the assumption that the title *Son* used of Jesus prescribes his subordinate status. If human analogies are left to one side and Scripture is allowed

---

[148]Robert Letham, *The Holy Trinity in Scripture, History, Theology, and Worship* (Phillipsburg, N.J.: P&R, 2004), 390–401.

[149]Ibid., 401.

[150]Doyle, "Are We Heretics?" 15.

[151]Ibid., 15.

[152]Robert Doyle, "God in Feminist Critique," *Reformed Theological Review* 52, no. 1 (1993): 21.

[153]Baddeley, "The Trinity and Subordinationism," 7.

to speak, this assumption fails. The Bible does not define divine sonship in terms of subordination. Jesus is the royal Son who rules in majesty and authority, having a loving intimate relationship with his Father with whom he is "one." John Frame says in fact that the "New Testament references to Jesus' sonship typically emphasize his equality with the Father."[154] If God the Son is equal God and the Lord, then there is no *necessity* for him in particular to become incarnate, although this is what he did. To argue otherwise would deny God's freedom—God's right to be sovereign God. According to Paul, Christ chose freely and willingly to take the form of a servant for our salvation. It was not by necessity (Php 2:4–11). In arguing this way I am not advocating anything novel or idiosyncratic. The idea goes back to Athanasius. It was his view, says Richard Hanson, that in freely choosing to become incarnate the Son was not "doing something which the Father, because of his higher status, could not do."[155] Barth is of exactly the same opinion. He agrees that it was fitting that the Son became incarnate, but he will not allow it was a necessity, because that would impinge on the freedom of God.[156]

Conclusion

There is much that evangelicals would want to differ on with Karl Rahner. However, I do not see any evidence that he breaches historic orthodoxy on what he says on the Trinity, let alone that he supports the doctrine of the eternal subordination of the Son in function and authority. If anything he emphasizes divine unity and equality when discussing the Trinity, limiting the divine distinctions to differing relations. He makes a helpful point when he insists that it was Christ as the second person of the Trinity who reveals the Father, not just God in general. His argument that the Logos by necessity had to be the one to become incarnate seems to curtail the freedom of God to be God, and for this reason among others must be questioned. His Christology in its "liberal" or "Ebionite" strand is another matter. This should be judged by evangelicals and other orthodox Christians as dangerous and be rejected.

---

[154]Frame, *The Doctrine of God*, 660.

[155]R. P. C. Hanson, *The Search for the Christian Doctrine of God: The Arian Controversy, 318–381* (Grand Rapids, Mich.: Baker, 2005), 424.

[156]Barth, *Church Dogmatics*, 1.2, 34–35.

CHAPTER

SUBORDINATION AND OBEDIENCE IN THE THEOLOGY OF KARL BARTH

In both this book and my earlier book *The Trinity and Subordinationism*, my primary historical authorities on the doctrine of the Trinity are Athanasius, the Cappadocian Fathers, Augustine and Calvin, the Nicene and Athanasian Creeds, and the Reformation confessions. I only refer to other church fathers, past theologians, or contemporary ones, particularly Barth, Rahner, Moltmann, Pannenberg, and Erickson in so far as they bear on the question of subordinationism. What they teach was not a primary concern of my first book, and it is not for this one. Some of the critics of my book *The Trinity and Subordinationism* seem to have missed this fact. They want to argue that Barth is central to my case; and contrary to my claim that he does not teach the eternal subordination of the Son in function and authority, they say he does. He is on "their" side, not "mine." Among Australian conservative evangelicals who argue for the permanent subordination of women and the eternal subordination of the Son, what Barth teaches on the subordination of the Son has unexpectedly emerged as an issue of great importance. So strident has this appeal to Barth become I have decided to write a chapter on this question. If what Barth teaches on the Trinity is of no great interest to evangelical readers of this book, they could skip this chapter

Robert Doyle, head of systematic theology at Moore College Sydney, accuses me of "misreading" Barth, who, he says, "refutes the egalitarian position," teaching rather the "eternal relational subordination" of the Son.[1] Mark Baddeley, his colleague, makes virtually the same charge.[2] He holds that I have "failed to understand him [Barth] at every significant point. He [that's me] gives the impression that Barth is arguing for a position that he in fact opposes in the strongest possible terms."[3] For Barth, says Baddeley, "There is 'One' within the Godhead who commands and 'Another' who 'without any cleft of differentiation but in perfect unity and equality' obeys."[4] And again, "Barth rejects a purely economic submission as modalism."[5] If I am completely and utterly wrong on Barth, who Baddeley thinks is one of the "linchpins" of my case, then he reasons I must be completely and utterly wrong in my whole thesis. Orthodoxy does affirm the eternal subordination of the Son in function and authority. It is I who have departed from the "mainstream position,"[6] not those I criticize.

In my home city of Melbourne, Peter Adam, another Australian evangelical theologian, made the same charges against me in a seminar organized by the primate of the Anglican Church of Australia, Archbishop Peter Carnley.[7] The archbishop and I argued in our papers that the way many conservative evangelicals committed to the permanent subordination of women are construing the Trinity is a form of subordinationism.[8] In reply to me Dr. Adam said, "You have misunderstood Barth. You believe that Barth represents your own views and repudiated the views of your opponents.... In fact Barth supports the very view you want to marginalise."[9] To prove his point he quotes several passages where Barth speaks of a subordination in God.

In Great Britain this appeal to Barth in support of the eternal subordination of the Son is also found in writings by evangelicals committed to the permanent subordination of women. Thomas Smail makes the most of this argument. He appeals

---

[1] Robert Doyle, "Are We Heretics? A Review of *The Trinity and Subordinationism* by Kevin Giles," *Briefing* (April 2004): 15.

[2] Mark Baddeley, "The Trinity and Subordinationism," *Reformed Theological Review* 63, no. 1 (2004): 3–6.

[3] Ibid., 6.

[4] Ibid. He does not give the reference but he is alluding to Karl Barth, *Church Dogmatics* (Edinburgh: T&T Clark, 1975), 4.1, 202. To get a real feel for what Barth is saying in these words, his last paragraph on p. 202 and the first paragraph of p. 203 needs to be read. Barth is far more subtle and dialectical than Baddeley's quote suggests.

[5] Ibid.

[6] Ibid., 3.

[7] Held in Trinity College, Melbourne, on August 20, 2004. All the papers given at this seminar are now published in *St. Mark's Review* 198 (2005): 1–44.

[8] Archbishop Carnley, to be exact, accused the Moore College theologians of Arianism. He put this in print in his book *Reflections in Glass* (Sydney: HarperCollins, 2004), 232–41.

[9] Peter Adam entitled his lecture "Honouring Jesus Christ." He kindly gave me the typed script. This quote is on p. 5. Later this article with a few corrections was published in *The Churchman* 119, no. 1 (2005): 35–50 and yet later again in the symposium papers printed in *St. Mark's Review* 198 (2005):1–44.

to Barth in support of his doctrine of the eternal subordination of the Son first in his book *The Forgotten Father*[10] and then in his later book *Like Father, Like Son*.[11] It is his belief that the Son of God is eternally subordinated in function and authority to the Father, apart from ontological subordination, and this is exactly what Barth teaches.[12] On this premise, in *The Forgotten Father* he exhorts his readers, men and women, to gladly submit to the authority of the divine Father as Jesus did, and in *Like Father, Like Son*, he exhorts woman in particular to gladly submit to the authority of men set over them in the home and in the church as Jesus eternally subordinates himself to the Father's authority.[13] It is his view that any authority that the Son has is "derived from the Father."[14] The Father has "absolute priority" of will.[15] Several times he quotes Jn 14:28 ("The Father is greater than I") as proof of his position. Jesus for him is fully divine and one in being with the Father, yet in function and authority he is eternally subordinated to the Father. He rejects Calvin's teaching that the obedience and the subordination of Christ are limited to his time as the incarnate Son.[16] Instead he follows what he thinks is Barth's position, namely that Christ is eternally subordinated, being bound always to obey the Father.[17]

In the United States appeals to Barth in support of the eternal subordination of the Son in authority are rare. This is mainly because in the more conservative wing of American evangelicalism Barth is considered to be theologically suspect.[18] One conservative Reformed scholar who has read Barth and appreciates his work is Robert Letham. In his book *The Holy Trinity*, he has a full chapter giving a fair and accurate account of Barth's thinking on the Trinity.[19] At no point in this discussion does he suggest that Barth teaches the eternal subordination of the Son in any way whatsoever. He warmly commends Barth for stressing divine unity and for distinguishing clearly the divine persons, or "modes of being." Most of what Letham says in his book speaks against the belief that the Son is eternally set under the Father in function and authority. It is only in his distinctively evangelical digression on pages 394–404,

---

[10] Thomas Smail, *The Forgotten Father* (London: Hodder and Stoughton, 1980).

[11] Thomas Smail, *Like Father, Like Son* (Milton Keyes, Bucks.: Paternoster, 2005), 76–77.

[12] Smail, *Forgotten Father*, 116; Smail, *Like Father, Like Son*, 76–77.

[13] Smail, *Like Father, Like Son*, 240–66.

[14] Smail, *Forgotten Father*, 16; Smail, *Like Father, Like Son*, 105.

[15] Smail, *Forgotten Father*, 16.

[16] Ibid., 118.

[17] Ibid., 118–21.

[18] Many evangelicals, however, are of another mind. One of the two editors and a translator of Barth's *Dogmatics* was G. W. Bromiley, a professor at Fuller Theological Seminary, the largest evangelical seminary in America. See further on this matter, Gregory Bolich, *Karl Barth and Evangelicalism* (Westmont, Ill.: InterVarsity, 1980).

[19] Robert Letham, *The Holy Trinity in Scripture, History, Theology, and Worship* (Phillipsburg, N.J.: P&R, 2004), 271–90.

which I have mentioned previously, where he seeks to support the permanent sub-ordination of women by appeal to an "ontological" basis for this in the Trinity, that he goes off the track. Unexpectedly he begins arguing for "the submission of the Son [to the Father] eternally."[20] What he wants us to believe is that the "Son submits in eternity to the Father."[21] "His human obedience reflects his divine submission."[22] He appeals mainly to Barth for support of these ideas.[23] He notes that Barth speaks repeatedly of "the obedience of the Son of God,"[24] and that for Barth this obedience is not limited to the incarnation; it is eternal.

A Puzzling Silence

What surprised me as I began to consider whether or not Barth eternally subordinated the Son to the Father was that I could find no secondary literature that was of any direct help.[25] A comment in passing now and then appears in the scholarly literature raising this possibility, but I could find no detailed study on Barth and the subordi-nation of the Son. This led me to suspect immediately that my evangelical friends were wrong. How could it be that Barth taught the eternal subordination of the Son in work and authority and no scholar had taken him to task in any extended way?[26]

---

[20] Ibid., 398.

[21] Ibid., 402. His case for the eternal submission of the son is found in its entirety on pp. 389–404.

[22] Ibid., 403.

[23] Ibid., 392, 397–98, 492. Letham asks, Does this teaching on the eternal obedience of the Son "have support from Scripture?" (p. 403). He admits he can find "very little in the Bible" in support. Again he is right. The Bible, as we have seen, indicates the opposite. The Son's obedience is limited to "the days of his flesh" (Heb 5:7)—a text Letham quotes in support of the eternal submission of the Son (p. 403). He also appeals to Php 2:5ff., but again the text counts against his thesis rather than supports it (p. 403). Christ was equal God, then in the incarnation (his "infleshing") he took the form of a servant, was obedient even to death on the cross, and then was raised to rule as Lord.

[24] Ibid., 397.

[25] A. J. McKelway, "The Conception of Subordination in Barth's Social Ethics," *Scottish Journal of Theology* 32 (1979): 345–57, does not deal with subordinationism as we have been discuss-ing this topic. He explores rather how Barth understands the apostolic exhortations to be subordinate, especially in relation to wives. Barth does endorse the subordination of wives; see *Church Dogmatics*, 3.2, 286ff., as we would expect. He was writing immediately after the Second World War, twenty years before "Women's Lib" opened the eyes of theologians and exegetes. Some things he says might encourage contemporary evangelicals committed to the permanent subordination of women; much would not. On Barth and women see McKelway's article; Paul K. Jewett, *Man as Male and Female* (Grand Rapids, Mich.: Eerd-mans, 1975); and Gary W. Deddo, *Karl Barth's Theology of Relations* (New York: Peter Lang, 1999), especially 120–21.

[26] There are occasional comments in the secondary literature that raise this possibility. In a short section, mainly criticizing Barth for arguing that God suffers, G. C. Berkouwer in *The*

I thus turned to Barth's own massive twelve-part volumes of *Church Dogmatics* to see what the great German-speaking theologian himself said on this matter. I did not read the whole of the *Dogmatics*, but I did read carefully and noted many volumes and skimmed several more, reading the sections of interest to me. I present my findings as they emerged from this sequential reading of Barth. This is a selective reading of his *Dogmatics*, searching for anything in them for or against the eternal subordination and obedience of the Son, but it is not a one-sided reading. I was as concerned to find passages that speak of the eternal subordination of the Son as I was to find ones that call this idea into question.

Working out what Barth teaches on the subordination of the Son of God in function and authority, or any other theological topic, is not an easy task for a number of reasons. First, notwithstanding the constancy of certain key motifs in his work, Barth's thinking develops and changes over the years as one volume after another of the *Church Dogmatics* appears. For this reason, selected quotes from Barth may only tell us what he thought at one particular time. Professor John Webster says, "No one stage of" Barth's unfolding thinking "is definitive; rather it is the whole which conveys the substance of what he has to say."[27] Second, Barth almost invariably seeks to reformulate the historically developed understanding of each doctrine he explores, often in a quite radical way. This means we are never comparing apples with apples, as the saying goes. What Barth says on any doctrine is often completely novel, a new way of conceptualizing a fundamental Christian truth. Nowhere is this truer than with his thinking on the Trinity. Professor Bruce McCormack says Barth's theological revolution is "finally a revolution in the doctrine of God."[28] Simply to conclude that on some detail in his mind-expanding reformulation of a doctrine he differs from what everyone else has believed should not lead to the rejection of what he says on this matter, or to the conclusion he is in error. When all the pieces are seen together, the new construct may explain God's self-revelation of himself and his work in the world better than anything said previously. Thus in the issue before us we will find that Barth can speak of the subordination and obedience of the Son as God in a novel way, but what has to be asked is, Is he intending to directly contradict what Athanasius, the Cappadocians, Augustine, and Calvin taught, or simply reformulate their

---

Triumph of Grace in the Theology of Karl Barth (London, Paternoster, 1956), accuses Barth of this error. See pp. 301–7. Later in this essay we look at Berkouwer's charge.

[27] John Webster, "Introducing Barth," in *The Cambridge Companion to Karl Barth*, ed. John Webster (Cambridge: Cambridge University Press, 2000), 9. He makes the same point explicitly in relation to the Trinity in his superb introduction to Barth's life and to his *Dogmatics* in particular. See John Webster, *Barth Second Edition* (London: Continuum, 2004), 57.

[28] Bruce McCormack, "Grace and Being: The Role of God's Gracious Election in Karl Barth's Theological Ontology," in *The Cambridge Companion to Karl Barth*, ed. John Webster (Cambridge: Cambridge University Press, 2000), 93.

position? Third, Barth's theology is a huge challenge to master not only because of the thousands of pages he wrote but also because it is often difficult to know exactly what he is saying. He frequently uses paradoxical and "dialectical"[29] modes of thought, and at times he would seem to contradict himself. Professor George Hunsinger, in his important book *How to Read Karl Barth: The Shape of His Theology*,[30] speaks of the "interlacing and complex argument of the *Church Dogmatics*" where "dialectical and counterintuitive patterns," "self-contradictory, or at the very least perplexing modes of thought" are common.[31]

Church Dogmatics 1.1: The Doctrine of the Word of God

In *Church Dogmatics* volume 1.1 Barth introduces three basic ideas that underlie the whole of the *Dogmatics*:[32] (1) God is hidden and unknowable to human beings; (2) God has revealed himself in Jesus Christ, and in no other way; and (3) this revealed God is triune. What Barth wants to stress is that the initiative in revelation belongs entirely with God. Thus he speaks repeatedly of "the freedom of God." He writes, "That God reveals Himself as the Lord means that He reveals what only He can reveal, Himself. And so, as Himself, He has and exercises His freedom and lordship."[33] What is revealed is true and accurate, an "unveiling," but Barth will never allow that it circumscribes God—limits his freedom. What is revealed "does not take God's place.... God is always a mystery."[34] In the unveiling there is also a veiling.[35] This veiling occurs because of the way God chooses to reveal himself, namely as a man. For Barth the humanity of Christ as such does not reveal his divinity. He can even say, "The form of God's Word, then, is in fact the form of the cosmos which stands in contradiction to God."[36]

When Barth comes to speak of this triune God revealed in Jesus Christ, he places

---

[29] This is a technical word frequently used to describe Barth's theology. See Terry L. Cross, *Dialectic in Karl Barth's Doctrine of God* (New York: Peter Lang, 2001). On p. 2, he gives the following definition, "Dialectic is the language of paradox, a mode of thinking which attempts to deal with relations of reciprocal interaction ... mutual determination, and asymmetry." He argues that while dialectic may have been more pronounced in Barth's earliest work, it is always present.

[30] George Hunsinger, *How to Read Karl Barth: The Shape of His Theology* (New York: Oxford, 1991).

[31] Ibid., vii. See also Webster, "Introducing Barth," 1–16.

[32] Karl Barth, *Church Dogmatics*, trans. G. W. Bromiley (Edinburgh: T&T Clark, 1975). All quotes from *Church Dogmatics* 1.1 are taken from this translation. Those new to Barth should note that volume 1.1 has a 1937 translation by G. T. Thompson.

[33] Ibid., 1.1, 307.

[34] Ibid., 1.1, 321.

[35] Ibid., 1.1, 169, 174, 299, 320–21, 363.

[36] Ibid., 1.1, 166. On this theme see ibid., 1.1 pp. 163–66, 323–34 and 2.1, 287.

the emphasis on divine unity.[37] He will not allow that the "threeness" in God in any way undermines the unity of God. To say the one God is triune does not imply "threefold deity either in the sense of a plurality of Gods, or in the sense of the existence of a plurality of individuals or parts within the one Godhead."[38] Rather, "The name of Father, Son and Spirit means that God is the one God in threefold repetition, and this in such a way that the repetition itself is grounded in his Godhead, so that it implies no alteration in his Godhead, and yet in such a way also that he is the one God only in this repetition, so that his one Godhead stands or falls with the fact that he is God in this repetition, but for this very reason. He is the one God in each repetition."[39]

For Barth, "Only the substantial equality of Christ and the Spirit with the Father is compatible with monotheism."[40] In this "unity model" of the Trinity, it is not possible to think of each divine person as having his own will, with the Son needing to submit his will to the Father's. For Barth the triune God has one will.

Because he believes the word *person* necessarily implies three centers of consciousness, something that would undermine the unity of the Christian God, Barth chooses rather to speak of each of the divine three as a "mode or way of being" (German *Seinsweise*) of the one God.[41] He says he is not seeking to change the historic doctrine of the Trinity by changing the terminology but simply seeking to express better what orthodoxy has meant by the term *person* when used of Father, Son, or Spirit. He wants to avoid at any cost a tilt towards either tritheism by dividing the divine three or modalism by collapsing the eternal distinctions. For Barth, like all orthodox theologians, differentiation does not imply subordination. It is simply a mistake to latch onto the "being" side of the term "mode of being" and suggest that Barth is teaching that the divine persons are one-in-being in unity and different-in-being in distinction, as my conservative evangelical debating opponents suggest. Nothing could be more alien to Barth's doctrine of God. Repeatedly he opposes this idea. For example, he says, "His taking [human] form ... means something new in God, a self-distinction of God from himself, a being of God in a mode of being that is different from *though not subordinate* to His first and hidden mode of being as God."[42] And,

---

[37] Richard Roberts, *A Theology on Its Way: Essays on Karl Barth* (Edinburgh: T&T Clark, 1991), 87, says, "The emphasis on unity is predominant." See also for a similar opinion, Alan J. Torrance, *Persons in Communion* (Edinburgh: T&T Clark, 1996), 103, 107–15.

[38] Barth, *Church Dogmatics*, 1.1, 350.

[39] Ibid.

[40] Ibid., 1.1, 353.

[41] Ibid., 1.1, 359. In the preface to the 1975 edition of *Church Dogmatics* 1.1, p. viii, the translator, G. W. Bromiley, points out that the German word *Seinsweise* can be translated as either "way of being" or "mode of being." It refers back to the Cappadocians' equivalent to *hypostasis*, *tropos huparzeos* (way of existing).

[42] Ibid., 1.1, 316. Italics added.

"Whether it be a matter of the inner property or the outer form of God's essence, all that is said to be can and must be finally said in the same way of Father, Son and Spirit. No attribute, no act of God is not in the same way the attribute or act of the Father, the Son and the Spirit."[43]

For Barth the being of God is one and simple, yet this one being of God is in three modes, Father, Son, and Spirit.

Barth's theology in general and his theology of the Trinity in particular is radically Christocentric. Barth speaks of revelation as "the root of the doctrine of the Trinity,"[44] and revelation for him is what is given in Jesus Christ, or to be more exact, Jesus Christ is Revelation. Apart from him we would know nothing of the Father and the Spirit. Christ the Son of God is God, and he reveals God. "If He [the Son] reveals God, then irrespective of His creaturehood He himself has to be God. And since this is a case of either/or, He has to be full and true God without reduction or limitation, without more or less. Any such restriction would not merely weaken His deity; it would deny it. To confess Him as the revelation of His Father is to confess Him as essentially equal in deity with this Father of His."[45]

With Barth's stress on the unity of God and on Christ as the revelation of God highlighted, we can now look at some of the relevant comments he makes on the question before us.

1. *First of all we note that Barth says explicitly that he rejects "every form of subordination-ism."*[46] This error he defines as teaching "a more and less in God's being as God." It "rests on the intention of making the One who reveals Himself there the kind of subject we ourselves are." In opposition he argues it must be held that "Father, Son and Spirit are one single, and equal God."[47] In an earlier comment he says, "If revelation is to be taken seriously as God's presence, if there is to be a valid belief in revelation, then in no sense can Christ and the Spirit be subordinate hypostases."[48] And similarly, "The divine essence would not be the divine essence if in it there were superiority and inferiority and also then, various quanta of deity."[49]

2. *Father, Son, and Spirit are all "Lord."* They share in equal majesty and authority. Barth writes, "'God reveals Himself as the Lord' three times in different senses."[50] And later he adds, "He can be our God because in all His modes of being He is equal

---

[43] Ibid., 1.1, 362.
[44] Ibid., 1.1, 304.
[45] Ibid., 1.1, 406.
[46] Ibid., 1.1, 382.
[47] Ibid., 1.1, 381.
[48] Ibid., 1.1, 353.
[49] Ibid., 1.1, 393.
[50] Ibid., 1.1, 376.

to himself, one and the same Lord."[51] Then speaking specifically of the Son he says, "The term 'Lord' points in the first instance to the significance of Jesus Christ for us. In relation to us He is the Bearer of authority and power.... He commands and rules.... His lordship is not derivative nor grounded in a higher lordship. It is a lordship in the final and definitive sense of the word. It is self-grounded lordship."[52]

I could not word a paragraph better if I wanted to exclude the thought that the Son is in some way eternally set under the Father in authority, or that the authority he has is less than that of the Father, or derived from the Father.

3. The divine three cannot be separated because "God's essence is indeed one and even the different relations of origin do not entail separation,"[53] and because each fully interpenetrates the other.[54] "This means that the unity of their work is to be understood as the communion of the three modes of being along the lines of the doctrine of *perichoresis*, according to which all three, without forfeiture or mutual dissolution of independence, reciprocally interpenetrate each other and inexist in one another."[55]

Barth argues that the doctrine of *perichoresis* is absolutely fundamental because it excludes any suggestion of tritheism or subordinationism. The triune God is one in being, work, and authority.

Although Father, Son, and Spirit are one, each mode of being has distinctive works or functions, but this does not divide the persons or set one under another in any way. The "revelation of God attested in Scripture forces us to make this differentiation" in the modes of being, yet Barth says these "do not consist in distinctions in God's acts and attributes."[56] Their "functions" cannot be separated.[57] Barth thus endorses the maxim attributed to Augustine, "the external acts of God are indivisible."[58] "To the unity of Father, Son and Spirit among themselves corresponds their *unity ad extra*. God's essence and work are not twofold but one. God's work is His essence in its relation to the reality which is distinct from Him."[59] And, "It is clear that the work and therefore the essence of the Father and the Son are one and the same."[60]

It is thus of no surprise to find Barth endorsing the doctrine of *appropriation* as firmly as he does the doctrine of *perichoresis*. The doctrine of appropriation first found

---

[51] Ibid., 1.1, 383.
[52] Ibid., 1.1, 423.
[53] Ibid., 1.1, 70.
[54] Ibid.
[55] Ibid., 1.1, 396. A similar definition is given on 379.
[56] Ibid., 1.1, 372.
[57] Ibid.
[58] Ibid., 1.1, 394, 442.
[59] Ibid., 1.1, 371.
[60] Ibid., 1.1, 443.

in the Cappadocians,[61] taken up by Augustine, and developed by Thomas Aquinas teaches that although certain divine acts are rightly appropriated or assigned to one of the divine three, ultimately they are actions of the one God.[62]

For Barth the doctrine of *perichoresis* excludes tritheism and the subordination of any divine person in being or work/function or authority. The divine three so profoundly interpenetrate one another that they are ultimately one in being and work/function. The doctrine of appropriation quite specifically excludes operational or functional subordination. All the acts of Father, Son, and Spirit are ultimately the acts of the one God. "All that is to be said can and must finally be said in the same way of Father, Son, and Spirit. No attribute, no act of God is not in the same way the attribute or act of the Father, the Son and the Spirit."[63]

4. *Barth is emphatic that the three divine modes of being are eternally differentiated and ordered* but, "What is meant by what is distinguished and ordered in God as Father, Son and Spirit," he says, is one of the "most difficult" matters to resolve.[64] Nevertheless, on divine differentiation in the one God he is emphatic. The one God of Christian revelation cannot be other than one God in three different ways. This threeness in God is what distinguishes the Christian understanding of God. "This being in these three modes of being is absolutely essential to Him ... [it is] irremovable."[65] There is no "possibility that one of the modes of being might just as well be the other."[66] But what constitutes these differences? Following the tradition, Barth makes the primary factor differing relations of origin. "Father, Son and Spirit are distinguished from one another by the fact that without inequality of essence or dignity, without increase or diminution of deity, they stand in dissimilar relations of origin to one another."[67]

What he will not allow is that these distinctions are grounded in differing "acts or attributes,"[68] or differing authority. The three modes of being work as one and are equally omnipotent, even though they work "in the order and sense appropriate to them."[69]

5. *For Barth human fatherhood does not explain or define divine fatherhood.* The trajectory for Barth is in the opposite direction. "When Scripture calls God our Father it adopts an analogy only to transcend it at once. Hence we must not measure by natural

---

[61] Lewis Ayres, *Nicaea and Its Legacy: An Approach to Fourth-Century Trinitarian Theology* (New York: Oxford, 2005), 296–300.
[62] Barth, *Church Dogmatics*, 1.1, 372–74.
[63] Ibid., 1.1, 362.
[64] Ibid., 1.1, 355.
[65] Ibid., 1.1, 360.
[66] Ibid.
[67] Ibid., 1.1, 363.
[68] Ibid., 1.1, 372.
[69] Ibid., 1.1, 396.

human fatherhood what it means that God is our Father (Isa 63:16). It is from God's fatherhood that our natural human fatherhood acquires any meaning and dignity it has ... (Eph 3:15)."[70]

Subordination?

With this great stress on the unity and equality of the divine three ringing in our ears, it is with some surprise on reaching page 412 to find Barth, who until this point has been adamantly opposed to "every form of subordinationism," speaking of the subordination of the Revealer. He writes, "The person of the Revealer is the person of Jesus Christ, who is subordinate to the Creator revealed by it, yet who is also indissolubly co-ordinate with Him, who is with Him."[71]

How these words might be harmonized with what Barth has said up to this point is not immediately obvious, but we may presume he is fully cognizant of what he has said. It could be that he is simply saying that in *his person as the Revealer* Jesus is subordinated to the Father, although in himself as God the Son he is "indissolubly co-ordinate with him" (i.e., the Father). Theologians before him have said this, but Barth always stresses that Jesus Christ is God. He does not ascribe some things to his humanity and some to his divinity. It is thus perhaps better to conclude that in the first instance Barth is making the point that what takes place in revelation and reconciliation discloses that the Father and the Son are differentiated. Jesus perfectly reveals the Father and he is one with him, yet in reconciliation, "his *self*-revelation,"[72] he is distinguished from the Father because in his work as the Revealer and the Reconciler, it is he who takes flesh and is subordinated. "As the Reconciler He follows the Creator, that He accomplishes, as it were, a second divine act — not an act which we can deduce from the first."[73] The first divine act is of course creation, the second act is reconciliation where the Son takes human flesh, assumes the form of a servant, and dies on the cross. To clarify his point Barth adds, "This subordination and sequence cannot imply any distinction in being; it can only signify a distinction in mode of being. For reconciliation is no more comprehensible and no less divine than creation."[74]

In hindsight after reading volume 4.1 of the *Dogmatics*, where Barth speaks at greater length on the subordination of the Son, I see yet another dimension to this brief comment on the subordination of the Son in the work of revelation and reconciliation. It seems here Barth is flagging a concern he senses dimly at this point,

---

[70] Ibid., 1.1, 389.
[71] Ibid., 1.1, 412.
[72] Ibid.
[73] Ibid., 1.1, 413.
[74] Ibid.

which he will develop later when he has worked it through in his mind. There is in the Bible an unmistakable subordinationistic element that every trinitarian theologian has had to address. These comments give his first tentative solution, a solution that no one before him has dared to suggest. In his characteristic paradoxical and dialectical style, Barth argues that God is both high and humble, and Jesus Christ reveals this astounding fact. God the Son is equal God in all majesty, glory, and power, yet he comes to humankind in humility, servitude, and suffering. In the work of revelation and reconciliation we see him as subordinated God, God identified with man (humanity) in humiliation and lowliness.

As I conclude these comments on Barth's *Church Dogmatics* volume 1.1, two things are to the fore of my mind. First, in stressing divine unity, Barth shuts the door to tritheism and subordinationism. Both these errors can only emerge when the divine persons are separated and divided. It is thus of no surprise to find Professor Alan Torrance concluding his study of Barth's doctrine of the Trinity in this volume of the *Dogmatics* by saying that Barth leaves "no room whatsoever for any form of subordinationism. The *Seinsweisen* [modes of being] are, as Barth continually reminds his reader, *nicht untergeordnet* [not subordinated]."[75]

The second thing that is in my mind as I conclude this section is that Barth has said very little about the humanity of Christ, except that it veils his divinity. All the emphasis falls on Christ as God.[76] What he is in revelation he is "antecedently in himself ... true and eternal deity."[77] We thus find no mention made of the "double account" of the Savior, one as God incarnate who tires, hungers, suffers, and dies, and the other as equal God, or between Christ in the form of God and Christ in the form of man,[78] contrasts highlighted by virtually all theologians prior to Barth.

Church Dogmatics 1.2: The Doctrine of the Word of God

In the first three sections of this volume (numbers 13, 14, and 15), some correction is found to what I have just suggested could be a weakness in Barth's first volume. Now Barth affirms strongly that Christ is God in human flesh, although the emphasis still falls on Christ as God. These three sections logically progress the argument. First, in section 12, Barth asks, How is divine revelation possible? He answers it is only pos-

---

[75] Torrance, *Persons in Communion*, 111.

[76] In a moment I will note that in volume 1.2 Barth does stress the humanity of Christ. I was interested to find after I had noted this contrast simply by reading Barth that George Hunsinger, "Karl Barth's Christology; Its Basic Chalcedonian Character," in Webster, *Cambridge Companion to Karl Barth*, 127–42, had also seen this differing emphasis in different volumes of the *Church Dogmatics*.

[77] Barth, *Church Dogmatics*, 1.1, 415, 416, cf. 428.

[78] I note with interest that in this first volume of the *Dogmatics* the key text in the tradition, Php 2:4–11, plays little part. It is simply noted a few times in passing.

sible because God freely chose to reveal himself by becoming incarnate. In section 14 he asks, When did this revelation in Christ the God-man take place? He says it took place in the historical event of the incarnation. And third, in section 15 Barth asks, Who is this Jesus Christ? He replies he is "very God and very man."[79]

Barth begins by rejecting any attempt to define the incarnation in docetic terms (God only appeared as a man) or Ebionite terms (he was a man God deified).[80] He writes, "As the true humanity of Christ is ultimately dispensable for Docetism, so is the true divinity of Jesus for Ebionitism."[81] Rather we must accept that Jesus of Nazareth is God's Son or Word. He is fully human and fully God in one person. "God is this Man and this Man is God."[82] Because he is God and God is always supreme, his humanity in no way limits him. "God in his entire divinity became man" but not undifferentiated God. It was the Son and not the Father or the Spirit that became the "what" of revelation.[83] "It is in this mode of being as the Word or the Son that God is able to become manifest to us."[84] "His humanity is the covering which he puts on, and therefore the means of His revelation."[85] In revealing himself in this manner we see "God bending down to us as it were, by assuming this form familiar to us."[86] It was "a veiling of the divine majesty," but no loss in divine majesty.[87]

In section 14 Barth comes to the Christian understanding of time. The incarnation speaks of God coming to us in human time, a specific time. He argues, however, that there are three "times": created time, fallen time in which we live, and revelation time constituted by God's coming to us in history.[88] Created time is God's time; this is a "time hidden and withdrawn from us."[89] Unlike fallen time it is not linear. This means there is a difference between human time and divine time. This brief comment on Barth's initial thoughts on time may seem off our topic, but later we will see how Barth's understanding of time bears on his Christology.

In section 15 Barth asks, "Who is Jesus Christ?" The answer he finds is in Jn 1:14, "The Word was made flesh." The Word is God and never ceases to be God, yet this Word took human flesh. Indeed for Barth he took fallen human flesh, and thus was subject to God's wrath and judgment although he himself never sinned. Because

---

[79] Barth, *Church Dogmatics*, 1.2, 132–71.
[80] Ibid., 1.2, 16–21.
[81] Ibid., 1.2, 21.
[82] Ibid., 1.2, 31.
[83] Ibid., 1.2, 33.
[84] Ibid., 1.2, 34.
[85] Ibid., 1.2, 35.
[86] Ibid., 1.2, 36.
[87] Ibid., 1.2, 37.
[88] Ibid., 1.2, 47ff.
[89] Ibid., 1.2, 47.

he was sinless, the perfectly obedient second Adam, he reversed the consequences of Adam's fall.[90] He writes, "Jesus Christ's obedience consists in the fact that He willed to be and was only this one thing with all its consequences, God in the flesh."[91] This he did willingly, freely, and by his own choice—not at the command of the Father. "He did not become humbled, but He humbled Himself."[92] In this section Barth very strongly underlines that the Son or Logos took human flesh at a point in time. In revelation time what changed was that the Son eternally identified with man became temporally incarnate. Barth writes, "Incarnation of the Word means neither wholly nor in part any changing of the Word into something else, but the becoming flesh of the Word that remains the Word."[93]

In sections 13 and 15, Php 2:4–11 plays an important part.[94] This text explains how God could become incarnate, take the form of a servant, and go as obedient man to the cross. Barth notes the sequence. "(1) The divine mode of existence, equality with God, (2) equality with men, (3) a second and this time a fuller equality with God, the name of Lord."[95]

What surprised me in this volume, having read later volumes, was just how traditional Barth is at this point of time. Jesus Christ the eternal Son of God takes flesh without any diminution of his divinity, majesty, or authority, notwithstanding the fact that this involved taking the form of a servant and as representative man in perfect obedience going to the cross to win our salvation. He remains God, but in taking our flesh his divinity is "veiled."

Church Dogmatics 2.1: *The Doctrine of God*

In volume 2.1 Barth deals with the knowledge of God, the reality of God, and "the perfections of God." In the first three sections of this volume (numbers 25, 26, 27) he discusses our knowledge of God. He returns to his basic premise that in God's revelation of himself in the man Jesus there is a veiling and an unveiling of God as he is in himself. This is the "mystery" of revelation.[96] In speaking of the flesh "veiling" the divinity, Barth follows Calvin, but he goes further than the Genevan Reformer by speaking of this veiling as a concealing of the divinity. "He makes Himself known to us, but in the means and sign which He uses to be known by us, He makes Himself foreign and improper to Himself . . . in revealing Himself in this way, He also conceals Himself."[97]

---

[90] Ibid., 1.2, 157.
[91] Ibid., 1.2, 156.
[92] Ibid., 1.2, 160.
[93] Ibid., 1.2, 38.
[94] The text is referred to repeatedly. See ibid., 1.2, 13, 16, 18, 23, 147, 152, 156, 165.
[95] Ibid., 1.1, 16.
[96] Ibid., 2.1, 37ff., 54ff.
[97] Ibid., 2.1, 55.

Barth (section 28) next moves to "the reality of God" where the main topic is "the Being of God in Act." Here one of the most distinctive features of Barth's doctrine of God comes to the fore. Barth rejects the idea that God's being is static, once given. For him God is the living God. God's being is always being in act. In revelation, that is in Christ, we are confronted with God's act.[98] This is an "event," a "happening."[99] So Eberhard Jüngel subtitles his book on Barth's doctrine of the Trinity, "God's Being Is in Becoming."[100]

From this Barth moves on to discuss the divine perfections (sections 29, 30, 31). The perfections in God of which Barth speaks are those common to Father, Son, and Holy Spirit. The term *God* throughout these many pages refers to the triune God. The perfections of love, freedom, holiness, mercy and righteousness, patience and wisdom, omniscience, omnipotence, eternity, and glory are perfections of Father, Son, and Spirit in unity and in diversity. The divine three are in no way differentiated on the basis of differing attributes, let alone differing authority.

In concluding his discussion of the divine perfections, Barth returns to the question of time, or to be more exact the question of the Christian understanding of eternity.[101] He rejects that eternity speaks of the infinite extension of time backwards and forwards,[102] or that it is timelessness.[103] Rather he argues that God's eternity is "non-temporal," since beginnings and endings cannot dictate to God, and yet it is temporal because God is the Lord of all beginnings and endings.[104] What Barth wants to assert is that God is not subject to time, as if time was prior and superior to him, yet God acts in time. There is a difference between God's time, which he calls "supra-temporal,"[105] and human time. Human time is linear; God's time is "simultaneity."[106]

---

[98] Ibid., 2.1, 262.

[99] Ibid.

[100] Eberhard Jüngel, *The Doctrine of the Trinity: God's Being Is in Becoming* (Grand Rapids, Mich.: Eerdmans, 1976).

[101] Barth, *Church Dogmatics*, 2.1, 608–40. Barth's doctrine of time has evoked a lot of discussion. George Hunsinger in *How to Read Karl Barth*, 4–15, says that Barth's discussion of time and eternity leaves many issues unresolved. However, in his later essay, "Mysterium Trinitatis: Karl Barth's Conception of Eternity," in *Disruptive Grace: Studies in the Theology of Karl Barth*, ed. George Hunsinger (Grand Rapids, Mich.: Eerdmans, 2000), 148–209, he is basically descriptive and sympathetic of Barth's position. Colin Gunton, *Becoming and Being: The Doctrine of God in Charles Hartshorne and Karl Barth* (Cambridge: Cambridge University Press, 1989), 177–85, thinks Barth is weakest on his doctrine of time. John Colwell, *Actuality and Provisionality: Eternity and Election in the Theology of Karl Barth* (Edinburgh: Rutherford, 1989), 64–78, is of a similar opinion.

[102] Barth, *Church Dogmatics*, 2.1, 608.

[103] Ibid., 2.1, 611.

[104] Ibid., 2.1, 610ff.

[105] Ibid., 2.1, 623.

[106] This is the term Colwell, *Actuality*, 245, uses to describe Barth's conception of God's time.

This difference is essential because basic to Barth's whole enterprise is his resolve to ensure the freedom of God and to present Jesus Christ as eternally God and man, yet incarnated in time.

Church Dogmatics 2.2: The Doctrine of God

Immediately following his discussion of the perfections in God, Barth moves to the doctrine of election in volume 2.2. Here Barth makes his most radical departure from all previous theology. What he says on election takes us right to the heart of his developing and mind-expanding doctrine of God in general,[107] and Christology in particular.[108] Professor John Webster says, "The doctrine of election forms the centerpiece of [Barth's] doctrine of God; indeed it is one of the most crucial chapters in the *Church Dogmatics*, as a whole, summing up much of what Barth has had to say so far and pointing forward to essential features of the doctrine of creation and reconciliation."[109]

What shapes Barth's innovative doctrine of election is that Jesus Christ is both the subject of election and its object; he is the electing God and the elect human.[110] Both parts of this thesis catch our attention. First we are surprised to find Barth speaking of Christ as the electing God. "He is not only the Elected, He is also Himself the Elector, and in the first instance His election must be understood as active."[111] Election has characteristically been attributed primarily to God the Father. We should not, however, think that Barth divides the Trinity at this point. He is quite emphatic that Christ is the electing and determining God, yet he carefully makes the point that Christ's free decision expresses "the harmony of the triune God."[112] (For Barth the Father and the Son cannot have separate and distinct wills.) If Christ himself is self-determining God, he is not subordinated in authority to the Father.

Speaking of Christ as the "subject of election," by which he means he who elects, is noteworthy on its own, but how Barth speaks of Christ as the object of election is absolutely breathtaking. Christ as the subject of election speaks of the free decision of God not simply to become man in human time but to be man for all eternity. It expresses God's eternal self-determination to be God in covenantal relationship with humanity, and to be God in no other way. In this decision "this man Jesus Christ was

---

[107]Colin Gunton, "Karl Barth's Doctrine of Election as Part of His Doctrine of God," *Scottish Journal of Theology* 25 (1974): 381–92.

[108]Bruce L. McCormack, *Karl Barth's Critically Realistic Dialectical Theology* (Oxford: Clarendon, 1995), 458.

[109]Webster, *Barth*, 88. For a helpful outline of Barth's teaching on election see Michael O'Neil, "Barth's Doctrine of Election," *Evangelical Quarterly* 76, no. 4 (2004): 311–26.

[110]Barth, *Church Dogmatics*, 2.2, 103.

[111]Ibid., 2.2, 105.

[112]Ibid.

taken up into the will of God and made a new object of the divine decree, distinct from God."[113] All the initiative to do this lay with God. "The Son of Man" (Barth's title for man elected to be God) becomes by God's sovereign will "the Son of God" (Barth's title for God who has freely elected to be man).[114]

We are even more startled to find on reading further that the election of Jesus Christ involves both election to life and election to reprobation.[115] Christ as the object of election means on the one hand that he is chosen by grace and love and on the other hand that he is chosen to be obedient, suffer, and to die.[116] "The rejection which all men incurred, the wrath under which all men lie, the death which all men must die, God in his love transfers from all eternity to Him in whom He loves and elects them, and whom he elects as their head and in their place. God from all eternity ordains this obedient One in order that he might bear the sufferings which the disobedient have deserved."[117]

Whereas all theologians prior to Barth have thought of God becoming man in a point in history, so that a clear separation can be made between the preexistent Christ and the incarnate Christ, Barth telescopes the two together. In eternity God decides to be man, and the incarnation is simply the "actualization" of what has forever been true in eternity. Barth definitely does not deny the historicity of the incarnation, yet he holds "Jesus Christ was in the beginning with God."[118] "He is the pre-existent *Deus pro nobis*" (God for us).[119] For him the Logos prior to the incarnation was *asarkos* (without flesh),[120] but we must not imagine, he says, "a 'Logos in itself' which does not have this content and form, which is the eternal Word of God."[121] In the incarnation what was true from the beginning becomes "concrete reality and actuality."[122] Here Barth's dialectical understanding of time comes into play. This allows him to think of Jesus Christ as existing from all eternity as God and man, yet becoming concrete and actualized as Jesus of Nazareth in a point of time, and continuing in time after the resurrection.

Thus for Barth there can be no absolute separation between Christ in history and Christ in eternity. "We have to say that, as Christ is in revelation, so He is antecedently

---

[113]Ibid., 2.2, 162.
[114]Ibid., 2.2, 158.
[115]Ibid., 2.2, 162–63.
[116]Ibid., 2.2, 121–22.
[117]Ibid., 2.2, 123.
[118]Ibid., 2.2, 104.
[119]Ibid., 4.1, 53.
[120]McCormack, "Grace and Being," 92–110. Similarly, Paul Molnar, *Divine Freedom and the Doctrine of the Immanent Trinity* (Edinburgh: T&T Clark, 2002), 61–70.
[121]Barth, *Church Dogmatics*, 4.1, 52.
[122]Ibid., 4.1, 53.

in Himself. Thus He is antecedently in Himself light of light, very God of very God, the begotten of God, and not His creature. We have to take revelation with such utter seriousness that in it as God's act we must directly see God's being too."[123]

What Barth is saying in this and the other many "antecedent" comments is that just as Jesus Christ is God and man in historical revelation, so he is in eternity. He is not saying, as my evangelical debating opponents want to think, that just as Jesus Christ is subordinated to the Father in historical revelation so too he is unilaterally subordinated in eternity.

As far as Christology is concerned, this revolutionary understanding of the eternal God-man completely overthrows the traditional theological paradigm. In Barth's schema no absolute division can be made between Christ before and after the incarnation, or between what Christ does as man and what Christ does as God. Instead he postulates a division, or perhaps better a dialectical tension, between Jesus Christ as the sovereign and electing God and Christ as man elected to be God. This new paradigm means that Christ as God identified with man is also man in relation to God. It is Jesus Christ identified with man who freely chooses to be obedient to the Father, to suffer and to die. "God in His Son is Himself the person of man. God knows and confirms and blesses Him as His Son. God creates Him for His own Word. God vouchsafes to grant Him a part in His own suffering for man's frailty and sin and for the discord and judgment, which inevitably result from them. God justifies Him, raises Him from the dead, and gives Him a part in His own glory. All that man can and will do is to pray, to follow and to obey. The honor of the Son of Man adopted to union with the Son of God can and will consist only in promoting the honor of His heavenly Father."[124]

As God who has freely and sovereignly chosen to be man, Christ is obedient to the Father, not by constraint but freely and sovereignly. "The obedience which he renders as the Son of God is, as genuine obedience, His *own* decision and electing, a decision and electing no less divinely free than the electing and decision of the Father and the Holy Spirit."[125] And "of Jesus Christ we know nothing more surely and definitely than this—that in free obedience to His Father He elected to be man, *and as man, to do the will of God*."[126]

In seeking to comment on Barth's reformulation of the doctrine of election, one is at a loss for words. Barth has dared to walk where none have walked before. I comment only on the issues of importance to the question addressed in this book. Historic orthodoxy has limited Christ's subordination, obedience, and suffering to the time of his incarnation. Barth moves the goalposts. He attributes these things to Jesus Christ

---

[123]Ibid., 1.1, 428.
[124]Ibid., 2.2, 177.
[125]Ibid., 2.2, 105.
[126]Ibid., italics added.

as God, God identified with man for all eternity. It is not that he sees in the historic incarnate Christ subordination, obedience, and suffering and reads these things back into the eternal Trinity, as subordinationists with one accord do. Rather he begins with God in eternity who freely chooses subordination, obedience, and suffering so that he can be God for us and our salvation. At no point does Barth allow or suggest that in freely electing to be man Jesus Christ is less in any way than the Father or the Spirit. He insists that Christ is eternally sovereign God, he who elects. He is self-determining God. The humiliated, subordinated, suffering Jesus Christ is God who has elected to be man (humankind) in grace and reprobation.

This means that right at the heart of Barth's doctrine of God is a dialectical understanding of the Son. He is always at one and the same time the sovereign God and God identified with man in humiliation. He is, as he says many times, always "both Lord and servant." All appeals by evangelicals to Barth in support of their doctrine of the eternal subordination in authority of the Son miss this dialectical tension in Barth's doctrine of God. They rightly see him speaking of the Son of God as subordinate and obedient: what they fail to see is that for Barth Christ is always both the sovereign electing God who rules in all majesty and authority, equal with the Father and the Spirit, and God identified with man in obedience, subordination, and suffering.

Church Dogmatics 3.1 and 3.2: The Doctrine of Creation

Barth's exposition of the doctrine of creation takes us outside the focus of this book. I simply note a few of his comments in this volume of the *Dogmatics* that bear on our topic, the eternal subordination in function and authority of the Son. Although Barth connects creation primarily with God the Father, he says, "Jesus Christ is the Bearer of the power of the creator,"[127] and when speaking of God the Father as the Creator he says we mean, "the Father with the Son and the Holy Spirit."[128] "As Creator he [the Father] does not exist as a monad."[129] From God's work as creator discussed in volume 3.1, Barth in volume 3.2 moves to the apex of God's creation, the creature "man" (humankind). He argues that "man" can only be understood from God's perspective by reflecting on "the real man Jesus Christ." What determines the being of man in distinction to God is that man is called to be obedient to God.[130] Man and woman are free to obey or not obey. In his obedience Christ exemplifies what it means to be human. As God identified with man, he freely chooses to be obedient to the Father.

In the context of this discussion Barth elaborates on the significance of God choosing to identify himself with man. It means, he says, "to let His being, Himself,

---

[127]Ibid., 3.1, 35.
[128]Ibid., 3.1, 49.
[129]Ibid., 3.1, 363.
[130]Ibid., 3.1, 179

be prescribed and dictated and determined by an alien human being."[131] And returning to the theme of veiled revelation, he says his humanity "does not present God
in Himself and in relation to Himself, but in relation to a reality distinct from Himself."[132] Finally we note that in this volume Barth again argues that the person and
work of Christ cannot be divided. He says, "He not only does but is His work,"[133] and
in him "the doer and His deed are one."[134] "We cannot separate His person and His
work."[135] If the person and work of Christ cannot be divided, then also the being and
function of Christ cannot be divided, for these two pairings are synonymous.

Church Dogmatics 4.1 and 4.2: The Doctrine of Reconciliation

What Barth says on Christ as the elect man in volume 2.2 of his *Dogmatics* and what
he says on Jesus Christ as "the real man" in volume 3.2 prepares us for what Barth
develops in volume 4.1, "The doctrine of reconciliation." Bruce McCormack says,
here "he merely sets forth the implications of his earlier teaching."[136] The title Barth
gives to this whole discussion is "Jesus Christ as Lord and Servant,"[137] which indicates
immediately that we are going to confront the paradox inherent in thinking of Christ
as the sovereign electing God and the elected man. In this volume we meet with a
more "plural" understanding of the Godhead[138] than seen in volume 1.1, although
divine unity is never far away. This more plural conception of God appears when
Barth outlines his doctrine of reconciliation as a story or narrative of the journey of
the Son of God from his Father's home in glory to a far country where in obedience
he accepts humiliation, suffering, and death before he is exalted and welcomed home
by his Father.[139]

The title of his first sub-section, "The way of the Son of God into the far country," discloses how he sees reconciliation being achieved. It involves God leaving
"home" in a point in history. "He does something unnecessary and extravagant."[140]
"In His high majesty He is humble."[141] As God identified with man, he goes as the

---

[131] Ibid., 3.1, 214.

[132] Ibid., 3.1, 219.

[133] Ibid., 3.2, 60.

[134] Ibid., 3.2, 61.

[135] Ibid.

[136] McCormack, "Grace and Being," 96.

[137] Barth, *Church Dogmatics*, 4.1, 157.

[138] Rowan D. Williams, "Barth on the Triune God," in *Karl Barth: Studies in His Theological Method*, ed. S. W. Sykes (Oxford: Clarendon, 1979), 175, 178, 181; Samuel M. Powell, *The Trinity in German Thought* (Cambridge: Cambridge University Press, 2000), 224.

[139] The motif of the exaltation of the Son of Man is developed mainly in the first section of Barth's *Church Dogmatics*, 4.2.

[140] Barth, *Church Dogmatics*, 4.1, 158.

[141] Ibid., 4.1, 159.

obedient Son of Man, humbling himself, accepting suffering, and giving his life for the salvation of those he embodies and represents—and all this he does as God. These things are not limited to his human nature as in the tradition: they are actions of God. I would say actions of God the Son, but Barth characteristically speaks simply of "God": Jesus Christ is God.

But it is not only that Barth refuses in volume 4.1 as in volume 1.1 to allocate some actions to Jesus as God and some to Jesus as man, as orthodox theologians before him have done. In volume 4.1 he also refuses to endorse the post-Reformation sequential schema that speaks of Christ's state of humiliation in the incarnation followed by his state of exaltation after the resurrection. He makes the humiliation *and* exaltation of Jesus the Son of God simultaneous rather than successive, eternal rather than temporally determined.[142] The incarnation and resurrection simply reveal what has been true for all eternity. Thus humiliation and exaltation are two ways of viewing the one Jesus Christ. He is sovereign God and God identified with man in humility and obedience, at one and the same time both Lord and servant. Again Barth's distinctive conception of time—which distinguishes between God's time that has no beginning, middle, or end and salvation time or human time—allows him to argue in this way.

For Barth Jesus Christ is God and man in the one person, yet he insists that the divine always triumphs.[143] Jesus never ceases to be God. He is always "absolute, infinite, exalted, active, impassable, transcendent . . . the Creator."[144] At no time does his identification with man entail any diminution of authority or power, although it does reveal divine power in weakness, that God is both "high and humble."

> His [the Son's] omnipotence is that of divine plenitude of power in the fact that (as opposed to any abstract omnipotence) it can assume the form of weakness and impotence and do so as omnipotence triumphing in this form.[145]

> The mystery reveals to us that for God it is just as natural to be lowly as it is to be high, to be near as it is to be far, to be little as to be great, to be abroad as to be at home.[146]

> He is amongst us in humility, our God, God for us, as that which He is in Himself, in the most inward depth of His Godhead.[147]

---

[142] Ibid., 4.1, 132–35.
[143] Hunsinger, "Karl Barth's Christology," 139. Hunsinger rejects the thesis of C. T. Waldrop, *Karl Barth's Christology: Its Basic Alexandrian Character* (New York: Mouton, 1984), that Barth's Christology is distinctively Alexandrian.
[144] Barth, *Church Dogmatics*, 4.1, 187.
[145] Ibid.
[146] Ibid., 4.1, 192.
[147] Ibid., 4.1, 193.

Barth makes himself even clearer when he says that what he is talking about is "a determination of divine essence: not an alteration." God "elects and determines Himself for humiliation."[148]

Lurking in the wings of the stage behind most of what Barth says in volume 4.1 is the profound tension between thinking simultaneously of Christ as the sovereign electing God and as God identified with man and as such called to obedience, suffering, and death. This tension suddenly comes onto center stage in pages 195 to 203. All claims that Barth endorses the eternal subordination or submission of the Son of God appeal to what Barth says here, and usually nothing else. I was thus interested when reading the secondary literature on Barth's *Dogmatics* to find Professor Geoffrey Bromiley saying, "To read a given volume or a selection from different volumes in isolation from all the rest, is to run the risk of considerable misunderstanding."[149]

Barth begins this short section by admitting, "It is a difficult and even elusive thing to speak of an obedience which takes place in God Himself. Obedience implies an above and a below, a *prius* and a *posterius*, a superior and a junior and subordinate."[150]

To suggest this, he then says, would seem "to compromise the unity and then logically the equality of the divine being."[151] So he asks, "Can the one God command and obey?"[152] This leads him to consider other options. First that this obedience and subordination in Christ takes place only in the economy,[153] or secondly that it is restricted to his humanity,[154] but he rejects both options. As we have noted before, Barth opposes these traditional ways of explaining the subordination and obedience of Christ, because they imply temporal change in the Son and a division between the Father and the Son. For him Jesus Christ is eternally the God-man, who is both Lord and servant.

He thus comes to give his own solution. What we have to accept, he argues, is that, "The one true God being Himself the subject of the act of atonement in such a way that His presence and action as the Reconciler of the world coincide and are indeed identical with the existence of the humiliated and lowly and obedient man Jesus of Nazareth. He acts as the Reconciler in that—as the true God identical with this man—he humbles Himself and becomes lowly and obedient. He becomes and is this without being in contradiction to His divine nature ... but in contradiction to all human ideas about the divine nature."[155]

---

[148]Ibid., 4.2, 84.
[149]Geoffrey Bromiley, *Introduction to the Theology of Karl Barth* (Grand Rapids, Mich.: Eerdmans, 1979), xi.
[150]Barth, *Church Dogmatics*, 4.1, 195.
[151]Ibid.
[152]Ibid.
[153]Ibid., 4.1, 196.
[154]Ibid., 4.1, 197.
[155]Ibid., 4.1, 199.

This means, he goes on to say, that there can be no avoiding of "the offensive fact that there is in God Himself an above and a below, a *prius* and *posterius*, a superiority and a subordination,... that it belongs to the inner life of God."[156] These words at first sight might seem unambiguously to endorse the idea that the Son is eternally subordinated and set under the Father in authority. There is a division and separation between the Father and the Son. Nothing is ever so simple with Barth. What Barth actually speaks of is a subordination "in God himself." The one God "is both the One obeyed and Another who obeys."[157] "No, not an unequal but equal, not a divided but in the one deity, God is both One and also Another, His own counterpart, co-existent with Himself."[158] And then to make the picture even more complex he adds, "As we look at Jesus Christ we cannot avoid the astounding conclusion of divine obedience ... in equal God, the one God, is in fact, the One and also Another, that He is indeed a First and a Second, One who rules and commands in majesty and One who obeys in humility. The one God is both the one and the other without any cleft or differentiation but in perfect unity and equality."[159]

In these quotes two things cannot be missed. Barth speaks of a subordination in the one "equal God" and of a subordination seen in Christ that does not negate his ruling and commanding in majesty. This suggests that Barth is indicating that the subordination seen in Christ actually reveals something about all three divine persons—the one triune God. This becomes explicit in a comment in volume 4.2. In words devoid of ambiguity Barth says it is "the Godhead," not Christ alone, who is high and humble. "The Godhead of the true God is not a prison whose walls have first to be broken through if He is to elect and do what He has elected and done in becoming man ... His Godhead embraces both height and depth, both sovereignty and humility, both lordship and service.... He does not become another when in Jesus Christ He also becomes and is man."[160]

Taken in isolation many a comment in this section could be problematic, but Barth must always be read holistically and with a tuned ear to his checks and balances. When he speaks of the subordination of the Son, he uses elusive, paradoxical, and dialectical language that makes it impossible to "box in" what he is saying. Nowhere is this more clearly stated than at the end of this discussion on the subordination and obedience in the one God. He writes,

> The One who in this obedience is the perfect image of the ruling God is Himself—as distinct from every human and creaturely kind—God by nature, God

---

[156]Ibid., 4.1, 200–201.
[157]Ibid., 201.
[158]Ibid.
[159]Ibid., 4.1, 202.
[160]Ibid., 4.2, 84.

in His relationship to Himself, i.e., God in His mode of being as the Son in relation to God in His mode of being as the Father, One with the Father and of one
essence. In His mode of being as the Son He fulfils the divine subordination, just
as the Father in His mode of being as the Father fulfils the divine superiority. In
humility as the Son who complies, He is the same as is the Father in majesty as
the Father who disposes. He is the same in consequence (and obedience) as the
Son as is the Father in origin. He is the same as the Son, i.e. as the self-posited
God (the eternally begotten of the Father as the dogma has it) as is the Father
as the self-positing God (the Father who eternally begets). Moreover in His
humility and compliance as the Son He has a supreme part in the majesty and
disposing of the Father.[161]

How do we put this all together? Christ is "the perfect image of the ruling God,"
yet in his mode of being he fulfills "the divine subordination." "He is the same as the
Father in majesty who disposes," and "in His humility and compliance as the Son He
has a supreme part in the majesty and disposing as the Father." Of whom exactly is
he referring when he speaks of the condescension, self-humbling, and even of suffering and obedience *in God*? Is he speaking of the Son alone, or has he the Godhead in
mind? If there is but one God in threefold repetition and the Son perfectly reveals the
Father, and Barth has just said the Son is "the perfect image of the ruling God," we
must conclude that he has in mind at all times the one triune God revealed in Jesus
Christ. Possibly the most important and most reiterated theme in Barth's doctrine of
God is that Christ reveals the triune God. God is not other than he is in Jesus Christ.
If Christ is high and humble, so too is the Father and the Spirit.

In seeking to grasp what Barth is saying in this section, we must note yet again
that Barth's Christology is characterized by a dialectical understanding of Jesus Christ
as the eternally sovereign electing God and the eternally elect man: as both Lord and
servant. Christ is never the subordinated obedient Son *simpliciter*. Some contemporary
conservative evangelicals may appeal to Barth for support of their distinctive doctrine
of the eternal subordination or submission of the Son in function and authority, but
in their zeal to find an ally in Barth they have failed to see one half of Barth's distinctive Christology. With delight they see him speaking of the eternally subordinated,
obedient, and suffering Son, but they fail completely to see him speaking of the Son
at the same time as the sovereign, omnipotent, and electing God.

Barth and Subordinationism

What Barth is saying in this so-called "subordinationist strand" in his doctrine of the
Trinity has been read in one of three ways.

---

[161] Ibid., 4.1, 209.

1. Barth is a subordinationist; he endorses this dangerous error. The only theologian I found arguing that Barth is a subordinationist, apart from contemporary conservative evangelicals with their own agenda, was the evangelical and Reformed theologian G. C. Berkouwer. He thinks Barth has fallen into the error of subordinationism and as well the error of *theopaschitism* — the idea that God suffers. It is his view that in this teaching on subordination, obedience, and suffering *in God* Barth has broken with both what the Bible says and the clear witness of the tradition. He writes, "When Barth speaks of the suffering of God and even of an 'obedience of God' and this not as a bold manner of speaking but as an essential element in the being of God over against natural theology, he exceeds the boundaries of the revelation we have in Christ.... It introduces another dimension of thought into the reflection of the Church than that which we are confronted in the Biblical revelation concerning the subjection of Jesus Christ to the Father as the mediator between God and man."[162]

Berkouwer believes that in speaking of these things taking place in "God himself" Barth undermines Christ's mediatorial role. If the obedience and suffering of Christ are ascribed to him as God, God *ad extra*, without any caveats, how is he the God-man who mediates between God and humankind? On such a view it becomes difficult to understand how "Christ was under the curse of the law, that he endured the wrath of God, and that he was forsaken by God."[163] Barth, he says, speaks frequently of "God himself" in the person of the Son suffering, but there is a limit to this line of thought. He cannot speak of God dying.[164] To speak of God being obedient is equally difficult. How can omnipotent God be obedient to omnipotent God? Berkouwer does not think that Barth has embraced Arianism, but he does think that what he says on the subordination of Christ as God represents a theologically dangerous breach with Scripture and how Scripture has been interpreted by the best of theologians from the past (tradition).

Berkouwer, like many contemporary evangelicals, seems to miss the dialectic in Barth's doctrine of God. He does not recognize that for Barth Christ is both the sovereign ruling God and the subordinated, obedient, and suffering Son of Man. He also judges Barth according to the Reformed paradigm where there is a temporal distinction between Christ in his state of humiliation and Christ in his state of exaltation rather than in terms of Barth's own completely new paradigm. In this there is no temporal distinction yet still a distinction between Christ as the sovereign electing God and Christ as the subordinated, suffering, and obedient Son of Man.

---

[162]G. C. Berkouwer, *The Triumph of Grace in the Theology of Karl Barth* (Grand Rapids, Mich.: Eerdmans, 1956), 304.

[163]Ibid., 305.

[164]Ibid., 309.

2. Barth is a subordinationist; his teaching on this is to be commended. My evangelical debating opponents believe like Berkouwer that Barth *eternally* subordinates the Son to the Father, but in contrast to him they warmly commend Barth on this matter, arguing that his teaching represents an orthodox expression of subordinationism. They see in what he says on the subordination and obedience of the Son a vindication of their own position. If Barth teaches just what they are teaching, we are asked, how can belief in the eternal subordination or submission of the Son in function and authority be mistaken or heretical? They particularly warm to Barth's comments on the obedience of the Son, because this motif is basic to their case that just as the Son is *eternally* obedient to the Father so women are to be obedient *permanently* to the men set over them in the home and the church. Their interpretation of Barth's comments on subordination and obedience in God are endorsed without criticism because of their prior agenda, the subordination of women. It is sad that these evangelical theologians do not see that if this is what Barth is teaching then he is contradicting St. Paul and the Athanasian Creed. In Paul's thinking Christ is obedient to the Father as the second Adam, the righteous man who goes to the cross and is then exalted to reign as Lord. Paul does not teach that as the Son of God Christ is eternally subordinated or eternally obedient to the Father. The Athanasian Creed seeks to exclude the idea that the Son is eternally subordinated and obedient to the Father. It teaches that all three divine persons are "almighty" and "Lord" and "none is before or after, none greater or lesser ... [all are] co-equal."

My evangelical friends claim I have "misread Barth," who they believe endorses their doctrine of the eternal subordination and obedience of the Son *simpliciter*. Their reading of Barth teaches that there is One who eternally commands, the Father, and One who eternally obeys, the Son. My reading of Barth indicates otherwise. For Barth, Jesus Christ the Son is both the One who commands *and* the One who obeys. He is always at the same time both Lord and servant. They somehow miss completely this fundamental dialectic in Barth's Christology.

3. Barth is not a subordinationist. A few contemporary conservative evangelicals may appeal to Barth for support of what they already believe, but the majority of scholarly opinion today is that Barth does not endorse the eternal subordination in function and authority of the Son *simpliciter*. Rather he is one of the strongest and clearest opponents of all forms of subordinationism. This is how I read Barth. In summary these are my conclusions.

1. Following the first volume of his *Dogmatics* where Barth stresses the unity of the one God "reiterated" in three "modes of being," he begins to wrestle with the fundamental question of how Christ can be subordinate, obedient, and suffer as man and yet still be God. In the end he completely breaks with

the tradition that distinguishes between Christ as God and Christ as man, or between the exalted Son and the humiliated Son. Instead, at least from volume 2.1 of the *Dogmatics*, Jesus Christ for him is eternally both the sovereign electing God and the elect man, Lord and servant, high and humble. In this revolutionary Christology the subordination, obedience, and suffering of the Son is not ascribed simply to the Son's incarnate existence. Rather, it is ascribed to the Son for all eternity. He is eternally the sovereign electing God and God identified with man in subordination, obedience, and suffering. Christ never ceases to be sovereign God with the Father and the Spirit, but he is not the Father or the Spirit. He is distinctively the Revealer and the Reconciler. The Son as God identified with man freely chooses subordination, obedience, and suffering to reconcile human beings to God, while yet still omnipotent God.

2. Barth creates this new paradigm because he cannot allow any separation or division between Christ as he is in eternity and Christ as he is in historical revelation, except that in the incarnation he took flesh. Nor will he allow any separation or division between the Father and the Son. Even in the incarnation, "He [Christ] is not alone on the way"; the Father goes with him.[165] True, it is the Son who freely chooses subordination, obedience, and suffering, yet it is also the will of the Father. This means that in the final analysis, in his mode of being as the Son, Jesus reveals the Father or the one Godhead as both Lord *and* servant, as high and humble. What the Son is the Father is likewise. For Barth Christ "is the perfect image of the ruling God." Christ as servant does not speak of Christ in contrast to the Father but rather of Christ revealing the Father. What the Son is so too is the Father.

3. In this new paradigm Barth also rules out any separation or division between the person and work or the being and function of Christ. What Christ does and who he is are one. Barth stresses the unity of being, work, and authority of the divine persons. Thus he endorses the Augustinian principle that the external works of the Godhead are one, and the doctrines of *perichoresis* and appropriation. The idea that the Son is eternally "functionally" subordinated to the Father, or that in himself as equal God he *must be* obedient to God, is completely foreign to Barth. Christ is sovereign God in his person and work, being, and function: subordinated and obedient only by his own free and sovereign choice in identifying with humankind. To suggest that Barth teaches that the Son who is one and equal with the Father and the Spirit *must* (even if he does so gladly) submit his will to the will of the Father is simply false and misleading. For Barth the one triune God can have only one will.

---

[165]Barth, *Church Dogmatics*, 4.1, 195.

4. Finally we point out that however Barth is interpreted in detail, his basic insight that Christ is always both Lord and servant excludes categorically the possibility of finding any support whatsoever in Barth for the permanent subordination of women. If women by analogy are both lords and servants, then they are not unilaterally subordinated to men in the home and the church!

There is yet one final question that demands to be put. Is Barth's radical reconceptualization of how the subordination seen in the incarnate Christ is to be explained convincing? Has he improved and successfully transcended the old paradigm, which restricted Christ's subordination and obedience to his temporal incarnation? I for one am not convinced. I find his schema just too difficult and its biblical basis too thin. Thinking of Christ as at one and the same time the eternally sovereign and electing God and the subordinated, suffering, obedient, and dying Son is to introduce a dialectic that is hard to comprehend and something the New Testament does not endorse. Paul is quite clear that it was in becoming human in a point of human history (Gal 4:4; cf. Jn 1:14) that Christ entered into his state of humiliation and subordination. Prior to this he was equal God, and afterwards he was exalted to reign as Lord (Php 2:4–11).

Postscript

My debating opponents also appeal to Professors John Thompson and Colin Gunton, who largely adopt Barth's distinctive dialectical Christology, speaking of Christ as both Lord and servant. To complete this chapter I make a brief comment on their work.

John Thompson

Some years ago when I had just begun the task of reading the scholarly literature on the Trinity, I was very surprised when I came to page 48 of John Thompson's *Modern Trinitarian Perspectives* to find him speaking of the eternal obedience of the Son.[166] I had found nothing to parallel this wording in the historical sources I had read, or in any Roman Catholic or mainline Protestant text on the Trinity I had studied so far. At the time I did not realize that Professor Thompson was basically following Barth's distinctive paradigm that has Christ always at one and the same time both Lord and servant. I did not notice that alongside his comments on the eternal obedience of Christ he also had comments affirming his eternal lordship and coequality with the Father. After reading Barth I came back to Thompson, seeing then for the first time his balancing comments and affirmations of the Son's sovereignty. I then noted that in *Modern Trinitarian Perspectives* he also says, "The Son as obedient eternally to the Father is not simply compliant to the Father's will. It is an active passivity, one in

---

[166]John Thompson, *Modern Trinitarian Perspectives* (New York: Oxford, 1994), 48–49.

which he shares the power, disposing, and majesty of the Father by the Spirit." He then quotes Barth, " 'The one who rules and commands in majesty and the one who obeys in humility is the one God.' "[167]

In another book, summing up Barth's treatment of "the way of the Son into the far country" to win our reconciliation or atonement, John Thompson says, "The atonement wrought in Christ has its source in the divine nature *ad extra*—in the obedience of the Son. Humiliation is its expression not its contradiction. It affirms the equality and unity of deity and implies no limitation or subordinationism."[168]

And then later in an article on Barth's doctrine of the Trinity: "The Son's obedience must be conceived as an obedience as Lord with no inequality or inferiority in the divine Being. Paradoxically, the Son is not only obedient but shares with the Father in his majesty, just as on the way to the depths of the cross the Father accompanies the Son."[169]

Colin Gunton

I also noted in my early reading that Colin Gunton on occasion made comments on the Trinity that I saw in no other book by mainline Protestant or Catholic theologians. He not only spoke of the eternal obedience of Christ, following Barth, but also of the Son and Spirit's subordination. My debating opponents have made much of these comments, arguing that Gunton actually supports what I am opposing. What he says illustrates, they claim, that there is an orthodox subordinationism. Gunton was Professor of Christian Doctrine at King's College, University of London, until he tragically passed away in 2003. He was a fine scholar who had a lifelong interest in Barth and in the doctrine of the Trinity. Later, after having read Gunton more widely, I came to see that there are in fact three Colin Guntons, figuratively speaking. There is the Colin Gunton who is a disciple of Barth, there is a Colin Gunton who is an entirely orthodox English United Reformed pastor and preacher, and there is a Colin Gunton who is an innovative, questioning, and critically minded theologian.

As a disciple of Barth, he rightly recognizes that the doctrine of election is fundamental to understanding Barth's developing Christological and trinitarian thinking.[170] For Barth, Christ is always both the sovereign electing God and the elect subordinated, obedient, and suffering Son of Man. He is eternally Lord and servant.

---

[167] Ibid., 49.

[168] John Thompson, *Christ in Perspective: Christological Perspectives in the Theology of Karl Barth* (Grand Rapids, Mich.: Eerdmans, 1978), 49.

[169] John Thompson, "On the Trinity," in *Theology Beyond Christendom*, ed. John Thompson (Pennsylvania: Pickwick, 1986), 18.

[170] We have referred already to Colin Gunton's 1974 article, "Karl Barth's Doctrine of Election." On Gunton as a disciple of Barth see his book *Becoming and Being*.

Following Barth, Gunton often adopts dialectical modes of speech when speaking of Christ as the sovereign God and lowly servant. Although it seems to me he became more critical of Barth as the years passed, a good example of this is found in his last book, *Father, Son, and Spirit*. He says, "The Father who begets and the Son who is begotten are together one God in the κοινωνια of the Spirit. They are one because the Son and the Spirit are, in a sense, though God, subordinate in the eternal ταζις [order] as they are in the economy. But in another sense they are not subordinate, for without his Son and Spirit, God would not be God."[171]

Colin Gunton as the orthodox and conservative pastor and preacher is, however, the most visible persona. In his writings his own personal faith and commitment to historic Christianity shine through. In the first essay in *Father, Son, and Spirit* we find this Colin Gunton expounding the doctrine of the Trinity to a public audience. In this lecture he sums up his doctrine of the Trinity in four theses that exclude modalism, subordinationism, and tritheism.

1. "God the Son—the one made flesh in Jesus of Nazareth—and God the Spirit are as truly God as the Father."[172]
2. God is nevertheless truly one. "The unity of God" must not be "impugned."[173]
3. "The relation of plurality and oneness is expressed" by the concept of "person." "God is one being in three persons."[174]
4. "The three persons who make up the one being of God; who together are the one God, are bound up together in such a way that only one word can be used to describe their relation: love."[175]

Third, there is the innovative, questioning, and critically minded academic theologian, Colin Gunton. In this persona he wrestles with the tradition and debates with other theologians of his stature. With absolute clarity he sees that one of the most perplexing questions for those enunciating the doctrine of the Trinity is, How is the subordination of the Son seen in the incarnation related to the immanent Trinity? In confronting this question he is particularly critical of Augustine, whom he thinks borders on modalism.[176] He also takes T. F. Torrance to task, and by implication Athanasius, for seeking to "obviate any hint of subordinationism" by making so

---

[171] Colin Gunton, *Father, Son, and Spirit* (London: T&T Clark, 2003), 73, 74.
[172] Ibid., chapter I, "The Forgotten Trinity," 11.
[173] Ibid., 12.
[174] Ibid.
[175] Ibid., 17.
[176] See his essay, "Augustine, the Trinity and the Theological Crises of the West" in *The Promise of Trinitarian Theology*, ed. Colin Gunton (Edinburgh: T&T Clark, 1991), 31–57.

much of the *homoousian* principle.[177] It is his own view that in the Scriptures "there is an element of *economic* subordination—to be strictly distinguished from *ontological* subordinationism."[178] Thus he says, "We must concede that there is a sense in which the Son is indeed subordinate to the Father. As we have seen he is the Son sent, given and obedient."[179] So he asks, Should Irenaeus' suggestion that the Son and the Spirit be thought of as the Father's "two hands" be given fresh consideration?[180]

  This radical questioning of the tradition and criticism of giants like Athanasius, Augustine, and Torrance is all very stimulating and it has evoked much debate, but it must be recognized for what it is. It is the penetrating academic questioning of a clever mind. To quote these comments, as my debating opponents do, as proof that orthodox theologians embrace the eternal subordination of the Son in authority is unconvincing. To start with, Gunton speaks only of the "economic subordination" of the Son, and when he develops his thinking along these lines he makes it clear he is dissenting from the received tradition. This means that the comments from Gunton quoted against me represent his questioning or rejection of the tradition. They are not evidence that I have read the tradition wrongly.

---

[177] Gunton, *Father, Son, and Spirit*, 38. See Molnar, *Divine Freedom*, 317–30, for a defense of Torrance.
[178] Gunton, *Father, Son, and Spirit*, 39.
[179] Ibid., 67. Cf. 72.
[180] Ibid., 39.

CONCLUSION

As everyone has discovered who has ever written a research essay, there are surprises as one digs deeper and deeper. Things hitherto not imagined come to light. The writing of this book has taken me on a journey. I have uncovered information I did not expect to find. In my earlier book, *The Trinity and Subordinationism*, I came to the conclusion that my evangelical friends who were arguing for the eternal subordination or submission of the Son had broken with the tradition and were seriously in error. I did not realize at any depth then that how they were reading the Bible and depicting the Father-Son relationship almost one for one matched how the so-called "Arians" of the fourth century read the Bible and understood the Father-Son relationship. This became obvious as I read the historical sources more widely and more deeply. What I found is that almost everything my evangelical debating opponents were saying about the divine persons in the Trinity was opposed virtually word for word by Athanasius, the Cappadocians, Augustine, Calvin, the creeds, and the Reformation confessions. These theological authorities were arguing against the same errors as I am.

The parallels between what the fourth-century "Arians" and contemporary evangelicals who argue for the Son's eternal subordination in function and authority are teaching is quite amazing. The following are to be noted.

1. All the so-called fourth-century Arians could confess, "Jesus is God." What they could not do was confess that Jesus is "coequal" God, one in being, function, and authority with the Father. Conservative evangelicals have the same reservations. When pressed they will not agree that the Father and the Son are *in all things* "coequal," except that one is the Father and the other the Son.

2. All the fourth-century Arians appealed to the Bible for proof of their position. They pointed out that the New Testament speaks of the Son as being sent by the Father, begotten of the Father, and it depicts him as subordinate to the Father in his incarnate state. They virtually ignored the texts that speak of Christ as "equal God," "the Lord," and functioning as God. They had texts: what they did not have, as Athanasius and Augustine were quick to point out, was a holistic biblical theology that put the seemingly contradictory teaching of Scripture into a framework that made sense of the whole. Contemporary evangelicals are in the exactly same situation.

3. For the fourth-century Arians, subordination in being, work, and authority were inextricably linked. One implied the other two. The dominant

evangelical view is that it is possible to have *eternal* subordination in function and authority without implying subordination in being. It is my case that this is not possible. If my argument is compelling, then by implication all evangelicals who endorse the eternal subordination of the Son in function and authority embrace—without realizing it, and even often denying it—the subordination of the Son in being.

4. For the fourth-century Arians and for the contemporary evangelicals with whom I am in contention, the titles *father* and *son* when used of God are understood literally. God the Father is a father and God the Son is a son. For this reason the Father has preeminence. He commands; the Son obeys. Time and time again contemporary evangelicals come back to this argument. The Father rules over the Son, like men are to rule over their wives or women in the church. There are two problems with this reasoning. First, the divine Father-Son relationship is defined in human terms, which is idolatry, and second, the implication is that the Father and the Son each have their own will like a husband and a wife. This last idea spells the end of divine unity. Thus the Arians and evangelicals committed to the eternal subordination of the Son in function and authority not only distinguish the divine persons, they also divide and separate them. In doing this they fall into both the errors of subordinationism and tritheism.

5. For all the fourth-century Arians the Trinity is ordered hierarchically. The Father is over the Son, and the Father and the Son are over the Spirit. Order means hierarchy. Athanasius, the Cappadocian Fathers, Augustine, Aquinas, Calvin, and almost all contemporary Catholic and mainline Protestant theologians are of the opposite opinion. Divine ordering is not hierarchical. The three divine persons operate and relate in a coequal order, or we might say a horizontal order. In the contemporary evangelical literature advocating the eternal subordination of the Son, we are told repeatedly that the divine three are ordered hierarchically.

6. The fourth-century Arians with one voice put to the fore the *differences* between the Father and the Son. The Father alone is true God, absolute in power and authority. In contrast Athanasius, the Cappadocian Fathers, Augustine, and what has become known as "the Western" tradition culminating in Barth and Rahner, with one voice puts to the fore divine unity, equality, and simplicity, while always insisting on divine differentiation. In this book I accuse my debating opponents of dividing the one God just as the Arians did in the fourth century. In dividing the Father and the Son all subordinationists undermine revelation. If the Son is eternally other than and unlike the Father in function and authority, then he does not reveal the

Father. What he reveals is subordinated God to be contrasted with God the Father, the sovereign God. Barth's great contribution to trinitarian theology, developing Johannine teaching, was to argue that even the Son's subordination in the incarnation reveals the Father. The Son is not unlike the Father even at this point of time. The God of the Bible is both high and humble, Lord and servant. The divine three are eternally differentiated as Father, Son, and Spirit, but neither the Bible nor the tradition separate and divide them on the basis of their distinctive work, because they work inseparably, nor on the basis of differing power and authority, because they are indivisible in power and authority.

7. All the fourth-century Arians focused on what was revealed in the economy of salvation, arguing that the subordination of the Son seen in the incarnation was to be read back into the eternal Godhead, or as we would say today, the immanent Trinity. From the time of Athanasius onward, those who opposed thinking of the Son as eternally subordinated argued that while the Son does reveal the Father, he does not reveal the Father or himself exactly as they exist in communion with the Spirit in eternity. There is correspondence but not identity between the economic and immanent Trinity. Evangelicals who argue for the eternal subordination of the Son today follow the Arian trajectory. They argue that if Jesus was subordinated in the incarnation, he must be subordinated in eternity. The economic Trinity is to be equated with the immanent Trinity. I argue that Scripture makes the triune God as he is in eternity primary and foundational, seeing the revelation of the Father, Son, and Spirit in history and Scripture as accurately conveying truth about God but not comprehensively or exhaustively. God is greater than what he has revealed to frail human minds and what the human mind can comprehend. God the Son in the incarnation did take the form of a servant for our salvation, but Scripture also teaches that he is coequal God, the Lord. The incarnation is only one scene in God's unfolding revelation of himself in the Son. The Scriptures also reveal the Son as the cocreator and after the resurrection as the ruler of the universe. So I hold that what is known of the immanent Trinity is given in revelation, but the economy of salvation is not the totality of the revelation given by God of himself in Scripture, and the revelation given does not exhaust who and what God is.

Twenty-First-Century Arians?

Are then my debating opponents twenty-first-century Arians? The answer to this question is no. Arianism was a fourth-century error that is excluded by the creeds and Reformation confessions. All those with whom I am debating insist that they are not Arians and that they say they accept the creeds and confessions. I am sure Bishop Robert Forsyth speaks for all I have criticized when he says none of the Sydney Anglican theologians "consciously intended" in the 1999 *Sydney Doctrine Report* to deny anything in the creeds or to abrogate the *homoousian* principle (the Father and the Son are one in being).[1] My charge is rather that in arguing for the *eternal* subordination of the Son to support the doctrine of the *permanent* subordination of women, my debating opponents' primary and consuming concern, they have in ignorance broken with how the best of theologians and the creeds and confessions have concluded the Scriptures should be read and understood. Unintentionally they have embraced fundamental aspects of the Arian heresy in its varied forms, producing a strange amalgam of truth and error.

Orthodoxy as I See It

The many books on the Trinity available today all give good outlines of the doctrine of the Trinity, varying mainly on the depth of presentation and on the points of allowable dissent within the bounds of orthodoxy. However, none of them answer directly the questions that the post-1970s' reworded and reformulated conservative evangelical doctrine of the Trinity raises. This is what has been attempted in this book by returning directly to the Bible and the historical sources to make an answer. On the basis of this research I have reached the following conclusions. There is absolutely nothing new in these findings. What is new is that they directly counter point by point what my evangelical friends with whom I am debating teach. It is my case that orthodoxy is best expressed today by the following fundamental affirmations.

1. *The God of Christian revelation is one divine being and three "persons."* Unity and divine differentiation are both absolutes. The unity of God is not to be thought of in terms of one substance but rather as the most intimate, most loving, and most profound triune communion. The triune God's unity is the unique Being-in-Communion of the eternal Father, Son, and Holy Spirit. What ultimately grounds this divine union and communion is the mutual interpenetration (*perichoresis*) of the three divine persons. The divine persons, nevertheless, in their eternal and immutable distinctions as the Father, the Son, and the Spirit, are not to be thought of as three individuals or centers of consciousness, but rather as the one God in tripersonal existence and self-revelation, distinguished but not divided. The Father, Son, and Spirit exist as Being-in-Relation.

2. *The three divine "persons" are inseparable in operations.* Inseparability in being implies and necessitates inseparability in work/operation/function. The

---

[1] See my earlier discussion on the Sydney Anglican position in chapter 1.

divine three are one in who they are and what they do. In every divine action all three divine persons work in harmony and cooperatively. They are never divided or separated in their operations. The doctrine of inseparable operations, it must be added, does not imply identical operations. The Father sent the Son, the Son took human flesh and died on the cross, and the Spirit was poured out on the day of Pentecost. These and other things are indelibly associated with one or another of the divine persons. However, to divide and separate the work of Father, Son, and Spirit is to undermine the unity and simplicity of the one God.

3. *The three divine "persons" are indivisible in power and authority.* Because each divine person is fully God, each is omnipotent without any caveats. If the divine persons are one in being, equal God, they must be one in power and authority. If they are not one in power and authority, then they are not one in being and divinity: the Son is subordinated God, not just in function but in his person.

4. *The three divine "persons" have one will.* To be one in being, operations, and authority implies oneness of will. The thesis that the Son must eternally obey the Father suggests that the Father and the Son each have their own will. The Son must submit his will to the will of the Father. If the divine three each have their own will, then divine unity is breached and tritheism follows. To argue in reply that the Son can do no other than obey the Father, or that his obedience is freely given, does not solve the problem. If the Father and the Son (and the Spirit) have one will, the actions of one cannot be conceived as obedience to another. In the New Testament Jesus Christ is obedient as incarnate God. It is the human will of Jesus that is obedient to the one divine will. In the immanent Trinity the Father and the Son live in perfect unity and perichoretic communion, having one mind and will in all things. To speak of the Father eternally commanding and the Son obeying, freely or otherwise, is to depict the Father-Son relationship in terms of fallen human relationships.

5. *The three divine "persons" are eternally differentiated but not divided.* The Father, Son, and Spirit are not divided in being, work, power, or will, but they are eternally differentiated. In the tradition their distinctiveness is grounded principally on three things: individual identity (the Father is the Father and not the Son, etc., etc.); differing origination (the Father begets the Son, the Son is begotten, the Spirit proceeds); and differing relations (the Father is the Father of the Son, the Son is the Son of the Father, the Spirit proceeds from the Father, or the Father and the Son). Differentiating the persons in these ways does not divide them. Differentiating them in being or power does divide them, leading both to subordinationism and tritheism. The divine

three must not and cannot be differentiated on the basis of differing being. What they are in unity they are as differentiated persons. To suggest otherwise is to deny the *homoousian* principle, enshrined in the Nicene and Athanasian creeds. This principle points to the real distinctions between the three divine persons and their absolute oneness in being. It categorically excludes the idea that any one divine person is more or less true God.

6. *There is order among the divine three persons.* The way the divine persons are revealed, how they relate to one another, and how they work is never random or arbitrary. It is ordered. There is a pattern and consistency, a disposition, in the divine life that is unchanging. To argue that this order is a sub-ordering in being or power is to deny that the divine three are "coequal" in being and power. To utilize linear imagery, we may say the divine persons are ordered horizontally, not hierarchically.

7. *The Son is subordinated in the incarnation.* In taking human flesh, the Son of God voluntarily relinquished his status but not his divinity or being as God, assuming the form of a servant. What is revealed in Jesus of Nazareth is true and accurate knowledge of God, but it is a revelation of God in *kenotic* form, of God in human flesh, of self-subordinated God. This means what is creaturely in Christ must not be read back into the eternal or immanent Trinity. The Son continues as God and man after his resurrection, but his humanity is glorified and exalted. None of the limitations necessitated in taking human flesh are present. The Son now reigns as the sovereign mediator and Lord.

It is my case that the Bible implicitly and the historically developed orthodox doctrine of the Trinity explicitly affirm the following: divine unity; the eternal personal distinctions of Father, Son, and Spirit; the oneness of being of the divine three; their inseparable operations; their indivisible authority; their oneness of will and ordered and unchanging divine relations; and the temporal and voluntary subordination of the Son in the incarnation.

The Options

For those who until this point have supported the eternal subordination of the Son, there are three options that are equally difficult for them.

1. The first option is to go on arguing that the Bible and historical orthodoxy supports the eternal subordination of the Son of God in function and authority. I am sure many will embrace this option because for them the stakes are so high. To admit that the orthodox doctrine of the Trinity gives no support at all—if anything it challenges the belief that women are permanently subordinated to men—is not a possibility. To give way on this point would

be to weaken their whole case for the permanent subordination of women, which for them is the most important Christian truth to be upheld in this age. This response demands special pleading, like arguments for a flat earth or a world created about 7000 years ago. The compelling case against their position, such as I have given, has to be summarily dismissed. To be quite specific it demands the rejection of the Athanasian Creed, which unambiguously affirms the eternal coequality of the eternally differentiated divine persons. This first option allows those who take it to continue to believe in an eternally subordinated Son and permanently subordinated women.

2. The second alternative is to admit that basing the permanent subordination of women on a doctrine of an eternally subordinated Son has been a bad mistake. The doctrine of the Trinity should be construed solely by reference to the Bible and how the Bible has been understood across the centuries. The doctrine of the Trinity and the doctrine of man-woman relations are two separate doctrines that need to be studied independently. The primary doctrine of the Christian religion, the doctrine of God, should be studied first, and only then the secondary if not tertiary doctrine of how men and women should relate in the home and the church be studied. The first should inform the second but not determine what is believed; the second in no way should determine the first. This position allows one to embrace historical orthodoxy by affirming a coequal Trinity without reservations and continue to believe that women are permanently subordinated to men in the home and the church—this is God's ideal for the man-woman relationship.

3. The third option is to accept that the Bible, and how the Bible has been read by the best of theologians of the past and by most theologians today, allows for no eternal subordination in the Trinity. The Christian doctrine of God speaks of a triune God who is differentiated as Father, Son, and Spirit, yet is one in being and authority in a bond of love and self-giving. This understanding of God analogically reflects the ideal for all human relationships. It suggests that permanently subordinating a race, socioeconomic group, or sex is not pleasing to God. The subordinating of any person is a reflection of the realities of a fallen world, not God's ideal. This response demands believing that it is quite erroneous to eternally subordinate God the Son to God the Father and to permanently subordinate women to men. The first idea demeans the Son of God and the second demeans women. This response is the one I hope the readers of this book will embrace. This is my prayer.

SUBJECT INDEX

SCRIPTURE INDEX